The Case of the Animals versus Man Before the King of the Jinn

The Case of the Animals versus Man Before the King of the Jinn

A translation from the
Epistles of the Brethren of Purity

Translated by
Lenn E. Goodman and Richard McGregor

Foreword by
Nader El-Bizri

OXFORD
UNIVERSITY PRESS
in association with
The Institute of Ismaili Studies

OXFORD
UNIVERSITY PRESS

Great Clarendon Street, Oxford OX2 6DP

Oxford University Press is a department of the University of Oxford.
It furthers the University's objective of excellence in research, scholarship,
and education by publishing worldwide in

Oxford New York

Auckland Cape Town Dar es Salaam Hong Kong Karachi
Kuala Lumpur Madrid Melbourne Mexico City Nairobi
New Delhi Shanghai Taipei Toronto

With offices in

Argentina Austria Brazil Chile Czech Republic France Greece
Guatemala Hungary Italy Japan Poland Portugal Singapore
South Korea Switzerland Thailand Turkey Ukraine Vietnam

Oxford is a registered trade mark of Oxford University Press
in the UK and certain other countries

Published in the United States
by Oxford University Press Inc., New York

First published 2009
First published in paperback 2012

British Library Cataloguing in Publication Data
Data available

Library of Congress Cataloguing in Publication Data
Data available

ISBN 978-0-19-958016-3 (Hbk.)
978-0-19-964251-9 (Pbk.)
3 5 7 9 10 8 6 4 2

Typeset by Saqi Books
Printed in Great Britain
on acid-free paper by
MPG Books Group, Bodmin & King's Lynn

Lenn E. Goodman is Professor of Philosophy and Andrew W. Mellon Professor in the Humanities at Vanderbilt University. His books include *Islamic Humanism; In Defense of Truth: A Pluralistic Approach; Jewish & Islamic Philosophy: Crosspollinations in the Classic Age; Judaism, Human Rights, and Human Values; God of Abraham; Avicenna*; *On Justice*; *Creation and Evolution*; and his Gifford Lectures, *Love Thy Neighbor as Thyself.* A winner of the American Philosophical Association Baumgardt Memorial Prize and the Gratz Centennial Prize, Goodman has lectured widely in international venues. His original translation of *The Case of the Animals versus Man* appeared in 1978. He is also the translator of Saadiah Gaon's Arabic commentary of the Book of Job. His translation, with commentary, of Ibn Ṭufayl's *Ḥayy Ibn Yaqẓān* was published in 2009 in an updated edition by the University of Chicago Press.

Richard McGregor is Associate Professor of Religious Studies and Islamic Studies at Vanderbilt University. His primary field of research is mediaeval Egypt and Syria, with a focus on intellectual history, visual culture, and Sufism. He is author of *Sanctity and Mysticism in Medieval Egypt* (2004), a study of the evolution of theories of religious authority among mystics of mediaeval Cairo. He is also co-editor with Adam Sabra of *Le développement du soufisme en Égypte à l'époque mamelouke* (2006), and is currently at work on a study of religious practice centred on processions, banners, pilgrimage, and iconoclasm.

Contents

Acknowledgements ix

Foreword xi

Introduction 1

Technical Introduction 57

Epistle 22: The Case of the Animals versus Man Before the King of the Jinn 61

Prologue of the Ikhwān 63

The Fable 99

Appendix A: Authorities Cited 317

Appendix B: Geographical Regions 319

Appendix C: Iranian Kings and Heroes of History and Legend 331

Appendix D: Religious Traditions 337

Bibliography 343

Index Nominum 357

Index Rerum 365

Index Locorum 379

Acknowledgements

Over the long period that we have been working together on this project we have enjoyed the support of Vanderbilt University's College of Arts and Science. Research funds pertaining to the Andrew W. Mellon Chair in the Humanities were of significant help, and we see Vanderbilt's contributions to this edition, translation, and commentary as a material expression of our university's commitment to research in the humanities, and its new initiatives in Islamic studies. We thank Dr Daftary and Professors Landolt, Madelung, and Poonawala for their contributions to the *Rasāʾil Ikhwān al-Ṣafāʾ* series, and Nader El-Bizri of the Institute of Ismaili Studies for his steadfast support throughout the seven years of our engagement in this project. Dr El-Bizri has been ably assisted by Tara Woolnough of the Institute, and by Wendy Robinson in the early stages.

In the spirit of intellectual fellowship modelled by the Ikhwān, we have profited from the help of friends and colleagues. Andras Hamori generously lent his expertise in early Arabic poetry. Kalman Bland and David Walker surveyed the Hebrew version of this epistle and contributed several observations on fascinating points of comparison between the Arabic original and the Hebrew. Ismail Poonawala, Abbas Hamdani, and Carmela Baffioni responded to our queries on out-of-the-way hadiths. James Grady, Nicholas Oschman, and D. Gregory Caramenico were indefatigable in their support, and Robert Kelz helped as well. We are thankful to all these fellow passengers on the ship that the Ikhwān launched, now over a thousand years ago.

Foreword

The Brethren of Purity (Ikhwān al-Ṣafā') were the anonymous members of a fourth-/tenth-century[1] esoteric fraternity of lettered urbanites that was principally based in the southern Iraqi city of Basra, while also having a significant active branch in the capital of the ʿAbbāsid caliphate, Baghdad. This secretive coterie occupied a prominent station in the history of scientific and philosophical ideas in Islam owing to the wide intellectual reception and dissemination of diverse manuscripts of their famed philosophically oriented compendium, the *Epistles of the Brethren of Purity* (*Rasāʾil Ikhwān al-Ṣafāʾ*). The exact dating of this corpus, the identity of its authors, and their doctrinal affiliation remain unsettled questions that are hitherto shrouded with mystery. Some situate the historic activities of this brotherhood at the eve of the Fāṭimid conquest of Egypt (ca. 358/969), while others identify the organization with an earlier period that is set chronologically around the founding of the Fāṭimid dynasty in North Africa (ca. 297/909).

The most common account regarding the presumed identity of the Ikhwān is usually related on the authority of the famed *littérateur* Abū Ḥayyān al-Tawḥīdī (ca. 320–414/930–1023), who noted in his *Book of Pleasure and Conviviality* (*Kitāb al-Imtāʿ waʾl-muʾānasa*) that these adepts were obscure 'men of letters': Abū Sulaymān Muḥammad b. Maʿshar al-Bustī (nicknamed al-Maqdisī); the *qāḍī* Abū al-Ḥasan ʿAlī b. Hārūn al-Zanjānī; Abū Aḥmad al-Mihrajānī (also known as Aḥmad al-Nahrajūrī); and Abū al-Ḥasan al-ʿAwfī. Abū Ḥayyān also

1 All dates are Common Era, unless otherwise indicated; where two dates appear (separated by a slash), the first date is the hijri (AH), followed by CE.

claimed that they were the senior companions of a secretarial officer at the Būyid regional chancellery of Basra, known as Zayd b. Rifāʿa, who was reportedly an affiliate of the Brethren's fraternity and a servant of its ministry. Even though this story was reaffirmed by several classical historiographers in Islamic civilization, it is not fully accepted by scholars in terms of its authenticity. Furthermore, some Ismaili missionaries (*duʿāt*) historically attributed the compiling of the *Epistles* to the early Ismaili Imams Aḥmad b. ʿAbd Allāh (al-Taqī [al-Mastūr]) or his father, ʿAbd Allāh (Wafī Aḥmad), while also suggesting that the *Rasāʾil* compendium was secretly disseminated in mosques during the reign of the ʿAbbāsid caliph al-Maʾmūn (r. 198–218/813–833).

Encountering 'veracity in every religion', and grasping knowledge as 'pure nourishment for the soul', the Ikhwān associated soteriological hope and the attainment of happiness with the scrupulous development of rational pursuits and intellectual quests. Besides the filial observance of the teachings of the Qur'an and hadith, the Brethren also reverently appealed to the Torah of Judaism and to the Gospels of Christianity. Moreover, they heeded the legacies of the Stoics and of Pythagoras, Hermes Trismegistus, Socrates, Plato, Aristotle, Plotinus, Nicomachus of Gerasa, Euclid, Ptolemy, Galen, Proclus, Porphyry, and Iamblichus.

The Brethren promoted a convivial and earnest 'companionship of virtue'. Their eschatological outlook was articulated by way of an intricate cyclical view of 'sacred' history that is replete with symbolisms and oriented by an uncanny hermeneutic interpretation of the microcosm and macrocosm analogy: believing that the human being is a microcosmos, and that the universe is a 'macroanthropos'. The multiplicity of the voices that were expressed in their *Epistles* reflects a genuine quest for wisdom driven by an impetus that is not reducible to mere eclecticism; indeed, their syncretism grounded their aspiration to establish a spiritual refuge that would transcend the sectarian divisions troubling their era.

In general, fifty-two epistles are enumerated as belonging to the *Rasāʾil Ikhwān al-Ṣafāʾ*, and these are divided into the following four parts: Mathematics, Natural Philosophy, Sciences of the Soul and Intellect, and Theology. The first part consists of fourteen epistles, and it deals with 'the mathematical sciences', treating a variety of topics in arithmetic, geometry, astronomy, geography, and music. It also includes five epistles on elementary logic, which consist of the following: the *Isagoge*, the *Categories*, *On Interpretation*, the *Prior Analytics*, and the *Posterior Analytics*. The second part of the corpus groups together seventeen epistles on 'the physical or natural sciences'. It thus treats themes on matter and form, generation and corruption, metallurgy, meteorology, a study of the essence of nature, the classes of plants and animals (the latter being also set as a fable), the composition of the human body and its embryological constitution, a cosmic grasp of the human being as microcosm, and also the investigation of the phonetic and structural properties of languages and their differences. The third part of the compendium comprises ten tracts on 'the psychical and intellective sciences', setting forth the 'opinions of the Pythagoreans and of the Brethren of Purity', and accounting also for the world as a 'macroanthropos'. In this part the Brethren also examined the distinction between the intellect and the intelligible, and they offered explications of the symbolic significance of temporal dimensions, epochal cycles, and the mystical expression of the essence of love, together with an investigation of resurrection, causes and effects, definitions and descriptions, and the various types of motion. The fourth and last part of the *Rasāʾil* deals with 'the *nomic* or legal and theological sciences' in eleven epistles. These address the differences between the varieties of religious opinions and sects, as well as delineating the 'Pathway to God', the virtues of the Ikhwān's fellowship, the characteristics of genuine believers, the nature of the divine *nomos*, the call to God, the actions of spiritualists, of jinn, angels, and recalcitrant demons, the species of politics, the cosmic hierarchy, and, finally, the essence of magic and talismanic incantations. Besides the fifty-two tracts that constitute the *Rasāʾil Ikhwān al-Ṣafāʾ*, this compendium was accompanied by a treatise entitled *al-Risāla al-jāmiʿa* (The Comprehensive Epistle), which acted as the *summa summarum* for the whole corpus and was itself supplemented by a further abridged appendage known as the *Risālat jāmiʿat al-jāmiʿa* (The Condensed Comprehensive Epistle).

In spite of their erudition and resourcefulness, it is doubtful whether the Brethren of Purity can be impartially ranked amongst the authorities of their age in the realms of science and philosophy. Their inquiries into mathematics, logic, and the natural sciences were recorded in the *Epistles* in a synoptic and diluted fashion, sporadically infused with gnostic, symbolic, and occult directives. Nonetheless, their accounts of religiosity, as well as their syncretic approach, together with their praiseworthy efforts to collate the sciences, and to compose a pioneering 'encyclopaedia', all bear signs of commendable originality.

In terms of the epistemic significance of the *Epistles* and the intellectual calibre of their authors, it must be stated that, despite being supplemented by oral teachings in seminars (*majālis al-ʿilm*), the heuristics embodied in the *Rasāʾil* were not representative of the most decisive achievements in their epoch in the domains of mathematics, natural sciences, or philosophical reasoning. Moreover, the sciences were not treated with the same level of expertise across the *Rasāʾil*. Consequently, this opus ought to be judged by differential criteria as regards the relative merits of each of its epistles. In fairness, there are signs of conceptual inventiveness, primarily regarding doctrinal positions in theology and reflections on their ethical-political import, along with signs of an intellectual sophistication in the meditations on spirituality and revelation.

The *Rasāʾil* corpus is brimming with a wealth of ideas and constitutes a masterpiece of mediaeval literature that presents a populist yet comprehensive adaptation of scientific knowledge. It is perhaps most informative in terms of investigating the transmission of knowledge in Islam, the 'adaptive assimilation' of antique sciences, and the historical evolution of the elements of the *sociology* of learning through the mediaeval forms of the popularization of the sciences and the systemic attempts to canonize them. By influencing a variety of Islamic schools and doctrines, the Brethren's heritage acted as a significant intellectual prompt and catalyst in the development of the history of ideas in Islam. As such, their work rightfully holds the station assigned to it among the distinguished Arabic classics and the high literature of Islamic civilization.

The composition of this text displays impressive lexical versatility, which encompasses the technical idioms of mathematics and logic, the heuristics of natural philosophy, and the diction of religious pronouncements and occult invocations, in addition to poetic verses, didactic parables, and satirical and inspirational fables. Despite the sometimes disproportionate treatment of topics, the occasional hiatus in proofs, irrelevant digressions, or instances of verbosity, the apparent stylistic weaknesses disappear, becoming inconsequential when a complete impression is formed of the architectonic unity of the text as a whole and of the convergence of its constituent elements as a remarkable *oeuvre des belles lettres*.

Modern academic literature on the *Rasāʾil Ikhwān al-Ṣafāʾ* is reasonably extensive within the field of Islamic studies, and it continues to grow, covering works dating from the nineteenth century up to the present, with numerous scholars attempting to solve the riddles surrounding this compendium. The academic rediscovery of the *Rasāʾil* in modern times emerged through the monumental editorial and translation efforts of the German scholar Friedrich Dieterici between the years 1861 and 1872. Several printed editions aiming to reconstruct the original Arabic have also been established, starting with the *editio princeps* in Calcutta in 1812, which was reprinted in 1846, then a complete edition in Bombay between 1887 and 1889, followed by the Cairo edition of 1928, and the Beirut editions of 1957, 1983, 1995, and their reprints.[2] Although the scholarly contribution of these Arabic editions of the *Rasāʾil* is laudable, as they valuably sustained research on the topic, they are uncritical in character, and they do not reveal their manuscript sources. Consequently, the current printed editions do not provide definitive primary-source documentation for this classical text. Given this state of affairs, the Institute of Ismaili Studies (IIS) in London has undertaken the publication (in association with Oxford University Press) of a multi-authored, multi-volume Arabic critical edition and annotated English translation of the fifty-two epistles. The annotated

2 The principal complete editions of this compendium that are available in print consist of the following: *Kitāb Ikhwān al-Ṣafāʾ wa-Khullān al-Wafāʾ*, ed. Wilāyat Ḥusayn, 4 vols. (Bombay: Maṭbaʿat Nukhbat al-Akhbār, 1305–1306/ca. 1888); *Rasāʾil Ikhwān al-Ṣafāʾ*, ed. Khayr al-Dīn al-Ziriklī, with two separate introductions by Ṭāha Ḥusayn and Aḥmad Zakī Pasha, 4 vols. (Cairo: al-Maṭbaʿa al-ʿArabiyya bi-Miṣr, 1928); *Rasāʾil Ikhwān al-Ṣafāʾ*, ed. with introduction by Buṭrus Bustānī, 4 vols. (Beirut: Dār Ṣādir, 1957); and an additional version, *Rasāʾil Ikhwān al-Ṣafāʾ*, ed. ʿĀrif Tāmir, 5 vols. (Beirut: Manshūrāt ʿUwaydāt, 1995).

English translation of Epistle 22 of the *Rasāʾil Ikhwān al-Ṣafāʾ*, which is contained in the present volume, is based on an earlier version that was also prepared by Professors Lenn E. Goodman and Richard McGregor, and published in 2009 alongside their Arabic critical edition of this tract, as part of the OUP–IIS *Epistles of the Brethren of Purity* series. This epistle, *The Case of the Animals versus Man Before the King of the Jinn*, is arguably the best known of the contents of the *Rasāʾil*, on account of its ecological fable, which casts the exploited and oppressed animals pursuing a case against humanity. The excellence in scholarship that underpinned the original OUP–IIS publication of this epistle, and the positive responses it received in academic circles, all reinforced the interest in printing it in this present paperback format. It is my delightful duty to express my gratitude in this context to Professors Goodman and McGregor for granting me the privilege of working closely with them in bringing this work to publication. I am also honoured to be given once more the opportunity to contribute a foreword to this remarkable epistle. Special thanks are due to the editors at OUP, and to Dr Farhad Daftary (Co-Director, IIS), for their generous endorsement of the publication of this paperback edition, and to Ms Tara Woolnough for facilitating the reuse of the original typeset English text that she copyedited with thoughtfulness and care at the IIS.

Nader El-Bizri
(General Editor, *Epistles of the Brethren of Purity*)

London, June 2011

Introduction

Lenn E. Goodman

'The Case of the Animals versus Man Before the King of the Jinn' (Epistle 22) is the longest of the fifty-two essays written in the 960s or 970s by a group of authors who took the pen name Ikhwān al-Ṣafā' wa-Khullān al-Wafā' (the 'Sincere [or 'Pure-Hearted'] Brethren and True Friends'). The collection was meant to spread philosophical, scientific, and mathematical understanding, scriptural lore and legend, and Persian, Indian, Muslim, Greek, and Hebraic values and traditions among the new Arabic literati of the lands of Islam. But in this essay, widely read and translated in the Middle Ages and since, the Brethren break away from their usual expository format and fly up into the realm of fable. Their aim, as they explain, is 'to consider the merits and distinctions of the animals, their admirable traits and pleasing natures, and to touch on man's overreaching, oppression, and injustice against the creatures that serve him — the beasts and cattle — and his heedless, impious thanklessness for the blessings for which he should be grateful.'

Once given words, the animals have much to say, both about their own plight and about the human condition. They present themselves not as mere objects of study but as subjects with an outlook and interests of their own. That casts the essay into a moral mode: the animals warmly appreciate the bounty of creation but passionately criticize human domination and systematically indict its underlying rationales as the products of human arrogance. The ingenious and insightful design of every creature, say the animals, testifies to God's creative and providential beneficence. But the natural piety, generosity, courage, and trust of the animals model virtues that human beings too often lack. The animals become living, speaking rebukes of human waywardness, faithlessness, negligence, and insensitivity.

Although it is actually the animals that have brought their case before Bīwarāsp the Wise, King of the Jinn, the humans see themselves as the plaintiffs. They expect animals simply to serve their needs. Outside the precincts of the court, in their own domains, they readily berate and belabour any domestic beasts that seem to shirk that role. Some even question God for creating beasts that they find useless, noxious, or repulsive. All creatures, the animals argue, have a place in God's plan. All play their roles in nature. But, beyond such merely defensive remarks, the animals turn the tables on their adversaries, goaded to a wide-ranging denunciation of human weaknesses. Their aim is to discredit the claim that man's innate superiority makes humans the owners of nature and gives them a perfect right to treat all creatures as they please. Much of the fable is taken up with the animals' ripostes to such arrogance. In the end, most but not all of the claims the humans make are found groundless.

The zoological and ethological information that the Ikhwān table, whether scientific in the Galenic and Aristotelian mode or fanciful in the manner of midrashic tales and ancient bestiaries, is never dry or merely technical. By allowing the animals to speak, the Ikhwān clearly hope to sweeten the didactic pill. But by letting them speak critically, they add a bit of salt as well. The method that serves their moral aim is Aesopian. But the fable embedded in the essay form rapidly bursts the bounds of the familiar Aesopian tale. It is longer, broader in scope, and more varied in focus. Without the great battle scenes or stagey clinches of the epic, the fable's narrative is far more arresting to the interests of a grown-up than any simple allegory or morality play; and the narrative ends with no single pithy punchline but by integrating its insights into a single thesis, promised at the outset: 'Man at his best, we shall show, is a noble angel, the finest of creatures; but at his worst, an accursed devil, the bane of creation.' To this the Ikhwān add: 'We've put these themes into the mouths of animals, to make the case clearer and more compelling — more striking in the telling, wittier, livelier, more useful to the listener, and more poignant and thought-provoking in its moral.'

Reception of the *Risāla*

The narrative strategy of the Ikhwān's fable in Epistle 22 made it a highly popular work. Its manuscripts, widely copied in the Middle Ages, survive in many a library. The text was translated into numerous languages. There was a Latin version. There were Hebrew translations by one Rabbi Joel and, later (around 1240), by Rabbi Jacob ben Elazar. Those two Hebrew versions seem to be lost. But the 1316 Hebrew translation by the Provençal Jewish philosopher Kalonymos ben Kalonymos (ca. 1286–ca. 1337) survives.[1] Kalonymos also made a Hebrew translation from the Arabic of the tales of *Kalila and Dimna*, the fables from India that so charmed the Ikhwān when they wrote their own, 'The Case of the Animals'. His version of the animal essay of the Ikhwān was later translated into Yiddish (by one Hanokh Segal, 1768), and also into German. The Hebrew version was printed in Warsaw in 1877, and then by I. Toforovski and A. M. Haberman in Jerusalem in 1948. The Arabic text was translated into Urdu in Calcutta in 1810, by one Ikrām Alī, at the request of Abraham Lockett, a colonial official. English translations from the Urdu were made by John Dowson, a Sandhurst professor, and by others: James Atkinson, T. P. Manuel, John Platts, and A. C. Cavendish. Arabic, Turkish, and Persian editions were made and have continued to appear in modern times. As recently as 2005, Rabbis Anson Laytner and Dan Bridge in Louisville produced an illustrated popular adaptation from the Hebrew.

1 Kalonymos came from Arles and returned there after studies in Barcelona and work in Naples with regular visits to Rome. He translated texts for Charles Robert, Duke of Anjou, who held sway over Hungary as well as Naples and Anjou. Kalonymos' Latin version of Averroes' *Incoherence of the Incoherence* is extant, a clear mark of his philosophical outlook. Over thirty of his Hebrew translations from the Arabic survive. They include translations of works on geometry, astronomy, and philosophy from Kindī to Averroes, Galen's works on phlebotomy, colic, and clysters, and Averroes' commentaries on Aristotle. Kalonymos wrote several satirical works of his own, including, as a *jeu d'esprit*, a pretended Talmudic tractate on Purim that captures the light-hearted spirit of that holiday. I am indebted to David Walker for information in this note.

The original Arabic text was edited by the prolific orientalist Friedrich Dieterici (1821–1903) in 1879, under the title *Thier und Mensch vor dem König der Genien* (Beast and Man Before the King of the Jinn). Dieterici devoted decades of his life to editing, translating, and commenting on the tale. Buṭrus al-Bustānī, a Lebanese Christian scholar (b. 1898, not to be confused with his famous namesake, the encyclopaedist, 1819–1883), edited the work again in his four-volume edition of the *Rasāʾil Ikhwān al-Ṣafāʾ*. My own translation, based on the texts printed by Bustānī and Dieterici, appeared in 1978 as part of the Library of Classical Arabic Literature, under the general editorship of my teacher Ilse Lichtenstadter. Alma Giese made a new German translation in 1990. The present translation and critical edition forms part of the first complete critical edition and translation of the *Rasāʾil*.

Aesopian Satire

Putting critical thought into the mouths of animals can help shield authors from counter-strikes. The device was used by Aesop (his name is thought to be a variant of '*Aethiops*') and many another outsider. We know it from La Fontaine and, more familiarly, from Joel Chandler Harris' Uncle Remus and his tales of Brer Rabbit. Native American tales of the coyote as a trickster serve a similar function, as lightly veiled satire and social critique. The fictional Uncle Remus, like the shadowy, ancient Aesop, is a black man, and the protagonist of his tales, Brer Rabbit, like some of the animal speakers in our fable, owes more to sass and wit than to brute strength like Brer Bear, or to cruel cunning like Brer Fox. George Orwell used barn-yard animals to devastating effect in *Animal Farm*, his trenchant satire of the Bolshevik revolution and the rapid betrayal of its pretended ideals. Orwell's fable (begun in 1943) was withheld from publication until 1945, lest the war effort against the Nazis and their Axis allies be sapped by its unflattering portrayal of Stalin as the pig Napoleon, whose revolution promotes the slogan, 'Four legs good, two legs bad', and transmogrifies its dictum 'All animals are equal', to make 'some more equal than others'. Like Orwell, the Ikhwān are morally and intellectually at war with the mores of a seemingly invincible and widely incorrigible society, which they find airless and too often at odds with its own professed ideals.

The use of animals to say what may seem unsayable is, of course, much older than Orwell, or even Aesop. In the Hebrew Bible, Balaam's ass turns her head around and remonstrates with her rider: 'What have I done to you that you have beaten me now three times? ... Am I not your she-ass, whom you've always ridden to this day?' (Numbers 22:28, 30). The ass has seen what the seer is blind to — an angel, with sword unsheathed, blocking the way. In an ironic reversal, the beast takes the high moral ground that might have been a prophet's province, speaking truth to power, as they say. The scriptural narrative underscores the irony. For Balaam's first response to his ass is this: 'You're playing with me! If I had a sword in my hand, I'd have killed you by now!' (Numbers 22:29). But then the hired holy man, or spell caster, must confess that his she-ass has not been balky in the past. That sets up a higher irony. For Balaam may be venal, but he is also truthful. In the end he will see the truth and tell his patron that Israel cannot be cursed: their just ways place them under God's protection.

Reflecting on the ass's speech, the Midrash embroiders homiletically:

> The Holy One, blessed be He, respects human dignity and knows our needs. He shut the mouths of beasts. For if they could speak it would have been impossible to put them in service to man or to stand up against them. Here was this ass, the dullest of beasts, and there was the wisest of men. But no sooner had she opened her mouth than he could not hold his own against her. (Numbers Rabbah 20:15)

Like the Bible, the Ikhwān use dramatic irony to expose moral weaknesses. When the humans, in their fable, meet to plan their response to the animal complaint, they consider bribing the jinni vizier and any of the jurists who seem unsympathetic. The satiric mirror casts the humans in a lurid light when they anticipate demands for documentary evidence of their title to the animals, and the Arab proposes: 'We'll say we had the documents, but they were lost in the Flood.' And if asked to swear an oath, 'We'll say the burden of swearing falls on the respondent. We are the plaintiffs.' Legalism, prevarication, and a gnawing urge to cheat justice displace honest argument in human counsels.

Fable, then, lends a satirical slant to the *risāla*. Rather than describe animals from a human standpoint, expatiating on their uses to human beings, the Ikhwān write their zoology from the standpoint of the animals, generalizing the idea of use, by focusing on God's gifts to all living things and relativizing the idea of beauty: utility must be understood as usefulness to the organism, the product of God's grace in the design of animal bodies, providing for their survival and procreation. Form serves function, whether in the floppy ears that give shade to a rabbit's tender skin, or in the features that attract prospective mates and allow each type to perpetuate its kind. But adopting an animal perspective also means looking askance at human foibles. That gives the Ikhwān ample opportunity to model what is best in human nature and to censure freely human vices, globally and locally.

So, as Kalonymos remarks in introducing his Hebrew version, this fable is serious at the core. It is no mere burlesque. And, as the printed texts of the Arabic also testify, again no doubt reflecting the response of early readers, neither is this narrative some mere fairy tale. Its speeches and devices may entertain, but the fable is not a mere entertainment like the tales of Sindbad. The work does use supernatural motifs, and it has much to say about the jinn. But it is no ghost story. In folklore, the jinn are bogies and mischief-makers, blamed for souring the milk or laming the calf. But here the jinn ridicule such charges, challenging anyone to come forward who has ever seen such things.[2]

In Sindbad tales like the ones Sheherezad tells to stir the imagination of a jaded monarch and stay her own execution, genies have amazing powers. They regularly show their gratitude on being released from age-long confinement in a bottle by fulfilling a hapless mortal's wishes for limitless wealth, or instant transportation to or from the ends of the earth. But here there's a bit more emphasis on how the jinni got into the bottle. For Solomon's seal, which keeps that prison tightly sealed, is meant to symbolize the sovereignty of the one God and the subservience of all lesser powers.

2 See Chapter 6 below.

The Ikhwān don't care much for vulgar superstition; and the unearned fortunes of Aladdin's cave that so delight the rabble who gather in the marketplace to listen to tales like those collected in the *Thousand and One Nights* evoke what the Ikhwān would see as entirely the wrong kind of fantasies. For such idle dreams only further tangle the tinsel chains that bind human souls to this world and prevent our liberation to a better one. The Ikhwān urge their reader to ride with them 'in the rescue ship' that carries minds and hearts far from all such deceptions. Their jinn do not conjure with dreams of concupiscence, images of bejewelled palaces and flawless maidens. Their powers, like those of all God's creatures, are limited. So, in fact, is their wealth. And jinni history is a chequered affair, especially as regards relations with human beings.

There are good jinn and bad, faithful ones, and rebels like the accursed Satan Lucifer, the Iblīs of Muslim demonology, who was raised among the angels but grew too proud to bow with them to Adam at God's command. Rising beyond fable to the plane of metaphysics, where the true natures of all beings are considered, the jinn, for the Ikhwān, are vehicles of God's governance, natural forms and forces. For, as in al-Fārābī's Platonizing philosophy, the Ikhwān expect readers to shed the trappings of imagination when they think conceptually. Thinking, on their account — conceptual thinking as opposed to day-dreaming — frees us from the traps of appetite and passion, and connects us with the world of pure ideas.

Still, it's risky to try to raise others beyond the plane of imagination. Most people, most of the time, do not think conceptually. Few will welcome the invitation to drop their familiar and all-too-cosy simulacra. The Ikhwān, Kalonymos writes, understandably kept their work anonymous. Evidently they hoped to duck the prejudices that might impede or react against their message. Clearly, Kalonymos goes on to remark, dissension was rife in their day — as it was in his own.

Part of what the Ikhwān gain by giving speaking parts to animals is what postmoderns insist is impossible: they find a way of getting outside oneself, beyond the constructs and constrictions of the familiar culture and even the shared biases of humanity. Viewed from a suitable distance, human self-deception and self-aggrandizement are cast in sharp relief. Yet, the distance afforded by the fanciful setting and the use of animal voices allows the Ikhwān to mount a fairly radical critique without losing the ear of the audience they seek to cultivate and win over. The critique *is* broad, and hard-hitting. But it does not fall into the bitter invective of Juvenalian satire. At the same time, it does not lose itself in the ambiguity of a Horace, seeming to condone even what it condemns by speaking just a hair too knowingly.

The Essay Form

The essay is the medium favoured by the Ikhwān. The genre, well developed in antiquity, evolves from the epistolary form. An essay sets itself apart from other sorts of prose by its discursive, even digressive, shape, its love of anecdotes, asides, and by-play. It does not hew to the tight thematic structure of a treatise. So it need not announce and may not even use thematic rubrics. The chief characteristic of the essay is its intimacy of tone. A treatise uses a public, impersonal voice, at times stentorian, meant for a large audience. The essay cultivates a softer voice and seeks rapport with the reader, in part by presuming it, inviting one into the author's moral universe on terms of friendship and shared confidences, as it were.

Where an orator lays out enthymemes meant for completion by his hearers, bringing them on board with appeals to common interests, the essayist, expanding on the letter-writer's salutation and complimentary close, welcomes the reader into a smaller, closer circle defined by shared values and ideals. The orator presses a societal sense of unity, and that public posture lives on in the treatise. The essayist evokes the interest of his reader in more personal, even confessional tones. He appeals not just to common fears or wants but to shared ideals and experiences, building a sense of fellowship. With the Ikhwān, that ideal, the ideal of shared ideals, is not just a tool of rhetoric but a capstan of the message. One might call it a subtext, were it not so explicit.

Moderns know the essay form from Bacon and Montaigne, and perhaps from Addison and Steele, Elia or Emerson. But Seneca, the Stoic philosopher of ancient Cordoba, the tragedian and tragic tutor to Nero, was a past master of the epistolary essay. Kindī, the philosopher of the Arabs, pioneered the philosophical essay in the early days of Arabic prose, a century before the Ikhwān. His essay 'On How to Banish Sorrow' uses its dedicatory salutation to frame its problematic, and what follows weaves a fabric of anecdote and allegory into a vigorous case for spurning the goods of worldly attachment that are so soon lost and so often a source of grief and disquiet, instead urging embrace of the abiding, readily accessed goods of the mind. Maimonides, another philosopher from Cordoba (although he spent his mature years in Egypt), used the essay form brilliantly in the *Guide to the Perplexed* to pre-qualify his reader for the arduous and risky journey across the no man's land between the world's determinacy and God's infinite perfection.

The essay form was a favourite of the so-called secretarial class in the early Islamic *imperium*. As officers, administrators, and court officials, they communicated with one another in letters and reports, lightened and brightened with patches of style. The use of rhyme in prose was a favoured way of displaying verbal virtuosity without too great a loss of clarity. Office-holders who were in regular touch with one another could readily presume familiarity with the *status quo ante*. The mildly secular members of the secretarial class (*kuttāb*) relished information, treasured learning, and respected learned men — not to mention their awe at the prodigious memories and repertoires of some of the song girls, whose presence might bring a sense of luxury and delight to an especially memorable evening.

When the men of the secretarial class sought erudition and edification, even wisdom, they did not always look to the blinding obliquity of the ancient Arabic ode, the *qaṣīda*, or to the high hilarity and pyrotechnics of the *maqāma*, the satiric genre that Hamadhānī devised and that Ḥarīrī would perfect. They liked a good yarn and didn't mind if it pointed a moral. *Adab*, after all, gave refinement to the literate. It was, along with history, a chief instrument of *ta'dīb* — culture, discipline, cultivation.[3]

3 See Lenn E. Goodman, *Islamic Humanism* (New York: Oxford University Press, 2003), pp. 83–84, 101–110, 120, 147, 199.

The Outlook of the Ikhwān

Several times in our *risāla*, the Ikhwān allude to the fables of Bidpai, known in Arabic as *Kalīla wa-Dimna*. Those stories look rather crude compared to theirs, as Kalonymos, who translated both, remarks. But the lion, camel, and jackal brought to life by Bidpai set a precedent for the Ikhwān, who, for the first time in an original Arabic work, give speech to animals. Beyond that, the Sanskrit fables set the tone for the worldly animal delegates who make their appearance in the fable of the Ikhwān, and for the biting comments they put into the mouth of their especially outspoken jinni critic of human groups and cultures. Fighting cynicism with cynicism, the animal personae of the Ikhwān readily undercut the self-serving boasts of their human adversaries, displacing worldliness itself with higher, spiritual interests.

The texts most cited by the Ikhwān come from the Qur'an, supplemented at times by lines from the hadith (the sayings traditionally ascribed to Muhammad) and by fanciful materials from the *Qiṣaṣ al-anbiyā'* (legends attached to the lives and deeds of ancient prophets like Abraham and Solomon), tales about tyrants like Nimrod, monarchs like Bilqīs, the Queen of Sheba, fabulous animals like the griffin, the sea-serpent, and the Simurgh, and, of course, the jinn themselves. Like other mediaeval authors, the Ikhwān use scripture creatively, dovetailing its verses to their purposes and adroitly finding proof-texts to underscore and underwrite their moral theses.

The views the Ikhwān embrace, as well as those they mean to pillory or deflate, are for the most part embedded in the speeches of their *dramatis personae*. The framing of passages quoted and legends retold by figures who speak their lines in a fictional context allows the Ikhwān some distance from earnest appropriation of every trope and tradition, gloss and reading they entertain. Fable enhances the distance that dialogue imparts. Muslim contemporaries like the grammarian Abū Sa'īd al-Sīrāfī (d. 979), who castigated philosophical logic and logicians as invasive weeds among the Arabic sciences, and predecessors like the Shi'i agent Abū Ḥātim al-Rāzī (d. 934), who ridiculed the philosophical ideal of intellectual autonomy, also used the dialogue form. But both of these critics present their dialogues as the records of actual disputes with real philosophers — the Nestorian

Christian logician Abū Bishr Mattā (d. 940) in the first case, and the independent-minded physician-philosopher Muḥammad ibn Zakariyā' al-Rāzī (Rhazes, d. 925 or 935) in the second. They do not use the debate format to gain distance but only to show how brilliantly they have skewered the rationalism of an adversary. The Jewish philosopher-poets Solomon Ibn Gabirol (ca. 1020–1075) and Judah Halevi (ca. 1075–1141) both mount fictional debates. Ibn Gabirol's *Fons Vitae* was to become a metaphysical classic, and Halevi's *Kuzari* stands as a masterfully crafted alternative to philosophical intellectualism. However, each of these works relies on a question-and-answer format. Dialectic, in the main, is just the authors' way of introducing their own ideas: questions are raised to be answered; objections, to be dealt with. The views presented are put through their paces. But the alternatives acknowledged are foils much more than live options.

Dialogue in this *risāla* of the Ikhwān is quite a different matter. The tale takes seriously quite a variety of view-points. There will still be one right answer in the end, but dialectic here is critical in reaching it. The forensically focused dialogue of the Ikhwān does not approach the heights won by Plato's Socratic dialogues. Still, the outcome is hardly sheer eristic. There is dramatic irony, of course — as there would be whenever eavesdroppers overhear self-serving arguments. Yet fable naturally caricatures rival views, whereas Plato's mimetic virtuosity allows more realistically shaded views of human brains stuffed with the false conceit of wisdom. The result is that the figures limned in Plato's vignettes, drawn from life, will work their way far deeper into the quicksands of self-parody. For their unexamined opinions and unreflective words often remain unanswered and thus sink unaided. The Ikhwān move more swiftly to provide thoughtless pronouncements with an answer. And, like Aesop and unlike the Plato of the Socratic dialogues, they are not averse to stepping in to point a moral. Even when the anonymous authors stay in the background, their shadows are pretty clearly discernible and their voices are pretty clearly heard behind the scrim.

The adversarial context of a fictive court case does not promote a commitment as strong as that of Cicero's speculative writings to the use of dialogue as a means of producing philosophical results. The distance the Ikhwān gain from the dialogue technique, like their cloak of anonymity and their use of animal and jinni speakers, is more defensive than philosophically constructive. But the authors' earnestness shines through. Their masks are diaphanous. Their sympathies, to be specific, are intellectualist and voluntarist: God is wise, and good. He shines His living Ideas into the natural world as the vehicles of his providence. Man, not despite that emanation but because of it, is free and therefore responsible — above all, for making a choice to seek his own salvation. For God has not left the souls He shed on the world without a rope ladder to shimmy up again and regain their true home.

The Ikhwān fight shy of factionalism. Like Muḥammad ibn Zakariyā' al-Rāzī, they loathe sectarianism. It foments bloodshed, perverting the spiritual quest that is man's *raison d'être* into a violent struggle for domination. Indeed, the Ikhwān have little good to say of the 'Abbāsid state and its functionaries. They offer their own outlook as an alternative, speaking as exponents of a spiritual brotherhood whose teachings they hope to spread among kindred spirits. Although their Shi'i and Mu'tazilite sympathies are soft-pedalled, they do uphold the 'Alid cause when they have the 'outspoken jinni' blame the human Muslims for rebelling, forsaking the faith, and slaying their finest leaders, that is, the early caliphs honoured by the Shi'a and Sunnis alike. Along with the Mu'tazilites, the Ikhwān link human free will with God's justice. Indeed, raising the topic of the heavens' obedience to God's will, they use a Mu'tazilite gloss on the Qur'anic image (55:5–6) of the stars' prostration before God, much as al-Kindī, the first great Muslim philosopher, did a century before. That is, they read the verse as an affirmation that God governs nature through its laws, providence manifest in the steady rhythms of the cosmos.

There's a subtler subtext in the names the Ikhwān give some of the jinni spirits in their fable. Here and in several artful digs, they work into their narrative a steady undertone or undertow of sentiments aligned with the Shu'ūbiyya, the ethnic reaction against Arab hegemony. In theory, tribal pride and Arab chauvinism vanished when Persian and other non-Arab peoples embraced Islam after the Muslim conquest. But that ideal was far from being realized in fact, and the Ikhwān were keenly sensitive to the persistent stigma of lesser birth and blood among non-Arabs. They express pride in the Persian history and traditions that long antedate the coming of Islam. So it is the Arab delegate who is made the author of the sly plan of claiming that documentary title to the animals was lost in the Flood. And the Ikhwān proudly and tellingly cite the 360-day solar year of the Iranian calendar, for its pleasing Pythagorean symmetry, despite the ban on this way of counting the passing days under Islamic hegemony. Looking further afield, to Byzantine, Afghan, and Turkic lands and peoples, and to Jewish, Christian, Hindu, Buddhist, and Zoroastrian traditions, the Ikhwān find virtues and vices, strengths and weaknesses, sincerity and insincerity in all ethnicities and faiths.

The ontology of the Ikhwān is Neoplatonic: ideas have a higher reality than sensory things. The cosmos draws its being, goodness, unity, beauty, and intelligibility from the Forms that God projects on nature through the mediation of the heavens — that is, the stars and planets, the spheres in which they are embedded, and the intellects that set their courses. It is to these intellects that God entrusts nature's governance. They fulfil their charge by generously giving life and order to all that lies below. Fancifully and liturgically, these intellects are angels, spirits, or jinn; but in reality they are minds and Platonic Forms that show their fealty to God in the invariance of their actions and effects.

Animals, as the Neoplatonists long argued, are made not for human exploitation but, in the first instance, for their own sakes. They have needs and interests of their own. As for the celestial bodies, they are compounded, the Ikhwān argue. So they are not eternal. Still, their revolutions have endured far longer than any casual reading of scriptural history might lead the unwary to believe. The stars and planets mark the rise and fall of each regime in the world below, not as rulers in their own right but as legates, messengers — the troops and vassals, as the Ikhwān put it, of the Lord who made them all and governs their every movement.

The Animals' Complaint

Irony is the distinctive mark of satirical literature, a delight to sophisticates proud of catching the in-joke that mocks a target's gravitas.

Irony gives a barb to prophetic criticism too, exposing outcomes that mock a wrongdoer's aims.[4] The animals in our fable relish the irony when humans boast of their fine garments and furnishings only to be reminded that mankind's choicest fabrics are of silk, wrested from the spittle of a lowly worm. The woollens and hides with which humans bedeck themselves are stripped from the backs of animals. Honey, the most delicious of human foods, praised as a health-giving elixir in the Qur'an, is robbed from bees. As the rabbit urges in his complaint:

> '[. . .]these humans drink the milk of cattle as they drank their mother's milk and ride on beasts' shoulders as they rode on their father's shoulders when small. They use animals' wool and fleece for coats and upholstery, but in the end they slaughter, flay, disembowel, and dismember them, set them to boil or roast, unfeeling and unremembering all the good, all the blessings, lavished on them.'

The animals' first pleas against human cruelty, a litany of torture and abuse, are laid knowingly, even calculatedly, before the jinni king, in order to arouse pity for the animals' plight. The ass, the ram, camel, elephant, horse, and mule raise a chorus of complaints against the beatings, proddings, and invective suffered by beasts of burden, and the flaying, roasting, and boiling of the animals that humans use for food. Each domestic beast in turn evokes the pity that any sensitive hearer would feel on witnessing such mistreatment. The ram's complaint is typical:

> 'You would have pitied us, your Majesty, had you seen us as their prisoners, when they seized our smallest kids and lambs and tore them from their dams to steal our milk. They took our young and bound them hand and foot to be slaughtered and skinned, hungry, thirsty, bleating for mercy but unpitied, screaming for help with none to aid them. We saw them slaughtered, flayed, dismembered, disembowelled, their heads, brains, and livers on butchers' blocks, to be cut

4 See Goodman in Saadiah, *The Book of Theodicy*, p. 420. Saadiah ben Joseph al-Fayyūmī, *The Book of Theodicy: Translation and Commentary on the Book of Job*, tr. Lenn Goodman (New Haven: Yale University Press, 1988).

> up with great knives and boiled in cauldrons or roasted in an oven, while we kept silent, not weeping or complaining. For even if we had wept they would not have pitied us. Where then is their mercy?'

The complainants do not fail to mention the foul language of mule-drivers, the pricks of the elephant goad, the wounds and risks faced by war-horses. These complaints against human cruelty are not forgotten as the case moves to a broader critique of human ways. So the outcome forecast at the beginning seems to stand at the end: even if domestic animals are not to be freed, and the exploitation of living species is to continue while human beings hold dominion, the demand for greater kindness and consideration — humaneness, as we like to say — survives each legal and moral challenge that the human beings in the fable make. Human hegemony rests on no intrinsic merit or superiority but solely on the grace of God, whose chief epithets are those of mercy and compassion, and whose cardinal expectation of His creatures is that they share His bounties with those less fortunate than they — as the stars shed God's grace on those below them.

Humans, as the animals complain, do not keep to a single habitat, nor do they await a set breeding season but breed indiscriminately. So humans have spread throughout the earth — over land and sea, mountain and plain. Men 'usurped the habitats of other animal kinds that lived on the earth, wrested from them their ancestral lands,' taking the whole earth as their dominion. 'We are roused to mount but once a year, and not with overmastering passion or at pleasure's call but for the survival of our race.' Human appetites and ambitions, by contrast, seem to know no limit.

Human overreaching, as the Ikhwān present it through the animals' eyes, is both a product and a stimulant of arrogance. Recognition that the gifts we boast of are not of our own making but are God's boons is thus critical to the case. The criticism points not just to the gratitude we owe God but also to the humility that befits us as creatures within nature, not apart from it. Human talents, skills, and attainments are gifts, not self-creations. Nor are they quite as splendid as we often like to think.

It is here that the animals press their satiric role, comparing human powers, arts, and institutions to the capabilities of our animal counterparts: humans see well, but many a bird sees far better. Humans have weapons, traps, snares, and stratagems, but we are weaklings compared to the beasts of prey, let alone the dragon, the sea-serpent, or the mighty Simurgh. And even the mightiest of animals have a softer side that humans match all too rarely. Thus the griffin:

> 'How many ships tossed by the tempest on the fathomless deep have I led back on course! How many shipwrecked and drowning men have I brought safe to islands or shores, only to please my Lord and give thanks for the blessing of my massive frame and huge body, to show due gratitude for His bounty toward me. *For He is our meed and faithful Protector.*'

Again, the lion,

> '[. . .]largest of predators and the mightiest in frame, the strongest, fiercest, most terrible and majestic. His chest is broad, his waist narrow, his haunches shapely, his head massive, his face round, his brow ample. His jaw is square, his nostrils flared. His paws are stout; his fangs and claws, strong as iron. His eyes flash like lightning. His voice is deep, and his roar mighty. His shanks are like granite, his heart bold, his aspect terrible. He fears no one. Water buffaloes and elephants do not alarm him, nor do crocodiles, or even men, with all their powers to do injury — not even armed horsemen with weapons that can pierce a coat of mail. He is doughty and steadfast. Whatever he undertakes, he sees to it himself and asks no help from his forces or vassals. But he is generous. When he's taken a prize, he eats his share and leaves the rest liberally to his followers and dependents. He disdains worldly things and will attack neither woman nor child — nor orphan. For his nature is noble. If he sees a light far off, he approaches through the dark of night and stands at a distance, his ferocity lulled and savagery gentled. If he hears a sweet melody he comes near and settles down peacefully.[. . .]'

Humans are proud of their arts and industries, cities and institutions. But bees build brilliantly without line or compass, ants live in organized societies, and all creatures praise God naturally and spontaneously — birds in their songs, beasts in their every movement and the very framing of their bodies.

As might be expected in an adversarial setting, some of the animals' arguments are self-serving. Some are *jeux d'esprit* of the Ikhwān. It is a bit sophistical, after all, to condemn hoarding, whilst praising the bee for its ingenious, airtight storage cells, and the ant for cutting grains in half to keep them from sprouting. The Ikhwān are just as thrilled by the grasshopper's carefree life as by the ant's industry and thrift. They admire the wasp's trusting expectation of rebirth in the spring just as enthusiastically as they mark the silkworm's metamorphoses. A celebratory, didactic intent peeks through the satiric overlay. Clearly, the critique of human weaknesses is only part of the tale's intent, a foil for the underlying exposition of the marvels of animal life. The *risāla* is, after all, a chapter on zoology in a larger, encyclopaedic collection. Nonetheless, the social critique eclipses the biological exposition, heightening the contrast between false vanity and what humans rightly prize.

It is a little contradictory to insist that beasts of prey don't eat much, and yet to marvel at the huge intake of the sea-serpent. But even in his case, the larger, morally freighted theme of the divinely imparted balance and justice in nature reasserts itself:

> '[. . .]All marine animals fear him and flee before his vast power and strength. When he moves, the sea itself rocks with his swift swimming. His head is immense, his eyes flashing, his teeth numerous, his mouth and gullet tremendous. He swallows countless hordes of sea creatures each day, and when his belly is full and he finds it hard to digest them, he arches and bends like a bow, supporting himself on his head and tail, and raises his mid-parts out of the water into the air, gleaming like a rainbow in the sunlight, huffing and puffing about, sunning himself to aid his digestion. But sometimes, in this posture, he swoons, and the rising mists lift him up from below and bear him through the air to dry land, where he dies, and the beasts feed on his hulk for days — or he is borne to the shores of the

land of Gog and Magog, who live beyond the great barrier, two nations of human form but savage spirit, who know neither order nor government and have no commerce or trade, industry or craft, ploughing or sowing, but only hunting and fishing, plundering, raiding, and eating one another.

'Know, your Majesty, that all marine animals flee in terror before the sea-serpent. But he fears nothing, save only a tiny beast resembling a mosquito, which he cannot harm and against whose sting he is defenceless. Once it stings him, its poison percolates through his body and he dies. Then all the sea animals gather to feed and gorge on his carcass for days. For small beasts do feed on the larger when they can. The same is true with birds: sparrows, larks, swallows, and their ilk eat grasshoppers, ants, gnats, flies, and the like. Then sparrow-hawks and falcons and their kind hunt and devour the sparrows and larks. Hawks and eagles hunt and eat these in turn. But when large animals die, they are eaten by the smallest — ants, flies, and worms.[. . .]'

The Ikhwān are having fun when they put snatches of celebrated Arabic elegiacs into the mouth of the owl, and homilies into the skylark's song. But their critique of human institutions is in earnest: ablutions and purifications are mandated only to cleanse impurity, moral as well as hygienic. Trades and industries trap the human spirit in an exhausting, endless, greedy, ultimately futile quest. Even human piety is too often self-serving:

'But most people, you find, scurry to the doctor at the first sign of illness but turn to God only if treatment is protracted and the medicine prescribed unavailing. When they've given up hope of a medical cure, they pray desperately, perhaps writing on scraps of paper to stick up on the walls of mosques, churches, or synagogues. They pray privately or make public penitential vows, saying "God have mercy on a troubled supplicant" — as He did in celebrated cases. This is the reward they expect for thieving or robbing or some such crime! Had they turned to God to start with and called on Him inwardly, not just publicly, it would have been well for them, far better than their public protestations and acts of penance.[. . .]'

The Ikhwān propose no utopian answer to the animals' brief. The fable envisions universal vegetarianism in the distant past, and one day that norm might revive. But no such outcome is demanded or expected by the story's dénouement. Still, the idea of revolution is never far from the thinking of the Ikhwān. And that thought takes on a vivid, graphic sense, piqued by the imagery of the Qur'an but hitched to thoughts of the revolutions of the heavens.

Revolution and Succession

Each heavenly body in the cosmos of the Ikhwān sheds its influence on what lies below. So every being reaps its share of grace from God, along with the obligation to pass on the bounty to lesser beings, as the rabbit explains:

> 'For example, the two celestial luminaries, the sun and the moon, received from God so bounteous a share of light, brilliance, splendour, and majesty that people often fell under the delusion that they were lords or gods, so clearly do the marks of divinity shine in them. That is why they were subjected to eclipses, to show the discerning that if they were gods they would not go dark. Likewise with the rest of the stars. They may be granted brilliant light, revolving spheres, and long lives, but they are not immune to flickering, or retrograde motion, or even falling, to show that they too are subordinate.[. . .]'

The heavenly bodies are God's subalterns. That is why they forecast creatures' fates: like the stars and planets, dynasties rise and fall. So do individuals, nations, whole species and kinds. Each creature and kind has its day, and each will be displaced by successors, until the final hour calls history to its close.

Biologists today study succession in the natural history of a forest or other ecosystem. That was an important theme in Darwin's thinking, confirmed by his experiments right on his own estate, when he fenced off a patch of grass and watched as ever-taller and more aggressive plants succeeded lesser types once the fence had put a stop to the nibbling of the sheep. But for the Ikhwān, as in the scriptural traditions they follow, succession is not a matter of biology alone. It is a morally fraught idea. The jinn have had their epoch in the ascendant, as their sages relate; humans are now dominant on earth. No created kind rules without limit. Taking up the Qur'anic archaeology, which sees in the ruins of vanished civilizations memorials to the fate their denizens suffered for spurning God's admonishers, the Ikhwān see every fall as a judgement, visited by God's justice and reflecting the limits to the worth and merit that each race and natural kind has exercised and enjoyed.[5]

All perfections stem from God, but none is absolute. Each species and genus has its strengths: the tiger may be powerful, but the gazelle has speed. And each kind has its weaknesses: the elephant fears the gnat, the lion is victim to the ant, the jackal must beware of dogs. Armoured warriors are harried by wasps, and the most brutal of human tyrants was brought low by a gnat. God always has the last laugh as the rhythms of worldly expansion, exploitation, oppression, and dependency resonate on the moral plane. Each creature and kind flourishes by its strengths and fades by its weaknesses. God's gifts are fair, answering to capability and need; and the rhythms of each life and reign are marked off by the steady circling of the heavens.

The turns of fate are implacable, but the Ikhwān are not fatalistic: dire outcomes can be dodged, as the parrot proposes in telling how one ancient city's people escaped a devastating flood.[6] The safest recourse, ultimately, is refuge in God's bosom. Nature will keep its course, as the heavens turn unquestioningly at His decree. But the moral and spiritual postures that human beings choose do make a difference — all the difference in the world, and beyond, as the Ikhwān see it. Even so, no creaturely strength endures forever. That is for God alone. For, as the Qur'an teaches, *All things are perishing but His Face* (28:88).

---

5 See, e.g., Qur'an 30:9; Tarif Khalidi, *Arabic Historical Thought in the Classical Period* (Cambridge: Cambridge University Press, 1994), p. 8; Goodman, *Islamic Humanism*, pp. 161–162; cf. Deuteronomy 29.

6 See Chapter 37 below.

Kindred Spirits

Montaigne (1533–1592), a modern master of the essay form, offers a nice parallel to the Aesopian critique of human foibles in the *Rasāʾil.* His *Apology for Raymond Sebond* aims 'to crush and trample underfoot human arrogance and pride' (p. 327)[7] — much of it grounded in a false confidence in human reason, 'the first foundation of the tyranny of the evil spirit' (p. 328). Montaigne's nominal aim is a defence of the Catalan theologian, whose work he had translated in 1569 at the instance of his father (who saw in Sebond's work a perfect antidote against Luther and the Reformation). But human pretensions lie closer to the bullseye of Montaigne's real target. Animals, he urges, have keener senses and seem in the end to lack no capacity that humans have. Just as the Ikhwān find a natural piety in the birds and beasts, Montaigne finds that elephants not only perform their ablutions but pray, make music, and dance (pp. 341–343).

Presumption, Montaigne argues, is mankind's endemic illness. Humans are puny, frail, and vulnerable. We live in the world's basement (p. 330) — the bowels of the cosmos, as some mediaevals liked to say. 'When I play with my cat,' Montaigne writes famously, 'who knows if I am not a pastime to her more than she is to me?' Granted, animals do not speak, but 'we do not understand them any more than they do us' (p. 331). That argument does not hew to the strictest standards of logical rigour. But modesty does not need rigour, and every philosopher, at least in reading others' works, if not in scrutinizing his own, has seen how readily the pride of too narrow a sense of rigour goeth before a philosophical fall.

The essay form allows Montaigne to argue playfully, as the Ikhwān do in setting down the paeans and praises of the birds, the elegies of the owl, and warning cries of the ominous raven. Hyperbole is the mask and mark of irony. But the spirit of mockery and raillery does not obscure the underlying point: the vanity of human self-assurance — which the Ikhwān locate not in reason but in sheer pretension, and pretentiousness.

---

7 References shown parenthetically here are to Donald Frame's translation: Michel Eyquem Montaigne, *Complete Essays*, tr. D. Frame (Stanford, CA: Stanford University Press, 1958).

Montaigne, like the Ikhwān, sings the praises of the bees:

> Is there a society regulated with more order, diversified into more charges and functions, and more consistently maintained? Can we imagine so orderly an arrangement of actions and occupations as this to be conducted without reason and foresight?

He goes on to quote Vergil, who cites those (i.e., the Stoics) who, like the Ikhwān, say that bees share in the mind of the divine (pp. 332–333). The swallows, Montaigne argues, return each spring and 'without judgment' find the perfect spots to build their nests. If nature guides animal instincts, why do we not acknowledge animal superiority? For human works, despite all we bring to them 'by nature and by art' are often surpassed by animals, when nature 'with maternal tenderness,' comes along, to 'guide them as by the hand in all the actions and comforts of their life; while she abandons us to chance and to fortune' (p. 333).

Like the Ikhwān, Montaigne cites the 'shells, husks, bark, hair, wool, spikes, hide, down, feathers, scales, fleece and silk' that nature gives all creatures, according to their needs. She 'has armed them with claws, teeth, or horns for attack and defence; and has herself instructed them in what is fit for them — to swim, to run, to fly, to sing — whereas man can neither walk nor speak, nor eat, nor do anything but cry, without apprenticeship' (pp. 333–334). Montaigne quotes Lucretius here, but his argument, like that of the Ikhwān, follows Galen's Stoicizing appeals, finding hallmarks of providence in all animal adaptations: every species, Montaigne writes, even ours, is equipped according to its needs. Even ants, he argues, quoting Dante and again paralleling the Ikhwān, are able to communicate the path to prizes they have found. But all creatures (another central theme for the Ikhwān) are equal, in a sense: 'We are neither above nor below the rest: all that is under heaven, says the sage, incurs the same law and the same fortune' (p. 336, echoing Ecclesiastes 3:14–15, 19).

Human imagination, Montaigne notes, allows us to conceive both what is true and what is false. That sets us above the beasts in one regard, but at a price. For all our vain wishes and unwholesome desires are fed from that spring (p. 336). Even free will, Montaigne writes, sets us at a disadvantage. For it makes human virtue contingent and unreliable, whereas animal behaviour is steady and fixed. Human desires far outrun the simple needs of nature (p. 346). The Ikhwān, of course, agree, and their thoughts find an echo when Montaigne adds, 'there is no animal in the world as treacherous as man' (p. 350). The Ikhwān write with knowing bitterness on that theme.

Picturing the wisest of men freely surrendering all human wisdom and virtue rather than give up the well-beloved human form, Montaigne concludes with a triumphant condemnation of human vanity:

> Well, I accept this naïve, frank confession. Indeed, they knew that those qualities about which we make so much ado are but idle fancy. Even if the beasts, then, had all the virtue, knowledge, wisdom, and capability of the Stoics, they would still be beasts; nor would they for all that be comparable to the wretched, wicked, senseless man. In short, whatever is not as we are is worth nothing. And God himself, to make himself appreciated, must resemble us, as we shall presently declare. Whereby it is apparent that it is not by a true judgment, but by foolish pride and stubbornness, that we set ourselves before the other animals and sequester ourselves from their condition and society. (p. 358)

Clearly Montaigne is drinking at the same well as the Ikhwān. They too have the animals reflect early in their fable on the human pretension — nursed in ancient and modern reflections on the differences between anthropomorphic and zoomorphic deities — that the human bodily form is somehow intrinsically nobler than the many and varied forms of the beasts. But Montaigne shapes the terrain to yield his own conclusion. For him, the nisus of the argument is human vanity. But the Ikhwān are after higher game: their chastening of vanity is a moral lever, meant to help a reader shift his gaze from trifles and ephemera to spiritual goods. And freedom, despite its many risks, is not disparaged. For freedom is what makes that shift possible, the key to man's redeemability.

The Ikhwān and Evolution

It has been both claimed and denied that the Ikhwān anticipated Darwin's evolutionary ideas.[8] Naturally, this cannot mean that they had the evidence that allows one to marshal virtually all of biology under the banner of evolution, in support of what Darwin called 'one long argument'. The biology the Ikhwān knew was that of Aristotle and Galen. They leaven their tale with fanciful lore about the coalescence of pearls from dewdrops in an oyster, the chivalry of the lion, poetry of the owl and nightingale, and generosity of the sea-serpent and the Simurgh. But regarding biology proper, they are no mean observers. They relish the chance to trace the flight of birds, take note of the savings in organ weights that make flight possible, and experiment with the balance that avian plumage affords. They delight in the anatomy of a grasshopper or a gnat, check off the multiple stomachs of a ruminant, and watch the foraging of ants, the scurrying and pecking of chicks, and the maternal ways of sheep. They blame geometers for puzzling over arcane mathematical problems and chasing seemingly useless facts when they could have studied the organs and workings of the human body.

The Ikhwān share the awe that every naturalist feels at the intricacy and ingenuity of nature's design and the symmetry and functionality of its structures in living beings. But they do not think in terms of natural selection. They see election in the history of natural (and supernatural) kinds. But the arbiter is God, and God's standard is grace, not creaturely fitness. One kind gives way to the next not because its efficiency in exploiting the environment has been outdone but because its allotment of bounty has been spent.

For the Ikhwān, adaptation is a fact, not a process. Every adaptation bespeaks God's mercy. Everything that fits a species to its métier and milieu is a sign of God's discerning providential care, the well-spring of all love and caring within nature,[9] exercised through the Forms

---

8 F. Dieterici, *Der Darwinismus im X. und XI. Jahrhundert* (Leipzig: J. C. Hinrichs, 1878); T. J. De Boer, *History of Philosophy in Islam*, tr. Edward R. Jones (London: Luzac, 1961), p. 91; S. H. Nasr, *Islamic Cosmological Doctrines* (Cambridge, MA: Harvard University Press, 1964), p. 71.

9 See Chapter 35 below.

that scriptural poetry calls angels but that Neoplatonism knows as the supernal souls and minds that animate the cosmos and direct the choric dances of the spheres.

Natural selection is not entirely a modern concept. The thought that living beings arose by chance and were culled according to their fitness was proposed by Empedocles (ca. 495–435 BCE), a millennium and a half before the Ikhwān put reed pen to paper. A more refined, atomistic version of the idea was salient in Epicurean naturalism. But the Ikhwān show no interest in such notions. Even a highly independent predecessor like Rāzī, who champions a brand of atomism not unlike the Epicurean, eschews appeals to chance in explaining life and order in the world. For Rāzī, only soul can yield soul, and only a divine intelligence can account for cosmic order.[10]

To the Ikhwān, too, the world is no whirligig; natural objects are powerless to cause or explain themselves. Nothing in nature is anything at all in and of itself. All reality and whatever properties manifest reality stem from God. That is why no species has a right to boast of what it is — any more than it can take credit for the sheer fact *that* it is. Every natural being is and does as God designed. Man cannot boast of his sciences, arts, or industries, because none of the distinctions that grace a creature is of its own devising. No finite being can reach out beyond the limits of its temporality and constitute its own essential character, as if to create itself.[11] All that is, stems from God's beneficence: we know God from the marks of His grace in nature, and we know that every reality in nature is a gift of grace — because it comes from God.

Certainly nothing could be further from the uses to which Darwinian naturalism is typically put today than that tightly argued circle, with the evidence of adaptation called to testify to God's creative grace, and grace

10 Goodman, *Jewish and Islamic Philosophy: Crosspollinations in the Classic Age* (Edinburgh: Edinburgh University Press, 1999), p. 43; and Goodman, 'Razi's Myth of the Fall of the Soul: Its Function in His Philosophy', in *Essays in Islamic Philosophy and Science*, ed. G. Hourani (Albany, NY: SUNY Press,1975), pp. 25–40.

11 Cf. Saadiah, *Kitāb al-Mukhtar fī'l-āmānāt wa'l-i'tiqādāt*, I.2, ed. J. Kafih (Jerusalem: Sura, 1970), tr. Samuel Rosenblatt as *The Book of Beliefs and Opinions* (New Haven: Yale University Press, 1948), pp. 46–50.

in turn made to vouch for nature's beneficence. There is, of course, a teleology in Darwinian adaptation. Any adaptive trait serves (or once served) the needs of a population. But Darwinian adaptation, as most commonly understood, is no product of intelligence. Evolution's cunning is inboard and built up over aeons, the work of regulated chance. As for Darwinian selection, it breeds with a sickle, rarely a loving eye. And its setting is an environment that is often hostile or presumed indifferent, not commodious like the world God made to be dwelt in by the creatures whose stories the Ikhwān unfold in the voices of the animals.

There is another reason why it's a misnomer to call the Ikhwān al-Ṣafāʾ Darwinians *avant la lettre*. They have no interest in deriving one species from another. They do casually call a giraffe a cross between a camel and an ass, but they don't seem to have an interest in recording — let alone making — such a cross. To them, such putative hybrids are just species at the intersection of discrete types. So the ostrich is a cross between a bird and a beast. But the idea of species change is, from the Neoplatonizing standpoint of the Ikhwān, not just unnatural but illogical. They make analogies between, say, animal and human parenting (to the advantage of the animals in the rhetoric of their fable's dispute), and they compare human savagery to animal predation, or contrast human lust with the seasonally regulated chastity of the beasts. But it never occurs to them to claim kin with the animals; and the monkey, to them, is a clown among the animals, not a progenitor.

Even the great chain of being, whose continuity might seem to forge moral bonds among God's creatures, is pled in support not of animal equity but of natural hierarchy. The Ikhwān do not think God's fairness demands that He treat all species alike, but only that he sustain each according to its needs: proportional, not arithmetic, equality is their Pythagorean message. What would it mean, after all, to give the gnat an elephant's trunk rather than the tiny proboscis God actually gave it, scaled to its frame?

The dragon, monarch of the crawling creatures, is moved to tears by the frailty and helplessness of so many of his subjects. But the cricket explains that worms, grubs, and parasites are compensated for their lack of limbs and organs by the ease and simplicity of their lives, their cosseted habitats, and ready access to all of their needs. All God's gifts are matched to need: what good would it do some intestinal worm to have organs of sense and locomotion that it will never use? The creature is perfectly adapted to draw in its food right where it is, without fear, pain, or trouble. There is a hierarchy of natural types, as Neoplatonism would expect. But there is no inequity in nature. So there is no need for the higher to emerge from the lower. Individuals may seek redemption. But that is for humans alone, a concomitant of human consciousness and freedom. Thinking can be done and freedom exercised by any human being, at any time — even a Nimrod might have repented. So global progress is never in question.

The taxonomy of the Ikhwān may seem crude. Beasts and predators, fowl and birds of prey, swarming and crawling creatures are grouped biblically, as it were — behaviourally, more by habitat than morphology. Some of the resultant divisions show their ragged edges, as when the parrot's hooked beak and claws make him out a raptor, or when the rhinoceros is pushed, by the imperatives of the fabulous, into the office of vizier to the Simurgh. Marks of narrative contrivance show up again when the frog is classed as a water animal. Evolutionists know that amphibians originate in an aqueous environment, as their juvenile forms reveal, and that is why a frog must lay her eggs in water. But the Ikhwān need to class the frog as a water creature partly to facilitate a land journey to the court of the jinni king by an aquatic delegate with a voice.

Still, the taxonomy of the tale is not unstable; its lines are fixed. All animals (even the unique and fabulous) belong to kinds. These are often spoken of in familial terms: humans are 'Adamites' (*banū Ādam*). The weasel is called by his traditional, almost totemic name, *'ibn 'irs'*. More than one bird calls his congeners 'brethren'. The bee king plainly regards his subjects as his children. The whale, we learn (with a hint of allegory), has kin in every sea and stream, shallow and brook. The dragon, despite his tender sympathies, lives far from the children of his kind. Dogs and cats are branded renegades for leaving their own ilk and going over to humankind.

But, despite the family resemblances and the mention of *murakkab*, or 'composite' species like giraffes and ostriches, cheetahs remain predators and horses remain beasts, even after leaving their fellows. Satan-Iblīs remained a jinni although living among the angels. Some species are hard to classify. The pig, for one, has a form and habits that place him ambiguously in many a classificatory scheme. But the Ikhwān do not make 'composite' species into mediating links in a chain of descent. And the ambiguities in classifying swine are treated satirically, as a mirror of human subjectivity and variance in cultural attitudes. The source of the ambivalence that humans manifest towards swine is not the pig's essence and is certainly not his fault. He is confused and bemused by all the things that are said of him, bewildered by the heated arguments that confidently make him out to be so useful or so loathsome. The disputes that tellingly affect his fate do not affect his nature, whatever it might prove to be. They only show how fickle and, indeed, pig-headed human individuals and societies can be. The Ikhwān do not attempt to exploit the views, so wavering from one culture to the next but so obstinate within each, by challenging the very enterprise of classification, fusing its categories, or dissolving its boundaries. For them, species fixity reflects the dependence of all things natural on the timeless, changeless Forms of the divinely projected intellectual realm. Fluidity and change, as in Aristotle's cosmos, affect only particulars, never essences. There is no transmutation of species.

Yet, unlike orthodox Aristotelians, the Ikhwān are not bound by the fixity of Forms to the view that so many of their predecessors, contemporaries, and successors took to be its strict entailment: the dogma of the world's eternity. Monotheistic philosophers were well aware that overly strict allegiance to invariant natural law and inviolable natural rhythms could militate against the idea of Creation. And Creation, proclaimed by the fable's speakers in a steady litany of variations on scriptural narratives, is the abiding theme of the cosmology of the Ikhwān. In this they stand with earlier Muslim philosophers like Kindī and Rāzī, who had not confronted the full authority of Aristotelian eternalism, as Fārābī and Ibn Sīnā would do — let alone answered the denial of Creation on its own terms, as Ghazālī and Maimonides were to do.

Creation and Judgement

The idea of Creation gives natural history a pungent moral flavour for the Ikhwān. The biblical account of the origins of natural kinds frames a linear alternative to Aristotle's eternal natural cycles; and the Qur'anic idea of Creation, with its counterpart of resurrection and judgement, of course, participates in that prophetic world view. The Ikhwān adopt the linear scheme and subordinate their cyclical vision to it: the revolutions of the heavens and the corresponding revolutions in hegemony that shift earthly dominion from one kind to another are, all of them, sequences within the larger linear history of the world. The lower animals, the Ikhwān reason, must have come before the higher, and plants before the animals they nourish. That's a matter of natural causality, but also of sustenance. So even here, in the sequence of life's appearance on earth, the Ikhwān see moral purpose.

History, Qur'anically, is a drama played out between the overture of Creation and the final curtain of resurrection. Life on earth is overshadowed everywhere by the looming fact of judgement — as the birds of our fable tirelessly remind all who can hear the hints hidden in their songs. Muhammad found cautions in the ruins of Arabia, much as he did in biblical histories and midrashic tales, fragments of the Alexander romance, bits of martyrology and legend. The lesson was unchanging: God's bounty turns to retribution when gratitude is forgotten, displaced by corruption and scorn of His admonishers. Repentance and contrite return to the upright life God demands might have saved the sinners. But disbelief portends a dire fate.

In Qur'anic terms, God's mercy is the source of grace. So even as Muhammad calls for repentance, he pictures God as granting or withholding a willing ear to hear.[12] For the Ash'arite contemporaries of the Ikhwān, therefore, both the grace to heed and believe and the gracelessness to scoff and ignore reflect *God's* freedom. But the Ikhwān hold the rival, Mu'tazilite view, affirming human liberty. Return to God is open, even in the face of destiny.[13]

12 See William Montgomery Watt, *Free Will and Predestination in Early Islam* (London: Luzac, 1948), pp. 12–17.

13 See Chapter 37 below in particular.

Every creature's tenure is no more than God has allotted. Animals, humans, jinn — every kind has its domain and its moment. Each species has its habitat and mode of life, the implements and skills it needs to carry on — to reproduce, in the case of higher animals; or to be reborn, for those that seem to arise by spontaneous generation. Ants and bees industriously stow their stores and guard their young. But even the careless grasshopper and negligent ostrich are looked after. So their kinds persist — but not forever. Each kind endures or flourishes for just the era God has allotted, marked out by the revolutions of the planets and the spheres.

Penitence and submission may win human beings a respite. But all creaturely gifts are finite — save only man's immortal soul, a ray of light shed by the Divine, still capable, even after descent into the world, of rising and returning to its spiritual home. So while man cannot boast that all the world exists for him alone, this return to God of what is divine in man gives a higher purpose to human life and a fuller meaning to creation than simply the flowing forth from God of the creative works that show His goodness.

Admonition and reproof, spiritual teaching and intellectual growth are not only possible, therefore, but vital. They open the portals to salvation that worldliness blocks and conceals. Yet earthly motives creep into every human undertaking, from the hubris of the *jihādī* who pursues a specious power in the name of a sham piety, to the arrogance, luxury, and caprice of worldly judges, the pride of the emulous devout, and the misanthropy of misguided ascetics and eremites whose spiritual aim is twisted by a crabbed vision and short-sighted complaints. For the highest piety, as the animals show by their own lives, is but a celebration of God's mercies and a quest for His compassion.

How Ecology Becomes Ethics

It is by projecting the idea of judgement onto the living world that the Ikhwān frame their notions of succession and ecological niche: species fit their habitats and find their place in the food chain. The environment, in turn, is suited to its denizens by divine design. No living being exists solely for its own sake. Each exploits and is exploited by others. Even the heavenly bodies suffer the insecurity of eclipses. Tyrants like Nimrod and Pharaoh are felled by gnats or lice. And it is by a similar poetic justice that the most awesome beasts fear some tiny foe — lest any creature seem invulnerable. Great predators like the sea-serpent, the dragon, and man, are not simply at the head of the food chain. In turn, they will be eaten by tiny insects and worms. The symmetry described by Linnaeus (1707–1778), long after the Ikhwān, describes not just a food chain but a food cycle; the linkages form a system.

In today's ecology, of course, there is no welcoming adaptation of environment to organism — except in symbiosis, where one creature's niche is afforded or enhanced by another through mutual adaptation, itself the work of natural selection, as in the co-evolution of flowering plants and their insect pollen vectors. The fitness of the environment is chalked up to chance, or to the impact of organisms themselves. Plants do throw off the oxygen that animal life requires, but no modern ecologist will say that they do so for the sake of animals. In the ecology of the Ikhwān, however, the mutual adaptation of organism and environment is read, as taught in the lessons of the Qur'an and the natural theology of the Stoics, as a gift of grace: animals would have only clay or earth to eat, were it not for plants. Just as organs and strategies were devised to meet specific challenges, the environment was made a setting in which the challenges of being alive could be met, and, within limits, happily resolved.

The spatial, temporal, and adaptive boundaries that hem in every species in the ecology of the Ikhwān are set by God. So, from the start, they're normative: the jinn of legend are fiery in substance and belong to the world's fiery regions. Birds, similarly, belong to the air, fish to water, beasts to land, and spirits to the heavens. Natural Forms and forces, the influences of celestial beings, perfuse and pervade the terrestrial realm. They bring gifts of energy and the order manifest in the numeric patterning of all creatures.[14] Each sublunary kind exploits its sector. Only man exceeds his needs and oversteps the usual natural bounds. Bees do store capital for the winter, but only according to their needs and those of their young. Birds take what they require, as one scholiast

14 See Chapter 16 below.

notes, echoing the Sermon on the Mount; but they leave the surplus for another day, tacitly proclaiming their trust in God's bounty.

In all the world, only man is a usurper, storing far more than he needs, depriving others, cramping his own quarters, and troubling his mind. He exploits animals for food, labour, shelter, and clothing, medicines, and luxuries, constricting wild creatures' habitats and disrupting their lives. Many have fled their ancestral ranges, which human habitation has destroyed or made unsafe. Resources that animals relied on for food or protection are pre-empted or engrossed. Many beasts are pressed into service for sport or war, or held captive for their milk or hair. Still others, like cats and dogs, rats and weasels, have been corrupted or debased, made sycophants, playthings, or sneak-thieves, fawning on humans, raiding their pantries, or skulking in their alleyways for scraps of food. Even carnivores, their delegate insists, were not always such. They were forced into predation by human selfishness and a dog-in-the-manger solicitude over the carcasses that carnivores once fed on. Turning the tables on those who blame them for their diet, the predators' case is that they learned to kill only from mankind's murderous practices in war and the conflict of brother with brother since the days of Cain.

Man's domination of nature, his reliance on enclosure, the spread of his burgeoning numbers, his subduing of the earth and exploitation of the animals, his amassing of capital far in excess of his needs, and his proliferation of crafts and industries that flatter and tease elaborate wants and educated tastes — as in the silk industry and in the great variety of human foodstuffs that no self-respecting wild beast would touch — are unique in nature. No other species lays claim to the entire environment or turns the world at large to the service of its wants.

The disenchantment of the Ikhwān with man the city builder, ditch digger, irrigator, user, and consumer, is plainly romantic. Waste land, from this standpoint, may seem fairer than the sown, and pastoralism looks more natural than urban or even agrarian life. Farmers and nomads know how dependent mankind is on animals. City people would as lief sell off the beasts, if it came to that, and take a cash profit. Country folk may not love their animals any more than their city cousins do, and the care they lavish on them stems not from compassion but from need — and greed. But they are close enough to nature not to have lost touch with a sense of their dependency. For they — and city dwellers too, although less cognizant of the fact — depend on animals. Without them, as they say, 'We'd be naked, barefoot, miserable, and sick. Death would be better for us than such a life. And the people of the cities would suffer the same fate.'[15]

Idealization of rural life, and pastoral life in particular, is as old as the Greek and Roman elegies and eclogues, as modern as Boucher's paintings and the Meissen images of silk-clad shepherds and shepherdesses. Even on the brink of the French revolution, Marie Antoinette played at being a milkmaid with a porcelain milk-pail. The idyll of rusticity is, of course, an urban fantasy, seeking escape from city life. Today's trekkers and survivalists cultivate a similar romantic sense — as hermits once did. But just as the anchorites and stylites of an earlier age relied on pious city people to bring them plates of food, today's wilderness sojourners count on their freeze-dried provisions and down-filled sleeping-bags, their satellite phones and GPS, all back-up support from the social system they dream they've left behind.

Raising crops and breeding stock are themselves cultural modes. They belong to civilization. And, ever since cities were first built, farmers, herders, and husbandmen have relied on the city, just as cities have depended on the countryside. The real contrast that stirs the romantic is not between town and country but between nature and artifice — *physis* and *nomos*, nature and convention in the sophists' dichotomy. The issue is no logical dichotomy but the fact of culture itself, which dramatically separates humans from the other animals — a source of mingled pride and shame, self-confidence and guilt. The tension that resonates in the fable of the Ikhwān arises in the fact that, although all beings are God's creatures, man sets himself apart, over and against the rest of nature. That is the source of the problematic that this essay of the Brethren seeks to address.

Biblically, all topics, even Creation — especially Creation — are cast in a moral light. The Qur'an adopts its own corresponding moral perspective, casting human culture in stark relief. Against that backdrop, the Ikhwān confront human uniqueness in moral terms and

15 Chapter 9 below.

seek a warrant for human claims. The sincerity of the Brethren, their spiritual sensibilities, and their candid commitment to the imperatives and obligations that those sensibilities evoke make this question of justification a live and active problem for them. Their fable and its inquiry is no mere exercise in the construction of a rationale.

Nature's balance, as they see it, is God's work. It is not the product of fortuitous circumstances, an invisible hand operating simply *among* natural species, blocking any from overrunning all the rest. Maimonides will later argue, on Epicurean lines, that in nature all things are provided according to the urgency of need: air, most freely, since it is most vital; then water; then simple, wholesome foods.[16] The Ikhwān think in just such terms; but, for them, nature's economy is yet more closely tailored: parasites are spared sense and sensibility, the conditions of pain as well as knowledge. Roaches and beetles, nature's scavengers, find their nutriment in nature's refuse. Nothing is wasted or left to pile up or drain away unused. Ample resource and the checking of each species by natural limits have been seen to in advance. Even the displacement of one kind by another is the work of divine wisdom. How, then, does man fit in, and how does the human case warrant our making an exception of ourselves?

Beyond Anthropocentrism

The Stoics marvelled that anything as noble as a soul should be lodged in a pig. Providence must have decreed its function, 'as if it were salt', to keep the meat fresh; for, all things, on the Stoic view, were made for man.[17] But if God was able to create man without the rest of nature — if even one thing might have been left out and man still flourish, Maimonides reasons, then it would have been otiose for God to create all that He did.[18] So, unless God acts in vain, some things in nature were not made for man's sake. As Job is reminded when God

16 Maimonides, *Guide* III.12; cf. Epicurus, *Letters, Principal Doctrines, and Vatican Sayings*, tr. Russel Geer (Indianapolis: Bobbs-Merrill, 1964), Principal Doctrine 15.

17 Porphyry, citing Chrysippus, in *De Abstinentia* III.20; tr. Thomas Taylor as *On Abstinence from Animal Food* (London: Centaur Press, 1965), p. 129.

18 Maimonides, *Guide* III.25

speaks to him from the storm wind, rain falls 'on the desert, where no man is, sating the wild waste and making the wild grass sprout' (Job 38:26–27). God gives that rain (38:25), but not for man's sake. The wild ox longs for no man's manger, and the wild ass revels in his freedom and looses a braying laugh against any would-be-taskmaster — God Himself has made him free (Job 39:5–12). Saadiah, a generation before the Ikhwān, shows keen sensitivity to those verses, in the Arabic commentary he wrote in Baghdad on the book of Job.[19] Porphyry, the Syrian disciple, editor, and biographer of Plotinus, used similar arguments against Stoic anthropocentrism. On the Stoic view, he said, horses would seem to have been made to carry men to war, dogs to aid in the hunt, and fierce animals like bears, lions, and leopards, to test men's mettle.[20] Maimonides voices the Neoplatonic alternative in monotheistic language. He finds God's glory in the creation of each natural being and kind for its own sake.[21]

That theme, rejecting anthropocentrism and celebrating the intrinsic worth and beauty of all the marvels of nature, resonates throughout the *risāla*: beetles, for example, scour the earth for their own sake, and for the world's. The whole system is the goal; and, high as man may rise in God's intent, no single member of God's symphony suffices to the exclusion of the rest. If what God has done is right and just, it would be wrong for any species, even snakes, to be swept away before its time. 'Don't you see', says one spokesman for the animals, 'that a slight to the work is an affront to its Maker?'

Clearly, animals besides man have purposes. Their organs and their acts serve the interests of the organism and its kind. This localized teleology makes animal deserts a locus of value and focus of concern. Nature is an object of God's care, and so should it be for humans, if we would only rise above selfish, exploitative perspectives, see the interest of animals in their fate, and recognize the aims they pursue.

Holding firmly to the Neoplatonic line of thinking, the Ikhwān extend beyond his original intent Aristotle's principle that nothing in nature is in vain. Their reasoning leads them to a justification of death

19 See Saadiah, *The Book of Theodicy*, tr. Goodman, pp. 385, 389, note 19.

20 Porphyry, *De Abstinentia* III.20.

21 See Maimonides, *Guide* III.13.

itself. In Aristotelian philosophy, death is explained, not justified, by the inevitable give and take among beings of a determinate nature. Only the species, which *as a class* instantiates a timeless form, is deathless. Individuals must perish in the unceasing cycle of natural transformations. But for the Ikhwān, even perishing has a purpose, giving symmetry and shape to the roles each player acts on God's stage. Species and their broader 'kinds', even the widest genera of living beings, perform their parts and then exit. The fitting pattern of each presence is writ plain in God's book, as the Ikhwān put it, echoing the Qur'an and vindicating the Mu'tazilite promise to find justice in all God's ways. The acts and scenes and sequence of appearances are justified by the merits and deserts allotted to each player. Each creature's part is the reflex of the worth God gave it — just as each creature's tools and skills mesh in answering to its needs: aesthetic and moral justice merge.

Theism offers entrée to the standpoint of each species: we can see the value of the viper's venom from the snake's perspective.[22] But monotheism also asks one to look at nature more dispassionately, from no one creature's viewpoint, but from the standpoint of the whole. And it is the serpent (naturally enough, since even in 'that garden', as the Ikhwān call Eden, it was the serpent who promised a divine perspective) who offers a fleeting God's-eye glimpse of life and death: death, too, has its uses, the serpent hisses. Human kings and others who know life's vicissitudes are well aware how welcome they might find the venom in the fangs of vipers. But death is necessary more broadly: to cleanse the air, clear the earth, and sustain the cycles of life. Aristotle's cycles, then, are not just necessary; their necessity makes them morally right.

Some modern advocates of the earth, especially those fixated on the triage of human populations, may clasp the serpent's words a bit too eagerly and closely to their bosoms, forgetting, as they find an ally in the praise of death, just who it is that is speaking. From a human standpoint, making death a positive good might look more like a positive evil. But if disinterest is the aim, the serpent must have his due. Evil enters when human individuals and institutions arrogate

22 See Chapter 18 below.

to themselves the role of arbiters of life and death, as if somehow empowered to decide which individuals and types deserve to be shed from the green and bounteous earth.

The Deserts of Animals

Kant declared that only a free, rational agent can be a subject and object of the moral law, since only such an agent can conceive itself as an end.[23] Clearly, it belongs to the logic of prescription that a moral agent must be a freely choosing being. But the idea of a moral law does not entail that only persons can be *objects* of moral treatment. A being may have worth or be an end objectively even if it cannot conceive itself at all, let alone conceive itself as a subject. The obligation of moral agents is to the claims of *any* being, insofar as they do not violate higher or parallel claims. For claims affirm a desert and warrant what they affirm unless some conflicting desert countermands them.

Whether a being is conscious or not, then, our *prima facie* obligation is to discern its nisus and treat it *as if* it conceived itself as an end. It is sheer invidiousness to confine our recognition and respect to beings whose subjectivity is the mirror of our own. To rely on sympathy or empathy for another that is like us in awareness is to pin our moral burden on far too flimsy and wavering a reed.[24] It risks surrendering the high ground of morals to passions and emotions that cannot readily preserve our choices from slipping into cruelty and destructiveness. Shall we protect only those creatures that we find warm and fuzzy? And what shall we do when we discover that some of us, sometimes, enjoy crushing or exploding precisely those creatures that *they* find warm and fuzzy?

Sympathy, as Spinoza explains in anatomizing the passive emotions, arises in the association of ideas: we feel for others insofar as we deem them like ourselves. It is for this reason, no doubt, that rhetorical pleas for animal sensibilities address themselves to empathy — less by way of argument than by images and sounds: animals are like us,

---

23 Immanuel Kant, *Groundwork of the Metaphysic of Morals*, tr. H. J. Paton, 2nd ed. (New York: Harper and Row, 1956), pp. 63–64, 95.

24 See L. E. Goodman, *Love thy Neighbor as Thyself* (New York: Oxford University Press, 2008), pp. 3–11.

we are reminded. Their cries, the textures of their skins, and their appealing, open eyes remind us of our children, helpless, perhaps, but endearing. The animals are cute or courageous, clever or responsive. And, lest we confine our concerns to the cuddly sort and ignore the ugly and unappealing, we are reminded, above all, that animals feel pain. The animals of the *risāla* open their complaint with this sort of emotive appeal. However, making ethical treatment a matter of a sentiment can go only so far. In the end, it surrenders ethics to unstable ground.

Trouble arises in the fact that sympathy varies widely from one person to the next. Empathy shifts and sways. It may take root in images, but they run deep into the erratic sands of culture, consciousness, and the unconscious. We should not need to know, before deciding how to treat some member of another species, why one person becomes physically ill at the sight of it, while another feels devoted to it, and a third would enjoy seeing it tormented, baited, worried, or killed in a dog-fight, bull-fight, cockpit or bear-pit. Why, the Ikhwān ask implicitly, do the same sensibilities that praise the form and coats of horses turn so readily to equine comportment on the battle-field, parade ground, or racecourse – admiring a horse for valour in a cause not its own, or smiling at the stamina and spirit that horses show when running in a contest of which they can have only the barest ken (beyond the spirit to run and readiness to set their strength and heart in emulous chase with one another, and service to a master or a rider)?[25]

Making emotion our moral mainstay subjects morals itself to the polyvalence of human affections about life and its violation, with the many and varied responses that human beings have to the *frisson* of the kill. For, the same event can evoke compassion or a savage thrill, the sort of thrill that cultures, from the start, have tried to capture or control, routinize, civilize, ritualize, or curb — in the hunt and the *corrida*, in athletic contests, in animal sacrifice and its many surrogates — even the meal-time grace and the niceties of table manners that seek to distance our social and familial table from the sight of blood or thought of death. The substrate underlying such rituals is far too protean to give a fair foundation to an ethics of the treatment of living beings.

25 See Chapter 6 below.

Our obligations find their proper warrant not in individual attitudes or social conventions but in the deserts of their objects. They rest not on our affinities with other living creatures, be those affinities objective or subjectively appropriated, but on the natures and claims of the beings themselves that our acts affect. Persons come first, for their ontic standing rather than their likeness to us. For appraisals of propinquity and distance only open the door to subjectivity and to ethnic and sexual invidiousness, the distancing that is the dialectical counterpart of the discovery and embrace of affinities. Objectively, what matters is that persons, that is, moral subjects, stand side by side with one another high on a plateau in the order of being. Their claims portend an objective worth well removed from that of animals or plants or inanimate objects. But all beings make claims, manifest in their natural tendency to persist. Rocks resist crushing and crumbling. Plants reach for light and air, water, and rooting. Animals struggle to survive, express, and preserve their natures.

Ethics, like science, asks us not to anthropomorphize, as if to see subjects where there are none. But, by the same token, it asks us not to deny or ignore the strivings we can see in every living being. The moral posture asks us not to affirm subjecthood where there is none, but, by the same token, not to deny the struggle to survive where we can plainly see it. *The most general ethical imperative is to treat all beings as what they are;* to respect them as one sort or another of ends in themselves — not always self-conscious ends or moral agents, but claimants, beings of intrinsic worth, whose efforts tacitly declare their purposes and make them worthy of regard.

The obligation to respect all creatures, and living creatures in particular, is derivable directly from the theism of the Ikhwān. For, the objectivity that it calls for is not a posture of neutrality or unconcern. It militates against anthropocentrism but not against teleology. Nor does it demand the abandonment of human interest. On the contrary, it presumes distinctive interests in all creatures, which it is their nature and *prima facie* desert to pursue. The Ikhwān, in the end, will not drop human claims to pre-eminence. They will continue to see humans as the worthiest beings in nature — although they will press their own account of the basis of that pre-eminence. But human supremacy for the Ikhwān does not exclude the intrinsic worth of other beings. For, all beings strive, as Spinoza put it, to preserve and promote their own being.[26]

Virtual Subjecthood

From the beginning, the focus of the Ikhwān in the fable is moral. 'Our purpose', they write, 'embraces, of necessity, all that allows man to better his life on earth and to assure his happiness and salvation in the eternal world.'[27] A core thesis of their essay on the animals is that every animal species and, in a way, even every living individual is precious — although none but man is an actual moral subject. Poetically, the device of giving speech to the animals drives home the point by allowing the animals to articulate what are normally unspoken pleas, encouraging readers to project themselves into another creature's place. The animals in the fable use much the same querulous tones as Balaam's ass. But the personification of the animals by the Ikhwān points not to projected human motives but to the natural, God-given needs and strengths, zest, and élan of all animals, striving after life.

We humans quite naturally see needs, interests, resources, challenges, and drives in human terms. But animals have needs and interests of their own, which the Ikhwān call on their reader to conceive more broadly. Granted, animals are not subjects; they are not persons; their souls, as the animals confess, are not immortal; animals are not free, responsible moral agents; redemption, as Islam conceives it, and even as Islamic philosophers conceive it, will never be theirs. Still, their lives are gifts of God. It is the intrinsic worth of animals that underwrites the poetic conceit of assigning speech to them. The fable, in other words, gives voice to the animals' *virtual* subjecthood, their striving to pursue interests of their own, interests that they would speak for, could they but speak.

26 Spinoza, *Ethics* I, Appendix; ibid. III, Proposition 7; *Short Treatise on God, Man, and his Well-Being*, 5.1, in *The Collected Works*, tr. E. Curley (Princeton: Princeton University Press, 1985), p. 84.

27 Quoted by Nasr in *Islamic Cosmological* Doctrines, p. 30, from the *Rasā'il* (Cairo, 1928), vol. 4, p. 218.

Plutarch writes that only human convention makes animals inarticulate:

> We deprive a soul of the sun and light, and of that proportion of life and time it had been born into the world to enjoy. And then we fancy that the voices it utters and screams forth to us are nothing but certain inarticulate sounds and noises.[28]

Animals do, after all, communicate. Their calls and cries, screams of pain or anger, sounds of warning or courtship, do express their wants and needs. Some higher animals will grieve; many play and show affection, or protectiveness. But signs and cries, and even language, are not the real test of moral standing, interests are. Virtual subjecthood is signified and marked by the fiction of animal speech. But it's not just a matter of what a beast would say if it could speak. Virtual subjecthood is the reflex of striving: it is having and pursuing interests that makes animals virtual subjects. It's immaterial whether those interests actually find a voice.

The Prudential and the Moral

The interdependence of living species is commonly propounded in warnings against tampering with the environment, since such meddling can have wildly unsuspected consequences. There's a hint of such suasions when the country people in our fable stress human dependence on domestic animals. The serpent, too, touches on the web of interdependencies when he alludes to the food chain. So do the Ikhwān, in their own voice, when they remark drily that without plants we animals would have only clay and earth to eat. Such arguments are typically anthropocentric. But prudential concerns are often tangential to ethics. Prudential ecology may fail to warn against exploitative acts and policies if the depredations are taken to serve human interests, even

28 Plutarch, 'On the Eating of Flesh' I.4, in *Moralia*. Plutarch does not insist on vegetarianism but urges that if flesh is to be consumed, the killing should be merciful rather than thoughtless or in a conscious quest of pleasure, as in the hunt, the commercial slaughter-house, or the wanton tormenting of beasts. He inveighs against the spitting of live swine, trampling of cows' udders, and like barbarities.

though they degrade or jeopardize the larger ecosystem. Too often the appeals focus narrowly on human interests: true, the rain forest may hide a cure for cancer, but that chance does not sum up the worth of biodiversity. And it would be better to find the missing cure, if it lies hidden there, without destroying the forest looking for it.

It's powerful rhetoric to ask, as Rachel Carson did, what nature would be like without birds to rid the crops of insects, or without insects that birds can feed on. But the risk lies in making it sound as if all species exist for human profit or enjoyment, if only for the satisfaction of knowing that they're there, the romantic's pleasure at the thought of wildlands that no human being will ever see — or none but the few and hardy. It is refreshing, by contrast, to find the Ikhwān couching their main ecological concerns more objectively, by speaking of the impact of human acts and choices on other species and on the land and sea at large.

The Ikhwān broaden their essay's moral horizons by assigning speech to the animals. But, unlike animal speech, the virtual subjecthood to which it gives voice is not fictive. And the aim here is not to arouse or heighten sympathy, but to recognize another's moral standing. The moral point the Ikhwān make is not that animals ought to be cherished for being created in our image, but that they deserve humane treatment despite being so very unlike us. As with any moral imperative, it helps to put ourselves in the other's situation. But our ethical obligation is heightened, not diminished, by the difference ethics calls on us to bridge. We are not asked to become like beasts or to learn to live as they do, nor to treat them any better than we are morally obliged to treat our fellow human beings. Our obligation is simply to recognize and respect the goals that animals have as living creatures: their ends are not just means to fulfilment of our own.

The virtual subjecthood of animals, and the goal orientation implicit in their doings and in the life processes that go forward, all unthinking in their bodies, undergird the moral arguments in their behalf. Special consideration is still called for towards humans, as it is humanity, for the present, which gives us our only actual contact with persons, that is, moral subjects. Persons are not virtual but actual subjects. Human dignity, the dignity of personhood, brings with it a special category of deserts, namely, rights and privileges, special obligations that are not at all germane to beasts, summed up in the obligation to love our fellow *human* as we love ourselves. In this strong form, the principle embodied when we are called on to put ourselves in one another's shoes cannot be applied to beasts. Yet there are obligations to beasts nonetheless, and rules against cruelty lie at the heart of those duties.

The means by which the Ikhwān highlight the moral standing of animals should not be overlooked, as if all that mattered were the outcome of an argument, and not the reasoning that reached it. For, an argument sets limits to its conclusion. Virtual subjecthood rests on teleology. If teleology is void, or valid only in the case of human hopes, then nature is just a great sand-box, and we humans can use it, waste it, play in it as we like. Indeed, if teleology is inapplicable even to man, there is no reason for circumspection in our choices: all our work becomes play, and all our play deadly futility. Without the categories of ends and means, there is no relevance for the very idea of choices. But if there are human purposes, then our choices may be apt or inept to their attainment. And if there are goals in nature, our choices belong to a system, and the work of ethics becomes political, a matter of finding and rightly assessing and assigning priorities to ends that may diverge, compete, serve, or complement one another.

For the Ikhwān, clearly, man is a uniquely precious end, not because all Creation exists for us alone, but because the gift of consciousness and choice renders man alone accountable. All animals are unique in some way, as each tailored niche can testify. But in other creatures, behaviour follows the dictates of their endowments. In humans alone, by a special grace, there is a choice between good and evil, truth and falsity, faith and negligence. Man does stand at the peak of the sublunary world, even above the angels, as the Qur'an would have it, since humans act freely and angels cannot. That is why the angels were commanded to bow down to Adam. And that is why the Ikhwān rank the universal human soul as presiding over the animal soul in each one of us.[29] Still, man is not the sovereign, lord, and master of Creation, as we too readily pretend or tacitly presume. Man may be the noblest of embodied beings — as the Qur'an teaches when it tells of the humbling

29 See Chapter 35 below.

of angels and jinn before Adam. But supremacy is not sovereignty. God still rules. And service as God's vice-regent (*khalīfa*) on earth does not confer absolute or indiscriminate powers. For, a rightful ruler, as the Ikhwān insist, governs in the interests of his flock, much as God's angels faithfully oversee the realms assigned to them.[30]

Islamic norms, like those of the biblical tradition from which Islam springs, sharply divide man from beast. That calls for clear criteria of the unlikeness of living kinds. Consciousness alone does not suffice. After all, consciousness, as the natural history of the Ikhwān suggests, is a continuum, varying from one species to the next. Human intelligence does matter. But if intelligence means skill, the Ikhwān find animals no less fittingly and generously endowed than humans. Not only do many animals have remarkable strengths of perception and discrimination, but instinct, as the animals argue, anticipating Montaigne, also has its advantages: it is more reliable in some ways than thinking, precisely because it's not quite as flexible or free — one could say it is more natural. But the Ikhwān make the point with a Qur'anic trope: instincts are directly inspired by God.[31] If freedom trumps instinct, it must be by the grace God affords in allowing persons (and only persons) the delegated authority to make choices, and lives, of their own.

A Mirror for Princes

The Aesopian framing of their tale allows the Ikhwān to make specific creatures paragons of specific virtues. The fable's kings, viziers, messengers, and subjects become models of their roles. At the court of the King of the Jinn, justice and impartiality rule, ministers are incorruptible, the monarch consults broadly and openly with wise and experienced counsellors, who are urged to speak freely and encouraged to question and critique proposed strategies and tactics. Regarding what constitutes an ideal messenger, the Ikhwān have the following to say:

> 'First, he must be a person of intelligence and character, well spoken, eloquent, and articulate, able to remember what he

30 Ibid.

31 See Chapter 25 below.

> hears and cautious in what he answers. He must be loyal, faithful, true to his word, circumspect, and discreet, adding nothing to his message but what he sees is in the sender's interest. He must not be grasping or avaricious. For a greedy person who meets with generosity from his hosts may shift his loyalties and betray the sender, adopting the new country for the good life he enjoys there, the blandishments and gratifications he finds. Rather, he must be faithful to his sender, his brethren, countrymen, and kind, deliver his message, and return promptly to those who sent him with a full report from start to finish of what passed on his mission, omitting nothing for fear of causing displeasure. For clarity is the whole duty of a messenger.'

The delegate of the swarming creatures in the dispute is Yaʿsūb, the bee king.[32] He discusses political theory freely with his fellow monarch, the jinni king. The jinni praises the loyalty and devotion of his own subjects, the best of whom follow their king as the stars and planets follow the sun, each heavenly body performing its role, as commanded by the angels that govern the spheres. That nexus is compared, in turn, to the service of the senses to the rational soul, bringing their reports 'without lag or delay' — as might be expected when the commands are intellectual. The celestial ideal contrasts sharply with the human case:

> 'But the nature and temper of humans are quite the opposite. Their obedience to their chiefs and monarchs is mainly hypocrisy and dissembling, gulling and grasping for stipends, payments, rewards, vestments, and prizes. If they don't get what they're after, they come out in open defiance and rebellion, shed their outward allegiance, secede from the commonwealth, and bring dissension, civil war, bloodshed, and destruction to the land. [. . .]'

Animal rulers care for their subjects with deep solicitude, the parrot explains. When the jinni monarch senses a hint of allegory in that remark, the leading jinni philosopher explains that the reference is to the ideal. A king is the caretaker of his subjects, their shepherd indeed. Beyond that, he must also be their angel:

32 Even in Aristotle, the bees have a king, not a queen; *Historia Animalium* IX.40.923b.

> '[. . .]The word "king" [*malik*], you know, derives from "angel" [*malak*]. And kings' names are taken from those of angels. For there is no kind of animal, no species or individual among them, great or small, that does not have a band of angels charged by God with overseeing its growth, preservation, and welfare, at every stage. Every class of angels has its chief to look after it. And these chiefs are kinder, gentler, and more compassionate than mothers toward their tiny sons or infant daughters.'

Here, with the help of a fanciful etymology, emanation, as the work of angelic emissaries[33] and the vehicle of providence, becomes the model of good governance — an ideal that human monarchs, and their subjects too, are bluntly charged with failing to follow:

> 'The monarchs of animal kinds, however, outshine human kings and leaders in emulating God's ways. The king of the bees looks to the interest of his subjects, troops, and vassals, and he seeks their well-being. He does not serve his own private whims or even the caprices of his people, but acts in their interest and protects them from harm, favouring not even one who supports his own wishes but acting solely in compassion and concern, kindness, and affection for his subjects, troops, and supporters. So do the king of the ants and the king of the cranes, who oversees their flight, and the king of the sand-grouse, who leads their flight and alighting. The same with all other animals who have leaders and rulers. They seek no recompense or requital from their subjects for their rule, just as they seek no reward, recompense, return, or show of filial gratitude from their offspring, as Adamites do. For, every animal that leaps and mounts, conceives, bears, nurses, and rears its young, and every kind that mounts, lays, broods, tends, and minds chicks or hatchlings, we find, seeks no reward, recognition, or recompense from its offspring but raises its young and cares for them kindly, tenderly, gently, compassionately, on the model of God, who created His creatures, raised, nurtured, and looked after them kindly and generously, asking nothing in return and seeking no reward or requital.[. . .]

33 See Goodman, 'Maimonidean Naturalism', in *Neoplatonism and Jewish Thought*, ed. Goodman (Albany, NY: SUNY Press, 1992), pp 139–172.

Religion and Politics

Human boasts are vain and empty, the animals argue. Even revelation is little more than the reflex of human unworthiness:

> 'Were it not for the ignoble nature of humans, their base characters, crooked lives, vicious mores, vile doings, foul acts, ugly, misguided, and depraved customs, and rank ingratitude, God would not have commanded them: *Show gratitude to Me and toward your parents, for unto Me shall ye come in the end.*[34] He gave no such command to us and our offspring. For we show no such disrespect or thanklessness. Command and prohibition, promise and threat are addressed solely to you, the human race, not to us. For you are creatures of mischief. Conflict, deceit, and disobedience are ingrained in you. You are more fit for slavery than we! We are more worthy of freedom.[. . .]'

Called upon to explain why dogs have betrayed their own kind and gone over to human habitation, the bear, who has made no such mistake, replies:

> 'Dogs were drawn to the precincts and abodes of men simply by their kindred nature and character. With men they found food and drink that they relish and crave — and a greedy, covetous, ignoble, stingy nature like their own. The base qualities they found in men are all but unknown among carnivores. For dogs eat putrid meat from the carcasses of slaughtered animals, dried, stewed, roasted, salted or fresh, good or bad. They eat fruit, vegetables, bread, milk (sweet or sour), cheese, butter, syrup, oil, candy, honey, porridge, pickles, and every other sort of food that humans eat and that most carnivores would not eat and do not know. They are so gluttonous, greedy, and mean that they cannot allow a wild beast to enter a town or a village, lest it compete with them for something there. So if a fox or jackal happens to enter a village at night to steal a hen, a cock, or a cat, or even drag off some discarded carcass or scrap of meat from a dead animal, or a shrivelled piece of fruit, just see how the dogs set upon him, chase him, and drive him out! They are so wretched, lowly, abject, beggarly, and covetous that when they see a human being, man, woman, or child, holding a roll, or a scrap of bread in his hand, or a date,

34 Qur'an 31:14.

> or any morsel, they beg for it and follow him about, wagging their tails, bobbing their heads, gazing up into his eyes, until the person feels embarrassed and throws it to them. Then see how they run for it and quickly snatch it, lest another reach it first. All these base qualities are found in humans and dogs. So it was their kindred nature and character that led dogs to leave their own kind and shelter with men, as their allies against the hunting animals who were of their own race.'

The humans in the story claim superiority to animals on the grounds of human unity: the animals vary in shape, whereas humans are all of one kind. The appeal rests on the Neoplatonic idea that unity rises closer to God's oneness than heterogeneity. But the animals answer that although humans share a single bodily type — racial disparities have vanished now, despite an earlier slur about presumed diversities in the choice of mates — humans are at odds in spirit, whereas animals are one in soul, despite their varied appearance. Here the animals raise the ante with a Neoplatonic postulate of their own: that all animal life springs from a single soul.

Displaying the underlying variance of human minds, the nightingale contrasts the many human sects and schools with the professed consensus of the animals in the natural monotheism of the *ḥanīf*. Animal faith is cast as an ideal, since it is spontaneous and free of doubts, wrangling, and dissension. The Persian delegate retorts that humans, too, agree in faith, at least in the essentials, although their paths to God may differ. But this leads the jinni king to ask: 'Why, then, do you slay one another, if your religions all have the same goal, of encounter with God?' The answer is telling:

> 'You're right, your Majesty', said the thoughtful Persian. 'This does not come from faith, for there is *no compulsion in faith*.[35] It comes from faith's specious counterpart, the state.'

As the Persian goes on to explain:

> 'Religion and the state are inseparable twin brothers. Neither can survive without the other. But religion is the elder. The

35 Qur'an 2:256.

> state is the younger brother, the follower. A state cannot do without religion for its people to live by; and religion needs a king to command the people to uphold his institutions, freely or by force. That is why the votaries of different religions slay one another — seeking political primacy and sway. Each wants everyone to follow the institutions of his own faith and the rules and practices of his own religion. [. . .]'

He then distinguishes spiritual from worldly struggle:

> 'The slaying of selves is practised in all faiths, creeds, and confessions, and all earthly dominions. But in religion, the mandate is for self-sacrifice. In politics it usually means slaying others to gain power.'

The King knows all too well how struggles for power lead to bloodshed, 'But how is it that seekers in the different religions slay themselves?' The Persian delegate replies:

> 'I'll explain. You know, your Majesty, that in Islam, this is clearly and plainly one's duty. For God says, *Lo, God hath bought of the faithful their substance and selves, since they shall have Paradise. Let them battle for God, slay and be slain. This is His promise, confirmed in the Torah, Gospels, and Qur'an. And who is truer to his pact than God?*[36] After which He says: *Rejoice in the sale of yourselves ye have made, a splendid triumph!*[37] And, *God loveth those who do battle for Him, in ranks like a close-knit structure.*[38] In the Torah tradition, He says, 'Turn to your Creator and slay your selves. Your humbling is good in the eyes of your Creator.' And Christ says in the Gospels, "*Who are my aides in the service of God?*" The Disciples answered "*We are God's helpers.*" He replied, "Prepare for death and the cross if you wish to aid me. Then shall you be with me in the Kingdom of Heaven, with my Father and yours. Else you are none of mine." And they were slain but did not forsake Christ's faith. [. . .]'

---

36 Qur'an 9:111.

37 Ibid.

38 Qur'an 61:4,14.

So, the true jihad is the battle for self-mastery. All the rest is politics, a sordid struggle for specious goals that detract and distract from the spiritual battle, which is universal:

> 'The Brahmins of India slay themselves and burn their bodies in their spiritual quest, convinced that the penitent comes closest to the Lord, exalted be He, by slaying his body and burning it to atone for his sins, certain of resurrection. And the godliest Manichaeans and dualists deny the self all gratifications and carry heavy loads of religious obligations, to slay the ego and free it from this realm of trial and degradation.
>
> 'The same pattern of self-sacrifice is found in the varied practices of people in all religions. All religious laws were laid down to deliver the soul, to save it from hell-fire and win blessedness in the hereafter, the realm to which we return and where we shall abide.[. . .]'

It's part of the dry humour of the Ikhwān that no sooner has the Persian delegate rested his case for human unity than the Indian speaker pins human hopes on diversity. With a flourish, he reels off an impressive catalogue of regions and races well known to the authors of the fable and clearly meant to impress their audience.[39] Once again, there is a subtext. For, most of the lands mentioned lie within reach of the Islamic empire. There is a sense of triumphalism in this mini-atlas of cultural geography, and the authors know well that many of the peoples mentioned have not readily and peacefully accepted the faith that the Ikhwān themselves so warmly profess. Ethnic discontent and religious nonconformity remained strong in many of these lands, and the Ikhwān themselves are not out of sympathy with such diversity. How, then, can one assay their remarks about jihad?

Cosmopolitanism, like religious politics, is a double-edged sword: the diversity that the Ikhwān allow the Indian spokesman to show off is intellectual rather than political. The authors are proud of their knowledge of the panoply of nations and creeds that the Indian mentions. They recognize and value diversity. But it is empire, after all, that makes possible such confident cosmopolitanism as theirs. The

39 See Chapter 40 below.

Ikhwān legitimize monarchy for enforcing the dictates of a religion — imposing both practical and intellectual obligations. Yet, enforced spiritual conformity is just as antithetical to the ideals of the Ikhwān as coerced faith is to the tenets professed in their religion.

The discussion of diversity and unity, then, introduces a genuine tension into the tale. The Ikhwān like the idea of natural monotheism, the natural faith of the animals. And they readily give the term '*islām*' a generic sense that would include any honest quest for God and acceptance of His decree. Yet there is a latent ambiguity in their use of terms like '*ḥanīf*' and even '*islām*'. For, the terms are not sheerly generic. They are also brand-names, and that side of their meaning taints the welcome affirmation of many pathways to God with an air of exclusivity. The ambiguous sense that lingers in their use of these generic/particularistic terms may cloak a genuine ambivalence on the authors' part: the Ikhwān celebrate diversity even as they hold up unity as the ideal; and even as they admire the spirit of self-sacrifice that they find in the faith of Hebrews, Hindus, and Christians, they still see the message of Islam and the warnings of its Prophet as universal.

A Surprising Dénouement

The humans of the fable are no match for the animals in diversity. So the Indian's appeal, impressive as it is, wins the human side no new ground. It is only when new arguments seem to have dried up that an orator from the Ḥijāz mentions immortality: resurrection is a distinction the animals cannot match. The nightingale gamely answers that every scriptural promise of reward has its counterpart in dire threats of chastisement. But the asymmetry remains:

> 'How are we equal?' demanded the Ḥijāzī. 'How do we stand on a par, when among us we have prophets and their devisees, imams, sages, poets, and paragons of goodness and virtue, saints and their seconds, ascetics, pure and righteous figures, persons of piety, insight, understanding, awareness and vision [. . . .]'

Only now do the animals and jinn acknowledge that the humans have finally struck the truth and found something worth valuing — as if the humans had stumbled onto the answer to a riddle that lay in plain sight all along, too obvious to notice. The Ḥijāzī holds up prophets, imams, and saints as persons of true discernment, and the animals concede the case and eagerly ask to hear more about these figures, whose very existence seems to make human life worthwhile and whose intercession, it is hoped, will atone for many of the human wrongs so vividly reported by the animals. But no one seems able to say much about these holy figures. Arguments have come to an end, and the whole court — animals, jinn, and humans — remains in thoughtful silence.

The Ḥijāzī, too, is left behind. Hailing from the region of Mecca and Medina, he seems to speak for all Muslims. But the last words in the fable adopt the wider perspective of the cosmopolitan faith that the Ikhwān propose. For their speaker embodies the fairest Jewish, Christian, Greek, Muslim, and Indian values and virtues and is blessed to the fullest with good breeding, faith, asceticism, science and spiritual insight:

> Finally arose a learned, accomplished, worthy, keen, pious, and insightful man. He was Persian by breeding, Arabian by faith, a *ḥanīf* by confession, Iraqi in culture, Hebrew in lore, Christian in manner, Damascene in devotion, Greek in science, Indian in discernment, Sufi in intimations, regal in character, masterful in thought, and divine in awareness. 'Praised be God, Lord of all worlds,' he said, 'Destiny of the faithful, and foe to none but the unjust. God bless the Seal of Prophets, foremost of God's messengers, Muhammad, God's elect, and all his worthy house and good nation.
>
> 'Yes, just Majesty and assembled hosts,' he began. 'These saints of God are the flower of creation, the best, the purest, persons of fair and praiseworthy parts, pious deeds, myriad sciences, godly awareness, regal character, just and holy lives, and awesome ways. Fluent tongues weary to name their qualities, and no one has adequately described their inmost core. Many have cited their virtues, and preachers in public assemblies have devoted their lives down through the ages to sermons dilating on their merits and their godly ways, without ever reaching the pith of the matter.'

The true elect of humanity are the saints (*awliyā'*), pure and noble paragons. But these saints, on whose virtues and insights so much now proves to depend, are only barely and tantalizingly mentioned. Even the ultimate, universal, and complete man, as it were, cannot adequately recount their virtues. Preachers through the ages have praised their attributes, we are told. But the words inevitably fall short. For, the character of these holy figures sets them side-by-side with the angels, as the Ikhwān suggested in introducing their tale. All humans, of every creed or race, are called on to rise to, or towards, this lofty spiritual plane. Here the Ikhwān reach out, as committed Muslims, to embrace all that is wise and worthy in the heritage they share with their Greek, Indian, Jewish, Christian, and other neighbours. The animals' challenge has provoked and confirmed the ringing affirmation of a universal human communion.

Immortality gives weight to the human condition, but only as the emblem of moral and spiritual freedom and responsibility. That is why the holy figures who come into view as the tale draws to a close are critical to the argument. For, even immortality is no blessing if all it brings is eternal wrath. The saints, like the angel rulers mentioned by the chief jinni philosopher, are models not of what human beings are but of what we can become. That is why their intercession has weight. Indeed, their wisdom and their way of life are what make human lives uniquely precious.

The case is ultimately resolved in favour of the humans, since a basis is found for human superiority. The issue on which the fictive court case was premised is all but forgotten — but not entirely. After all, the animals' complaints are not erased, and the cries that gave voice to their virtual subjecthood have not been silenced. If human exploitation of other species is wanton or cruel, it cannot be justified even by human worth — and least of all by the human potential for moral or spiritual purity and transcendence. For these would in fact heighten man's moral responsibility. Plainly, the aim of the Ikhwān is not to justify a tyranny over nature that their Aesopian personae have so thoroughly lambasted. The intent, rather, is to make clear that dominion imparts responsibility — for stewardship of nature and care for one's fellow humans and one's own precious soul. Humans stand high in the scale of being — but only by the spiritual potential present in every rational soul and realized, all too rarely, in God's saints.

The Ikhwān do not conclude that humans have no right to make use of other creatures. Such usage requires no special license. For artifice in humans is just as natural as flight in birds. Humans are not set into a class that alone is held guilty by virtue of predation, and therefore must live in guilt. Still, there is no mitigation of the demand to ameliorate the treatment of animals, insofar as the requirements of human life permit. So the Ikhwān do not unsay all that they have taken so much trouble not to leave unsaid.

What warrants calling the core of human identity a unique, immortal soul is a question as alive today as it was a thousand years ago. The arguments of the animals rule out many a familiar answer: it is not our powers of calculation or manipulation, our tool-making or perception, our social organization, or our proud powers of discernment that set human worth above mere utility and make the worth of personhood inestimable. Nor is it our arts and industries, or any of the ornaments on which we pride ourselves. It is not our business acumen and wealth, our rituals and purifications — and still less is it our powers of violence and destruction. Whatever we achieve in prolonging or enhancing human life, as the Ikhwān see it, is a gift won by use of our God-given powers, even though much of what we pursue by the use of those powers is, indeed, illusory — false goods and sham rewards, on which many a life is wasted. Consciousness, as the Ikhwān have argued through their fable, gives us more than the power to plan and build and fashion means to fit our ends. It gives us powers of choice, and that makes us responsible for the ends we choose and the means by which we pursue them. Responsibility brings accountability in train, making human beings subject to reward and retribution, and tipping the scales of the argument about the existential worth of the human person: the window on immortality lies open; the pathways it puts in view are marked by the footsteps of those paragons whose piety, insight, and generosity show that they have not just gazed through that window but have trodden the pavement of the path it reveals.

Freedom makes life a puzzle with no trivial solution. It opens choices to us that can go desperately wrong or that can lead beneath the surface of things, to realms beyond the reach of the senses. Freedom, the source of all the ugliest faults and failings that the animals cite, is also the source of the one unanswerable strength that places humankind above the beasts, and, in one respect at least, above the angels.

Technical Introduction

This translation is based on the reading of several manuscript copies of the original Arabic text. Given the great number of extant copies of this popular *risāla*, we have limited our scope to a body of ten manuscripts, selected for their antiquity, clarity of script, and completeness. We have divided this group of ten into three further groups, here listed as A, B, and C. The manuscripts of Group A form the core of our translation, and have been closely and systematically compared. Those in Group B were consulted at key points where copyists differed, or where passages remained unclear in Group A. The manuscripts of Group C were consulted only *ad hoc* for their treatment of particularly difficult terms or passages.

Group A

MS Atif Efendi 1681 (1182 CE), Istanbul [clear; fully vocalized; with comments and corrections in the margins by the same hand; complete text]

MS Köprülü Kütüphanesi 871 (AH 820/1417 CE), Istanbul [clear *naskhi* script; fully vocalized; with corrections in the margins by the same hand; complete text]

MS Esad Efendi 3638 (ca.1287 CE), Istanbul: Süleymaniye Kütüphanesi [clear; unvocalized; occasional corrections in the margins by the same hand; complete text]

MS Köprülü Kütüphanesi 870 (AH late ninth century/fifteenth century CE), Istanbul [clear; unvocalized; occasional corrections in the margins by the same hand; complete text; decorative heading in blue and gold for the *risāla* title]

Group B

MS Feyzullah Efendi 2130 (AH 704), Istanbul [cramped text; unvocalized; corrections, completions, and several additions often illegible in the margins by the same hand; complete text]
MS 6.647–6.648 (AH 695), Paris: Bibliothèque Nationale de France [unvocalized; corrections and additions in the margins by a second hand; complete text]
MS 5038 (ca. AH 600/1203 CE), Berlin: Königliche Bibliothek [clear; partially vocalized; occasional corrections in the margins by the same hand; incomplete text ending at our Chapter 21 of the *risāla*]

Group C

MS Laud Or. 260 (1560 CE), Oxford: Bodleian Library [cramped script; partially vocalized; complete text; many illustrations]
MS 2304 (AH 1065/1654 CE), Paris: Bibliothèque Nationale de France [clear; fully vocalized; with only one comment and two corrections in the margins by the same hand; complete text]
MS Casiri 923/ Derenbourg 928 (AH 862/1458 CE), Madrid: El Escorial [cramped *maghrebi* script; unvocalized; corrections and additions in the margins by the copyist and at least one other hand; complete text]

Quotations from the Qur'an are sourced neither in the original manuscripts nor in the printed Arabic editions. In our translation we have italicized all passages from the Qur'an, and cited them by *sūra* and *āya* (chapter and verse) in the footnotes. Passages from the Hadith, traditions of the Prophet, appear simply between quotation marks, with their source given in a footnote.

Occasionally in the footnotes we will make mention of the printed Arabic editions. A full list of these can be found on the first page (343) of our *Bibliography*. With minor exceptions, the division of the text into sections (1–18) and chapters (1–42) follows that typically used in the manuscripts. Where the manuscripts have provided section and chapter titles, we have included them in translation.

The *Encyclopaedia of Islam*, 2nd edition, ed. H. A. R. Gibb (Leiden: Brill, 1960–2004) is abbreviated as *EI2*.

Epistle 22
The Case of the Animals versus Man Before the King of the Jinn

(Being the eighth epistle from the second section of the *Epistles of the Brethren of Purity*, on the Natural Sciences)

In the name of God, the Compassionate, the Merciful

1

We have now completed our essay 'On Plants' [Epistle 21], touching on their origins, growth and development, their numbers, genera, differentia, species, traits, benefits and harms. We have shown that the lowest plants verge into the highest mineral gems, and the highest plants into the lowest animals.[1] In the present essay, once again, we wish to treat the history of animals, their origins, numbers, growth, and development. We will survey their genera, differentia, and species, their distinctive traits and diverse habits.[2]

Once again, we will show that the highest animals verge with the lowest rank of human beings; and the highest rank of humans, with the lowest of the angels.[3] The pure-hearted and clear-headed, whose minds can weigh evidence, will find in this continuum clear evidence that the entire hierarchy, the whole order of being, springs from a

1 'Nature proceeds gradually from things lifeless to animal life, making it impossible to fix the exact line of demarcation, nor on which side an intermediate form should lie. Thus, after lifeless things come plants; and of plants one differs from the next in apparent vitality. So, in a word, the whole plant kind, while lifeless compared to animals, is endowed with life compared to other corporeal things.' Aristotle, *Historia Animalium* VIII.1.588b4–11; see *The Complete Works of Aristotle*, ed. J. Barnes, 2 vols. (Princeton: Princeton University Press, 1984). Cf. Ikhwān al-Ṣafā', *Rasā'il Ikhwān al-Ṣafā'*, ed. Buṭrus Bustānī, 4 vols. (Beirut: Dār Ṣādir, 1957), vol. 4, p. 224 (hereafter, citations are to this edition, unless otherwise specified).

2 As their tale unfolds, the Ikhwān show an enduring interest in biodiversity, a fitting theme since Neoplatonists hold that every creature and kind exists for its own sake, not just to serve humankind. Towards the end of the fable, they seek to ease the tensions between the principle of plenitude and the Neoplatonic privileging of unity: the animals will argue, in Chapter 39, that animal souls are one and human souls diverse. The uniqueness of each individual, a detriment in Neoplatonic terms, is a salient positive value in scriptural monotheism.

3 Describing the perfected human being, Yaḥyā ibn 'Adī (d. 974), the Monophysite Christian ethicist, who was a philosophical follower of al-Fārābī and a contemporary of the Ikhwān, writes: 'If a person reaches this level he is more like the angels than like humankind.' Yaḥyā calls such a person a 'perfect human being' (*insān kāmil*), transposing into an Arabic idiom the Aristotelian ideal of the *spoudaios* and anticipating the Sufi ideal of the perfect man. See Yaḥyā ibn 'Adī, *Tahdhīb al-akhlāq*, tr. S. Griffith as *The Reformation of Morals* (Provo: Brigham Young University Press, 2002), p. 92. The Ikhwān present their image of the perfect man as they bring their tale to a close.

single Cause and Source, just as the numbers issue from unity, which is prior to duality.[4] We shall show, as well, that the human form is to the forms of other animals as head is to body: man's soul is the leader, as it were, and theirs the led.[5]

We have explained in our essay 'On Ethics' [Epistle 9] that the human Form is God's vice-regent[6] on earth; and we've made it clear that every human being should live thus, so as to deserve to be one of God's intimates, worthy of His blessings.[7] Most of our earlier essays highlighted human virtue, man's admirable attainments and praiseworthy traits, his true insights, ingenious arts, and uplifting modes of governance, training, discipline and rule. Here we wish to

4 'To be one means to be the start of counting. For the initial measure is the start. It is that by which we count members of a class. So unity is the starting point in knowing any particular. But not all kinds have the same units. Here it is the quarter-tone, there the vowel or consonant. There is a different unit of weight and of movement. But in every case the one is indivisible in quantity or kind.' Aristotle, *Metaphysics* V.6.1016b17–24, translated after W. D. Ross and Richard Hope. In their essay on arithmetic, the Ikhwān write: '"One" is used in two ways: properly and metaphorically. Properly, it is what cannot be split or divided. So everything indivisible is one in that respect. Metaphorically, every aggregate that is considered as a unit is called a unity. So ten is called a unit, and so are a hundred and a thousand. What is one attains its unity by way of oneness, just as what is black is such by virtue of blackness: unity is the character possessed by what is one, just as blackness is the character possessed by what is black. But a plurality is a collection of units.' *Rasāʾil*, Epistle 1, vol. 1, p. 49 (tr. Goldstein). Cf. Nicomachus of Gerasa, *Thābit ibn Qurra's arabische Übersetzung der Arithmêtikê Eisagôgê des Nikomachos von Gerasa*, ed. Wilhelm Kutsch (Beirut: Catholic University Press, 1959), p. 19: 'Absolute numbers… are composed of units.'

5 Here the authors announce their thesis, vindicated, in their view, only as the fable ends.

6 Qur'an 2:30: *Then did thy Lord say to the angels 'Lo, I shall place a vice-regent* [*khalīfa*] *on earth.'* The reference is to Adam's creation. The angels object: *Wilt Thou place there one who will work corruption and shed blood there, while we celebrate Thy praises and sanctify Thee?* God answers: *I know what you know not.* See Chapter 8 below.

7 The claim that humans can deserve God's blessings may seem unproblematic. But in Ashʿarite theology, salvation depends on grace alone and cannot be won or earned. The Ikhwān press the claims of merit. The issue is reflected in the debates of their Sufi contemporaries; see, for example, al-Ḥakīm al-Tirmidhī, *Kitāb Khatm al-awliyāʾ*, ed. ʿUthmān Yaḥyā (Beirut: Catholic University Press, 1965), p. 406.

consider the merits and distinctions of the animals, their admirable traits, pleasing natures, and wholesome qualities, and to touch on man's overreaching, oppression, and injustice against the creatures that serve him — the beasts and cattle — and his heedless, impious thanklessness for the blessings for which he should be grateful. Man at his best, we shall show, is a noble angel, the finest of creatures; but at his worst, an accursed devil, the bane of creation. We've put these themes into the mouths of animals, to make the case clearer and more compelling — more striking in the telling, wittier, livelier, more useful to the listener, and more poignant and thought-provoking in its moral.

2

You must know, dear brother, God aid you and us with His sustaining spirit, that mineral substances are the lowest things that come to be. They include all bodies that arise as composites of the four elements: fire, air, water, and earth.[8] Plants, too, are compounded of these elements. But nourished by the elements, they can grow, expanding in all three dimensions: length, width, and depth.[9] Animals share with plants the functions of nourishment and growth but are distinguished by locomotion and sensitivity. Man shares these traits with plants and animals but adds his own distinctions: reason and discernment.

---

8 Plato argues that all bodies subject to change are generated (*Timaeus*, 28). Most mediaeval philosophers infer that all bodies are therefore also destructible. All sensory particulars, they reason, are composites and thus subject, in principle, to dissolution. But, following Aristotle, they reason further that whatever can happen must occur at some time, or it would not, in fact, be possible.

9 The idea of three dimensions was relatively fresh at the time of the *Rasā'il*; cf. Chapter 16 below. Contemporaries of the Ikhwān would have wondered whether one should speak of three dimensions or six, one for each direction. See Goodman, 'Rāzī vs Rāzī: Philosophy in the Majlis', in *The Majlis: Interreligious Encounters in Medieval Islam*, ed. Hava Lazarus-Yafeh et al. (Wiesbaden: Harrassowitz, 1999), pp. 94–95.

3

Know further, dear brother, that mineral and plant substances are all of them temporally prior to the animals. For they afford the matter from which living things are made, the underlying substrate of their forms and the nutriment of their bodies. They, that is, the plants, are the mother of the animals, as it were.[10] They take moisture from water and fine particles from the earth through their roots and into their stems. These they assimilate to their own nature, turning the good they derive from these materials into leaves, fruit, and ripe grain. From these, animals take pure, health-giving, wholesome nourishment, just as a mother eats wholesome food and her child gets the pure milk, delicious to drink. If plants did not provide this nourishment, animals would have plain clay or dry earth to eat, a dreadful diet to enjoy![11]

10 'Plants are created only for the sake of animals. . . . The activity of an animal is nobler and better than all those of a plant; and we find in an animal all the virtues that are present in a plant and many more. Empedocles says that plants came to birth when the world was still small and it had not yet reached maturity, and that animals came after it was complete. But this does not fit the facts, for the world is a whole, perpetual and eternal and has never ceased to produce animals and plants and all their species.' *De Plantis* I.2.817b25– 818a1. This work ascribed to Aristotle is no longer thought to be his, but it was translated into Arabic; and the view that plants exist for the sake of animals is Aristotelian. In *Politics* (I.8.1256b15), Aristotle reasons that, just as mammals provide nourishment for their young, 'we must infer that plants exist for the sake of animals, and other animals for the sake of man, the tame for use and food, the wild, if not all then most of them, for food, for the provision of clothing, and other supports of life.' The translation here follows Ernest Barker, as revised by R. F. Stalley (Oxford: OUP, 1995). The *Politics*, alone in the Aristotelian corpus, was not translated into Arabic. The Ikhwān would not accept the doctrinaire eternalism pressed in the *De Plantis*, nor would they accept its anthropocentrism. They see all creatures in nature's hierarchy as pursuing their own ends, in keeping with God's plan, not existing solely for the sake of 'their betters'.

11 'Plants get their nourishment from the earth by way of their roots; and this food is already worked up when taken in, which is why plants produce no excrement, the earth and its heat serving them in place of a stomach. . . . But animals, with scarcely an exception . . . are provided with a stomach sac, an internal substitute, as it were, for the earth. So they need some organ corresponding to the roots of plants, with which they may take up their food from this sac . . . The mouth, then, once its task is done, passes food to the stomach, and there something

See then, dear brother, how wise it was of God, glory be to Him, to place plants between animals and minerals, and let them use their roots to take up those fine mineral substances and extracts, digest, process, and purify them, so that animals, in turn, could savour the fine nuts and grains, bark, leaves, fruits, gums, buds, and blossoms — God's providential bounties for His creatures and largess for His creation. *Blessed, then, be God, the most generous creator,*[12] and *wisest of judges.*[13]

4

You must know, too, my dear brother, that some animals are more perfect than others in form and frame — those that carry and bear live offspring, which they suckle. Others are of lesser nature — those that arise in rotting matter, like the crawling and swarming creatures. Still others, intermediate types, mount, lay eggs, hatch and rear their young.

The lower animals, you must know, were created before the more perfect.[14] For the former develop rapidly, and higher natures need

must receive it — this being the blood vessels that run all along the mesentery from its lowest part up to the stomach.' Aristotle, *De Partibus Animalium* II.3.650a21–30.

12 Qur'an 23:14.

13 Qur'an 11:45.

14 Were the Ikhwān evolutionists? They do date one species prior to another and find a succession of dominance among living beings. But they do not derive one species from another: the Forms that impart natures to each kind are God given and unchanging. Living creatures are adapted to their habitats and métiers. But adaptation here is a fact, not a process; and it results not from natural selection but from God's providential bounty. Nasr writes, 'The chain of being described by the Ikhwān possesses a temporal aspect which has led certain scholars to the view that the authors of the *Rasā'il* believed in the modern theory of evolution.' But 'according to the *Rasā'il* all changes on earth occur as acts of the Universal Soul and not by an independent agent acting within bodies here on earth'. Further, 'according to the Ikhwān this world is a shadow of another world more real than it, and the "idea" of everything in this world actually exists in the other, so that there is no question of a species changing into another . . . In the words of the Ikhwān: "The species and genus are definite and preserved . . . because their efficient cause is the Universal Soul of the spheres".' Seyyed Hossein Nasr, *Islamic Cosmological Doctrines* (Cambridge, MA: Harvard University Press, 1964), pp. 71–72. See Friedrich Dieterici, *Der Darwinismus im X. und XI.*

more time, for reasons that would be tedious to explain here,[15] which are touched on in our essays 'On Embryology' [Epistle 25] and 'On the Actions of the Soul' [Epistle 49]. Water animals, we add, preceded land animals. For water came before land, sea before earth in the original creation.

5

You must know, dear brother of mine, that the more perfectly built animals first arose from clay — male and female — and then began to increase and multiply. They spread over the earth, mountain and plain, land and sea, from the equator, where night and day are equable. There the seasons are balanced between hot and cold, and the matter best suited to receive form is ever present.[16] Adam too arose there, our forefather, the ancestor of all humankind; likewise, his wife. They also began to increase and multiply, and so did their progeny, filling the earth — mountain and plain, land and sea, down to the present day.

Know, dear brother, that all the other animals arose before man. For they all exist for his sake, and whatever exists for the sake of something else antedates it. That is self-evident and needs no prior premise or inference. For unless these animals had preceded man, man would not have what he needs to survive comfortably, or live properly,

Jahrhundert (Leipzig: J. C. Hinrichs, 1878); and the response by T. J. De Boer in his *History of Philosophy in Islam*, tr. E. Jones (London: Luzac, 1961), pp. 91–92. As De Boer notes, the Ikhwān see stronger human affinities with elephants or horses than with apes, despite the 'bodily likeness'. See Goodman's discussion, pp. 24-34 above.

15 Aristotle explains, in *De Generatione Animalium* II.4.740a24–35: 'Since the embryo is already potentially an animal but an imperfect one, it must take its nourishment elsewhere. So it uses its mother's uterus as a plant uses the earth, to get nourishment, until it is mature enough to move about. . . . This is why the animal remains in the uterus . . . '

16 Compare Ibn Ṭufayl, *Ḥayy ibn Yaqẓān*, tr. Lenn E. Goodman (updated edition, Chicago: University of Chicago Press, 2009), pp. 103–104.

pleasantly, and well. His life would be poor, wretched, and sorry, as we shall explain in a later chapter.[17]

6

Plants, you must know, live upside down. Their heads point towards the centre of the earth, their bottoms to the circling spheres.[18] Man is just the opposite. His head is in the heavens, and his feet point to the earth's centre, wherever he stands on the earth's surface — north, south, east, or west — and whichever way he faces.[19] Animals are in

17 See Chapter 9 below. The text continues with a cross reference: '. . . just after the urban spokesman has concluded his remarks, where it is stated what life would be like without the animals.' So, the animals do exist for man's sake — but not solely for his sake, as is clear from the fact that they are active in pursuit of their own interests. The Ikhwān stress that animals preceded man on earth, partly to underscore the moral point with which the fable opens: animals were here first and lived in freedom until the humans, who had once feared them, began to enslave and exploit them.

18 'Empedocles is wrong in adding that growth in plants is to be explained, as regards the downward rooting, by the natural tendency of earth to travel downwards, and as regards the upward branching, by the corresponding natural tendency of fire to travel upwards. For he misinterprets up and down; up and down are not for all things what they are for the whole world: if we are to distinguish and identify organs according to their functions, the roots of plants are analogous to the heads of animals.' Aristotle, *De Anima* II.4.415b30–416a6.

19 Aristotle writes: 'The reasons have now been stated why some animals have many feet, some only two, and others none; why, also, some living things are plants and others animals; and lastly, why man alone of all animals stands erect. Standing erect, man needs no forelegs, and has been given arms and hands instead. Now Anaxagoras has it that having these hands is the cause of man's being the most intelligent animal. But it makes more sense to suppose that man has hands because of his higher intelligence. For the hands are instruments, and the constant plan of nature in distributing the organs is to give each to the animal that can use it; nature thus acting as any prudent man would. For it is a better plan to take a person who is already a flute player and give him a flute, than to take someone who has a flute and teach him the art of flute playing: nature adds the less to the greater and more important, and not what is greater and more precious to what is less.' Aristotle, *De Partibus Animalium* IV.10.687a3–16. Stoics read the erect stature of human beings as one of the many lavish gifts of a wise and provident nature: 'First, she has raised them from the ground to stand tall and upright, so that they might be able to behold the sky and so attain knowledge of the gods. For men are sprung from the earth not as its tillers and

between, neither upside-down like plants nor right-side-up like man. Rather, their heads face one way, horizontally, and their tails the other, as they turn this way and that and go about their business.[20]

This order or scale of plants, animals, and humans, as we've described it, is divinely ordained, an expression of God's wisdom and sovereign providence,[21] a sign and a testimony *for all with eyes to see*,[22] who ponder the mysteries of creation. All who probe the true natures of things and

---

settlers, but to be, as it were, the viewers of things celestial and supernal, a vision no other species shares.' Cicero, *De Natura Deorum* II.57.140 (tr. after Horace Rackham, pp. 257–259).

20 Compare Plato's 'friendly burlesque' (at *Timaeus* 91–92), as A. E. Taylor calls it in his *Commentary on Plato's 'Timaeus'* (Oxford: Clarendon, 1962), p. 640. We render after Cornford: 'Birds were changelings, growing feathers in place of hair. They came from harmless birdbrains who chittered about the marvellous heavens but foolishly supposed the best evidence about such things came through the eyes. Land animals came from men who had no use for philosophy and just ignored the heavens. . . . They took their lead from those parts of the soul located in the breast. Given that kind of life, they let their forelimbs and heads be drawn down, by their natural affinity, towards the earth for support. Their heads grew elongated and were so unused that they took any shape their circles were pressed into. So their race were quadrupeds from birth, or multi-footed. The more witless they were, the more supports they needed, to connect them ever more fully to the earth. The most senseless of all, whose bodies stretched out along the earth, no longer needed feet, so the gods made them footless, crawling on the ground.' Cf. Ovid, *Metamorphoses* I.76ff.; and Montaigne, *Apology for Raymond Sebond*, in *Complete Essays*, II, 12, tr. Donald Frame (Stanford, CA: Stanford University Press, 1958), p. 356. See also, Ibn 'Arabī, *Fuṣūṣ al-ḥikam*, ed. A. 'A 'Afīfī (Beirut: Dār al-Kitāb al-'Arabī, 1966), p. 224. In Ḥunayn ibn Isḥāq's Arabic translation of Galen's *Precis of the 'Timaeus'*, the passage reads: 'God made the race of birds from people devoted to gazing at the celestial courses. The wild creatures that walk, He created from people that profited not at all from any form of learning; and the swimming animals, from those people who were the most utterly ignorant and the least knowledgeable or cultured'; in *Plato Arabus*, vol. 1, ed. with Latin tr. Richard Walzer and Paul Kraus (London: Warburg Institute, 1951), [Arabic] p. 34, [Latin] p. 96. Walzer and Kraus signal their suspicion that a line is missing from the text, but the final sentence suggests that Galen or Ḥunayn may have simply paraphrased Plato's Greek, as this text does consistently. The translation here is Goodman's.

21 For the principle of plentitude as an explanation of the diversity and hierarchy of beings and thus as the basis of a theodicy of nature, in which each kind has its place and contributes in its own way to the excellence of the whole, see Arthur Lovejoy, *The Great Chain of Being* (new ed., Cambridge, MA: Harvard University Press, 1976).

22 Qur'an 3:13.

scan the horizon to learn from the portents they find there will see that the powers of the Universal Soul shed their influence on the world from the highest circling sphere to the deep core of the earth.[23] Some flow straight down from the outermost sphere to the earth's centre, some return from the centre, rising toward the encircling sphere, and some are broadcast in all directions across the heavens. Every ray is filled with God's hosts, charged with preserving the world and managing its creatures, governing the whole, and other tasks whose inmost workings are known but to God, exalted be He.[24]

We've explained in an earlier essay that the powers of the Universal Soul are the first to flow towards the earth's core from the supernal level of the circling sphere into the depths of the physical. Streaming through the spheres, stars, elements, and living creatures, they finally reach the centre of the earth, the nadir and furthest limit of their journey. Then they double back to the outermost sphere. This is the sublime ascent, the ultimate rebirth and return.[25]

---

23 The outermost sphere, the *muḥīṭ*, or encircling sphere, 'was added by Muslim astronomers to the spheres of Ptolemy to account for the precession of the equinox', as Nasr notes. The Ikhwān 'follow the Ptolemaic system of epicycles in order to explain the retrograde motion and changes in the periods of the planets'. They differ from most Greek astronomers in treating the epicycles as solid spheres. Nasr believes that the celestial system which the Ikhwān describe is probably taken from Farghānī (Alfraganus, ninth century), whose book survives in Arabic and was translated into Latin by both John of Seville and Gerard of Cremona, and into Hebrew by Jacob Anatoli. Valued for its brevity and simplicity, Farghānī's book was widely studied in the Middle Ages and printed with extensive commentary in the Renaissance. See Nasr, *Islamic Cosmological Doctrines*, p. 76; and H. Suter, 'Al-Farghānī', *EI2*, vol. 2, p. 793.

24 For the Ikhwān, angels are Forms and forces projected onto nature by the Intellects (themselves Forms) that govern the spheres. In pagan Neoplatonism, the star souls were gods mediating between nature and the One, Plato's God, the Form of the Good. As Nasr notes, the Ikhwān freely identify the 'natural forces' of the philosophers with what religion calls the 'angels and troops of God', charged with the nurture of plants, the generation of animals, the composing of minerals and 'partial spirits' (*Islamic Cosmological Doctrines*, p. 92). Like the Ikhwān, Maimonides adapts the Neoplatonic approach to monotheism. See Lenn Goodman, 'Maimonidean Naturalism', in *Neoplatonism and Jewish Thought*, ed. Lenn Goodman (Albany, NY: SUNY Press, 1992), pp. 157–194.

25 The Ikhwān read the soul's destiny in terms of the Neoplatonic drama of the cosmic fall of the Universal Soul into embodiment and particularity, and

Consider, then, dear brother, how your soul rises from this world towards that. For it is one with the power that flows from the Universal Soul through the world. It has reached the core and begun its return,[26] rescued now and risen beyond the plane of minerals, plants, or animals — beyond the inverted life of plants and the bowed life of animals. Now it stands erect, in the straight way.[27] This is the human form.

If you rise higher and break loose from this tangle, you reach Paradise by one of its gates and take on angelic form, won by your right choices, good works, sound insights, true beliefs, and virtuous character.[28] Strive for this, dear brother, before your life is snuffed out and you perish — before the end draws nigh.

its ultimate return. Muslim exegetes understand Qur'an 17:1 as proclaiming Muhammad's miraculous ascent to the heavens. See B. Schrieke et al., 'Miʿrādj', *EI2*, vol. 7, pp. 97–105; Josef Horovitz, 'Muhammeds Himmelfahrt', *Der Islam*, 9 (1919), pp. 161ff.; Ignaz Goldziher, *Muslim Studies*, tr. Samuel M. Stern (London: Allen and Unwin, 1971), pp. 45–52. Muhammad's journey is taken as a pattern for later descriptions of the rise of the soul in Islamic eschatology and mysticism. Al-Bisṭāmī tells of his own heavenly ascent, as recorded in ʿAṭṭār, *Tadhkirāt al-awliyā'*, ed. M. Istilami (Tehran: Intisharāt-i Zuwwār, 1968), pp. 161–172; see Michael Sells, *Early Islamic Mysticism* (New York: Paulist Press, 1996), pp. 242–250. Ibn ʿArabī pictures a philosopher and a believer rising together. But the philosopher cannot ascend beyond the seventh heaven. See Miguel Asín Palacios, *Islam and the Divine Comedy*, tr. Harold Sutherland (repr., London: Frank Cass and Co., 1968), pp. 44–51.

26 The Universal Soul flows through the world, giving form to minerals and life to plants, animals, and human beings. Man's rise towards the angelic marks the realization of human potential and the consummation of God's plan. See Epistles 28, 38, 43, and the discussion of the 'Science of Return' in Godefroid de Callataÿ, 'The Classification of Knowledge in the *Rasa'il*', in Nader El-Bizri, ed., *The Ikhwān al-Ṣafā' and their 'Rasā'il': An Introduction* (Oxford: OUP–IIS, 2008), pp. 70–71. The heavens revolve, as the Ikhwān reason, so that the Universal Soul may be fulfilled and matter attain perfection: 'the final term of the union of the soul with matter' is its return to its divine Source. See Nasr, *Islamic Cosmological Doctrines*, p. 81.

27 Qur'an 1:6. Two Arabic manuscripts here add '*ākhar darajāt muḥtabika*' ('the final stage in the interweaving'), that is, of earthly matter with celestial Form, the intertwining that for Neoplatonists epitomizes creation. The Dār Ṣādir text, evidently influenced by the idea of salvation, substitutes '*ākhar darajāt jahannam*' ('the ultimate level of hell'). But the Ikhwān here are pretty clearly speaking of the soul's immersion in corporeality, and thus of its escape from embodiment.

28 Once again, the Ikhwān speak for a Muʿtazilite merit theology.

Ride with your brethren in the rescue ship,[29] God grant you His

29 For the motif of the rescue ship, see *Rasā'il*, vol. 4, p. 418; and Ian Netton's discussion in *Muslim Neoplatonists: An Introduction to the Thought of the Brethren of Purity*, (London: George Allen and Unwin, 1982), pp. 105–108. Chapter 19 below voices a far less guarded espousal of a Platonic ontology, placed in the mouth of the vizier to the King of the Jinn. Kindī, writing just over a century before the Ikhwān undertook their project, urges his reader to seek the enduring and accessible goods of the mind: 'Men are like passengers in a ship travelling home. The captain has put in for supplies and left the ship at anchor while they disembark for provisions. One secures what he needs and returns to the ship without dawdling. . . . Another stands gazing at the meadows filled with flowers of all colours and kinds, smelling the fragrant blossoms, wandering in the flower-filled fields, losing himself in the lovely woods, so full of strange new fruits, listening to the lovely calls of unseen birds, observing the soil of that land, with its varieties of brilliantly coloured rocks, so delightful to see, and its enchanting sea-shells with their strange forms and wonderful designs. . . . He returns now to his old place, since the better, wider, and more comfortable berths are taken. A third kneels to collect the shells and rocks and the nearby fruits and flowers, forgetting the needs that brought him ashore. He returns loaded down with rocks, shells and flowers, as though in service to the things he has taken from the earth. But already the flowers are fading and the fruit has begun to turn. . . . others have beaten him back to the ship and taken the better places. He must settle into a cramped, narrow, hard, and rough spot. The rocks, shells, flowers and fruit he has loaded upon himself don't leave him space for comfort like the rest. . . What little repose he gets is disrupted by the lack of space, by worry about his things, and by a throng of anxieties — over his possessions, his powerful emotional attachment to his little place and the small legacy he has won. . . . Another has no sooner entered those meadows and woods than he forgets the ship and the whole purpose of his journey. Engrossed in gathering rocks, shells and flowers, he plunges deeper and deeper into the woods. Entranced by the taste of the fruits, he loses all thought of his homeland. . . . But he is hardly carefree. He is beset by one crisis and agony after another. . . . When the captain calls the passengers back to set sail . . . some have wandered so far afield and strayed so deep into the woods that the voice of the ship's master does not even reach them. The vessel departs, leaving them behind. . . . Those who board with the heavy loads they have amassed . . . soon see their flowers fade, their stones lose their lustre, lacking the moisture that made them gleam and sparkle. The sea-shells alter as they sleep and now stink horribly. . . . Before they put in at port they are sick with the putrid odours of all that they've brought on board. . . . This is the most fitting parable of our passage through this world to the world of reality and the most appropriate allegory of our condition as travellers here. How shameful to be gulled by pebbles from the earth, shells from the water, flowers from trees, and the dry stalks of plants that will all too soon become a burden so loathsome that we can escape only burying it back in the earth or the depths of the sea, or committing it all to the flames. We hold our noses at the stench and avert our eyes from the hideous form, seeking to get as far as we can from the unbearable ugliness. . . . If sorrow we must, we should grieve for our exile from our true home, for being launched on seas whence no ship can carry us back to our homeland. For in that land

compassion. Do not linger with those who drown, or tarry in the company of devils.[30]

7

Know, dear brother, that an animal is a body that moves and senses, takes nourishment, grows, and has perception and locomotion.[31] Some of the highest are almost human — those with five senses, fine powers of discrimination, and receptivity to training.[32]

Others, the lowest, are almost on a par with plants. They have but one sense, that of touch. Such are the diverse worms that breed in clay, water, vinegar,[33] snow,[34] fruit pits, grain, the seeds of plants and trees, or the

---

there are no tragic losses, no privations or lacks, no missed opportunities, since nothing there is unreal and nothing is desired that is unworthy of desire. What is desired is there, present to one who wants it, never to be parted with, harmed or lost.' Al- Kindī, *Essay on How to Banish Sorrow*. For the Arabic text, see *Uno Scritto Morale*, ed. Helmut Ritter and Richard Walzer (Rome: Accademia dei Lincei, 1938). The translation here is Goodman's.

30 'Our purpose', the Ikhwān write, 'embraces, of necessity, all that permits man to ameliorate his life on earth and assure his happiness and salvation in the eternal world'; quoted by Nasr in *Islamic Cosmological Doctrines*, p. 30, from *Rasā'il* (Cairo, 1928), vol. 4, p. 218. Nasr epitomizes this spirit in a hadith which the Ikhwān echo: 'The world is the prison of the faithful and the paradise of the unbelievers' (p. 30). The Brethren contrast their sacred mission of salvation with the demonic call of those who are unwilling to let go of worldliness. But notice, again, the voluntarism of their plea: one can win eternal life through one's own moral and spiritual efforts. Heaven here is no merely temporal realm, and it is merited through effort and renunciation, not by sheer grace.

31 In the Aristotelian mode, the Ikhwān introduce their topic with a definition in terms of genus and differentia. Their functionalist formulation is itself Aristotelian.

32 Cf. Aristotle, *Historia Animalium* I.1.488b; *De Caelo* II.12.292b.

33 'Flies grow from grubs in the dung that farmers have gathered up. . . . A grub is tiny to begin with. At first — even at this stage — it takes a reddish colour. Then, having been quiescent, it takes on the power of motion, as though born to it. It then becomes a small motionless grub. Then it moves again, and again relapses into immobility and then comes out a perfect fly and moves off under the influence of the sun's heat or a puff of air. The horse-fly is engendered in timber. The budbane . . . in cabbage-stalks. The cantharis comes from the caterpillars found on fig-trees or pear-trees or fir-trees. For grubs breed on all of these — and also from the caterpillars found on the dog-rose. The cantharis takes eagerly to foul-smelling substances, since it was engendered in ill-scented woods. The conops comes from a grub engendered in the slime of vinegar.' Aristotle, *Historia Animalium* V.19.552a21–552b.

34 See *De Plantis* (attributed to Aristotle) II.3.825a4: 'we often find plants

gut of larger animals. Their bodies are fleshy and tender; their delicate skin, absorptive all over. They perceive by touch alone and have no other sense: no taste, smell, hearing, or sight, only tactile sensation. Animals of this sort arise quickly and soon perish, decay, and decompose.

But others are more solidly built and have more perfect form. They include all the various worms that breed and crawl on leaves, blossoms, the flowers of trees and other plants. They have taste as well as touch. Still others, more perfect and better formed, include the animals with taste, touch, and smell, but not hearing or sight. They live in the depths of the sea and other dark places.[35]

Others, higher and more perfect, are the varied swarming and crawling creatures that burrow in dark places. They have touch, taste, smell, and hearing, but not sight. For it is by touch that they stay alive, by taste that they discern their nutriment, by scent that they locate their food, and by hearing that they sense the tread of assailants and arm against attack.[36] But they are given no sense of sight, since they live in dark places and have no need to see. If they had sight they would only have the trouble of guarding it and shielding their eyes from debris.[37] For divine wisdom gives no animal any organ or sense that serves no need or affords it no benefit.[38]

---

appearing in snow, and animals of all kinds, especially worms, for they are bred in the snow'. The notion that insects and worms breed in snow arises from the striking appearance of such creatures at the start of the spring thaw, their eggs or larvae unobserved.

35 See Aristotle, *De Anima* II.3.

36 The Dār Ṣādir text reads: 'Ticks are an example. For it is by touch that they affix their bodies, by taste that they discern their nutriment, by scent that they locate their food, and by hearing that they trace the footsteps of those who would harm them before they actually reach them and vanquish them.'

37 'The eyes of moles and of some burrowing rodents are rudimentary in size and in some cases quite covered up by skin and fur. This state of the eyes is probably due to gradual reduction from disuse, but aided perhaps by Natural Selection... As frequent inflammation of the eyes must be injurious to any animal, and as the eyes are certainly not indispensable to animals with subterranean habits, a reduction in their size with the adhesion of eyelids and growth of fur over them, might in such case be an advantage . . . '. Charles Darwin, *Origin of Species*, in *The Works of Charles Darwin*, ed. Paul H. Barrett and R. B. Freeman (London: Pickering, 1988), vol. 15, p. 99.

38 Aristotle argues, famously, that nature does nothing in vain, *De Anima* III.12.434a30–32. Maimonides puts it in more explicitly theological terms:

More perfect still and more fully formed are animals with all five senses: touch, taste, smell, hearing, and sight. These too divide into the higher and the lower.

8

There are animals that inch along like the snow worm, or creep like the oyster, slither like the snake, scurry like the scorpion, scamper like the mouse, or flit like flies or gnats. Of those that crawl or walk, some go on two legs, some on four or six or more, like those that make their way on many legs.[39] Among flying insects, some have two wings, some four. Some have six legs, four wings, a snout, claws, and horns, like the grasshopper.[40] Others have a proboscis, like gnats and flies.[41] Still others, a venomed dagger like the wasp.

Of the crawling and swarming creatures, some, like ants and bees, have thought and discernment, the ability to manage their lives in organized societies. They live co-operatively in communal homes and hamlets, storing food and provender for the winter, so they survive

'Far be it from God to produce any organ in vain'; *Maimonides' Treatise on Resurrection (Maqāla fī teḥiyyat ha-metim): The Original Arabic and Samuel ibn Tibbon's Hebrew Translation and Glossary*, ed. Joshua Finkel (New York: American Academy for Jewish Research, 1939); the translation here is by Goodman, but see also *The Essay on Resurrection*, in *Crisis and Leadership: Epistles of Maimonides*, tr. Abraham Halkin (Philadelphia: Jewish Publication Society of America, 1985), p. 214. Darwin specifies: 'What Natural Selection cannot do is modify the structure of one species, without giving it any advantage, for the benefit of another species; and though statements to this effect may be found in works of Natural History, I cannot find one case which will bear investigation.' *Origin of Species*, ed. Barrett and Freeman, vol. 15, p. 64.

39 Centipedes and millipedes, in the subclass Chilopoda, may have from 24 to 340 legs.

40 The grasshopper does indeed have claws. The 'horns', of course, are the antennae. Some manuscripts give the grasshopper four legs and six wings, but that reading belies the careful observation of the Ikhwān.

41 'As for insects, some, like ants, have the part that serves as a tongue inside the mouth . . . in others it is externally placed. In the latter case it resembles a sting and is hollow and spongy, serving at once for tasting and for sucking up nutriment. This is plainly seen in flies and bees and all such animals . . . ' Aristotle, *De Partibus Animalium* II.17.661a16–21.

through the year and often longer. Other crawling and swarming creatures — gnats, fleas, flies, grasshoppers, and the like — do not live out the year. The extremes of heat and cold destroy them, and their kind must arise anew the next year.

9

Better-formed, larger, and better-built are all the animals whose bodies have variously shaped, jointed, and specialized limbs, with bones long or short, thick or thin, straight or curved — backed by sinews and ligaments, filled out with flesh, channelled with veins, cased in skin, and wrapped in hair or fur, wool or feathers, shell or scales. Internally, they have certain chief organs — brain, lungs, heart, liver, spleen, kidneys, bladder, intestines, bowels, arteries, stomach, rumen, crop, gizzard, and the like. Their outer organs include legs, hands, wings, tail, claws, beak, footpads, or hooves, cloven or uncloven. This wealth of resources serves ends known fully but to Him who framed and formed them, raised them up, and brought them to the peak of perfection.

These are the various kinds of cattle and beasts, carnivores, wild beasts, fowl, birds of prey, some water animals, and certain crawling animals, like snakes.[42] The cattle include all animals with cloven hooves; beasts, those with hooves. Predators are those with fangs and claws. Wild beasts may or may not have these attributes. Fowl have wings, feathers, and beaks. Birds of prey, too, have wings, but curved beaks and hooked talons. Aquatic animals are those that can live in water. Swarming creatures are those that fly but have no feathers. Crawling creatures go on two legs or four, or creep or slither on their bellies, or loop along on their sides.

42 'The tracks left by snakes are such that although they are seen to lack feet, they nevertheless crawl on their ribs with forward thrusts of their scales . . . which are like nails, and with their ribs, which are like legs. So if a snake is crushed by a blow to any part of its body, from the belly to the head, it cannot make its way but is crippled, because the blow, wherever it falls, has broken its spine, which activates its rib "feet".' Isidore of Seville, *Etymologies*, tr. S. A. Barney et. al. (Cambridge: CUP, 2006), 12.4.45–46.

10

You should know, further, that huge, hulking animals with massive bones, thick skins, tough sinews, broad veins, and big limbs, such as the elephant, camel, water buffalo, and the like, need long gestation in the womb — for two reasons: first, to gather all the materials their natures need to build their bodies and complete their form. Second, to allow the sun to circle and the right constellations to be in trine, to fix their natures properly,[43] sending down the spiritual influences that the stars shed on the world of generation and decay, which every creature bred must receive to perfect its vegetative powers of growth or its sensory, animal powers, as we explained in one part of our essay 'On Embryology' [Epistle 25].[44]

Know, dear brother, that all the larger-bodied, more perfectly formed animals, those with the more imposing forms, were formed in clay at first, male and female, at the equator, where day and night, heat and cold, are ideally balanced. This was in sites sheltered from shifting winds and rich in matter of the sorts receptive to form. But places of that character were wanting on the earth at large. Therefore, females were given wombs with just such balanced natures, so that these animals could fan out over the earth, able to procreate and multiply wherever they might be.

Most people are stunned at the thought that animals came from clay. But they are not surprised at their own development in the womb, from

43 Greek and Arabic astrology section the heavens according to the signs of the zodiac, whose relations were widely thought to govern the formation of all species and to mark the rise and fall of human fortunes. Triplicity or 'trine' is the most favourable aspect of two planets, at 120° from each other. See F. Dieterici, *Die Anthropologie der Araber im zehnten Jahrhundert n. Chr.* (Leipzig: J. C. Hinrichs, 1871), pp. 72–74; W. Hartner, 'Muthallath', *EI2*, vol. 7, pp. 794–795.

44 See Epistle 25; the material constituents assembled in the womb are the substrate for the receipt of the proper Form, which emanates from the stars. Matter, receptive to Form, lays down the parameters of a creature's genus. The substantial Form, bestowed from on high, brings the vital powers that impart specificity. Matter must await the astrologically opportune moment to receive its proper Form. For the gestation of the elephant, see Pliny, *Natural History* VIII.10.28, ed. and tr. H. Rackham (Cambridge, MA: Harvard University Press, 1940), vol. 3, pp. 22–23.

foul water,[45] a more awesome exercise of power. For some people can fashion an animal in clay or wood, iron or copper, as is familiar from the work of sculptors. But no human being can fashion an animal from water, since a liquid does not hold a shape. So the generation of these animals in the womb or in an egg, from foul water, is more marvellous, a more awesome use of power than making them from clay.

Most people, too, find an elephant's creation more amazing than a gnat's. But the gnat is more marvellously built and more elegantly designed. The elephant has his great size, his four legs, and trunk. But the tiny gnat has six legs, a proboscis of her own, four wings, a tail, mouth, oesophagus, stomach, intestines, bowels, and many other organs, unseen by the eye. Despite her size, she's deadlier and more baneful than an elephant, and he cannot get the better of her.[46] Besides, a human artisan can form a perfect elephant of wood, iron, or such. But no craftsman can model a perfect gnat of wood or iron.

A human arises from that first droplet, grows to a foetus in the womb, an infant in the cradle, a child at school, and, with experience

45 Qur'an 77:20. See note 66 below.

46 Babylonian Talmud, Shabbat 77b: 'A gnat terrifies a lion, and a mosquito can harm an elephant.' Aesop tells of the lion's shame at his fear of the cock. His chagrin was allayed when he learned that the elephant fears the gnat, which might kill him if it got into his ear. For a cock is surely more fearsome than a gnat! Aesop chuckles at the hubris of the ass, who supposed that a lion, fleeing the cock's crow, was running from him. The foolish ass gave chase and was eaten as soon as the lion was out of earshot of the cock. See Aesop, *The Complete Fables*, tr. Olivia and Robert Temple (London: Penguin, 1988), items 210 and 269. Sextus Empiricus, reeling off the grounds of relativism in support of his scepticism, retails as commonplaces: 'The elephant flees from the ram, the lion from the cock, sea monsters from the crackle of bursting beans, and the tiger from the sound of a drum.' Sextus Empiricus, *Outlines of Pyrrhonism*, tr. R. G. Bury (Cambridge, MA: Harvard University Press, 1933), vol. 1, p. 58; cf. Lucan, *Pharsalia* IX.859–861, where the elephant, despite his bulk, is vulnerable to the serpent's bite. Pliny relates that the elephant so hates mice that he will reject food touched by one, *Natural History* VIII.10.29, ed. and tr. H. Rackham, vol. 3, pp. 22–23. Cf. Isidore for the elephant's fear of mice; *Etymologies* 12.2.14–16. Recent work by Todd Palmer shows that acacia trees in Kenya are guarded by stinging, biting ants that inhabit enlarged thorns and feed on the rich sap. When the trees are protected from elephants, giraffes, and other ruminants, they cut back on nectar production and are abandoned by the ants, leaving the trees vulnerable to devastating invasions by beetles. See *Science*, January 11, 2008, vol. 319, 5860. See also Chapters 14, 21, 23, 38 below.

of life in the world, a man of prudence and discernment.[47] But more wondrous changes and more awesome acts await, when he is raised from the grave on Resurrection Day and men issue from the earth *like a locust swarm.*[48]

We see twenty chicks emerge from beneath the breast of a single broody hen, or thirty from a single pheasant that lays a clutch of eggs. Within an hour they scurry after grain and flee anyone who chases them, so you can hardly catch them. That's more a marvel than the dead issuing from their graves on Resurrection Day. So, what, besides its singularity, makes doubters deny this, when they see the other with their own eyes, a more astounding, more awesome display of power.

11

Experience, dear brother, holds steady. The familiar offers little surprise and arouses little thought or reflection, passing all but unremarked, as if people's spirit were dead, or asleep in unknowing. So be aware, dear brother, not oblivious. Be one of those whom God describes in his Book: *those who are ever aware of Him, standing, sitting, or lying down, pondering the creation of heaven and earth, and saying: 'O Lord, Thou didst not create this in vain. Praise be to Thee, and do Thou save us from the torment of the Fire!'*[49] For He blames those who slight Him

47 The ages of man, well known to English readers from Shakespeare's set piece in *As You Like It* (2.7), were well defined in antiquity and in the Hellenistic literature that nourishes the Ikhwān. See Paul of Aegina, *The Seven Books*, ed. Francis Adams (London: Sydenham Society, 1844–1847), vol. 1, p. 104. The commentary cites further textual sources from Oribasius and Aetius, and ultimately Galen (*Hygiene*, Part I). For the Arabic reception of the idea, see the passages edited and translated from Baladī's *Habala* (composed in Fāṭimid Egypt in the 980s), 2.47–48, in Peter E. Portman, *The Oriental Tradition of Paul of Aegina's 'Pragmateia'* (Leiden: Brill, 2004), pp. 104–105. Ibn Ṭufayl uses the ancient scheme in periodizing the life of Ḥayy ibn Yaqẓān.

48 Qur'an 54:7.

49 Qur'an 3:191. The reasoning being that if man were born just to die, His creation was in vain. Cf. Saadiah ben Joseph, *The Book of Theodicy*, tr. L. E. Goodman, pp. 42, 362, where Saadiah's language echoes Qur'an 23:115; cf. Qur'an 44:38.

in their thoughts: *How numerous are the portents in heaven and on earth! But they pass them by and turn away.*[50]

12

Know, dear brother, that all animal bodies, higher or lower, are composed of limbs and organs of varied shapes, functions, and configurations — like the head, hand, foot, back, belly, heart, liver, lung, etc. All have their uses and benefits, known ultimately to God alone, who created them and formed them as He pleased. We shall touch on them briefly, to confirm the truth of our account and the soundness of our description.

There is no organ, great or small, that does not serve and minister to some other, sustaining and supporting it or enhancing its function and improving its usefulness.[51] The brain, for instance, is king of the human body, hub of the senses, quarry of our thoughts, home of our ideas, storehouse of memory, abode of the soul, and seat of reason.[52]

50 Qur'an 12:105.

51 See Aristotle, *De Partibus Animalium* I.5.645b27: 'When one function is ancillary to another, a like relation obviously holds between the organs that discharge these functions.' Cf. Macrobius, *Saturnalia* VIII.

52 Hippocrates saw the brain as the source of sensation and muscular motion (*De Insomniis* I). Galen confirmed that the brain governs all animal powers, at least in higher animals. He traced to the brain the nerves that control six throat muscles. Only 'those who know nothing of what is to be seen in dissection', he argued, would ascribe the motion of these muscles to the action of the heart. Al-Fārābī held to the (Aristotelian) view that, 'The heart is the ruling organ, uncontrolled by any other organ of the body. Below it in rank is the brain.' *Kitāb Mabādi' ārā' ahl al-madīna al-fāḍila*, ed. and tr. R. Walzer as *Al-Farabi on the Perfect State* (Oxford: OUP, 1985), p. 175. He was apparently unaware of or unconvinced by Galen's discovery of the function of the recurrent laryngeal nerve, which proved that the brain controls voluntary actions like speech. As Margaret Tallmadge May writes, Joseph Walsh, in a 'splendid article', identified Galen's description of this action in *De Usu Partium* (written at Rome between 169 and 176) as embodying 'the actual lecture given by Galen and taken down stenographically on the occasion when he demonstrated publicly the structure of the larynx, the muscles moving it, and their innervation'; Galen, *De Usu Partium* VII.14, tr. M. May as *On the Usefulness of the Parts of the Body* (Ithaca, NY: Cornell University Press, 1968), vol. 1, pp. 362–363. Walsh wrote: 'This discovery established for all time that the brain is the organ of thought and represented one of the most

The heart is the brain's servant, charged with carrying out its orders in governing the body and controlling its functions. It is the well-spring of the arteries[53] and source of our body heat.[54] Serving the heart, and

important additions to anatomy and physiology, being probably as great as the discovery of the circulation of the blood.' Joseph Walsh, 'Galen's Discovery', *Annals of Medical History*, 8 (1926), p. 179; cf. Galen, *De Placitis Hippocratis et Platonis*, in *Opera Omnia*, ed. C. G. Kühn (Leipzig: Knobloch, 1821–1833), vol. 5, which inveighs steadily against the Aristotelian siting of thought in the heart and not the brain. Galen's dissections, as May notes, relied on animals, chiefly, small, tailless primates like the Barbary ape, although he also used pigs, goats, and bovine specimens (Galen, *De Usu Partium*, tr. May, p. 40). In his *De Compositione Medicamentorum per Genera* III.2 (in *Opera Omnia*, ed. Kühn, vol. 13, p. 604), Galen praises the use of apes as a guide to human dissection, which would otherwise be as blind and profitless as the work of butchers, even when the opportunity for human anatomical dissection arises, as it did, he remarks, when the bodies of enemy combatants were made available in the German war. Ibn Ṭufayl, himself a physician, includes extensive dissection in the naturalistic phase of Ḥayy ibn Yaqẓān's life.

53 Galen found it critical that the blood vessels stem from the heart — although he did not clearly distinguish veins from arteries. His *De Usu Partium* was translated into Syriac by Sergius of Resh ʿAyn, a priest who had studied Greek and medicine at Alexandria. It was translated again by Ḥunayn ibn Isḥāq. Ḥunayn's nephew Ḥubaysh began an Arabic translation directly from the Greek, a task Ḥunayn completed in old age. See May's introduction to her translation, p. 20; Max Meyerhof, 'New Light on Ḥunayn Ibn Isḥāq', *Isis*, 8 (1926), pp. 685–724.

54 Aristotle, *On Youth, Old Age, Life and Death, and Respiration*, 6.740a20: 'Everything living has a soul, and, as we have said, cannot exist in the absence of natural heat.' Innate body heat, called radical heat in medical texts, is vitally necessary in Galenic physiology. The Stoic philosophers saw body heat not just as a sign of life but as the actual divine spirit in each living being. Drawing on Hippocrates, Aristotle, and the Stoics, Galen equates a living being's nature and soul with this heat. If not the essence of the soul, he writes, this heat is clearly its first instrument. Hippocrates had called heat the immortal basis of life and intelligence. In Aristotle's view, both nutrition and reproduction depend upon the heat he traces to the heart in animals with blood, and to some analogous centre in other animals. Both Hippocrates and Aristotle see the body heat as sustained by respiration, but Aristotle holds that it must be tempered by 'refrigeration' in the brain — a notion that Galen vehemently denies. Centring the heat in the heart, especially the left ventricle and the arteries that spread it throughout the body, Galen rejects the view of Erisistratus, Praxagoras, Philotimus, Asclepiades, and 'innumerable others' that the heat that distinguishes living from non-living beings is externally derived. See Hippocrates, *De Temperamentibus*, 1.9, in *Opera Omnia*, ed. C. G. Kühn, vol. 1, pp. 569–570; Galen, *De Usu Partium* IV.6, VI.7, VII.9, VIII.4; cf. May's introduction, vol. 1, pp. 50–53; and Richard Broxton Onians, *The Origins of European Thought about the Body, the Mind, the Soul, the World, Time, and Fate* (Cambridge: CUP, 1951).

assigned to act in its behalf, are three other organs: the liver, lungs, and arteries.

The liver, where liquids lodge, is served by five other organs: the stomach, veins, spleen, gall-bladder, and kidneys.

Likewise, the lungs, seat of our breath, are served by four other organs: the chest, pleura, windpipe, and nostrils. Air enters through the nostrils. It is drawn into the windpipe, where its temperature is adjusted. From there it reaches the lungs, where it is filtered, and proceeds to the heart. There it ventilates the radical heat and percolates through the arteries, reaching all the extremities of the body, under the name of the pulse.[55] The heated air is released from the heart to the lungs and back to the windpipe, whence it exits through the nostrils or the mouth. The chest serves the lungs by expanding for them on inhaling and contracting for them on exhaling. The pleura protects the lungs from injury by a blow or bodily disturbance.

The liver, on the same pattern, is served by the stomach, which digests the chyme before it reaches the liver, and by the veins, which fetch and carry for it. The spleen serves by drawing into itself the muddy dregs of the chyme, the thick, burning residue.[56] And it is served by the gall-bladder, which takes up the yellow bile, cleansing the blood of it, and by the kidneys, which absorb the thin, finer fluids, whence the urine.[57] It is also served by the hollow arteries, which take up the

---

55 Chrysippus (apud Calcidius, 220 = H. von Arnim, ed., *Stoicorum Veterum Fragmenta* [Stuttgart: Teubner, 1903–1905], vol. 2, item 879, henceforth *SVF*): 'the soul is found to be the natural breath . . . The soul's parts flow from their seat in the heart, as if from a spring, and spread throughout the body. They continually fill all the limbs with vital breath and rule and govern them with countless different powers'; A. A. Long and D. N. Sedley, *The Hellenistic Philosophers* (Cambridge: CUP, 1987), English trans., vol. 1, p. 315, Latin text, vol. 2, pp. 313–314.

56 Galen argues, against Erisistratus, that the spleen does have a purpose: it draws off the 'thick muddy residue… the thick, earthy, atrabilious humours formed in the liver', as if by a canal — a duct, that is — and holds it in its spongy tissue, thus purifying the liver. To Galen, the spleen's placement, like its function testifies to the divine artisanship of nature. *De Usu Partium* IV.4, IV.15, tr. May, vol. 1. pp. 210, 232; De *Naturalibus Facultatibus* II.9.

57 On the Galenic account, the liver draws nutriment from the stomach via the veins and fabricates nutriment-rich blood, which circulates throughout the body. John Actuarius, a Byzantine physician who sums up Galenic and later medical work including that of the Muslim physicians, writes: 'Digestion is performed

blood and transport it to all the extremities of the body, as matter for the body's parts.

The oesophagus, teeth, and mouth, similarly, serve the stomach. For the mouth is the gateway through which food and drink pass to the body's interior. The teeth serve by crushing and grinding. The oesophagus, by swallowing food and drink and conveying it to the stomach. The bowels take up the wastes and expel them from the body.

On the same pattern and plan every organ in an animal's body helps carry out the body's functions and is served in turn by other organs with functions of their own. The ultimate purpose of them all is to promote the survival and well-being of the organism and its kind for as long as possible, as a species and genus, as well as an individual.

13

You must know, dear brother, that some animals are mute, having neither voice nor speech. Such are the crabs, turtles, fish — and most water animals,[58] but for a few like frogs. Others have voices, those that breathe air. Still others do not make sounds by blowing air but by moving their wings — like gnats, flies, wasps, crickets, grasshoppers, and the like.[59]

---

by moderate heat and moisture.' *De Spiritu Animali* II.1. Further: 'When the food in the stomach is changed and digested, the meseraic veins, which derive their origin from the liver, by their vein called *ramalis*, suck the stomach and intestines; and having emulged, as it were, the purer part, (namely, the food converted into chyle) and having drawn it as if through a strainer, they convey it to the concave part of the liver, and deliver it over to the sanguinificatory power. Here, then, if nothing impede it, when it is changed into blood, whatever is subtile and acrid is received by the gall-bladder, which is placed at the convex part of the liver, and draws off the bile; but whatever the blood possesses of a terrene and melancholic humour is drawn to the spleen, by some natural faculty, whereby every part draws off whatever suits its nature. Thirdly, the serous humour remains. It is drawn off by the kidneys.' *De Urinis*, quoted in Paul of Aegina, *The Seven Books*, vol. 1, p. 99.

58 'Since fish live in the water, they have no use for a voice.' Galen, *De Usu Partium* VI.9, tr. May, vol. 1, p. 296.

59 'Order, Orthoptera — The males in the three saltatorial families belonging to this Order are remarkable for their musical powers, namely the Achetidae or crickets, the Locustidae . . . and the Acridiidae or grasshoppers. The stridulation

Air-breathing animals have a great many calls, long or short, rough or smooth, great or small, loud or soft. Their buzzes and chirps, songs and melodies all match the length of their neck, the breadth of their throat and nostrils, the clarity or coarseness of their natures, their lung power, and the balance of bodily spirits that they attain by cooling the radical heat in their hearts and within their bodies.[60]

The reason why most water animals are mute is that they have no lungs and do not breathe air. They have no voices because they do not need them. For God's wisdom and sovereign providence gave every animal the limbs and organs suited to its needs:[61] veins and arteries,

---

produced by some of the Locustidae is so loud that it can be heard during the night at the distance of a mile; and that made by certain species is not unmusical even to the human ear . . . the sounds serve either to call or excite the mute females. . . . The house cricket when surprised at night uses its voice to warn its fellows. . . . In both sexes a remarkable auditory apparatus has been discovered by Von Siebold, situated in the front legs. . . . In the males of the Achetidae both wing-covers have the same structure; and this in the field cricket (*Gryllus campestris*) consists, as described by Ladois, of from 131 to 138 sharp, transverse ridges or teeth on the under side of one of the nervures of the wing-cover. This toothed nervure is rapidly scraped across a projecting, smooth, hard nervure on the upper surface of the opposite wing. First one wing is rubbed over the other, and then the movement is reversed. Both wings are raised a little, so as to increase the resonance. . . . In the Locustidae the opposite wing covers differ in structure. . . . The left wing, which acts as the bow of the fiddle, lies over the right wing, which serves as the fiddle itself.' Darwin, *The Descent of Man*, in *The Works of Charles Darwin*, ed. P. H. Barrett and R. B. Freeman, vol. 22, pp. 294–295.

60 As the Ikhwān clearly knew, and as Erasmus showed with the success of *In Praise of Folly*, ridicule is the surest form of erasure. Laurence Sterne buries the physiology of radical heat in *Tristram Shandy*, Book V, Chapters 33–37, when Tristram's father bloviates: 'The whole secret of health depending upon the due contention for mastery betwixt the radical heat and the radical moisture.' As the authorial persona comments: 'With two strokes, the one at Hippocrates, the other at Lord Verulam, did my father achieve it. The stroke at the prince of physicians, with which he began, was no more than a short insult upon his sorrowful complaint, of the *Ars longa*, — and the *Vita brevis*. — Life is short, cried my father, — and the art of healing tedious! And who are we to thank for both the one and the other, but the ignorance of the quacks themselves . . . '. As for Bacon, 'O my lord Verulam! . . . What shall I say to thy internal spirit — thy opium — thy salt-petre, — thy greasy unctions, — thy daily purges, — thy nightly clysters, and succedaneums?' The Galenic canon is dismissed with no more ceremony or apology than Cervantes used in sinking the canon of chivalric romance.

61 God's gifts match the needs and capacities of the recipients, a theme elaborated in the cricket's speech to the dragon, king of the crawling creatures, in Chapter 17 below.

coverings and reservoirs that allow it to seek what is good for it and avoid what is harmful, to survive, mature, and win its ultimate end: preservation of its kind, using its sexual and reproductive organs to procreate and breed offspring.[62]

The more perfect any animal's frame and form, the more it needs a great variety of organs and implements to help it survive and reproduce. The more wanting its body and the lower its type, the less it needs varied organs and implements to survive and perpetuate its kind.

To explain, there are three kinds of animals: the highest and most perfect mate, conceive, bear live young, nurse and rear them. Below these are all that mate, lay eggs, and brood them. Lower still are those that do not mate, lay eggs, or bear young, but breed in rotting matter and do not live a full year but perish in extremes of heat or cold, since their bodies are open pored and loose knit. They have no thick skin, wool or hair, fur, feathers, or shell, no bone or sinew. So they do not need lungs, spleen, gall-bladder, kidneys, or urinary bladder. They do not breathe air to cool the body heat. For the breeze penetrates their tiny, porous bodies. It regulates the body heat that sustains their constitution, maintaining the balance of the elements within.

The larger animals have massive frames, leathery skins, and much flesh, they have membranes, veins, solid or hollow bones, ribcages, entrails and intestines, rumen and stomach, heart and lungs, spleen and kidneys, urinary bladder and skull, hair, fur, wool, feathers, or a shell or similar covering to keep out the draft and maintain the body's vital heat. Some are given lungs, throats, and a space within for the breath, so the outer air can reach the inner chambers and cavities of the body and temper the body heat, preserving them for a definite

62 Aristotle, *De Generatione Animalium* II.1.731b : 'Some things that exist are eternal and divine; others may or may not exist. The noble and divine is always, by its nature, the cause of the better in things that may be better or worse. . . . But soul is better than body, and the living, being ensouled, is thus better than the lifeless, which is not. Being is better than non-being, living than non-living. These are the reasons for the generation of animals. For it is impossible for such sort as animals to have an eternal nature. So what comes to be is eternal in the only way possible: it cannot be eternal as an individual . . . but it can as a species.' Aristotle adds: 'That is why there is always a class of men and animals and plants.' That last conclusion, the Ikhwān, of course, do not share.

lifespan. Such is the rule for animals that are complete and perfect, that breathe the air and live in it.

The animals that live in water permanently do not need to breathe air. The Creator in his wisdom, glory be to Him, formed them in the water, made it their home, and gave them an aquatic nature. He so framed their bodies that the cool, wet water penetrates and relieves the body heat, making breathing unnecessary for them. To each species He gave limbs suited to its body, tailored and apt to it, and a garb of shell or scales of various kinds, to guard against heat and cold — an inner coat and an outer, to shield against injury and accident. Some He gave wings and a tail, to swim through the water as birds fly through the air. He made some the feeders and others the food, the race of the prey more numerous than the predators — all to preserve the individuals in life and sustain their kinds over time, as long as their natures would allow.

As for the varied birds that fill the air as its denizens, the wise Creator, glorious be His praise, trimmed their allotted organs, as compared to the land animals that bear and nurse their young, to lighten them for taking off and flying through the air. The Creator gave birds no teeth or visible ears, no stomach, rumen, urinary bladder, or vertebrae,[63] no thick hide. Their bodies have no hair, wool, or fur. Instead, He gave them feathers as their cover, to keep out the heat and cold. This is the wrap and comforter that protects them from injury and accident. He aided them in taking off and flying by substituting a beak for teeth, a crop for the stomach, a gizzard for the rumen. In place of every missing organ He supplied another, scaled and adapted to their bodies and suited to their needs in pursuing what is good for them and avoiding what is harmful — all, again, to promote their

---

63 In a typical bird such as the domestic fowl, 'The neck contains about 16 cervical vertebrae, each with saddle-shaped articular surfaces that permit free movements in feeding, preening, and other activities. The trunk vertebrae are closely fitted together; those of the thorax have rib articulations laterally, and the remainder are fused into a solid synsacrum to which the pelvis attaches. No lumbar region is evident. The four free caudal vertebrae and the compressed terminal pygostyle (= 5 or 6 fused vertebrae) serve in movements of the tail feathers.' T. I. Storer and R. L. Usinger, *General Zoology* (New York: McGraw Hill, 1957), p. 547. Perhaps it is the fused structure of some avian vertebrae that the Ikhwān have in mind.

individual survival and the perpetuation of their kinds for as long as their natures and constitutions allow.[64]

To land animals that eat plants the Creator gave wide mouths that allow them to graze on herbage and pasturage. He added sharp, shearing incisors and rugged molars to grind the tough parts of plants — the grain and leaves, husks and kernels. He gave them full, slick gullets, to swallow what they've chewed and an ample rumen to hold all they've taken in when they've had their fill. For when sated they return to their byres and folds, lie down, and rest.

Some chew their cud: they regurgitate what they've swallowed and grind it a second time and then swallow it down again to a different stomach with a different nature, more suited to the cookery that their vital heat requires and capable of digesting it further to make it good for them. They separate thick from thin and send the grosser parts to the bowels, which vent them through special outlets.[65] The filtered,

---

64 'Birds also differ in the part that serves to receive the food, for the same reason. For here too it is because the mouth fails to do its job. For birds have no teeth at all, nor any instrument at all with which to bite or grind their food. So in some what is called the crop comes ahead of the stomach and does the mouth's work, while in others the oesophagus is broad, or a part of it bulges just before it reaches the stomach, forming a preparatory storehouse for the unreduced food; or the stomach itself has a bulge somewhere, or is strong and fleshy, so as to be able to store food for a considerable period and concoct it, even though it has not been ground to a pulp. For nature compensates for the inefficiency of the mouth by increasing the efficiency and heat of the stomach. Other birds, such as have long legs and live in marshes, have none of these provisions, but just a long oesophagus. The reason is the moist character of their food. For all these birds feed on easily reduced substances.' Aristotle, *De Partibus Animalium* III.14.674b19–36.

65 Cf. Aristotle, *Historia Animalium* IX.50.632b1–11: 'All animals that ruminate derive profit and pleasure from the process, as they do from eating. It is the animals that lack the upper teeth that ruminate, such as cattle, sheep, and goats. In the case of wild animals no observation has yet been made, except for animals occasionally domesticated, like the stag, and it chews the cud. All animals that ruminate generally do so lying on the ground.' Cf. also Aristotle, *De Partibus Animalium* III.14.674a23–674b15: 'The stomach is single in all sanguineous and viviparous animals that are ambidentate. So it is single in all the polydactylous kinds, like man, dog, lion, and the rest. Likewise in all solid-hoofed animals, like the horse, mule, and ass, and all those which, like the pig, though their hoof is cloven, yet are ambidentate. But when an animal is of large size and feeds on substances so thorny and ligneous as to be difficult of concoction, it may as a result have several stomachs, as is the case with the camel. A similar multiplicity

finer parts return to the liver for a second concoction. They are purified once again, and the gross parts flow to vessels suited to receive them, like the spleen, gall-bladder, kidneys, and hollow veins, which are like rivers and streams in the body, allowing the purified blood to course through them to all the extremities, replacing what has broken down. For all animal bodies are subject to flux and break-down.

Even better, the bodies of males are provided by their wise Creator with organs, conduits, and channels that conduct the bead of semen to the female's womb when they couple, mount, and mate.[66] To the females He gave organs, conduits, and channels that let the fluids He provided as a complement to the semen unite with it. In the days and months that follow, the resulting mass will coalesce and grow, and the Creator gives it a form like that of one parent, as He may please, as we explained in our essay 'On Embryology'. The whole causal sequence is the means by which the wise Creator , glory be to Him, providentially preserves individuals and their progeny for as long as possible, and thus sustains their kinds. Blessed be God, Lord of the awesome throne, best of creators, wisest of the wise and most merciful of the merciful.[67]

---

of stomachs is found also in horned animals. For horn-bearing animals are not ambidentate. The camel too, although it has no horns, is not ambidentate. For it is more essential for the camel to have multiple stomachs than to have front teeth. So its stomach is constructed like that of non-ambidentates, and its teeth match its stomach. Otherwise they would be of no use. Besides, its food being thorny and its tongue fleshy, perforce, nature uses the earthy matter saved from the teeth to give hardness to the palate. The camel ruminates like the horned animals, since its multiple stomach resembles theirs. For all animals that have horns, the sheep for instance, the ox, goat, deer, and the like, have several stomachs. For since the mouth, owing to its lack of teeth, only imperfectly does its job with the food, the stomachs receive the food from one another in succession, the first taking the unreduced substances, the second the same when somewhat reduced, the third when reduction is complete, and the fourth when the whole has become a smooth pulp. That is why there is this multiplicity of parts and cavities in animals with such dentition. The names given to the several cavities are paunch, honeycomb bag, manyplies, and reed.'

66 The Ikhwān echo the language of Qur'an, where the droplet of semen is a persistent theme: 16:4, 18:37, 22:5, 23:13–14, 35:11, 36:77, 40:67, 53:46, 75:37, 76:2, 80:19; cf. Mishnah Avot 3.1. Setting the Qur'anic language into a physiological context, the Brethren fuse the Qur'an's spiritual response to the act of generation with the scientist's analytic understanding.

67 Causality was controversial in the time of the Ikhwān: occasionalist *mutakallimūn* denied any efficacy to horizontal (natural) causes, lest God's universal control be

14

Beasts of prey, being carnivores, have quite a different nature. Their internal and external organs differ in structure from those of herbivores, and their drives and urges are not the same. The Creator made them meat-eaters and made the carcasses of other animals the matter for their bodies. So He gave them powerful fangs and strong, hooked claws, stout forearms, light, bounding steps, long, powerful leaps, enabling them to catch and maul their prey, rend its hide, tear out its viscera, break its bones, and mangle its flesh without mercy or remorse.

Most thinkers are troubled on contemplating this, perplexed as to its reasons, wondering how this could be wise on God's part. But we have explained its wisdom and rightness in our essay 'On Causes and Effects' [Epistle 40] and will touch on it in another section of the present essay.[68]

15

You must know that the Creator gave the diverse animal kinds forms, natures, and habits of four different types: some live in the air — most species of birds and all swarming creatures. Some swim in the water and make it their home. Some live on land — the quadrupeds, cattle, and carnivores. Some live in the earth — the crawling creatures. God ordained that among these classes some would be predators and others prey. So, among birds, some eat grain or fruit; others, meat — namely, the raptors, all those with hooked claws and curved beaks that cannot gather grain or eat fruit.[69] Likewise with water animals: there are the

---

slighted. See Majid Fakhry, *Islamic Occasionalism and its Critique by Averroes and Aquinas* (London: Allen Unwin, 1958). The Brethren show no such compunctions. God, in their view, acts *through* nature, by way of the Forms that give all things their natures and efficacy. By ascribing natural causality to providence and interpreting providence, in turn, in terms of natural causality, the Ikhwān take aim at the occasionalists: God acts not by arbitrary interventions but through the mediation of proximate causes. See Epistle 40: 'On Cause and Effect'.

68 See Chapter 32 below.

69 Aristotle, *De Partibus Animalium* IV.12.693a 11–15: 'The beaks of birds also

eaters and the eaten. And again with the earth animals, crawling creatures like snakes, lizards, and geckos.[70]

16

You must know too, dear brother, that when the wise Creator made the perfectly formed animals, He framed them in matching halves, left and right,[71] like the start of the number series and all dualities, as we explained in our essay 'On Principles' [Epistles 32 and 33].[72] He placed

---

vary with their modes of life. For in some the beak is straight, in others crooked: straight, in those that use it merely for eating; crooked, in those that live on raw flesh. For a crooked beak is an advantage in fighting; and these birds must, of course, get their food from the bodies of other animals, in most cases by violence.'

70 Nature forms a system, wisely devised: some parts depend on others, and all are provided for. Again, the Ikhwān mount a mild anti-occasionalist polemic. The argument left implicit is that if one creature's welfare did not depend on the presence of another, as the occasionalists imply in ascribing all events to God's direct and immediate act, then many creations would be unneeded and much of God's creative work would be otiose.

71 The reference is to bilateral symmetry in animals that bear their young.

72 The Ikhwān envision the world in Neopythagorean terms. Numbers, as Nasr explains, relate the world's diversity to God's unity, and by bringing to light the world's pervasive harmony, afford manifest evidence of its wise creation; see *Islamic Cosmological Doctrines*, pp. 45–47. Foundational here is the Neopythagorean work of Nicomachus of Gerasa (ca. 60–ca. 120). His 'Introduction to Arithmetic', translated into Arabic by Thābit ibn Qurra (826–901), lays out the following case: 'We see all things in the world's natural order to be artfully fashioned, overall and in each of their parts — solely because the Creator based them on certain ratios, distinguishing and balancing them so beautifully and admirably, by building into them the pattern He meant them to pursue. He made these numbers a paradigm and plan, pre-drawn in the knowledge of God, their Creator'; see Nicomachus, *Arithmêtikê Eisagôgê*, (Arabic) ed. W. Kutsch (Beirut: Catholic University Press, 1959), p.18. Translation here is Goodman's. Numbers, for the Ikhwān, and ratios in particular, are not just a means of counting and calculating, they are, as the followers of Pythagoras taught, foundations of the rational order of the cosmos, and thus, for the Ikhwān, directly intelligible expressions of the wisdom God embedded in His creation. Symmetries, rhythms, and harmonies, discovered in the abstract in number theory and geometry and manifested concretely in, say, music, astronomy, and anatomy (and the parallels among them) not only bespeak divine craftsmanship but also help guide the soul on its return voyage to its divine home. See Epistle

them on three broad levels — upper, lower, and in between — like the first odd number and all things with two extremes and a middle.[73]

He compounded their bodies of four humours, matching the first square number and the four natures of the elements.[74] He gave them five senses that apprehend sensible forms, matching the first round number[75] and the four natures plus the fifth, the celestial.[76] He gave them the power to move in all six directions, corresponding to the first perfect number and the faces of a cube.[77]

He gave their bodies seven active faculties, corresponding to the first complete number and the number of the planets.[78] He gave their bodies

---

5: 'On Music'; and Owen Wright, 'Music and Musicology in the *Rasā'il Ikhwān al-Ṣafā*'', in Nader El-Bizri, ed., *The Ikhwān al-Ṣafā' and their 'Rasā'il'*, pp. 215–216.

73 Water is between earth and air, just as two lies between one and three.

74 The four Galenic humours are: blood, phlegm, black bile, and yellow bile. The four natures: hot, cold, wet, and dry. Blood, like air, is hot and wet. Phlegm, like water, is cold and wet. Black bile, like earth, is cold and dry. Yellow bile, like fire, is hot and dry.

75 In their epistle 'On Numbers' [Epistle 1], the Ikhwān explain: 'We say that 5 is the first round number, because when multiplied by itself it returns to itself; and if that number is multiplied by itself, it again returns to its essence and so on forever. Thus 5 x 5 = 25, and if this number is multiplied by itself, the product is 625, and if this number is again multiplied by itself, the product is 390,625, and if this number is multiplied by itself, the product is another number ending in -25'; translated after Bernard Goldstein's 'A Treatise on Number Theory', *Centaurus*, 10 (1964), p. 142. See Nicomachus of Gerasa, *Arithmêtikê Eisagôgê* II.17, ed. W. Kutsch, p. 87 = fol. 154a, Arabic MS 426.15 (in the British Museum), p. 112.

76 Nasr writes, 'the Ikhwān conceive of a unified cosmos in which the quintessence also possesses the four qualities. Otherwise it would not be possible to assign to the planets and the signs of the Zodiac the qualities which are the basis of astrology.' But he adds: 'The Ikhwān do, however, agree with the Peripatetics that the ether is beyond corruption and heaviness and lightness. Sometimes they even imply that it is beyond the four qualities, but most often assign the qualities to the planets and signs of the Zodiac.' *Islamic Cosmological Doctrines*, p. 62.

77 The first perfect number is 6: the sum of its factors is its equal: 1 + 2 + 3 = 6.

78 'It was said that 7 is the first complete number, because it contains the ideas of all the preceding numbers. For all the numbers are even or odd: 2 is the first even number, and 4 is the second; 3 is the first odd number, and 5 is the second. If the first odd number is added to the second even number, or the first even number is added to the second odd number, the sum is 7. . . . And if 1, which is the source of all numbers, is taken with 6, a perfect number, their sum is 7 . . . '; tr. after Goldstein, 'A Treatise on Number Theory', p. 143. The seven planets of

eight temperaments, four simple and four paired,[79] corresponding to the first cube ($8 = 2^3$) and the octave. He composed their bodies of nine layers, matching the first odd square number and the tiers of the celestial spheres.

He gave their bodies twelve orifices, portals for the senses and other bodily needs, corresponding to the first excessive number and to the signs of the zodiac.[80] He anchored their frame on the spinal column, of twenty-eight vertebrae, matching the perfect number and the phases of the moon.[81] He gave them 360 veins, in which the blood flows to all the body's extremities, corresponding to the degrees in the circle of the zodiac and the days in the year.[82]

---

the ancient astronomers are the moon, Mercury, Venus, the sun, Mars, Jupiter, and Saturn.

79 In *De Temperamentis*, a work well known in Arabic, Galen counts nine temperaments: in the ideal, a perfect balance (*eukrasia*) is maintained. In four, hot or cold, moist or dry predominates. In four others, a pair of qualities predominates: hot and moist (sanguine), hot and dry (choleric), cold and dry (melancholic), cold and moist (phlegmatic). See Oswei Temkin, *Galenism: Rise and Decline of a Medical Philosophy* (Ithaca, NY: Cornell University Press, 1973). For temperament as a harmony, see Aristotle, *De Partibus Animalium* I.1.642a18–30; *De Anima* I.4.408a5.

80 'It was said that 12 is the first excessive number, because if all the divisors of a number are added up and their sum exceeds it, the number is called excessive. The first such number is 12. It has a half, which is 6, and a third, which is 4, and a fourth which is 3, and a sixth which is 2, and a twelfth, which is 1. If these divisors are added up, the total is 16, which exceeds 12 by 4.' Translated after Goldstein, 'A Treatise on Number Theory', p. 144.

81 The second perfect number is 28, as: 14 + 7 + 4 + 2 +1 = 28. The Ikhwān count twenty-eight days in the lunar cycle, from new moon to new moon.

82 The Muslim lunar year has 354 days. So it loses some 3 per cent annually against the solar year. It keeps in phase with the moon, but dates and holidays shift each year. They cycle through the seasons completely about three times in each century. The Qur'an (9:36–37) forbids adding a corrective intercalary month. But, strikingly, the Ikhwān here voice their preference for the ancient Iranian solar calendar, which counts 360 days in a year, divided into twelve thirty-day months, each divided further to mark the phases of the moon. The Iranian system, adapted from the Babylonian, added a thirteenth month every six years, to keep the months in phase with the seasons. The 360-day year was preserved when the Achaemenids (650–330 BCE) standardized their empire's calendar. The Ikhwān express their Iranian cultural allegiance by favouring the solar, 360-day year, finding support for it in the congruence of nature and mathematics — although, of course, the ancient Babylonian assignment of 360 degrees to the circle was itself a calendrical convention.

In the same pattern and plan, if any bodily organs are studied and numbered, they are found to match some sort of real things, showing what the Pythagorean sages meant by saying that all reality follows the nature of numbers. Such is the decree of the All-wise and Almighty.

17

On the Varied Habits of Birds — Their Seasons of Courting, Mating, Building of Nests and Aeries, Sizes of Clutch, Periods of Incubation, and Rearing of Young.

You should know that some birds, like doves, pair and court, aroused to mate all through the year, and the male helps the female brood the eggs and raise the young. Others, like the rooster, give no help. They do not brood the eggs or help raise the chicks. Some are stirred to mate but twice a year, in the more equable seasons of spring and autumn or in the summer. But most birds are primed to mate only as winter ends and spring comes on. Then they lay their eggs, incubate them and rear their young, knowing that the weather then is good, the air mild, the land open, and food abundant and readily found.

Some birds build their nests among the branches and leaves of trees. Some, like the partridge, francolin, and quail, under shrubs, in the grass and thorns. Others nest in a hollow in the wall or in tree-trunks; others, under the eaves, atop walls, or in ruins; and still others, in mountain crags and on hill-tops. Some nest on river-banks or sea-shores, while others build their nests in the desert among the rocks.[83]

---

83 'Birds generally lay their eggs in nests, but such as are not suited for flight, like the partridge and quail, lay them not in nests but on the ground and cover them over with loose material. The same is true of the lark and tetrix. These birds nest in sheltered places; but the one called *eirops* in Boeotia, alone of all birds, burrows into holes in the ground and hatches there. Thrushes, like swallows, build nests of clay, on high trees, and build them in rows all close together, so the resulting structure, one nest beside another, looks like a necklace of nests. Of all the birds that hatch for themselves, only the hoopoe builds no nest at all. It enters a hollow tree trunk and lays its eggs there, not making any sort of nest. The martin builds either under a house roof or on cliffs. The tetrix, called *ourax* in Athens, builds neither on the ground nor in trees, but on low-lying shrubs.' Aristotle, *Historia Animalium* VI.1.558b–559a.

There are some water birds that hold their eggs against their breast with one leg and swim with the other until the chicks hatch and emerge. Some birds lay and brood two eggs, some four, some six, some eight, some ten, some twelve, some twenty or thirty.

Some birds feed their chicks on macerated grain carried in their crops. Others feed them with their beaks, on grain, or fruit, or prey. Some, like the ostrich, incubate some of their eggs and wean their chicks on others.[84] Others, like the chicken and francolin, scratch in the dirt and fling grain or herbage to their chicks.

Some birds, like the swallow, fly swiftly all through the day. Others fly rather heavily, like the quail. Some, like the sand-grouse, can go without water for a considerable time. Some range far, like the raven. Others, like the sparrow, never leave home. Still others, like the crane, fly in lines, in long trains, like a camel caravan. Others fly in serried ranks like men at prayer, and others in broken flocks. Some fly into the wind and some with it, some fly upright and some aslant. Some soar and swoop and tack left or right, others fly straight.

Some run along the ground for a few steps before they take flight. Others take off with a single bound. Some take the air circling, as if climbing a minaret. Others take a zigzag, switchback course in flight, as if climbing a mountain path. Some stop moving their wings once they take the air, others flap them occasionally and rest in the mean time. Some tuck their heads when ready to descend and hurl themselves into a dive, plummeting like rain on a blustery day. Others land spiralling, as if coming down stairs in a minaret. Some descend wheeling right or left, like a beast descending a mountain path.[85] Others fold their wings and swing out their feet — dangling or thrust forward.

But every kind of bird has wings of a length, width, and weight suited to it. Each wing has fourteen courses of feathers, all with a stiff, hollow shaft. These feathers are arrayed in rows symmetrically, down each side, with other fuller feathers running down each side to close off any chink. On their bodies, birds have still shorter feathers that serve as their clothing; and between these are rows of fine, tiny feathers that form a nap, their undergarment and covering against heat and cold.

---

84 See Chapter 36 below.

85 The description might fit a raptor's wheeling descent after rising on thermals.

Most birds, moreover, have a tail proportioned to their wings, and tail-feathers numbering around twelve rows, more or less.

Some birds, like the peacock, have broader tails than wings. Others, like the crane, have long, ample wings but a stubby tail. Some birds, like the francolin and chicken, hatch out covered with feathers. Some, like the chicks of the dove, hatch featherless and are fledged as they mature.

Some, like water birds, have an oily substance on their feathers, to keep them from soaking through. Some moult each year and sprout new plumage. Some have webbed feet. Some water birds take flight straight from the water; others leave the water to take flight.

Some birds have long legs, wings, necks, and beaks; others have short necks and long beaks; yet others, long necks, and short beaks. Most birds tuck up their legs in flight. But some, like cranes and storks, stretch them back with their tails. Some birds fold their long necks in flight. Others, like the heron stretch them forward.

Some birds of prey seize other birds in mid-air and fly off with them. Others overtake them, fly underneath, clutch, and tumble them into a spin. Still others swoop and snatch their prey from the ground. Some dive at the heads of gazelles or wild asses, sink in their talons, flap their wings in their eyes, raise them into the air, and kill them.

The carrier-pigeon knows by sight from the air the terrain he will cover — the river courses and wadis. He navigates over foothills, flanking mountain ranges on the left or right, avoiding turbulent air. That is how the birds that winter in warm lands and summer in cooler ones find their way.

Most birds have a keen sense of sight, smell, taste, and hearing, but a weaker tactile sense, because of the feathers on their skin.

All birds of prey have a wide wing-span, broad tails, powerful flight, stout legs and necks, long thighs, powerful talons, and hooked beaks, unsuited to gathering grain, since they eat meat and hunt other birds. Some birds gather grain or eat fruit, or hunt insects and crawling creatures, or eat plants and herbage.

Some birds fly by night, not by day. But most fly by day and not by night. Some roost at night, others by day. Some shelter in the hills and mountain-tops or atop walls or towers; others, in woods or jungles; still others, in holes, nests, or burrows, or under the eaves. Others nest on islands in a stream or some other body of water. Some live in the desert or on the beach or a river-bank, seeking protection from harm by the shore. Some simply live in the air.

Some birds wake at dawn and sing melodious paeans,[86] or set out early[87] seeking food. Some are up at daybreak, some by morn, some in the forenoon. Then they set out to forage, to ease their bellies and feed the emptiness within.

Some birds hatch in the morning, some in the evening, some at midday, some on cloudy days, and some on clear days, some on rainy days, some when it's very hot, others when it's very cold, and some on windy days.

18

You must know, dear brother, that some birds, like swallows and starlings, take a wedge shape in flight, spreading and stretching their wings and tails in a set pattern. Others, like cranes and storks, take a

86 It's easy to dismiss the idea of bird-song as prayer, since the functions of such song in declaring territory are now well established. See Bernard Altum, *Der Vogel und sein Leben* (Münster: Niemann, 1868); H. E. Howard, *Territory in Bird Life* (London: John Murray, 1920). But at least one twentieth-century philosopher found a celebratory sense even in such territorial declarations: 'It has been said (Sibley, 1952) that we cannot hope to understand what a song means to a bird, which sometimes mixes singing with fighting trespassers. But consider man's war songs and dances. He, too, combines music with many sorts of actions. And just as patriotism can have both harshly negative or hostile aspects and very positive and happy ones, as in the love of country, so perhaps can a bird combine vivid liking for his territory and his place in it with potential hostility toward trespassers. And here is a difference between birds and the two men fighting that Sibley mentions: the men hate each other as individuals; not so two avian rivals for territory. So long as the proper spacing with the recognized singing neighbors obtains, "God's in his heaven, all's right with the world." The animal feels that the entire situation, as it impinges on his life, is good. So the old cliché, birds sing to praise the Lord, like the other cliché, they sing to please their mates, has not been shown to be entirely devoid of truth or relevance. Why not sing when so much is going well? Surely a bird has happy feelings about its territory, which gives it food, shelter, and so much else.' Charles Hartshorne, *Born to Sing: An Interpretation and World Survey of Bird Song* (Bloomington, IN: Indiana University Press, 1973), p. 54.

87 The line echoes the opening verse of the hunt scene in the famous *qaṣīda* of Imru' al-Qays. See Lenn E. Goodman, *Islamic Humanism*, p. 54.

squarish shape, their wings spread, long necks thrust forward, long legs trailing behind, and a stubby tail. Some insects, like grasshoppers, gnats and wasps, assume a hexagonal shape in flight, their four wings spread, two on each side, their heads forward and tails behind.

If you examine and study the bodies of birds, or of insects, you know, you will find that all are balanced and symmetrical in length and breadth, weight and lightness, left and right, fore and aft. So, if a bunch of feathers were pulled out of either wing, a bird's flight would be hobbled, like the limp of a cripple with one leg shorter than the other. If a bunch of feathers were plucked from their tails, again their flight would be hampered. They would tumble head over heel like a skiff, or a reed boat launched with too heavy a bow and too light a stern. That is why some birds, like the crane, extend their feet behind them when they stretch their necks forward, to balance the weight at the neck with that of their legs — and why others, like the heron, crook their necks to their breasts and tuck their legs to their bellies in flight.[88] Likewise with the flight of other birds and of insects.

88 The heron in fact flies with feet extended and neck extended too, although distinctively crooked.

Chapter 1
The First Creatures

It is said that when the race of Adam began to reproduce and multiply, humans spread across the earth, land and sea, mountain and plain, everywhere freely and securely seeking their own ends. At first, when they were few, they lived in fear, hiding from the many wild animals and beasts of prey, taking refuge in the mountain-tops and hills, sheltering in caves, and eating fruit from trees, vegetables from the ground, and the seeds of plants.[1] They clothed themselves in tree leaves against the heat and cold, wintering where it was warm and summering where it was cool. But then they built cities and villages on the plains and settled there.[2]

They enslaved such cattle as cows, sheep, and camels, and beasts like horses, asses, and mules. They hobbled and bridled them and put them to work — riding, hauling, ploughing, and threshing. They wore

1 The vegetarianism of the first humans is a wide-spread motif, suggested as early as Genesis. In Eden, Adam is given to eat 'of every tree', except, of course, the Tree of Knowledge of Good and Evil (Genesis 2:16–17). Even after their exile, Adam and Eve are to eat 'thorns and thistles' and 'the herb of the field' (3:18). But Noah is allowed animal food (9:13). These passages readily suggest that human meat-eating post-dated a vegetarian epoch, and that is what the Ikhwān assume. But the stress in Genesis is on the permission to eat all fruits but one, and on the hardship and toil of the life we know, compared to the life of Eden. Noah and his offspring are permitted meat, so long as living flesh is not consumed. But that suggests that meat was already part of the human diet. The notion of a primal vegetarian diet has mythic roots. Claude Lévi-Strauss elicits from a host of mythic materials a broad theme that makes food stories and ritual practices emblematic of the contrast of nature with culture; see *The Raw and the Cooked*, tr. John and Doreen Weightman (New York: Harper and Row, 1970). In both Genesis and the *Rasā'il*, we find a moral meaning in that theme: Genesis overlays a humane sensibility on food culture. In the *Rasā'il*, the shared primal narrative is read in mildly ascetic and ecological terms.

2 Natural man, it seems, although not as civilized as his descendants, was also not as dominating. Like other animals, he kept to this own turf. But by finding shelter from the elements and from other species, he gained flexibility in habitat. Thus began human hegemony: in the invasion of new terrain. Nomadic life here, as in Chapter 9 below, is 'closer to being good', than settled life, as Ibn Khaldūn puts it in the *Muqaddimah*, 2.4, tr. F. Rosenthal (New York: Pantheon, 1958), vol. 1, p. 253; gathering, too, seems more natural than agriculture. But the Ikhwān seem to be innocent regarding the ecological impact of that way of life.

these creatures out in service, with toil beyond their strength. Beasts that had roamed the woodlands and wilds unhindered, in search of pasture, water, and all their needs, were checked and trammelled.[3]

Other animals — the wild asses, gazelles, and beasts of prey, wildlife and birds that had been docile and lived in peace and quietude in their ancestral lands — fled the haunts of men for far-off wastes, forests, mountain peaks, and glens.[4] But the Adamites set after them with all sorts of devices for hunting, trapping, and snaring, convinced that the animals were their runaway or rebellious slaves.

The years went by, and Muhammad[5] was sent, may God bless him. He called men and jinn to God and to Islam. One band of jinn answered his call and became good Muslims.[6] In the course of time, a king arose

3 Like today's animal-rights advocates, the Ikhwān count the frustration of animals' inborn urges as an abuse of domestication. Peter Singer notes the inability of hens to form a pecking order in crowded, battery conditions, and the unnatural confinement of calves raised for veal (lest grazing and muscular activity add sinew and iron to their muscle). The stalls, he writes, are too small to let calves turn to groom themselves with their tongues; see his 'Down on the Factory Farm', in *Animal Liberation* (New York: Harper Collins, 1991). Here liberal premises are stiffened with an appeal to nature: creatures should be left to do what comes naturally to them, since natural inclinations are wholesome and best for all concerned. Cf. Epicurus, *Principal Doctrines*, 8, 15, 25; *Vatican Fragments*, 21, 52; Lucretius, *De Rerum Natura* I.10–23. For a counter-argument, finding vegetarianism and a broad rejection of the use of animals itself unnatural, see Walter E. Howard, *Animal Rights vs. Nature*, (Davis, CA: privately published, 1991).

4 Man lays claim to what is best and most advantageous; the animals must be content with the leavings, driven to extreme environments at the fringes of human settlement or relegated to the most remote and inhospitable habitats.

5 The Ikhwān begin from the beginning, like the Arabic universal histories; see Goodman, *Islamic Humanism*, Chapter 4. The aim is to establish the aboriginal relations of humans and other animals. But the authors are also anxious to start their own story; they will fill in the cosmogonic narrative, viewed from quite a variety of perspectives, as the case proceeds. So here they move swiftly past the Creation.

6 The reality of the jinn, the demons and sprites of Arabic parlance (cf. Latin *genii*), was taken for granted in popular and traditional Islam. Rejecting rationalistic and naturalistic glosses on the idea of jinn, of which the Ikhwān offer an early example, a traditionally oriented but very recent Qur'an commentary urges: 'Both the Qur'an and the Hadith describe the Jinn as a definite species of living beings. They are created out of fire and like man, may believe or disbelieve, accept or reject guidance. The authoritative Islamic texts show that they are not merely a hidden force, or a spirit. They are personalized beings who enjoy a certain amount of free will and

over the jinn, Bīwarāsp the Wise, known as Mardan, King Heroic.[7] His capital was on an island called Ṣāʿūn, lying near the equator in the midst of the Green Sea.[8] The air and soil were good. There were sweet rivers, burbling springs, broad fields, and sheltered dells, a wealth of trees and fruit, lush meadows, streams, herbs, and spices.[9]

It happened in those days that storm winds cast up a sea-faring ship on that island's shore.[10] Aboard were men of commerce, industry, and learning, and others of the human kind. They disembarked and explored the island, finding it rich in trees and fruit, fresh water, healthful air, fine soil, vegetables, herbs and plants, all kinds of cereals and grains that flourished in the rain from heaven. They saw all sorts of animals — beasts, cattle, birds, and carnivores — all living in peace and harmony with one another, secure and unafraid.[11]

---

thus will be called to account.' The Holy Qur'an, ed. The Presidency of Islamic Researches IFTA (Medina: King Fahd Holy Qur'ān Printing Complex, n.d.), p. 372, note 929. The Qur'an (Sura 72) tells of a band of jinn listening intently to Muhammad as he received and recited his revelations. The listeners confessed the error of their ways and embraced Islam. Tradition makes them emissaries to other jinn. So there were many Muslim jinn, just as there were good and wicked jinn, as the jinn themselves explain in Chapter 26 below. As Kalonymos notes, the fable makes the jinn impartial judges between animals and humans, but the Ikhwān, as he also notes, do not take demonology literally. In discussing the obedience of the jinn to God in Chapter 26 they give a Neoplatonic reading to the idea of the jinn. They treat tales of jinni interference in human affairs as sheer superstition, as the jinn suggest in Chapter 6 below, but cf. p. 240. Kalonymos suppresses the mention of Muhammad's appeal to the jinn.

7 For Bīwarāsp , see Appendix C.

8 Some texts have Balāsaghūn, a Soghdian town about 125 miles (200 km) south of Lake Balkhash. It figured in the military history of the Qara-Khans, et al. But the Ikhwān place their jinni realm on a fanciful island in the Green Sea, the Eastern Indian Ocean. Kalonymos shifts the story's setting to the antipodes, to retain the aura of a fairy tale.

9 The Ikhwān carefully list the natural resources that made this island a favoured spot for animal or human habitation. Likewise with other lands. No habitat is treated unfavourably; even the most extreme environments have features beneficial or necessary to their denizens.

10 Kalonymos expatiates here, with a dramatic account of the storm, the pitching sea, the prayers of the fearful passengers. That last touch echoes the Book of Jonah (1:4–5). David Walker notes parallel set pieces in Judah Halevi, al-Ḥarīzī, and Jacob ben Elazar.

11 The animals will argue in Chapters 12 and 32 below that predation and even competition among animals stem directly or indirectly from human doings.

Delighted with the place, these folk decided to settle there. They built dwellings and soon began to meddle with the beasts and cattle, forcing them into service, riding them and loading them down with burdens, as in their former lands. But these beasts and cattle balked and fled. The men pursued and hunted them, using all manner of devices to take them, convinced that the animals were their runaway and rebellious slaves. When the cattle and beasts learned of this belief, their spokesmen and leaders gathered and came before Bīwarāsp the Wise, King of the Jinn, to complain of the injustice and wrongs of mankind against them and to protest the human notions about them. The King sent a messenger to summon the parties to his court.

A group from the ship, some seventy men of diverse lands, answered the summons. When their arrival was announced, the King ordered a fitting welcome for them. After three days he brought them in to his council chamber.[12] Bīwarāsp was a sage, just, and noble king, fair minded and open-handed, hospitable to guests and a refuge to strangers. He had mercy for the afflicted and would not brook injustice but ordained the good and forbade evil,[13] seeking only to please God and be worthy of His favour.[14] Appearing before the King, the men saw him seated on his royal throne and hailed him with wishes of long life and prosperity. The King then asked, through his interpreter, 'What brought you to our island? Why did you come uninvited to our land?'

---

12 Kalonymos shortens the wait to three hours and allows the jinn to speak admiringly of human qualities.

13 The obligation to ordain what is right and forbid what is wrong (Qur'an 3:110, etc.) is a keystone of the Sharīʿa. For the elaboration of this norm in Islamic jurisprudence, see Michael Cook, *Commanding Right and Forbidding Wrong in Islamic Thought* (Cambridge: CUP, 2000).

14 Bīwarāsp is a model king, a princely mirror to be emulated. He combines the Platonic kingly virtue of justice with the traditional virtues of magnanimity, liberality, clemency, and compassion. The frequent reflections on royal virtues and tyrannous vices in our text clearly outline the political message of the Ikhwān. They are meant to stimulate princely pursuit of the ideal and to castigate royal failings. Al-Ghazālī makes pursuit of God's favour the highest human aim, chary of voicing the ideal of virtue in terms of the pursuit of what is right for its own sake, lest that seem to impart too much autonomy to ethics and personal choice; see Goodman, *Islamic Humanism*, p. 115. But note again here that God's favour is won by merit, not arbitrarily bestowed.

One of the humans answered, 'We were drawn by all that we have heard of the virtues of the King, his many glorious deeds, his great generosity and noble character, his justice and impartial judgement. We have come before him that he might hear our case and the arguments we shall present, and judge between us and these runaway slaves, who deny our authority. God will uphold the righteous cause and guide your Majesty to a sound decision. For He is *the wisest of judges*.'[15]

'Speak as you wish', said the King.[16]

'I shall, your Majesty', said the human spokesman. 'These cattle, beasts of prey, and wild creatures — all animals in fact — are our slaves. We are their masters. Some have rebelled and escaped. Others obey grudgingly and scorn our service.'

The King replied, 'What proof or evidence have you to back up your claims?'

'Your Majesty,' said the human, 'we have both traditional religious arguments and rational proof of our position.'

'Very well,' said the King, 'let us hear them.'

So a human orator of the line of ʿAbbās[17] rose and mounted the rostrum, opening his speech with the following exordium: 'Praised be God, Sovereign of the universe, hope of those who fear Him and foe to none but the unjust. God bless Muhammad, Seal of the Prophets,[18] chief of God's messengers, and intercessor on the Day of Judgement.

15 Qur'an 11:45; cf. 95:8.

16 The King grants freedom to the disputants to make out their case. Free speech is not presented here as an inherent or universal right. But again the King's generosity is meant to be taken as a model. See *Pañcatantra* I.110, ed. Olivelle, p.93

17 ʿAbbās ibn al-Muṭṭalib was half-brother to Muhammad's father and eponym of the ʿAbbāsid dynasty, which traced its descent through ʿAbbās's son. He fought the Muslims at the battle of Badr but, after accepting Muhammad's mission in 629, gave his wife's sister to his nephew, the Prophet, as a bride. At the battle of Ḥunayn, he is said to have turned the tide in favour of the Muslims with a mighty shout. The Ikhwān assign pride of royal place to the orator who is his descendant, and show what they think of the ʿAbbāsid dynasty by allowing his arguments to be refuted by a mule, who is also given a special place among the animal spokesmen.

18 In Islamic theology, the line of prophecy, begun with Adam and continued through Jewish and Christian figures (including Jesus), is sealed, that is, completed — some say confirmed — by Muhammad. Kalonymos suppresses the reference to Muhammad as Seal of the Prophets.

Praised be God *who formed man from water,*[19] and formed his mate from him. He broadcast their seed, men and women, bore them over land and sea, favoured them with dominion, and sustained them with all manner of delights, saying, *Cattle did He create for you, whence you have warmth and many uses. You eat of them and find them fair when you bring them home to rest or drive them out to pasture. They carry your heavy burdens for you to lands you might reach only with great trouble to your souls.*[20] He also said, *You are borne upon them and on ships,*[21] and, *Of the cattle some are for burden and some for meat.*[22] And again, *horses, mules, and asses for riding and for splendour, and much that you know not,*[23] and *Praised be God who said: that ye may be seated on their backs and consider your Lord's favour as you ride.*[24] There are many other verses in the Qur'an, Torah, and Gospels[25] which show that they were created for our sake and that they are our slaves and we their masters. God grant pardon to you and to myself.'

'Cattle and beasts,' said the King, 'you have heard the Qur'anic verses this human has adduced to support his claims. What say you to this?'

At this a spokesman for the beasts, a mule, rose and said:[26] 'Praised be God, one, unique and alone, peerless, impassive, ever-abiding, and

19 Qur'an 25:54

20 Qur'an 16:5–7.

21 Qur'an 40:80. Animals here, like ships, are afforded for man's ease. Granted, ships are not a part of nature. But the presence on earth of seas and navigable waterways is an act of grace: *He it is who subdued the sea, that you might eat moist flesh from it and bring forth from it jewellery to wear, and see ships cleaving it, that you may seek His bounty and mayhap be thankful. He pitched towering mountains on the earth, lest it shake you; rivers and passes that you may find your way, and landmarks — for by the stars are they guided* (16:14–16). God's grace is manifest in the fitting of nature to human needs.

22 Qur'an 6:142.

23 Qur'an 16:8.

24 Qur'an 43:13.

25 Kalonymos obliges by supplying two passages from the Torah to fill out the speaker's coda, but he drops the mention of the Gospels.

26 As a proper formal discourse should, the mule's remarks, like those of the 'Abbāsid representative, open with a *khuṭba*, or exordium, in praise of God. Like an overture, the *khuṭba* in a thematic discourse often sets the tone and foreshadows the themes to come. Since the mule will deal with the rights and wrongs of animal-human relations, his *khuṭba* harks back to the creation and God's first commands, laying a groundwork for an appeal to God's expectations regarding relations among species. Many of the subsequent speakers, animal and human,

eternal, who was before all things that come to be, beyond all time and space, who then said, *"BE!"*[27] at which there was a burst of light, which He shined forth from His hidden fastness.[28] From this light He created a blazing sea of fire and a surging sea of watery waves, and out of this fire and water He created spheres studded with constellations and brilliant stars.[29] He raised up the heavens and spread out the earth, anchored the mountains and framed the many-storeyed heavens as the archangels' abode, and the spaces between the spheres as dwelling places for the cherubim.[30] The earth He gave to living beings — animals and plants. Next He created the jinn from the fiery simoom, and humans out of clay. *He gave man posterity*[31] *— from vile water in a vessel sure,*[32] and allowed man's seed to follow one another in succession on the earth, to dwell in it, not lay it waste,[33] to care for the animals and profit by them, not abuse or mistreat them. God grant pardon to you and to me.'

'Your Majesty,' the mule continued, 'there is nothing in the passages

---

follow the mule's example. The biblical vision of cosmic time and universal history casts its spell over the authors' imaginations in these little introductions.

27 Cf. Qur'an 2:117, 16:40. Kalonymos translates these Qur'anic echoes without attribution.

28 Cf. Genesis 1:3 and the centrality of light in Neoplatonic imagery.

29 In the allegorical exegesis of the Ikhwān, the sphere of the fixed stars is the pedestal of God's throne, and eight are said to bear it (Qur'an 69:17; cf. 2:255). The throne itself (Qur'an 9:129, 69:17) is the outermost sphere, most high (Qur'an 83:18–19; the Arabic word is *"illiyyīn*'; cf. the Hebrew *"elyon*'). See Chapter 2 of Epistle 16: 'On the Spheres', in *Rasā'il*, vol. 2, p. 26; *Rasā'il*, vol. 3, p. 187; ibid., vol. 4, pp. 214, 240 ; Yves Marquet, *La philosophie des Iḫwān al-Ṣafā'* (Algiers: Société Nationale d'Édition et de Diffusion, [1975]), pp. 110–111; Nasr, *Islamic Cosmological Doctrines*, pp. 61–62, 76. Such allegories are sharply at variance with the literalism pursued in authoritative Islamic creeds. The *Waṣīyat Abī Ḥanīfa*, § 8 reads: 'We believe that Allah has seated Himself on His throne. . . . He occupies his throne and what is outside it . . . ' In a tradition ascribed to Ka'b al-Aḥbār, all the heavens, as compared with the throne, are said to be 'like a lamp hanging between heaven and earth'. The intent is to magnify the throne and dim the allegory. Other authorities, in the same vein, cite a hadith traced to Abū Dharr, which has Muhammad saying: 'the seven Heavens are, as compared with the chair [called the pedestal by Nasr], as a ring thrown away in the desert. And the relation between the throne and the chair is as the relation between this desert and the ring.' See A. J. Wensinck, *The Muslim Creed: Its Genesis and Historical Development* (London: Frank Cass, 1965), pp. 127, 147–149.

30 Even in the heavens there are diverse habitats, each with its own proper denizens.

31 Qur'an 32:8.

32 See Qur'an 23:13.

33 Cf. Isaiah 45:18, 'So saith the Lord, Creator of the heavens, God who framed

this human cites to support his claim that they are masters and we slaves. These verses point only to the kindness and blessings God bestowed on mankind. God said *He subjected them*[34] *to you* — just as *He subjected the sun and moon,*[35] *the wind and clouds.*[36] Are we to think, Majesty, that these heavenly bodies too are their slaves and chattels, and men their masters? Hardly! God made all His creatures in heaven and earth. He set some in service to others, for their good or to preclude some evil. He subjected animals to man only to help humans and keep them from harm,[37] not, as they deludedly suppose and slanderously claim, to make them our masters and us their slaves.[38]

'Your Majesty,' the spokesman of the beasts continued, 'we and our fathers lived on earth before the creation of Adam, forefather of the human race. We dwelt in the countryside and roamed the country trails. Our herds went to and fro in God's land, seeking sustenance and taking care of ourselves. Each of us minded his own affairs, kept to the

---

the earth, founded it and made it: not as a waste did He create it. He formed it to be settled.'

34 Camels, that is; Qur'an 22:37.

35 Qur'an 13:2.

36 Qur'an 2:164.

37 See Chapter 9 below, where the agrarian and pastoral delegates spell out what humanity would lose if they gave up the animals.

38 Maimonides deems it the height of arrogance to suppose that the celestial bodies were created just to serve mankind: 'Do not be misled by its saying of the stars "to light the earth and rule by night and by day" (Genesis 1:17–18), supposing it to mean that they exist to do this. It is simply describing their nature. . . . The good they constantly shed may seem to the recipient to mean that they exist solely for his sake. But that is like a city dweller's supposing that the government exists just to safeguard his house from robbers at night. That's true in a sense, for his house is protected, and he does benefit in that way from the government. So, speciously, house protection looks like the government's raison d'être.' Maimonides, *Guide to the Perplexed* III.12–13, ed. with French translation by S. Munk (Osnabrück: Zeller, 1964), vol. 3, p. 25b. The translation here is Goodman's. The mule reads Sura 16 rather differently than does the scion of the House of 'Abbās: the Qur'an (16:12) does speak of the subjection of sun, moon, and stars, and even of night, and day. But what they are subject to is God's command. They need not be seen to serve just for man's sake. As in Biblical usage, the Qur'an may express a result as a purpose. For all outcomes are foreseen by God. Man does benefit from God's ordering of nature. And even a casual beneficiary should feel the gratitude Muhammad calls on from the discerning: we are given a commodious environment, but that does not make us its lords or owners, free to deal with nature as we like.

place best suited to his needs — moor, sea, forest, mountain, or plain. Each kind looked after its own, absorbed in raising our broods and rearing our young on the good food and water God allotted us, safe and unmolested in our domain. Night and day we praised and hallowed God, and God alone, assigning Him neither rival nor peer.[39]

'Ages later God created Adam,[40] the ancestor of humankind, and made him His vice-regent on earth. His offspring reproduced, and his seed multiplied, spreading over the earth, land and sea, mountain and plain. Humans encroached on our ancestral lands. They captured sheep, cows, horses, mules, and asses from among us and enslaved them, subjecting them to the exhausting toil and drudgery of hauling, ploughing, drawing water, turning mills, and being ridden. They forced us to these tasks with beatings, bludgeonings, and every kind of duress, torture, and chastisement throughout our lives.

'Some of us fled to deserts, wastes, or mountain-tops, but the Adamites pursued us, hunting us with every kind of wile and device. Whoever fell into their hands was yoked, haltered, caged, and fettered. They slaughtered and flayed him, ripped open his belly, cut off his limbs and broke his bones, tore out his sinews, plucked his feathers or sheared his hair or fleece, and set him on the fire to cook, or to roast on a spit, or put him to even harsher tortures, torments ultimately beyond description. Even so, the sons of Adam are not through with us. Now they claim this is their inviolable right,[41] that they are our masters and we their slaves. They treat any of us who escapes as a fugitive, rebel, and shirker — all with no proof or reason beyond main force.'[42]

---

39 The animals observed the laws of nature. That was their worship. The animal spokesman freely sets his rational arguments alongside appeals to tradition and makes no show of favouring tradition over reasoning, as Islamic traditionalism in the times of the Ikhwān was coming to demand.

40 The close of Chapter 8 below reveals strikingly how little stock the Ikhwān place in a literal six-day Creation.

41 As readers of mediaeval texts know, ideas of rights flourished long before the Tennis Court Oath, albeit not in the same sense assigned, say, in the English Glorious Revolution of 1688 or later.

42 The Ikhwān, like most philosophers, especially those in the wake of Plato and the monotheistic scriptural tradition, reject the notion that might makes right.

Chapter 2

When the King heard this, he ordered a herald to carry the news throughout the kingdom and summon his forces and followers, vassals from all tribes of jinn, the folk of Sāsān,[43] the offspring of Khāqān,[44] and the children of Shayṣabān — judges, justices, and jurisconsults, the folk of Idrīs and the sons of Bilqīs.[45] Then he took his seat to judge the case of the animals against the delegates and advocates of men. He addressed the human leaders first: 'What have you to say of the injustice, oppression and usurpation charged against you by these beasts and cattle?'

'They are our slaves', said the human spokesman. 'We are their masters. It is for us, as their lords, to judge them. To obey us is to obey God. Whoever revolts against us is a rebel against God.'

The King replied, 'Only claims grounded in clear proof are accepted in this court. What proof of your claims do you offer?'

'We have philosophical arguments and rational proofs that our claims are sound', said the human.

---

43 Clifford E. Bosworth describes the Banū Sāsān as the fraternity of beggars, swindlers, confidence men, tricksters, and conjurors. The legendary founder of that way of life was one Shaykh Sāsān, dispossessed son of the legendary Persian Shah Bahmān ibn Isfandiyār, who took to vagabondage among the Kurds. Persians as a nation, Bosworth writes, were said in one legend to have been reduced to beggary after the Arab conquest and the fall of the Sāsānian dynasty. So there is an ethnic edge in the inclusion of the people of Sāsān among the jinni jurists. See C. E. Bosworth, 'Sāsān, Banū', *EI2*, vol. 9, p. 70; and Bosworth, *The Mediaeval Islamic Underworld: The Banū Sāsān in Arabic Society and Literature* (Leiden: Brill, 1976).

44 The Khāqān would be a Turkic ruler, grand khan of a tribal federation; see J. A. Boyle, 'Kh̲āḳān', *EI2*, vol. 4, p. 915. Superstition may associate such nomads with the jinn, especially if dispossessed and relegated to a life as tricksters and mendicants.

45 The summons addresses fairy creatures of all sorts, the King's own vassals and those of the Khāqān, the progeny of Bilqīs, the wise Queen of Sheba, and those of Idrīs, the eponymous father of all learning, equivalent to the Hebrew Enoch. The vagabonds here are not the human jongleurs and tricksters of whom Hamadhānī and others wrote, but errant sprites and spirits that folklore pictures as roaming the earth with their tricks and japes. Shaysabān, as Bosworth notes, seems to derive his name from the late Hebrew and Syriac '*shoshbīn*', or 'best man', itself taken from the Latin '*socius sponsi*'. The noun became the name of a particular angel and in Muslim usage, a jinni; cf. Bosworth, *The Mediaeval Islamic Underworld*, vol. 1, pp. 122–123, note 75.

'What are they?' asked the King.

'Our fair form, erect stature, upright carriage, and keen senses, our subtle powers of discrimination, our sharp minds and superior intellects all show that we are the masters and they, our slaves.'[46]

The King turned to the spokesman of the beasts. 'How do you answer these allegations?'

'There is nothing in what he says to support what this human claims.'

'Is it not a royal trait to sit erect and stand upright, and aren't bent backs and bowed heads the marks of slaves?' asked the King.

'God aid your Majesty to the truth', the animal spokesman answered. 'Listen and you shall know that God did not give them this form or shape them in this way to mark them as masters. Nor did He create us in the form we have to brand us as slaves. He knew and wisely ordained that their form is best for them and ours for us.'

Chapter 3
An Explanation of the Divergence of Animal Forms

The animal delegate continued: 'God created Adam and his offspring naked and unshod, without feathers, fleece, or wool on their skin to protect them from heat and cold. He gave them fruit from the trees as their food and the leaves of trees for their clothing.[47] Since the trees

46 'In man, the forelegs and forefeet were replaced by arms and by what we call hands. For of all animals man alone stands erect, in keeping with his godlike nature and being. For it is the work of the godlike to think and to be wise; and no easy task were this under the burden of a heavy body, pressing down from above and obstructing by its weight the motions of the intellect and general sense. When the weight and bodily substance become too great, in fact, the body inevitably tilts towards the ground. Nature, in such cases, to support the body, has replaced arms and hands by forefeet, and so made the animal a quadruped. For, as every animal that walks must necessarily have two hind feet, such animals become quadrupeds, their bodies leaning down in front from the weight the soul cannot sustain. For all animals except man are dwarflike in form: the upper part large, and that which bears the weight and is used in going forward, small. . . . This is the reason no animal is as intelligent as man.' Aristotle, *De Partibus Animalium* IV.10.686a27–b22.

47 Cf. Genesis 3:7, 3:21: Adam and Eve cover their nakedness, once they notice

spread high in the air, He made man stand erect, to reach the fruit and leaves readily. Since He gave us the grass on the ground as our food, He made us face downward, to make it easy for us to reach it.[48] This and not what he claims is why God made them erect and us bent over.'

'What, then, do you say of God's words, *We formed man at the fairest height*?' asked the King.[49]

The animal replied, 'The prophetic books have interpretations and explanations that go deeper than the surface, known to *those well rooted in knowledge*.[50] Let the King inquire of scholars expert in the Qur'an.'

---

it, by sewing fig leaves together. But God clothes them in animal skins on their expulsion from Eden.

48 Each species is adapted to its niche. It is not inherent beauty or intrinsic merit that determines the forms of any species, including humankind.

49 Qur'an 95:4. Kalonymos identifies the point as 'an Ishmaelite' thesis. In the debate surrounding al-Ghazālī's claim that nothing could be better than the world God made, Ibn al-Munayyir reads the verse as meaning that man is the best of God's actual creatures, not the best He *could* have made. See Eric Ormsby, *Theodicy in Islamic Thought: The Dispute over al-Ghazālī's 'Best of all Possible Worlds'* (Princeton: Princeton University Press, 1984), p. 164. The Ikhwān allow the jinni sage to interpret the verse freely, taking advantage of the possibilities that its diction and syntax afford.

50 Later Islamic hermeneutics distinguishes the freer interpretation of *ta'wīl* from the closer type, *tafsīr*. Both kinds are necessary, but the former carries greater risks. Qur'an 3:7 alludes to those whose knowledge is deep. As punctuated by Sunnis, it reads: *He it is who sent you down this Book in which are sure verses, the substance of the Book, and others that are unclear. Those who waver in their hearts pursue its uncertainties, eager for strife and avid to explain them. But none but God knows the interpretations. And those well rooted in knowledge [al-rāsikhūn fī al-ʿilm] say 'We believe in it. All is from our Lord.' Yet none can heed it but those with hearts to understand.* The passage seems to warn Muhammad's hearers not to try to gloss the Qur'an for themselves. But later generations saw in the mention of problematic verses an invitation to interpretation: the well rooted in knowledge were the exegetes most able to interpret hard passages well; numbered among the faithful, they were destined for a divine reward (Qur'an 4:160). Qur'an 3:7 is a key proof-text for the juridical concept of *muḥkamāt*, revealed verses whose sense is plain, requiring no elaborate interpretation — as distinguished from *mutashābihāt*, verses acknowledged to be obscure and in need of interpretation. Sufi and Shiʿi exegetes understand 'those well rooted in knowledge' (*rāsikhūn fī al-ʿilm*) to be a specific class of experts. They punctuate the verse to read: *But none but God and those well rooted in knowledge know the interpretation*. Hence the interpretive authority of the Shiʿi imams. See al-Ṭabarsī, *Majmūʿ al-bayān fī tafsīr al-Qur'ān*. Sufis, similarly, validate the

So the King asked the jinni sage, 'What is the meaning of *at the fairest height*'?

'On the day God created Adam,' the jinni replied, 'the stars were at their zeniths, the points of the signs of the zodiac were solid and square, the season was equable, matter was ready to receive form. So his body was given the finest form and soundest constitution.'

'That would suffice to warrant their boasts of nobility and excellence', said the King.

The wise jinni said, 'The passage has another meaning, in the light of God's words: *who proportioned thee in just the form that pleased thy Lord.*[51] This means, He made you neither tall and thin nor short and squat but at a mean.'

The animal spokesman said, 'He did the same for us. He did not make us too tall and too thin or short and squat but well proportioned. So we, the same as they, have a graceful and graciously given form.'

'How can you think that animals are well proportioned and evenly formed?' the human asked. 'We see the camel's long neck, small ears, and short tail. The elephant has enormous bulk, great tusks, and broad ears, but tiny eyes. The cow and water buffalo have long tails and thick horns, but no tusks. Rams have two great horns and a thick tail, but no beard. Goats have a fine beard, but no fat tail — leaving their private parts exposed. Rabbits have a small body but loppy ears, and so it goes.

---

authority of saintly figures; see Rūzbihān al-Baqlī, *'Arā' is al-bayān fī ḥaqā'iq al-Qur'ān*. The Ikhwān here are careful not to relegate such interpretive words to one of the animals.

51 Qur'an 82:7–8. Taken literally, the verses might suggest that God physically handled Adam's clay. Al-Ghazālī wrote a commentary on them, and Ibn Ṭufayl (d. 1185) reverts to them in his *Ḥayy ibn Yaqẓān*, in view of the opening they afford for a discussion of the interaction of matter and spirit. The Ikhwān read the passage as referring to the modulation of matter for the receipt of form. They use the Qur'anic reference to form as a way of naturalizing their own Neoplatonic idea of Form, as a divinely imparted intellectual principle that gives each being its specific essence and strengths. Ghazālī refers unfavourably to the Ikhwān, calling their work 'the dregs of philosophy'; see *Al-Munqidh min al-ḍalāl*, in *The Faith and Practice of al-Ghazālī*, tr. William Montgomery Watt (London: Allen Unwin, 1953), p. 53. But in the same work (pp. 41–42) he urges that one judge claims on their merits: if one rejected all that is contained in works, say, of *falsafa*, one would have to reject much of the Qur'an and hadith, simply because so much from these sources is cited by the Ikhwān al-Ṣafā'.

Most animals — wild beasts, carnivores, birds, and crawling creatures are unevenly built and misproportioned.'

'Not at all, O human', said the animal spokesman. 'You've missed the beauty and wisdom of their creation. Don't you see that a slight to the work is an affront to its Maker? You should start from the recognition that all animals are the work of the wise Creator, who made them as He did with reason and purpose, to benefit them and protect them from harm.[52] But this is grasped only by Him and *those who are well rooted in knowledge*.'[53]

'Tell us, then,' said the human, 'if you are the learned spokesman of the beasts, why is the camel's neck so long?'

'To match his long legs,' he answered, 'so he can reach the grass on the ground — and also to help him rise with a load, and so that he can reach all parts of his body with his lip to scratch and rub them. The elephant's trunk takes the place of a long neck. His big ears serve to shoo flies and gnats from the corners of his eyes and mouth. For his mouth is always ajar. He can't fully close it because of his protruding tusks. But those are his defence against predators. The rabbit's big ears give him cover. They are his blanket in winter and shade in summer. For his skin is tender and his body delicate. In just this way we find that God adapted the parts of every species to its needs in seeking the beneficial and avoiding harm. This is what Moses meant, peace be upon him, when he spoke of *Our Lord who gave its nature to every thing and guided all things.*[54]

---

52 Inquirers must presume the wisdom of Creation. Just as scientists assume that efficient causality is universal and seek causes, not stopping whenever evidence falters to ask whether causality has petered out, so biologists must presume the universality of functional causality, that is, teleology, the subordination of form to function. The assumption is not arbitrary but educated by experience and rewarded by understanding. Yet it *does* reach beyond the evidence at hand, as it must if it is to work heuristically. Nature would be unintelligible without the assumption of causality, and biology would be impossible without teleology.

53 Qur'an 3:7.

54 Qur'an 20:50. Both anatomical form and ethological function are God's work: form is the product of creation; function, of divine guidance. Galen holds a similar view, but he situates himself, and other Greeks like Plato, in a middle ground between what he sees as the Mosaic story, that God simply ordered, say, the eye-lashes to stay short and the forehead to be mobile, and the view of Epicurus, ascribing all adaptations to chance. Galen prefers Moses to Epicurus,

'As for the fair form you boast of, there's nothing in that to support your claim that you are masters and we slaves. An attractive form is simply one that sparks desire between males and females in any species, drawing them together to pair and mate, to produce progeny and new generations for the survival of the species. Our males are not aroused by your female beauties, nor are our females drawn to the charms of your males — just as blacks don't find the charms of whites attractive, or whites those of blacks, and just as boy-lovers have no passion for the charms of girls and wenchers have no desire for boys.[55] So, Mr Human Being, your boasts of superior beauty are groundless.'

Chapter 4
On the Acute Senses of the Animals

'Your vaunted powers of perception and discernment are not unique. There are animals with finer senses and sharper discrimination. The camel, for one, despite his long legs and neck and the elevation of his head so high in the air, finds his footing on the most punishing and treacherous pathways in the dark of night, where you could not make out your way and not one of you could see without a lantern, torch, or candle. A fine charger can hear distant footsteps in the dead of night.

---

for linking purpose with design. He does not think chance adequate to yield useful traits. But he faults Moses for neglecting the material basis of adaptations, slighting science, as if God had only to command hair and skin to obey. See *De Usu Partium* II.14–15, in *Opera*, ed. Kühn, vol. 2, pp. 156–164; tr. May, pp. 530–537; see also Walzer, *Galen on Jews and Christians* (London: OUP, 1949), pp. 11–37.

55 Since form follows function, physical beauty must be subjective, answering to adaptive needs. It does not reflect a being's standing in the ontic hierarchy. The Ikhwān argue from the putative variations in attraction among individuals and cultures. Cf. Montaigne, *Apology for Raymond Sebond*, in *Complete Essays*, II, 12, pp. 355–356, citing Seneca; Darwin, *Descent*, ed. Barrett and Freeman, vol. 22, p. 630. The animal delegate does not place blacks and whites in different species. Any divergence of taste would serve his case. He might have argued simply that males are attracted to females of their own species, and *vice versa*. But the homosexual case evidently seemed clearer cut to the Ikhwān — despite the absence of any immediate reproductive benefit; and the presumed racial differences in tastes are adduced to heighten the sense of subjectivity. For Islamic views on race, see Bernard Lewis, *Race and Color in Islam* (New York: Harper and Row, 1971).

Often he will wake his master nudging him with a forefoot to warn him of an enemy, a predator, or an impending raid.[56] An ass or cow is often seen to find its way home when led off on a path it did not know and abandoned by its master. Yet some men can travel the same road time and again and still stray from it and lose their way.

'In a flock of sheep and ewes a great number may give birth in a single night. Then, early in morning they're driven out to pasture, not to return until nightfall. Yet when the young, a hundred or more, are released, each is seen to find its dam, without any doubt by the mother or confusion by the young.[57] For humans, a month or two or more must pass before they can distinguish their own mother from their sister, or their father from their brother. So where are the wonderful senses and discernment you boast of against us?

'As for your supposedly superior minds — we find not the least trace or sign of that. If you had such powerful intellects you would not have boasted over us about things which are not your own doing or won by your own efforts but which are among God's manifold gifts, to be recognized and acknowledged as acts of grace. The intelligent take pride only in things of their own doing — wholesome arts, sound views, true sciences, upright conduct, just practices, ways pleasing to God.[58] As far as we can see, you have no advantage to boast of but only groundless claims, baseless allegations, and bootless choler.'

---

56 Pliny the Elder tells of horses that allowed only their master to ride, or defended a master in battle, or grieved at his death; *Natural History* VIII.64–65.

57 See Isidore, *Etymologies* 12.1.12, tr. Barney et al., p. 247: The sheep 'recognizes its mother before other animals, so that even if it has strayed within a large herd, it immediately recognizes the voice of its parent by its bleat'.

58 Cf. Jeremiah 9:23–24: 'Thus saith the Lord: Let not the wise man glory in his wisdom, or the hero glory in his might, or the rich man glory in his wealth. But let him that glories glory in this: knowing and understanding Me. For I am the Lord that worketh grace, right, and justice on earth. It is in these that I delight, saith the Lord.' The animals adopt the Stoic axiom that one is accountable only for what one controls. For the Stoics that meant only the inclination of one's own will. Kant similarly deemed only the good will an unqualified good. But the animal spokesman suggests a wider scope for justified pride: there are arts, industries, sciences, views, actions, and practices that one might claim as one's own. The Ikhwān see these, too, as gifts of God but do not treat that fact as incompatible with human responsibility.

Chapter 5
The Animals Charge Humans with Oppression

The King then said to the human, 'You have heard their reply. Have you anything to add?'

'Yes, your Majesty. There is more evidence that we are their masters and they our slaves. We buy and sell them, feed and water them. We clothe and shelter them from heat and cold, and protect them from predators that would tear them to pieces. When they fall ill, we treat their illnesses and care for them.[59] We train them when they're raw, bear with them when they're mad, put them out to pasture when they're spent — all in kindness and compassion for them. But these are things masters do for their servants and owners for their property.'

'You've heard his claims', said the King. 'Answer as you see fit.'

The spokesman of the beasts replied, 'He argues that they buy and sell us. The same is done by Persians to Greeks and Greeks to Persians when they conquer one another. So which is the slave and which the master? The Indians treat the Sindians the same way, and the Sindians, the Indians; the Abyssinians, the Nubians; and the Nubians, the Abyssinians. The Arabs, Turks, and Kurds do the same to each other. Which, pray, are the slaves and which the masters?[60] Are these

59 Aristotle, *Politics* I.5.1254b10–11: 'All tame animals are better off when ruled by man; for then they are preserved.'

60 The Ikhwān reject the triumphalist bent of thinkers like Aristotle and al-Fārābī, who entertain the thought that the fortunes of war might tend to enslave those who are fit only to be slaves, or who, at the very least, seem likely to profit from their servitude by acquiring a higher level of culture or religion. See Aristotle, *Politics* I.9.1256b23: 'From one point of view, the art of war is a natural art of acquisition, for the art of acquisition includes hunting, an art which we ought to practise against wild beasts, and against men who, though intended by nature to be governed, will not submit; for war of such a kind is naturally just.' Al-Fārābī writes that a prince employs two classes of persons to form the character of his subjects: 'a group employed by him to form the character of whoever is susceptible of having his character formed willingly, and a group employed by him to form the character of those who are such that their character can be formed only by compulsion.... The [province of the] latter is the art of war, the power by which one excels in organizing and leading armies and using the implements of war and warlike people to conquer nations and cities that do not willingly do what will lead them to happiness.' Al-Fārābī, *Fī taḥṣīl al-saʿāda*, trans. after Muhsin Mahdi in *Alfarabi's Philosophy of Plato and Aristotle* (Ithaca: Cornell University Press, 1962), pp. 36–37.

not, just Majesty, the mere turns of human fortune, with the changing influences of the stars and conjunctions of the constellations? As God Himself said, *These are but the days whose revolutions I bring about among men.*[61] But *none comprehends but the learned.*[62]

'As for feeding and watering us, as he says, and everything else he says they do for us, these things are not done out of kindness or compassion, as he claims, but for fear lest we die and they lose their investment in us and the benefits they take from us — drinking our milk, wearing our fleece or wool or fur, riding on our backs, and having us carry their burdens.'

Then the ass spoke up and said, 'Your Majesty, had you seen us as prisoners of the sons of Adam, our backs laden with rocks, bricks, earth, wood, iron, and other heavy loads, struggling and straining to

61 Qur'an 3:140. The verse in full: *If ye are stricken with a wound, so are the enemy stricken with a wound. These are but the days whose revolutions I bring about among men — that God may know who is faithful, and take martyrs from among you. For God loves not wrongdoers.* Muhammad comforts his followers on a defeat. The Ikhwān read the passage allegorically. Hence their aside, that no one understands it but the learned. The 'days' often mentioned in pre-Islamic poetry are battle days — thus, the fortunes of war, whose turns or 'revolutions' God is said to bring about. Since the Qur'an speaks of revolutions in human fortunes, the animals see an allusion to the turning of the heavens: in rising and falling constellations learned astrologers read visible signs of destiny. The Ikhwān fuse ecological and dynastic with astral succession. Temporal dominance, the animals infer, is no proof of absolute supremacy or warrant of hegemony in God's plan: today's victor is tomorrow's victim. The thought is immemorial — in a lament for the fall of Ur (ca. 2004 BCE), the city's patron, Nanna the moon god, is abjured from weeping: 'The sentence of the gods assembled is not to be reversed. . . monarchy was given to Ur, but not eternal rule. From of old when the land was founded and folk multiplied, who has ever seen a royal realm endure? Ur's dominion was long. Now it is spent. Weary yourself no more, my Nanna. Leave your city', paraphrasing Jack Sasson's rendering (after Noah Kramer) in *Hebrew Origins: Historiography, History, Faith of Ancient Israel* (Hong Kong: Chung Chi College, 2002), p. 103. The lament is quoted more fully in William Hallo, 'Lamentations and Prayers in Sumer and Akkad', in Sasson, ed., *Civilizations of the Ancient Near East* (Peabody, MA: Hendrickson, 1995), vol. 2, p. 1873; the full text can be found at the Oxford Faculty of Oriental Studies (2006):
http://etcsl.orinst.ox.ac.uk/cgi-bin/etcsl.cgi?text=t.2.2.3&charenc=j#
Fate and the gods have issued their decree. No moral or spiritual fault is cited to warrant its severity. But a similar lament for the destruction of Sargon's capital, Agade, blames the hubris of King Naram-Sin. See Sasson, *Civilizations of the Ancient Near East*, vol. 2, p. 838.

62 Qur'an 29:43.

go forward, while they stood over us, stick in hand to beat us brutally about the face and back in anger, you would have pitied us and shed tears of sorrow for us, merciful King. Where then are their mercy and compassion?'[63]

The ox said, 'Had you seen us, your Majesty, as prisoners in the hands of the Adamites, yoked or bound to a water wheel or mill, with muzzles to our face and blinders on our eyes, as they beat us with sticks and clubs about the face and flanks, you would have pitied us and shed tears. Where, then, is their mercy? Where is the compassion they speak of?'

The ram said, 'You would have pitied us, your Majesty, had you seen us as their prisoners, when they seized our smallest kids and lambs and tore them from their dams to steal our milk. They took our young and bound them hand and foot to be slaughtered and skinned, hungry, thirsty, bleating for mercy but unpitied, screaming for help

63 The Ikhwān assign virtual subjecthood to the animals, ascribing interests to them and interpreting their inarticulate struggles and strivings. By giving speech to the animals, the fable breaks the barrier of their inarticulacy and gives voice to their desires and hurts. The Torah uses the same device when Balaam's belaboured ass turns and addresses him about the angel blocking his way: 'She said to Balaam, "What have I done to thee that thou hast struck me three times now. . . . Am I not thy she-ass that thou hast ridden all thy life, down to this day? Have I ever done such a thing to thee?"' (Numbers 22:28–30). Vergil assigns virtual subjecthood to the wounded deer in *Aeneid* VII.781–783, filling the woods with its groans, as if begging to be spared. The lines are echoed and translated by Montaigne, Pope, Dryden, and many others; see Montaigne, 'Of Cruelty', in *Complete Essays*, II, 11, p. 316; Hassan Melehy, 'Montaigne and Ethics: The Case of Animals', *L'Esprit Créateur*, 46 (2006), pp. 96–107; Philip P. Hallie, 'The Ethics of Montaigne's "De la cruauté"', in *O Un Amy! Essays in Honor of Donald M. Frame*, ed. Raymond C. La Charité (Lexington, KY: French Forum, 1977), pp. 156–171. As Melehy and Hallie note, Montaigne prefers evoking empathy to invoking the convention of animal speech, partly as an expression of scepticism about reason (and scripture?) and partly to meet the suffering stag and other inarticulate sentient creatures on their own ground. In classical Arabic criticism, negative capability rests on *tagh yur* ('changing places'), a move anticipated by Balaam's she-ass. Pre-Islamic poets often apostrophized wolves, camels, or horses — and, of course, abandoned campsites. But, as the scholar poet Abū Tammām remarked, the addressees 'were not in the habit of answering'. Geert Jan van Gelder observes, 'Speaking animals do not occur regularly' in Arabic literature, 'before the fables of *Kalīla wa-Dimna*' (p. 332) — a source warmly acknowledged by the Ikhwān; see Geert Jan van Gelder, 'The Conceit of the Pen and Sword: On an Arabic Literary Debate', *Journal of Semitic Studies*, 32 (1987), pp. 329–360.

with none to aid them. We saw them slaughtered, flayed, dismembered, disembowelled, their heads, brains, and livers on butchers' blocks, to be cut up with great knives and boiled in cauldrons or roasted in an oven, while we kept silent, not weeping or complaining. For even if we had wept they would not have pitied us.[64] Where then is their mercy?'

The camel joined in, 'Also had you seen us, your Majesty, as prisoners in the Adamites' hands, our muzzles bound with rope, our halters gripped by drivers who forced us to carry heavy loads in the dead of night, while all others slept, making our way through dark defiles and arid plains over a rocky track, bumping into boulders and stumbling with our tender pads over rocks and rough, broken ground, hungry and thirsty, our sides and backs bruised and sore from the rubbing of our saddles, you would have pitied us and wept for us. Where then is their mercy?'

The elephant said, 'Had you seen us, your Majesty, as prisoners of the sons of Adam, with chains on our feet and cables about our necks while they held iron goads in their hands to beat us about the pate and drive us left or right, powerless to defend ourselves, despite our great bulk, our mighty frames, long tusks, and immense strength, you would have pitied us and wept for us. Where then are the tenderness and compassion this human claims they feel for us?'

Then the horse spoke, 'Your Majesty, had you seen us as their prisoners on the field of battle, bits in our mouths, saddles on our backs, plunging unprotected through clouds of dust, hungry and thirsty, swords in our faces, lances to our chests, and arrows in our throats, awash in blood, you would have had pity on us, O King.'

The mule said, 'Had you seen us, your Majesty, as their captives, with hobbles on our feet, bridles at our throats, bits in our mouths, and locks at our crotches to curb us from satisfying our natural desires, loaded down with pack saddles, while those base, foul-mouthed men who rode atop them, our keepers and drivers, berated us with the vilest words at their command, whipping us about the face and hindquarters in such fury that often they were carried away and reviled themselves

64 Cf. Isidore, *Etymologies* 12.1.9: 'The sheep is a mild, wool-bearing sort of cattle, with a defenceless body and a docile temperament', tr. after Barney et al., p. 247.

and their human sisters, saying, "This ass's prick up the arse of the dealer's wife!" or the buyer's or the owner's — their own fellows! All these abuses turn back upon them, since they deserve them most.

'Your Majesty, if you consider how dense, vulgar, uncouth, and foul-mouthed humans are, you'll be amazed at how little they discern their own odious ways, vicious traits, depraved characters, and vile actions, their manifold barbarities, corrupt notions, and conflicting dogmas. They don't repent or take stock but ignore the warnings of their prophets and scorn the commands of their Lord, who said, *Let them show compassion and indulgence. Would you not wish God to show you mercy?*[65] And, *Tell the faithful to forgive those who have no hope in the days of God.*[66] He also says, *Every creature on earth depends for its sustenance on God, who knows their every lair and refuge.*[67] And, *There is no creature that treads the earth or flies on wings that is not a nation like you.*[68] And He said, *That you may sit solid on their backs and recall the grace of your Lord and say, praised be He who subjected them to us, for we could not have done it. And to our Lord we shall return.*'[69]

When the mule had finished speaking, the camel turned to the much-maligned pig and said, 'Stand up and speak. Tell of the Adamites' oppression of the swine. Set your complaint before the merciful King. Perhaps he will pity us and free us from their thrall, for you, too, are of the cattle.'

---

65 Qur'an 24:22: *Let not those with affluence and ease among you shun to share with kin and with the poor and with those who have emigrated in the cause of God. Let them show compassion and indulgence. Would you not wish God to show you mercy? For God is most merciful and compassionate.* Again, the Ikhwān assign universal scope to appeals spoken at a particular historical juncture. In the animals' plea, the unfortunate are the beasts; humans are the affluent who should show indulgence. The appeal to kinship is not in the portion of the verse quoted and is not relied upon in the appeal of the beasts.

66 Qur'an 45:14. Those who have no hope in the days of God — that is, in resurrection and redemption — here again, that means the animals, as revealed in the eschatology spelled out at the close of the *risāla*.

67 Qur'an 11:6.

68 Qur'an 6:38. The passage continues. *We have omitted nothing in the Book. Then to their Lord they will be gathered.* The animals here seem to presume the Mu'tazilite view that they too will be requited in the hereafter, although the Ikhwān reject that view in the end.

69 Qur'an 43:13–14.

But one of the jinni scholars said, 'No indeed! The pig does not belong to the cattle. He's a beast of prey. Don't you see that he has tusks and eats carrion?'

'No,' said another jinni, 'he belongs with the cattle. Don't you see he has hooves and eats grass and hay?'

Another said, 'No, he's a cross between cattle and wild beasts, like the elephant, or the giraffe, who is a cross between an ass and a camel.'[70]

Then said the pig, 'Good Lord! I don't know what to say or of whom to complain, with all the welter of conflicting things that are said of me. You've heard the opinions of the wisest jinn, and men differ even more about us. Their doctrines and sects are even further apart. Muslims call us accursed and grotesque. They loathe the sight of us and find our smell revolting and our meat disgusting. They hate even to say our name. But Romans eat our meat with gusto in their sacrifices and think it makes them blessed before God.

'The Jews detest, revile, and curse us, although we've done them no harm or wrong, but just because of the enmity between them and the Romans and Christians.[71] Armenians treat us the same as others treat

70 'The giraffe, *camelopardus*, is so called because while it is covered with spots like a pard it has a neck like a horse, ox-like feet, and a head like a camel'; Isidore, *Etymologies* 12.2.19. As Mary Douglas explains, ambiguously classified animals may be sacralized. See Mary Douglas, *Purity and Danger: An Analysis of the Concepts of Pollution and Taboo* (London: Routledge and Kegan Paul, 1966), pp. 169–170.

71 The Beirut text adds in a note: 'This again is a chimerical notion on the part of the Ikhwān, since the Jews' loathing of swine antedates Christianity.' It is biblical, of course (Leviticus 11:7). The whole passage in the *risāla* is somewhat anachronistic. For 'Romans' (*abnā' al-Rūm*) would usually mean Byzantines, Greeks of the Eastern Roman Empire, but they did not eat pork with gusto in their sacrifices; pagan Greeks and Romans did. As Pliny writes in his *Natural History* VIII.72.206: 'A pig is suitable for sacrifice four days after birth.' But pagan Greeks and Romans did not think that sacrificing swine made them blessed before (the monotheistic) God. The Ikhwān may have in mind the sacrifices of swine that Antiochus Epiphanes (r. 175–163 BC) ordained in his own honour. This foe of the Hasmoneans ruled Syria, but his ardent Hellenism might allow him to be called a *Rūmī*. As for the 'sacrifices' of the Christians, see the jinni rejoinder to the Christian in Chapter 19 below. Muslim abhorrence of swine, a forbidden food in Islam, may stem from Muhammad's early Jewish contacts. The Jerusalem Talmud (Berakhot, 2) treats swine as a symbol of filth, and the

sheep or cows. To them our fat bodies, rich meat, and many young are special blessings. Greek doctors use lard in their treatments and prescribe it in their medicines and therapies.[72] Husbandmen mingle us with their cattle and feed us in the same stalls, believing that an animal's condition is improved by contact with us or even scenting our smell. Magicians and sorcerers use our skins for their books, spells, amulets, and magic devices. Saddlers and shoemakers prize our bristles and vie for the pluckings from our snouts, so badly do they need them.[73] No wonder we're confused. We don't know whom to thank and against whom to complain of injustice.'

When the pig had finished speaking, the ass turned to the rabbit, who was standing between the camel's forelegs, and said, 'Tell about the mistreatment rabbits have suffered at the hands of man. Set your complaint before the King. Perhaps he will look into our case in his mercy, take pity on us, and set us free.'

But the rabbit said, 'We are already free of the tribe of Adam. We no longer venture into their dwelling places but have withdrawn into forests and glens, safe from their wrongs. Still we are harassed by dogs, hunting birds, and horses, who abet men against us. They carry men to us and search us out for them, along with our brethren the gazelles, wild asses, wild cattle, mountain sheep, and mountain goats.

'It's excusable for dogs and birds of prey to aid man against us', the rabbit went on. 'They have a reason to eat our meat, since they're not of our kind but are carnivores. But the horse is a beast. Our meat is not for him. So he should take no part in aiding men against us, unless out of ignorance, stupidity — failure to grasp the true nature of things.'

Babylonian Talmud (Menuḥot 64b) regards one who raises swine as accursed; see also Goodman, *God of Abraham* (New York: OUP, 1996), pp. 230–232.

72 Paul of Aegina writes that fats and grease of 'all kinds dilute and warm the human body, but their powers vary according to the different temperaments of animals. That of swine, then, is the most humid of all, its powers being like those of oil. Hence it blunts sharp pains.' *The Seven Books*, vol. 3, pp. 354–355.

73 Isidore, *Etymologies* 12.1.26: 'The hairs of pigs are called bristles [*setas*] and are named from the sow [*sue*]. From these we name "shoemakers" [*sutores*], because they sew [*suant*], that is, stitch together leather with bristles.' Isidore's etymology may be fanciful, but the connection of sewing and suturing with the Latin for 'cobbler' is sound.

Chapter 6
The Pre-eminence of Horses over other Beasts

'Stop right there', the human interrupted. 'This goes too far! You would not have blamed horses in this way if you knew that they're the finest animals in man's service!'[74]

'Tell us', said the King, 'what great good you find in horses.'

'Their merits are many, both in their sterling nature and their marvellous character,' the man replied, 'in their handsome form and fine proportions, well-knit frames, pure colours, and glossy coats. They're fast and responsive, heading wherever a rider turns them, left or right, forward or back, pursuing or fleeing, charging or retreating. And horses are sharp witted. They have keen senses, and they're well mannered. Often they refrain from staling or fouling the ground while mounted; and, if their tails get wet, they hold them still so as not to spatter their master. A horse must have an elephant's strength to carry rider and weapons, helmet, and armour, besides its own saddle, bridle, and coat of mail. The iron equipage alone must weigh near half a ton at full tilt. A horse must be steady as an ass to face the thrust of spears at his chest and throat in battle. Yet he lopes like a ravening wolf, walks like a proud bull, bounds quick as a hare, and leaps like a great rock torn loose by a torrent. In a race he runs as if the prize were meant for him!'[75]

---

74 Horses are praised in pre-Islamic Arabic poetry, as in other sources, in part because the horseman works as one with his mount; power and speed are felt as if they were his own. In the Arabic *qaṣīda*, as Hellmut Ritter remarked, the *waṣf*, or description of one's mount, was almost never neutral. See van Gelder, 'The Conceit of Pen and Sword', p. 331. 'Horses have noble and beautiful heads, whether they are shaggy draught horses or refined Arabians. There is something about the elongated profile, the soulful eyes and delicately pointed ears, the mobile lips and sensitive flaring nostrils, that has always appealed deeply to human sensibilities.' Catherine Johns, *Horses: History, Myth, Art* (Cambridge, MA: Harvard University Press, 2006), p. 126.

75 Horses, Isidore relates, can smell warfare and are roused to battle by the sound of the trumpet (cf. Job 39:24), and they exult at winning a race and grieve when they lose; *Etymologies* 12.1.43. Pliny observes that horses respond to shouts of encouragement and applause in a race; they run on even when the charioteer has fallen from his car, *Natural History* VIII.65.159–162.

'True,' the rabbit answered, 'but with all these admirable traits and talents, horses have one great flaw that casts a shadow over all their virtues.'

'What is that?' asked the King. 'Explain what you mean.'

'Lack of insight', said the rabbit. 'A horse will as soon flee with his master's enemy, whom he's never seen before, as with the master at whose home he was born and bred. He will as readily carry an enemy to his master as the master after an enemy. He's just like a sword in this way, without sense, sentience, or spirit, as quick to behead the owner who burnishes it as anyone who wants to break it, twist or mar it, seeing no difference between them.[76]

'A similar fault', the rabbit went on, 'is found among men. A man will often turn on his parents, brothers, or kin, plot against them, and treat them as meanly as his worst enemy, who never showed him any kindness or gave him cause for gratitude.[77] Just so these humans drink the milk of cattle as they drank their mother's milk and ride on beasts' shoulders as they rode their father's shoulders when small. They use animals' wool and fleece for coats and upholstery, but in the end they slaughter, flay, disembowel, and dismember them, set them to boil or roast, unfeeling and unremembering all the good, all the blessings, lavished on them.'

When the rabbit had finished his censure of men and horses, the ass said, 'You should not be too reproachful. No creature is granted so many gifts and virtues as not to lack something greater, and none is deprived of at least some special gift. God's bounties are many. No one individual can compass them all, and no species or kind engrosses all God's goodness. God's bounty, rather, is shared by all creatures in

76 Montaigne's essay 'Of War Horses' is similarly ambivalent about war horses: 'There are many horses trained to help their masters, to rush upon anyone who wields a drawn sword at them, to hurl themselves with feet and teeth on those who attack and confront them; but they prove to hurt their friends oftener than their foes. Besides, you cannot call them off at will once they have engaged; you remain at the mercy of their combat. . . you stake your valour and your fortune on your horse; so his wounds and death lead to yours; his fear or hot-headedness make you either rash or cowardly; if he fails to respond to bit or spur, it is your honor that must answer for it.' *Complete Essays*, I, 48, pp. 210–211.

77 See Plato, *Statesman* 298. A sword cuts friend or foe alike; a physician may cure or kill. The artefact is blind; the disloyal friend, changeable.

greater or lesser proportion. But the clearer divinity shines in a being, the plainer is its servitude.[78]

'For example, the two celestial luminaries, the sun and moon, received from God so bounteous a share of light, brilliance, splendour, and majesty that people often fell under the delusion that they were lords or gods, so clearly do the marks of divinity shine in them. That is why they were subjected to eclipses, to show the discerning that if they were gods they would not go dark. Likewise with the rest of the stars.[79] They may be granted brilliant light, revolving spheres,[80] and long lives, but they are not immune to flickering, or retrograde motion,[81] or even falling,[82] to show that they too are subordinate.[83] So again

78 In Platonic wise, all creatures share in perfection, each in its own way. Creation is enriched by diversity; and every creature's unique perfection is a gift of grace vital to its survival. None challenges God's goodness. Indeed, the highest are the humblest. The Ikhwān here allude to the Qur'anic (55:5–6) obeisance of the celestial bodies. See note 443 below.

79 The Midrash, similarly, tells that the moon was diminished and the sun subjected to setting and eclipses, lest they pride themselves too much in their glory. Genesis (1:16) avoids naming the sun and moon, calling them only a greater and a lesser light, deflating notions of their divinity by affirming both their goodness and their creation by the one God. Philo, *De Opificio Mundi* 1.31: 'It would not be amiss to term. . . "all brightness" that from which the sun and moon as well as the fixed stars and planets draw, each according to its capacity, the light befitting each: that pure, undiluted radiance is bedimmed so soon as it begins to undergo the change entailed by passage from the intelligible to the sensible. For no object of sense is undimmed.'

80 Aristotelians held that the rotation of the heavens, unlike linear motion, has no opposite. For it occupies every position in turn and constantly returns to its point of origin. They infer the eternity of the heavens from this premise. Monotheists countered that the heavens might have turned in the opposite sense — so there is contingency in their revolutions, and the possibility of a reversal shows that even celestial bodies are destructible and owe their origin to God's creative act and their sustenance to His providence.

81 The retrograde motion of the planets is a sign of imperfection: they are not divine. Their powers are limited and delegated.

82 The Ikhwān reject the Aristotelian assumption that 'falling stars' come from within the encircling spheres and are thus not celestial bodies but *meteora* — changeable like the weather — a notion preserved today in the names 'meteor' and 'meteorite'.

83 The sixth-century Christian philosopher John Philoponus argued (against Aristotle) that the stars were not uncompounded substances (and, therefore, immutable, indestructible, and uncreated). Their diverse colours suggest that they are composed of diverse materials; and their flickering, that they are undergoing

with all the rest of creation — angels, men, or jinn. None of these is vouchsafed all virtues together, or all of God's gifts at once. Each lacks something beyond what it has. Perfection belongs to God alone, *one and triumphant*.[84] In this vein did the poet say:

> 'How can you keep a friend if you do not reprove his faults?
> Is anyone perfect?'[85]

When the ass had finished, the ox added, 'But whoever is richly endowed by God should show his thanks by sharing the excess with the less fortunate beings who lack those gifts. See how the sun pours light unstintingly on all creatures from its generous portion. The moon and stars too shed their influences, each according to its powers. Men should do the same, since they are granted divine gifts that other animals lack. They should share their gifts unsparingly.'[86]

---

some process. Therefore they must be originate. As terrestrial fires glare and glow with diverse hues depending on what fuels them, Philoponus argued, the stars must differ in composition. As Shmuel Sambursky noted, Philoponus here founds astrospectroscopy. See Philoponus, *De Caelo*, ed. J. L. Heiberg (Berlin: Reimer, 1894), p. 89; and Philoponus, *De Opificio Mundi*, ed. G. Reichardt (Leipzig: Teubner, 1897), p. 102; S. Sambursky, *The Physical World of Late Antiquity* (London: Routledge, 1962), pp. 158–166. Like the Ikhwān, Philoponus finds nothing in nature perfect or absolute. Where Aristotle held the heavens and the cosmos at large to be divine, eternal, and immutable, Philoponus insists that only God is beyond change.

84 Qur'an 14:48. The Ikhwān, pacifically and Neoplatonically, gloss the paired epithets as referring to God's unique, transcendent perfection.

85 The lines are from Nābigha al-Dhubyānī, one of the most celebrated pre-Islamic poets; see *Dīwān*, ed. G. Shaykh (Beirut: Mu'assasat al-A'lamī li'l-Maṭbū'āt, 2000), p. 10. See A. Arazi, 'Nābigha al-Dhubyānī', *EI2*, vol. 7, pp. 840–842.

86 The ox sees an ethical obligation in the cosmic principle of emanation. Like Plato in the *Timaeus*, he fuses *nomos* ('law') and *physis* ('nature') in the idea of natural law: the cosmos lives under a God-given rule, and human norms must accord with nature's law. Kant's awe at the twofold natural law is voiced in his famous words: 'Two things fill the mind with ever new and increasing admiration and awe, the oftener and more steadily we reflect on them: the starry heavens above me and the moral law within me.' *Critique of Practical Reason*, tr. Lewis White Beck (Indianapolis: Bobbs-Merrill, 1956), Conclusion, p. 166. The union of moral and cosmic law anchors scriptural monotheism, and monotheists welcomed Neoplatonism for seeing all reality as a procession (*prohodos*, 'emanation') of being/goodness/grace/truth from the One, that is, God. It is to this idea of emanation, elaborated by Plotinus, Porphyry, and

When the ox had finished speaking, the cattle and beasts all cried out together, 'Have mercy on us, just and noble King, and free us from the oppression of the tyrannous sons of men.'

The King of the Jinn then turned to the jinni scholars and sages assembled before him and said, 'Have you heard the complaint of the cattle and beasts and their account of the injustice, oppression, and ruthless trespass they have borne at the hands of men?'

'We have heard all that has been said', they replied. 'It is true and correct, night and day, everywhere to be seen, and hardly lost on the aware. It was for this very reason that the race of jinn, too, fled from among men to deserts, wastes and moors, mountain-tops, hills, valleys, or sea-shores. We too saw their vicious ways and vile mores and shunned the lands where they dwelt. Even so, men never overcame their bias against us. They still see jinn as tempters of men and authors of their aches and pains, making us the bogies of women, children, and the ignorant. They seek to ward us off by wearing talismans, amulets, charms, and such. Yet no one has ever seen a jinni harm or kill a human, snatch his clothes, steal his things, break into his house, filch from his pocket, cut his sleeve, pick his lock, waylay a traveller, rebel against a ruler, mount a raid, or perpetrate a kidnapping. All these, rather, are human specialities, acts of men towards one another night and day, *heedless and unrepentent.*'[87]

When this speaker had finished, a herald announced, 'Honoured delegates, night has come. Repair to your lodgings in honour. And, God willing, return safe in the morning.'

Proclus, that the Ikhwān here allude. Putting the idea of emanation into the mouth of the ox, allows them a discreet distance from Greek versions of the idea, since emanationism was somewhat heterodox, often read by strict Neoplatonists not just as an interpretation of Creation but as its rival. Even so, emanation is an insistently recurrent theme in the cosmology of the Ikhwān, as in their ethics and politics.

87 Qur'an 9:126.

Chapter 7
The Benefits of Consultation

Having recessed the court, the King remained closeted with his vizier,[88] Bayrān, a grave and sagacious person and a wise philosopher. Said the King, 'You have seen the session and heard the arguments on both sides. You know what they're here for. What do you think is right, and what do you advise us to do?'

The vizier said, 'God strengthen your Majesty and guide him to the right course. I think it would be best for the King to summon the judges, jurists, scholars, and thinkers of the jinn to gather at his court and consult on this matter. For this is a fraught and momentous case, highly contentious and deeply problematic. There are considerations on both sides, but consultation lends weight to an opinion. It guides the uncertain and assures the committed.'

'You're right', the King answered. 'What you say is sound. Your plan is excellent.'[89]

The King then summoned the jinni judges of the family of Birjīs and the jurists of the family of Nāhīd,[90] jinni thinkers of the tribe of Tīrān and scholars of the stock of Luqmān, experienced jinn from the tribe of Māhān, philosopher jinn of the tribe of Kaywān, and hard-headed, forthright jinn of the House of Bahrām.[91]

---

88 The jinni king, like a human monarch, has a vizier, chief minister, adviser, and spokesman beyond his court. For the office of vizier, the chief power in many a Muslim regime, see Dominique Sourdel, *Le Vizirat 'Abbāside de 749 à 936* (Damascus: Institut français de Damas, 1959–1960).

89 The Ikhwān take care to portray the wise jinni king as taking advice from ministers and counsellors, in keeping with the Islamic and ancient Arab ideal of consultation.

90 Birjīs and Nāhīd are the planets Jupiter and Venus, a fitting retinue for the jinni king, since the Ikhwān link the jinn Neoplatonically with the governance of the planets.

91 See Appendix C, Bahrām. The Ikhwān show pride in their Iranian heritage by using this name, which antedates the birth of Islam and the rise of Arab power. Further Persian elements are highlighted by the Iranian tribal names mentioned in this passage. The Tirān tribe gave its name to a city in central Iran, near Isfahan. The Māhān are associated with the city and region of the same name some twenty miles east of Kirmān, in south-east Iran; see E. G. Browne, *A Literary History of Persia* (Cambridge: CUP, 1964), vol. 1, p. 263, note 2.

When they were assembled before him, he met with them in private audience and said, 'You have learned of these parties who have landed on our shores and entered our country. You've seen them here at court and have heard their claims and charges and the complaints of these captive animals against the injustice of men. The animals have sought our aid and protection. What are your views? What do you recommend be done?'

Then the chief jurist of the House of Nāhīd said, 'God strengthen the King's hand and guide him aright. The course I would suggest is that the King order these beasts to write a brief laying out the injuries they have suffered at the hands of humans and seeking a ruling from the jurists. This will give them a way to gain their freedom and escape this tyranny. For the judge will doubtless rule in their favour and decide either that they should be sold or freed or that their tasks be lightened and they be better treated. Then, if the tribe of Adam fails to heed the judgement, no crime can be charged against the animals should they take flight.'[92]

'What do you think of this proposal?' the King asked the assembly.

All agreed that it was a fine and sensible idea, except the forthright jinni of the House of Bahrām. 'Have you considered', he said, 'who will lay out the price to buy the animals if the Adamites agree to their sale?'

'The King', said the jurist.

'With what?' asked the King.

'With the funds of the Muslim jinn.'

'There is not wealth enough in the treasury of the Muslim jinn to meet the cost', said the jinni thinker. 'Besides, many humans will be loath to sell them. They need them too badly, and some don't need

92 'Oriental despots' may wield extensive power in theory, especially in 'righting wrongs' brought before them, but their powers of enforcement were very limited, de facto, beyond the court. Mediaeval 'mirrors for princes', and folk literature retail the ruses monarchs used to execute their designs. The *Siyāsat-nāma* of Niẓām al-Mulk, tr. H. Darke (London: Routledge and Kegan Paul, 1960), is filled with examples. The ruses recounted by Machiavelli in *The Prince* belong to the tradition of political manoeuvring that saw virtuosity in the manipulation of small force to maximal effect. Pleas like Locke's for the limitation of sovereignty reflect the efficacy and efficiency of the rising modern state, which deployed power on a scale unknown in the Middle Ages — even for the jinn.

the money — kings, nobles, and the well-to-do, for example. Such a sale could never be brought off. So don't weary yourselves thinking about it.'

'What do you think is the right plan?' asked the King.

'I suggest', said the jinni theorist, 'that the King order all the cattle and beasts in captivity to humans to make a plan to flee, all on the same night, far from the realm of men, as the wild asses and gazelles have done. When the humans wake in the morning they'll find no beast to ride or carry their burdens. They won't be able to pursue the animals because of the great distance and the difficulty of the road, and the animals will be free.'[93]

The King was resolved to follow this plan and asked the others what they thought of the thinker's proposal.

The chief scholar, of the House of Luqmān,[94] said, 'In my opinion this won't work. It's too ambitious. Most of these beasts are tied up or stabled at night. So how could they all manage to flee in a single night?'

The hard-headed jinni said, 'The King could send bands of jinn that night to open the gates for them and loose their bonds and tethers. We could distract the watchmen until the beasts had travelled far enough from human habitation. Your Majesty should know there would be great reward for him in doing this. I speak candidly, since I'm touched by their plight. God is aware of the sound and open-hearted intent of the King's resolve. His aid will ensure success. To help the oppressed

93 The radicalism of the speculative jinni needs tempering by the learning and the historic sense of other jinn; cf. Michael Oakeshott, *Rationalism in Politics and Other Essays* (2nd ed., Indianapolis: Liberty Press, 1991). As Hamdani notes, the Ikhwān 'exhort their readers to study every type of literature', be it philosophical, juridical, mathematical, natural, or theological, since knowledge is the 'nourishment and the very life of the soul, in this world and the next' (*Rasā'il*, vol. 3, p. 538); Abbas Hamdani, 'Religious Tolerance in the *Rasā'il Ikhwān al-Ṣafā*', in Y. Tzvi Langermann and Josef Stern, ed., *Adaptations and Innovations: Studies on the Interaction between Jewish and Islamic Thought and Literature from the Early Middle Ages to the Late Twentieth Century — Dedicated to Professor Joel L. Kraemer* (Paris, Louvain, and Dudley, MA: Peeters, 2007), p. 138.

94 Luqmān, the subject of numerous magical folk tales, is mentioned for his wise teachings in Qur'an 31:11–19 (the sura bearing his name). Arabic historians see him as a fabulist and author of proverbs. Some Western authors identify Luqmān with Aesop (*Aethiops*) because of his alleged Ethiopian ancestry and slave origin.

and free the enslaved is the best thanks for God's blessings.[95] In one of the books of the prophets, they say, it is written that God said, 'O King that reigns, I did not give you power that you might gather riches and gratify your lusts and passions but that you in My place might answer the entreaties of the oppressed. For I do not repulse them even if they be unbelievers.'[96]

At this the King was all the more determined to follow the speculative jinni's advice. He said to the assembly around him, 'What do you think of this suggestion?'

They all agreed it was a generous and noble plan. All voiced their approval, except the philosopher of the House of Kaywān, who said, 'God give you insight, your Majesty, and show you the unseen side of things and the ills that lie hidden in tactics. The project is fraught with great dangers that are insuperable, flaws neither remediable nor rectifiable.'

'Tell us your view', said the King to the philosopher. 'Explain what you fear and of what you are so wary, so that we may be alerted and on guard.'

'I shall, your Majesty. Something was left out of this proposal for the beasts' escape from the Adamites' hands. When the race of Adam wake in the morning and find these beasts gone, fled from their lands, will they not be certain that this was not the work of humans nor planned by the beasts themselves, but surely by the wiles of the jinn?'

'Doubtless', said the King.

'Isn't it so', the philosopher continued, 'that whenever men later come think of all the benefits and comforts they've lost by the animals' flight, they'll be filled with grief, rage, and regret over their loss, and spite, malice, and hatred toward the jinn? They'll devise secret schemes and tricks to ensnare us, hunt us everywhere, and everywhere lie in

95 The outspoken jinni cites the prospect of a divine reward for taking the course he advises. But that is not the chief motive he urges. He uses the notion of a reward to introduce the expectation of God's aid and approval, appealing to moral and religious ideals in support of his desire to free the enslaved and oppressed. His activism addresses not the mob but the King. So it is not overtly subversive. Yet his plea is pregnant with the affirmation of the legitimacy of direct action, should conditions demand it.

96 We have not been able to identify a source for this line, but its liberality is striking.

wait for us. In place of our once secure life, the race of jinn will know only trouble, hostility, and fear.

'One who is prudent and astute', the wise jinni added, 'makes peace among enemies and does not draw enmity on himself.'

All agreed that the wise philosopher was right. Then one jinni scholar said, 'What have we to fear from human enmity? You know well that we jinn are light, fiery spirits that rise by nature. The sons of Adam have gross, earthly bodies that fall by nature. We see them, but they do not see us. We can strike them, but they cannot touch us. What have we to fear from them?'

'Ah,' the jinni sage replied, 'you miss their greatest, gravest advantage. Don't you know that although the sons of Adam have gross, earthly bodies, they also have heavenly spirits and angel-like rational souls that set them above us? There are lessons to be learned, you know, from the histories of ancient times and all that passed between us and the humans in ages gone by!'[97]

At that the King said, 'What did happen, wise one? Tell us the story of our relations with them?'

'I shall, your Majesty', said he. 'There is a deep-seated enmity, a savage and fanatic division and mutual hostility that would take long to explain.'

'Tell us a little about it,' said the King, 'starting with its origins.'

Chapter 8

The Enmity between Men and Jinn and How it Came About

'In ancient times,' the wise jinni said, 'before the creation of Adam, forefather of the human race, we jinn were the earth's denizens. It was we who covered the earth, land and sea, mountain and plain. Our lives were long and filled with blessings in profusion. We had kings, prophets, faith, and law.[98] But we grew wanton and violent, ignored our

97 *Adab*, the learning and literature of the Arabic literati, was prized, in part, because history was seen to hold lessons crucial for the growth of character and the guidance of policy. See Goodman, *Islamic Humanism*, esp. Chapters 2 and 4.

98 Religion in Arabic can be called *dīn* or *sharīʿa*. '*Dīn*' is often understood as one's confession; '*sharīʿa*', as a system of law. But the meanings of the terms

prophets' precepts and ever worked corruption on earth,[99] until finally the earth and its denizens joined in crying out against our wrongs.

'When that era was drawing to a close and a new age was dawning, God sent a host of angels down from heaven to settle the land, and they scattered the vanquished jinn to the far corners of the earth. Many they took captive — among them, the accursed Satan Lucifer,[100] Adam's pharaoh,[101] then still a callow lad. Raised among the angels, Lucifer acquired their knowledge. Outwardly he resembled them, and inwardly he adopted their nature and stamp.[102] As the ages passed he became a chief among them, and for aeons they followed his commands and bans. But that era too came to an end, and a new age began. God revealed to those angels that were on earth: "*I shall place a vice-regent on earth* in place of you; and you shall I raise to the heavens." The earth angels

overlap: both bear connotations of law and a way of life. Mediaeval Judaism, Christianity, and Islam share this twofold conception of religion, thus giving a special emphasis to the practical and ritual expression of religious commitment. The Reformation return to Pauline discomfort with law and ceremony privileges grace and faith above 'works'. Enlightenment thinkers exploited the Protestant turn, to prise apart morality from theology, deeming faith a matter of conscience, which must be free, and locating practice in a moral realm kept high and dry, apart from the realm of faith, often dismissing ritual as 'empty formalism'. Thus, in modern usage, religions are often called creeds or faiths, as though thought and action, symbol and ceremony, were unconnected — or their nexus, either morally void or socially suspect.

99 The phrase is biblical (Genesis 6:11, Numbers 35:31–34, Deuteronomy 21:22–23), ethicizing nature, as J. H. Hertz felicitously termed it. The Ikhwān, too, see the earth as unfit for habitation by those who have fouled it with corruption; see Goodman, *God of Abraham*, pp. 219, 224–225.

100 Satan Lucifer, here called Iblīs Azāzīl in the Arabic.

101 The Ikhwān use the terms 'pharaoh' and 'nimrod' generically for any evil ruler; see note 461 below. They count pharaohs as the most vicious of mortals. As Qur'an 25:31 relates: *To every prophet we have assigned a foe.* The Ikhwān class the substance of tar as lowest among minerals, oleander as the lowest of plants, swine as the lowest of animals, barbarous humans as the lowest of the species, and pharaohs as the worst of the wicked. Extending in the opposite direction, on the scale of nobility are gold, aloes, the horse, imams, and prophets. See Nasr, *Islamic Cosmological Doctrines*, p. 71.

102 The Qur'an (18:50) assigns Satan a jinni origin, but it also counts him among the angels (2:34, 20:116). Saadiah finds the notion of a fallen angel theologically bizarre and refutes it at length; see *The Book of Theodicy*, tr. Goodman, pp. 154–159. The Ikhwān use their narrative to paper over the difficulty.

were loath to leave their familiar homeland[103] and answered, "*Wilt thou place there one who will work corruption there and shed blood*", as did the race of jinn, "*while we celebrate Thy praises and sanctify Thee?" God said, "I know what you know not*;[104] for I have sworn an oath upon Myself that in the end, after the age of Adam and his seed, I shall leave not one — angel, jinni, human, or any living creature — on the face of the earth."[105]

'When God created Adam, fashioned him, breathed of His spirit into him, and from him formed Eve, his mate, He ordered the angels on earth to bow down before the two and submit to their command. All obeyed except Satan. For he was haughty and arrogant. A savage, jealous frenzy seized him when he saw his dominion ending and knew that he must follow and be a leader no more.[106]

'God then ordered the angels to bear Adam, peace be upon him, up to the heavens into paradise,[107] a garden in the East atop a mountain of

103 As a little-known hadith explains: the angels and lesser jinn who dwelt on earth before Adam's creation objected to being displaced by humankind, even though they were raised up to heaven — since their worship of God on earth was of the highest kind. See Abū Ḥayyān al-Jayyānī, *Al-Baḥr al-muḥīṭ* (Riyadh: Maktabat al-Nashr al-Ḥadītha, 1960), vol. 1, p. 141; M. J. Kister, 'Adam: A Study of Some Legends in *Tafsīr* and *Ḥadīth* Literature', *Israel Oriental Studies*, 13 (1993), p. 121.

104 Qur'an 2:30.

105 The Arabic text continues: 'There is a mystery in this oath that we have explained elsewhere.' Bustānī's text softens God's oath by adding, 'except those whom I choose', but the manuscripts do not support the mitigation. Nasr helps us understand the oath: 'God does not create something after man as he created man after the animals, because man, by virtue of being able to return to his origin, fulfils the purpose of the whole of creation. All other orders of beings were created in order that this final stage of reunion might take place.' Nasr, *Islamic Cosmological Doctrines*, p. 73. The animals still exist for their own sakes. But theirs is a supporting role in the larger cosmic drama, centred on human destiny.

106 See Qur'an 2:30–36.

107 Adam, here, as in the narrative of al-Kisā'ī, is created on earth and then raised to paradise by angels, even though his animation by God's breath of life occurs in paradise. Al-Tha'labī has Adam created in paradise and borne through it by angels to learn all of its wonders; see al-Kisā'ī, *Qiṣaṣ al-anbiyā'*, tr. Wheeler M. Thackston as *The Tales of the Prophets of al-Kisa'i* (Boston: Twayne, 1978), p. 25; al-Tha'labī, *'Arā'is al-majālis fī qiṣaṣ al-anbiyā'*, tr. William Brinner as *Lives of the Prophets* (Leiden: Brill, 2002), p. 47.

jacinth[108] that no mortal man can climb. The garden's soil was good; its climate even, summer and winter, night and day.[109] It had many rivers, verdant trees and every sort of fruit, meadows, fragrant herbs, and flowers. The many animals did no harm, and the birds sang sweet, melodious songs.

'Adam and Eve both had long hair streaming down from their heads, lovely as ever graced a maiden, reaching their feet and covering their nakedness. This was the clothing they wrapped about themselves, their cloak and the ornament of their beauty. They would stroll by the river banks amid the plants and flowers, eating the many varieties of fruit from the trees and drinking water from the streams, without tiring their bodies or troubling their souls. There was no irksome ploughing, planting, irrigating, reaping, threshing, milling, or kneading, no spinning, weaving, or washing — none of the chores at which their children in our days toil, struggling to survive in this world. They

108 Jacinth (*yaqūt*, cognate with the Greek '*huakinthos*' and the Persian '*yākand*') is a special gemstone for Muslim mineralogists. Bīrūnī, writing in about 1000, calls it the most precious of gems. *Yaqūt* is crystalline corundum, an oxide of aluminium, given its brilliant red, yellow, or blue colour (in rubies, and yellow or blue sapphires) by traces of other oxides. The gem, which Muslim sources say neither melts nor calcifies like emeralds, features in the Qur'anic (55:58) description of the houris in paradise. Islamic sources assign it medicinal, magical, and talismanic properties. See Ghada al-Hijjawi al-Qaddumi, 'Yāḳūt', *EI2*, vol. 11, pp. 262–263. Nasr writes: 'Minerals, according to the Ikhwān, are not dead things but have a life of their own. They grow like fruits of trees and have love, desire, hatred, and repulsion, just as animals do. They have a hidden perception (*shuʿūr khafiy*) and delicate sense, like plants and animals. Minerals exist potentially in the earth and become actualized at the surface. They are grown, as are the animals, by the inception of the male sperm in the female womb of the earth'; *Islamic Cosmological Doctrines*, pp. 91–92. Mineral passions of attraction and repulsion were presumably helpful in explaining the alchemical reactions of diverse materials. But, as Nasr notes, the Ikhwān stipulate that the love and hate of minerals is known but to God.

109 The Ikhwān echo their description of paradise in the favourable descriptions they give of man's terrestrial environment. But they add features of a natural idyllic garden. For the impact of the concept of the enclosed garden, see Moses Hadas, *Hellenistic Culture, Fusion and Diffusion* (New York: Columbia University Press, 1959), p. 212. For a wider consideration of the 'Islamic garden', see Jonas Benzion Lehrman, *Earthly Paradise: Garden and Courtyard in Islam* (Berkeley: University of California Press, 1980); and Chapter 6 of Oliver Leaman, *Islamic Aesthetics: An Introduction* (Notre Dame: University of Notre Dame Press, 2004).

lived in the garden like any other animal, in leisure, contentment, and delight.

'God inspired Adam with the names of the trees, fruits, plants, and animals in the garden.[110] As soon as he could speak, he asked the angels about them, but they had no answer. So he sat down to teach them their names, benefits, and harms, and the angels followed his lead. For it was plain to them that he was their better.[111]

'Seeing this, Satan's envy and malice only grew. All through the morning and into the night he laid crafty, twisted plots against Adam and Eve. Then he approached them, as if with friendly counsel and said, "God has uplifted you, gracing you with articulate speech and discernment. But if you ate of this tree, you would grow yet wiser and surer. You would live here forever, safe, deathless, eternal." They were taken in by his words. For he swore he was, *a faithful friend.*[112] Transported, neither could wait to taste the forbidden fruit. But when they ate of it, their hair parted, exposing their nakedness. They were left bare, the sun's heat beating down on them, blackening their bodies. The animals shied away, seeing the change, and God ordered the angels to banish them from the Garden and cast them at the foot of the mountain.[113]

---

110 Cf. Qur'an 2:31.

111 To the Ikhwān, the humbling of the angels is emblematic of the subordination of nature to the rational soul.

112 Qur'an 7:21.

113 See Qur'an 7:11–25: *I created you, then formed you, then said to the angels 'Bow down before Adam!' and they bowed down — except for Satan, who did not join those who bowed. He said, 'What keeps thee from bowing as I commanded thee?' Satan said, 'I am better than he. Thou hast created me from fire and him from clay.' Then God said 'Then get thee down hence. It is not for thee to vaunt thyself here. Get thee gone, thou art diminished!' Satan replied 'Spare me until the day they are resurrected.' 'Thou art spared.' 'Since Thou hast misled me, will I lie in wait for them by Thy straight path . . .' 'Get thee gone, disgraced and banished! Whoever follows thee of them — Hell shall I fill with all of you together! O Adam, dwell thou and thy mate in the Garden, and eat where ye list, but come not near this tree, or ye shall be wrongdoers.' But the devil whispered to them, revealing to them their hidden shame: 'Your Lord forbade this tree to you only lest ye become angels or immortals.' He swore to them he was a faithful counsellor and so deceived them. When they tasted of the tree their shame was revealed to them, and they scrambled to cover up with leaves from the garden. But their Lord called to them, 'Did I not forbid that tree and tell you that Satan is your sworn enemy?' They said,*

'They fell into a stark wasteland without plants or fruits, and there they long remained, weeping and grieving at their loss and rueing their fate. At last God's mercy reached out to them. He pardoned them and sent an angel to teach them to plough and sow, reap, thresh, grind, bake, spin, weave, sew, and fashion clothing. They procreated and their seed grew numerous, and some of the jinni race mingled with them and taught them the arts of planting and building, showed them what was good for them and what was harmful.[114] Befriending mankind, the jinn won their affection, and for a time they lived together on the best of terms.

'But whenever the race of Adam recalled the enmity of the accursed Satan Lucifer and how he had cozened their forefather, their hearts filled with rage and rancour toward the jinni race. When Cain killed Abel, Abel's progeny blamed the prompting of the jinn and hated them yet more. They sought them everywhere and tried to catch them with every trick of magic, witchcraft, and sorcery they knew. Some they clapped in bottles and tormented with all manner of smoke and foul vapours, nauseating and revolting to the jinni race.

'So things went until God sent the prophet Idrīs.[115] He smoothed

---

'Lord we have wronged ourselves. If Thou dost not forgive us and have mercy on us, we are lost!' He answered 'Get you down, each a foe to the other. There is an abode for you on earth and provision for the nonce. There shall ye live and there shall ye die, and thence shall ye be brought forth.'

114 The widespread mythos of the supernatural origin of human arts and industries supports the animals' claim that culture and civilization, being adventitious to man's primitive nature, do not redound to human glory but are gifts of God's bounty. The earlier suggestion that sound arts deserve recognition is here sharply qualified.

115 Idrīs, sometimes identified with Elijah or al-Khiḍr, is the Islamic counterpart of Enoch or Hermes Trismegistus (as a scholium to the text preserved in the Dār Ṣādir edition notes). He is the bringer of occult knowledge to humankind and is cited in the Qur'an (19:57) as a prophet raised by God to a lofty place, along with Ishmael (Qur'an 21:85), worthy for his steadfastness or patience, a precious virtue in Muhammad's ethical scheme. Idrīs was a descendant of Seth and an ancestor of Noah. By one account he was close friends with an angel who bore him to the fourth heaven — the 'lofty place' of the Qur'anic allusion. His name is sometimes derived from that of Ezra, sometimes from that of the Christian apostle Andrew or the Andrew who was cook to Alexander the Great and becomes glorified in the Alexander romance; cf. J. Horovitz, *Koranische Untersuchungen* (Berlin: de Gruyter, 1926), p. 88. The name seems in fact to be a calque on the Hebrew for Enoch (Henoch), since both words denote learning and suggest esoteric learning. Idrīs becomes a central figure in hermetic Islamic thought. Ibn 'Arabī called him

relations between men and jinn through community of faith, law, submission, and religion.[116] The jinn returned to the realms of men and lived in concord with them from the time of the great Flood until the days of Abraham. But when Abraham was cast into the fire, men thought knowledge of the mangonel[117] had come to the tyrant Nimrod from the jinn.[118] And when Joseph's brothers cast him into the pit, this

---

'the prophet of the philosophers', taking the term 'philosopher' in a hermetic sense, referential to the lore and practices of theosophy — theurgy, astrology, alchemy — a sense preserved in references to the 'philosophers' stone'. Idrīs would thus be a natural conciliator of men and jinn.

116 Submission — the literal meaning of '*islām*', placing of one's life and destiny in God's care (see Qur'an 2:112). The term is used here generically to denote faith and trust, not just the faith of Muhammad's followers. In Islamic doctrine, Muhammad's teaching was precedented by numerous essays in essentially the same direction.

117 Warned of Abraham's subversive impact, Nimrod is urged by his people: 'Burn him, as he has burned our hearts!' — that is, by breaking their idols. Kisā'ī continues: 'Now Nimrod had an iron furnace; and whenever he grew angry with any of his subjects, he would order it lit, and that subject would be cast into it alive, to melt like lead. . . Wood was gathered for four years by men, women, children, and slaves. Then they set torch to it. The flames leapt up, and smoke rose to a height of four hundred cubits. When even a bird flew over, it caught fire and fell down dead. But they could find no means of getting Abraham into the fire. Satan appeared to them in the guise of an old man. . . he said to them, "Build a mangonel", and taught them how.' Translated after Thackston; *The Tales of the Prophets of al-Kisa'i*, p.147. The mangonel (*minjaniq*, from the Greek '*manganon*', meaning an 'engine'), is a catapult, a siege engine, used for casting great stones and other missiles in warfare and often described as a magical contrivance, as the connotations of the Greek term suggest.

118 According to the Qur'an (e.g., 21:51–70, 26:69–104), Abraham was cast into the flames for rejecting pagan worship. The Qur'anic narrative is laced with Midrashic accretions and coloured by Muhammad's changing relations with the Jews of Arabia. After Muhammad's break with the Jews of Medina and the reorientation of his followers towards Mecca, Abraham, the common forefather of the Arabs and Jews and founder of monotheism, takes on a more distinctively Islamic cast, founding a monotheistic cult centred in the Ka'ba and favouring Ishmael. The Ikhwān seem sensitive to the thought that Nimrod the Tyrant (as they consistently call him) reigned in their own Mesopotamian land. Their references to him as a persecutor bear overtones of a plea for toleration, especially by the contrast with Bīwarāsp the Wise, who generously welcomes all the diverse parties that appear before his court, urging them to speak freely and promising attentiveness to their arguments. The Ikhwān make explicit their plea for open mindedness in broad if somewhat cynical terms:

You must know that the human mind, before any knowledge or belief has

too was laid to the wiles of Satan, who was of jinni race.[119] When God sent Moses, he reconciled the jinn and Israel through religious faith and law,[120] and many of the jinn embraced his faith.

'In Solomon's time, God strengthened his dominion and subjected the demons and jinn to him.[121] Solomon subdued the kings of the earth,

---

arisen in it, is like a clean, white sheet of paper on which nothing has been written: once anything is written on it, whether true or false, it fills up the space, blocking anything else from being written, and it's hard to scratch out or erase. Likewise the mind: once it has attained any bit of knowledge or belief, habit or custom, that too becomes engrained; and, whether true or false, it is hard to uproot or erase, as the poet says:

> My passion for her came before I knew what passion was.
> It ravished my empty heart and took root within.

If things are as I describe them, dear brother, you should not trouble yourself with trying to improve dotty old men who have been committed from their youth to false beliefs, base habits, and vices. They'll only wear you out and not improve — or if they do improve, ever so gradually, it won't stick. You should focus on the young, whose breasts are unblemished and who are avid for higher culture and refinement, whose intellectual quest is just beginning, who are eager to find the pathway to the truth... and are not fanatical defenders of some school! (*Rasā'il*, Epistle 45, vol. 4, pp. 51–52; translation here is Goodman's).

119 The story of Joseph is told in the Qur'an, Sura 12. See Baiḍāwī, *Commentary on Sura 12 of the Qur'an*, ed. and tr. A. F. L. Beeston (Oxford: OUP, 1963).

120 Philosophically inclined Muslim thinkers view Moses, as Philo and al-Fārābī did: he was not merely a prophet but a lawgiver of the sort projected by Plato in his conception of the Philosopher-King. Earlier prophets, Maimonides explains, spoke of their personal spiritual experiences, addressing family members and others who came within range of their personalities. But Moses legislates for a nation. See *Guide* II.35–40; cf. Brannon M. Wheeler, *Moses in the Quran and Islamic Exegesis* (London: Routledge Curzon, 2002). Law, as the Ikhwān see it, links faith with action, becoming the moral and social interpretation and application of the truth discovered by spiritual insight. As in Fārābī's Platonizing account, belief and symbol, poetry, and rhetoric allow a prophetic lawgiver to bind human hearts to the practices leading to moral and intellectual, perfection, insofar as this is humanly possible.

121 Midrashic legends elaborate on Solomon's intimacy with the jinn, embroidering on the biblical ascription (1 Kings 5:9–11 in the Masoretic Text) of wisdom to the tenth-century BCE monarch of Israel. In 1 Kings 3:28 (MT), popular awe at Solomon's bold threat to cut the disputed babe in half, is early on read in supernatural terms. The lore of Sulaymān ibn Dā'ūd and the jinn enters Islam through the Qur'an and reverts to Midrashic and other sources and the fertile imagination of storytellers for constant enlargement of matter and detail, a process still visible in Kipling's delightful tale of the butterfly who stamped in the *Just So Stories*. For Solomon's divine inspiration, see Qur'an 2:102, 4:163, 6:84. At Qur'an 21:78–82, we read:

and the jinn boasted to mankind that he had achieved this by their help. Without their aid, they said, he would have been just another human king. The jinn led humans to believe that they had knowledge of the unseen. But, when Solomon died, and the jinn, still suffering their humiliating chastisements, knew nothing of his death, mankind realized that had the jinn possessed occult knowledge they would not have remained in such degrading torment.[122]

> *And David and Solomon, when they judged as to the tillage when the people's sheep strayed into it at night; and We confirmed their judgement. We gave Solomon to understand it, and gave them both judgement and learning. With David We subdued the mountains, that they might give praise, and the birds — We accomplished this. We taught him the art of making coats of mail for you, to protect you from your own violence. And are you thankful? And to Solomon We subjected the storm wind, to course, at his command, to the land We had blessed. For We knew all things. Some demons dived for him and did other work as well, as We watched over them.*

Cf. Qur'an 38:34–40. The subjection of the mountains reflects the poet's image of the mountains skipping like rams (Psalms 114:4–6). The Qur'anic passage reflects the tradition that David was a skilled armourer. As for the strayed sheep, the Muslim commentaries fill in the picture: a negligent shepherd had allowed his flock into a cultivated field, where they decimated the crops. David, according to the *tafsīr*, awarded the sheep to the field's owner. Solomon, just eleven at the time, wisely proposed that the sheep should be held by the farmer only until his losses were recouped, and David, sagely accepted the boy prince's judicious advice. Both father and son were inspired in their handling of the case.

122 See Qur'an 34:10–14:

> *We gave David of Our bounty: 'O ye mountains and birds echo back his song.' We made iron soft to him. 'Fashion ample coats of mail; measure out the links. And do what is right. I see what thou dost!' To Solomon We gave the wind, its morning course a month's journey, and its evening course a month's journey, and caused brass to flow for him from the font. Some of the jinn toiled before him by leave of his Lord, and any who turned from Our command We made to taste the chastisement of the Blaze. They made him whatever he pleased — shrines, images, basins like great troughs, and mountainous cauldrons. 'Work gratefully, O house of David. How few of My creatures know gratitude!' When We decreed his death nought showed them he had died but a tiny worm of the earth, that gnawed away his staff. Then, when he fell, the jinn realized that had they had knowledge of the unseen they would not have remained in such degrading torment.*

As William Montgomery Watt observes: 'The story is told that Solomon before his temple was completed, realized he was about to die and prayed to God that his death might be concealed from the jinn until their building of the temple was complete; then he died as he stood praying leaning on his staff, and his body remained standing for a year until a worm gnawed away the staff; by this time the temple was completed.' W. Montgomery Watt, *Companion to the Qur'an* (London: Allen Unwin, 1967), p. 196. In Islamic legends, it was a termite that

'Again, when the hoopoe brought his report of Bilqīs,[123] and Solomon said to the throng of jinn and men, *"Which of you will bring me her throne?"* The jinn bragged, and one sprite, Uṣṭur son of Māyān of Kaywān, said, *"I'll have it here before you rise from your place"* — that is, before court recesses. Solomon said, "I want it faster!" At that, *a man with knowledge of the Book*, Āṣaf son of Barkhiyya,[124] said, *"I'll have it here in the twinkling of an eye." And when he saw it already standing*

gnawed away Solomon's staff, allowing his jinni conscripts to realize that he was dead and make good their escape; see al-Kisā'ī, *Qiṣaṣ al-anbiyā'*, tr. Thackston, pp. 319–320. For the brass of Solomon's temple, see 2 Chronicles 4:18. As the Ikhwān understand the story, God gave Solomon a font of molten brass.

123 King Solomon's encounter with the Queen of Sheba (1 Kings 10:1–13, MT) is reported in Qur'an 27:15–45:

> *We gave knowledge to David and Solomon, and they said 'Praised be God who favoured us over so many of his faithful servants!' Solomon was David's heir. He said, 'O ye folk, we have been taught the discourse of the birds and given of all things — clearly an act of grace.' Mustered before Solomon were his hosts, jinn, men, and birds, advancing in battle array, until they came to the valley of the ants, and an ant said, 'Ants, get into your dwellings, lest Solomon and his troops trample you unawares.' He smiled, laughing at her words, and said, 'Lord, teach me to be truly grateful for Thy bounty toward me and toward my parents and to do what is right and pleasing to Thee. Enlist me, by Thy mercy, in the company of Thy righteous servants.' He reviewed the birds and said, 'Why do I not see the hoopoe? Is he missing? I shall surely chastise him sorely — or slay him, unless he has a good excuse!'*

The bird arrived not long after — with his report of Sheba; see Chapter 12 below. It is reported at 1 Kings 5:13 (MT) that Solomon discoursed of the trees, of the beasts, of the creeping creatures and of the fish, but the makers of legends took it that he spoke not *of* the birds and beasts but *with* them. The story of Solomon and the Queen of Sheba was a favourite of Muhammad's — perhaps because it brought the Biblical potentate into contact with Arabia — and a clear favourite of the Ikhwān, who are drawn by the role of the jinn in Solomon's service and the recurrent assertion of God's sovereignty, which is symbolized by the king's subjection of the jinn. The Qur'an and the embroideries on its narrative relish the contrast of Sheba's earthly (but highly portable) throne and the true and immovable might of God's throne. Since the Ikhwān regard the jinn as natural forms and forces, their subjection to Solomon is emblematic of the faustian position of *homo faber*, who may harness nature's powers with God's help but is lost without reliance on God's aid.

124 The biblical Āsaf (or Asaph) ben Berekhiah is listed among the Temple Levites carried off to Assyria (1 Chronicles 6:24, 15:17). Psalms 50 and 73–83 are ascribed to him in their titles, and he is called the father of the chronicler of Hezekiah's reign; 2 Kings 18:18, 37. In Jewish and Islamic lore he becomes Solomon's vizier.

steady at his side, he said, "This is by the grace of my Lord",[125] and he knelt in prayer. Man had clearly outdone the jinn. The court ended, and the jinn left, hanging their heads, the human rabble at their heels, tramping, gloating, and hooting at them.[126]

'After the events I have mentioned, a band of jinn escaped from Solomon, and one rebelled against him. Solomon sent troops after them and trained them to snare the jinn with spells, incantations, magic words, and revealed verses, using sorcery to confine them. He produced a book for this purpose, found in his treasury after his death. Until he died Solomon kept the rebel jinn at work with arduous tasks.

'When Christ[127] was sent, he called all creatures, men and jinn alike, to God and imbued them with yearning for Him. He showed them the way and taught them to mount to the Kingdom of Heaven. Several jinni bands embraced his faith. Keeping to a monastic path, they did rise up to heaven. There they overheard tidings among the celestial throng and relayed the reports to soothsayers.[128]

'When God sent Muhammad, God bless and keep him, the jinn were barred from eavesdropping and said, *We do not know whether evil is intended against those on earth or whether their Lord desires them to go right.*[129] Some jinni bands embraced Muhammad's faith and became good Muslims.[130] Ever since then, down to our own days jinni relations with Muslims have been peaceable.

---

125 Qur'an 27:38–40.

126 The humans are hardly good sports as the jinn perceive them. But the real lesson, learned at the jinn's expense was again God's sovereignty. Reliance on natural or magical forces is inevitably less efficacious than direct appeal to God, the source of all such powers. The jinni relied on his own power, which was derived from God. The human with knowledge of the Book appealed directly to God, avoiding obliquity. The weakness of the approach lies in making God just another tool — as in the use of God's name in kabbalistic theurgy, where it can be degraded to a mere magic spell. Legends place God's name on Solomon's seal. It keeps a jinni trapped for aeons in a bottle, announcing the subservience of magic to theism and demons to the divine — but at the risk of making God simply a super demon.

127 Muslims agree that Jesus was anointed, and recognize him as a prophet but deny his divinity. Kalonymos, in his Hebrew version of our story, omits the present references to Jesus.

128 See Qur'an 72:8–9.

129 Qur'an 72:10.

130 Qur'an 72:1–2.

'Assembly of jinn,' the jinni scholar concluded, 'do not antagonize them and spoil our relations with them. Don't stir up smouldering hatred or revive the ancient bias against us that is ingrained in their nature. For hatred is like the fire latent in stones[131] that appears when they're struck together: it lights the matches that can burn down houses and bazaars. God protect us from the triumph of the wicked and the sway of the iniquitous, which brings ruin and disgrace!'

When the King had heard this startling history, he bowed his head in thought. Then he said, 'Tell us, O wise one, what you think we should do in the case of these animals who have come seeking our protection? How can we let them leave content that our decision is just?'

The wise jinni replied, 'A sound view is reached only after much deliberation, diligent and thorough investigation, and study of the past.[132] I suggest the King hold a court of inquiry tomorrow, in the presence of the parties, and hear their arguments and explanations, so as to make clear to him all the aspects of the case. After that he will be able to deliberate on a course of action.'

The outspoken jinni said, 'If these beasts cannot hold their own rhetorically against the humans, for lack of clear and fluent speech and men best them with their glib tongues and their fine and facile explanations, do you think these animals should remain their prisoners, to be tormented by them forever?'

'No', he said. 'But the beasts must remain in durance and bondage until the cycle has run its course and resurrection is at hand. Then God will free and deliver them, just as he saved the House of Israel from the oppression of the House of Pharaoh,[133] the House of David from the tyranny of Nebuchadnezzar,[134] the House of Himyar from that of

131 See Anaxagoras, fragment 17, apud Simplicius' commentary on Aristotle's *Physics* I.163.20.

132 For the lessons of history, see notes 93 and 97 above.

133 See the Exodus story as recorded in the Qur'an 7:130–141, 10:90–94, etc.

134 Nebuchadnezzar is not named in the Qur'an. Some Islamic traditions make him a great grandson of Sennacherib or confound him with Cyrus or Ahasuerus. Bīrūnī strives heroically to disentangle the chronology, as Georges Vajda puts it; 'Bukht-naṣ(ṣ)ar', *EI2*, vol. 1, p. 1298.

Tubba',[135] the House of Sāsān from harassment by the Greeks,[136] and the House of 'Adnān[137] from the torment of Ardashīr.[138] The days of this world here below run in cycles allotted to its denizens, turning by God's leave and foreknowledge, and executing His pleasure, through the influences of the aspects of the stars as they revolve each 1,000 years, or 12,000 years, or 36,000 years, or 360,000 years, or each day of 50,000 years.'[139]

---

135 Qur'an 44:37, 50:14 alludes to Tubba', a recurrent name of the kings of Himyar who ruled in South Arabia from the late third to the early sixth century and conquered their Sabaean rivals not long before 300. In Islamic tradition the fall of Himyar is one of history's great object lessons.

136 Unlike Western histories that make, say, Marathon a great victory for civilization, the Ikhwān here seem more sympathetic to Iran.

137 'Adnān, thought of as a descendant of Ishmael, was the eponymous ancestor of the Northern Arabs according to the genealogy finalized by Ibn al-Kalbī around 800; see W. Caskel, "Adnān', *EI2*, vol. 1, p. 210.

138 Ardashīr (Artaxerxes) did battle with the Romans and built his empire on the ruins of the Seleucid successor state to Alexander's eastern conquests. For his reign, see Appendix C. Persian hegemony in Arabia ended decisively with the Muslim conquest of Iran after the Arab defeat of the Sāsānian forces at Qādisiyya in 635. The Ikhwān here picture both Persians and Arabs as liberated through the fortunes of war. The authors see freedom from alien hegemony as both just and natural, but they counsel patience until the epoch is fulfilled — hardly an unambiguously conservative, pacific, or quietist counsel.

139 The Ikhwān are thought to take their cycles from the Sindhind, a work adapted from the Brahmasphuta Siddhanta, composed in 628 by Brahmagupta in southern Rajastan, and brought by an embassy from Sind to the caliphal court at Baghdad in 773. Some Arabic authors thought '*sindhind*' meant 'eternal', since the work proposes a cosmos lasting 4,320,000,000 years. But the title, as David Pingree explains, was 'a clever calque (Sind and Hind) on *siddhanta* ("perfected")', a proud label typical of Hindu astrological works. Translated into Arabic by an Arab and an Indian, the work became the basis of the now lost work of al-Fazārī, an astronomer who developed astronomical tables and a manual for their use relying on Ptolemy and on a Sāsānian adaptation of Ptolemy's tables. The resulting Arabic text, also now lost, formed the core in turn of Khwārizmī's *Sindhind*, prepared in the 820s, which survives and was translated into Hebrew by Abraham ibn Ezra, and also into Latin. Within two centuries after Khwārizmī, advanced scholars like al-Bīrūnī, Pingree writes, saw his *Sindhind* as 'simply a curious antiquity'. But that text, revised at Cordoba around the time of the Ikhwān and further adapted in later generations, anchored European astronomy until the development of the Alphonsine tables in the fourteenth century. See D. Pingree, 'Sindhind', *EI2*, vol. 9, p. 640; Marquet, *La Philosophie*, p. 141. In the Ptolemaic system favoured by the Ikhwān, the motions of the heavens 'become slower and slower as one moves farther from the supreme heaven, which is the unerring sphere of diurnal movement', as Nasr writes. 'To this motion is added

Chapter 9
How the Assembly Sought to Divine the Secret Royal Counsels

That same day, while the King was closeted with his vizier, the humans met in a council of their own, seventy men of diverse lands, to consider the situation. One said, 'You've seen what went on today between us

---

the precession of the equinoxes, which is the rotation of the fixed stars about the signs of the Zodiac in the period which the Ikhwān consider to be 36,000 years. In fact, they equate the 'Great Year' of the Chaldeans (36,000 years, the time required for all the planets to be in conjunction at the spring equinox) with the time of revolution of the orb of the fixed stars found by Hipparchus to be also 36,000 years.' (Nasr, *Islamic Cosmological Doctrines*, pp. 79–80).
As the Ikhwān write, 'All that arises swiftly in this world lasts a short time and swiftly vanishes. . . . A slow movement of long duration that returns to its starting point after a long time is the course of the fixed stars about the sphere of the Zodiac, completed once in 36,000 years. . . . During this time span, civilization here in the world of generation and corruption shifts from one quarter to another. Continents replace seas, and seas replace dry land, mountains become seas and seas mountains. Every 3,000 years the fixed stars, apogees, and the nodes of the planets pass from one sign to the next, traversing each sign degree by degree. In 9,000 years they pass from one quadrant to the next. . . . So the zeniths of the stars and the incidence of their rays shift in relation to different spots on earth, changing the climate in diverse lands. . . . Through these remote and proximate causes, worldly sway passes from one folk to another, cultures rise and fall in sequence in the diverse quarters of the earth — all by the power that directs the astral conjunctions at regular times and sequences.' (*Rasā'il* [Cairo, 1928], Epistle 35, vol. 3, pp. 246–259, tr. after Nasr, *Islamic Cosmological Doctrines*, p. 80.)
For knowledge of marine fossils in mountains and other terrestrial areas, see ibid., p. 87. The precession of the equinoxes, calculated by Hipparchus between 147 and 127 BCE is today understood to result from the gradual shifting of the earth's axis, caused by the slightly oblate shape of our planet and leading to a movement by the earth's pole of one degree every 71.6 years. Some 5,000 years ago, the North Pole pointed at the star Thuban (Alpha Draconis); today, it sights Polaris. A precessional cycle is today calculated at some 25,765 years. Cosmic rhythms, being invariant, so far as ancient observers could determine, were at least from Aristotle's time (*Metaphysics* XII.6.1063a15–17; cf. *Physics* VIII.10.267b17) paradigms of the divine perfection of the cosmos. They were emblems of divine justice and invoked by Hellenistic philosophers as symbols if not engines of providence. The Ikhwān expect a moral as well as a physical balance of accounts to be struck by the completion of the celestial cycles. So, like evolutionary progressives, they temporalize the chain of being, but in terms of cycles, not progress. Cyclical history, therefore, might seem to have no end. But the Day of Judgement breaks the rhythm of the cosmic cycles that fold time into eternity and puts a close to history once it has served its purpose. Thus the mention of a day of 50,000 years, for that is the duration of the Day of Judgement according to the Qur'an (70:4).

and these slaves of ours. You've heard the arguments and the long speeches. Yet the case was not dismissed. What do you think the King has in mind?'

'We've no idea,' came the answer, 'but we suspect the King is unsettled and wrought up over this matter and will not sit tomorrow.'

Another said, 'I think he'll stay by himself with his vizier to seek counsel about the case.'

'In fact,' said a third, 'he'll probably gather the jurists to consult about it.'

'What do you suppose they'll advise him?' asked another.

Another offered, 'I think the King is friendly toward us. But I'm afraid the vizier leans the other way and will turn the King against our cause.'

'He's easily taken care of', the other said. 'We should give him a bit of a gift to improve his opinion of us and tilt him our way.'

'I'm worried about something else', said another.

'What's that?' they asked.

'The rulings of the jurists, the findings of the judge.'[140]

'They're easily handled. They should be given presents too, a little sop. Then they'll think better of us and find some loop-holes to help us out. They won't mind bending the rules.[141] Our problem, the one to watch out for, is that outspoken one. He's nobody's fool. He's hard-headed, independent, and wilful. And he's not afraid of anyone. If the King asks him for advice, I'm afraid he'll counsel him to help the slaves against us and teach him how to set them free.'

Another said, 'Just as you say. But if the King consults the philosophers and scholars, they're sure to disagree. Whenever scholars meet to consider some subject, each sees only one side of the issue and not what matters to another. So their counsels will conflict. They'll hardly reach a consensus.'[142]

---

140 A judiciary free of royal domination was an Islamic ideal, reflecting the role of jurists as exponents of religious law, which rulers ideally defend and enforce. The tensions between the normative and de facto roles of both groups were perennial concerns.

141 In the Aesopian context of the fable, this dig at jurists as a class will be taken amiss by jurists only at the risk of calling attention to their own problematic practices.

142 To philosophical sceptics, the conflict of opinions was a standard ground for

Another said, 'If the King consults jurists and judges, what do you think they'll advise about our case?'

'A jurist or judge could rule in just one of three ways', said another. 'Either the animals must be freed, or they must be sold for a mandatory settlement, or their lives must be eased with better treatment. The precepts of our law and our faith leave no alternative.'

'If the King consults his vizier,' another asked, 'what will he advise?'

Someone answered, 'I imagine he'll say, "These animals have appeared in our court seeking refuge and redress of wrongs. They're oppressed, and to aid the oppressed is a just king's duty. For kings are God's vice-regents on earth. He gave them dominion over His subjects and His land to rule justly and fairly as to His creatures' duties toward one another, to aid the weak, show mercy to the afflicted, crush injustice, and establish the sway of law in the world. Kings must judge among God's creatures in truth,[143] in gratitude for His blessings and in dread of the reckoning that He will demand of them on the morrow."'[144]

---

dismissing all claims to knowledge beyond the self-evident; see Sextus Empiricus, *Outlines of Pyrrhonism*, tr. R. G. Bury (Cambridge, MA: Harvard University Press, 1933). To the Ikhwān, the inference is not to scepticism but to a more syncretic and synthetic outlook. But the Brethren do seem to take some pleasure in pointing out the bootlessness of (much) philosophical disputation and the vanity of the pretensions of (most) professional thinkers.

143 In scriptural monotheism, justice and truth are traditionally fused.

144 The divine right of kings is founded in Muslim tradition on Qur'anic authority: *O ye who believe, obey God and obey the Messenger and those who have authority among you . . .* (4:59). Muhammad referred to his own role and specifically, as the balance of the verse makes clear, to the need for bringing disputes before duly designated leaders for adjudication, rather than, say, resorting to the tribal method of revenge. But jurists make this passage the *locus classicus* of the ordinance to obey established authorities and of the inference that to do so is to obey God. See al-Māwardī, *Aḥkām al-sulṭāniyya wa'l-wilāyāt al-dīniyya*, tr. Wafaa H. Wahba as *The Ordinances of Government* (Reading: Garnet, 1996), p. 3. The theory was naturally susceptible to abuse, but the Ikhwān here reject the notion of arbitrary power: authority is granted so that God's will regarding justice and compassion may be implemented in the world. No creaturely authority is absolute. If all power derives ultimately from God, it is also answerable to Him, as conscientious kings must remain constantly aware. For the development of the caliphate, see T. W. Arnold's classic study, *The Caliphate* (London: OUP, 1924; repr., New York: Barnes and Noble, 1966); H. A. R. Gibb, 'Al-Mawardi's Theory of the

'If the King orders the judge to rule in our case and the judge decides in one of these three ways,' asked another, 'what do you suppose we should do?'

They answered, 'We have no way of evading the rule of the King or the ruling of the judge. Judges are the prophets' successors, and kings are the defenders of the faith.'[145]

'Suppose the judge decides to release them and let them go free? What do we do then?'

'We shall say', answered another, 'that the animals are our slaves and chattels, inherited from our fathers and grandfathers. It's for us to decide whether or not to set them free.'

'And if the judge tells us to produce deeds, bills of sale, contracts, and witnesses attesting that they are our property, slaves inherited from our forefathers?'

'We'll say that we'll call our neighbours and reliable witnesses from our homelands.'

'But what if the judge says, "I can't accept one human's testimony in behalf of another that these beasts are your slaves. All men are their adversaries here, and partisan testimony is not admissible under the rules of our law"? Or suppose he says, "Where are the deeds, contracts, and bills of sale? Produce and present them, if you speak the truth"? Then what shall we do or say?'

No one in the assembly had an answer for that, except the Arab: 'We'll say we had these documents, but they were lost in the Flood.'[146]

Caliphate', in *Studies in the Civilization of Islam*, ed. S. J. Shaw and W. R. Polk (Boston: Beacon, 1962).

145 The clear division of authority: judges (not kings) are vice-regents of the prophets. Kings are protectors of the faith. The suggestion is that the title '*khalīfa*' — 'vice-regent', or successor to Muhammad — was usurped and belongs properly to jurists. Yet judges, too, fall short of the mark, being as susceptible to bribes as viziers. And here it is the monarch who orders or authorizes the judicial authorities to make a ruling.

146 By assigning this remark to the Arab delegate, the Ikhwān wryly suggest the tone of deprecation used against Arabs by Persians in the Shuʿūbiyya — the populist reaction against Arab hegemony that rose to a crescendo in the ninth century. In theory, Islam was egalitarian. But converts, known as *mawālī*, for their role as 'clients' to Arab tribes, often found themselves socially and economically disadvantaged in an Arab-dominated society and were not prone to suffer in silence. See H. A. R. Gibb, 'The Social Significance of the Shuʿūbiyya', in *Studies in the Civilization of Islam*, ed. Shaw and Polk (Boston: Beacon, 1962).

'And if he says, "Swear solemnly that they are your slaves"?'

'We'll say the burden of swearing falls on the respondent. We are the plaintiffs.'

'And if the judge administers an oath to these beasts, and they swear that they are not our slaves, then what do we do?'

One said, 'We'll say they've perjured themselves, and we have rational proofs and cogent demonstrations to show that they are our slaves.'

'And if the judge decides to sell them and make us take compensation? Then what do we do?'

The city folk said, 'Sell them and take the money. We'll make a profit.'

But the pastoral Arabs, Kurds, Turks, and nomads said, 'If we do that, by God, we perish! Great God! Don't even think about it!'

'How so?' the town folk asked.

'Why,' they said, 'if we did this, we'd be left with no milk to drink or meat to eat, no woollen clothes or blankets, no furnishings of hair or fleece, no shoes or sandals, no water skins, rugs, bedding, or covers. We'd be naked, barefoot, miserable, and sick. Death would be better for us than such a life. And the people of the cities would suffer the same fate. Don't sell them or free them, don't even consider it, and don't accept any judgement except to better their lives, lighten their load, and show them some kindness, sympathy, and pity. For they're flesh and blood like us. They feel and suffer. We have no special merit in God's eyes that He was rewarding when he subjected them to us;[147] and they haven't fallen short or sinned that they should be punished. But God does as He pleases and decrees as He wills. No one can alter His sentence or thwart His decree. None can contest His sovereignty or gainsay His knowledge. That is all I have to say. God forgive myself and you.'

147 The pastoral peoples are quicker than the city dwellers to recognize the dependence of man upon beast. The urban folk are engrossed with the abstractions of commerce. The pastoralists are also more readily sympathetic to the sentience of animals and hence, to the legitimacy of their demands for kinder treatment. Stock breeders cannot afford to risk their living capital, but they are also more ready to acknowledge that God's grace in subordinating animals to humans does not reflect man's absolute superiority in God's eyes. For, any advantage a creature enjoys must result from God's grace and thus cannot be its warrant!

Chapter 10

Meanwhile, after the King had risen from his audience and the court had dispersed, the beasts held a secret conclave. One said, 'You've heard the debates and arguments between us and our adversaries. A decision is yet to be reached. How do you view the situation?'

One animal said, 'We must return tomorrow and complain, weep, and demand redress. Perhaps the King will pity us and free us from bondage. He was touched today. Still, it is not proper for kings and judges to rule between claimants before clear proof and proper evidence have turned the issue one way or the other.[148] But arguments persuade only when presented clearly, articulately, and fluently. For, as the judge of judges, God's Apostle, says, "When you bring your cases before me, perhaps one of you is plainer in proof than another and I rule in his favour. So anyone I have allotted aught that is rightfully his brother's had best take none of it. All I have given him is his share in the Fire."[149] Considering that humans are more eloquent and articulate than we are, I fear the case might go against us and favour them when the arguments are heard.[150] So what course do you think best? Speak out.

148 The beast's point, often overlooked by today's advocates of animal rights, is that emotive appeals to sentiment, sympathy, and the visceral response of the flesh to the sentience of flesh have their place, but they are no substitute for reasoned argument. The observation marks a transition in the tale from appeals for sympathy to more objectively grounded arguments.

149 By ascribing the words to Muhammad rather than to God the text marks them as a hadith, a saying of Muhammad putatively passed down on oral authority before its transcription. The vast corpus of hadith materials, amounting to hundreds of thousands of sayings, was a fertile field in which the seeds of thoughts, from many sources, were cultivated — not least because hadith became a canon of authority in Islam second only to the Qur'an. There are several versions of the present hadith. The text cited here is closest to that attested in the *Muwaṭṭa'* of Mālik (*Kitāb al-Aqḍiyya*, Bāb 1). For other versions, see A. J. Wensinck, *Concordance et Indices de la Tradition Musulmane* (Leiden: Brill, 1992), vol. 1, p. 422.

150 It might seem that inarticulate creatures, lacking reason, cannot have rights like those of humans. But the exponents of animals often argue that poor, 'dumb' animals, unable to voice their needs and hurts, deserve solicitous concern all the more so for that. The Ikhwān archly treat the matter as a relative one. Setting aside the fiction of animal speech, the claim is that animals do communicate, albeit not as effectively as might be needed to sway a judge. As with the ancient Sophists, superior persuasive powers might make the unjust cause appear just. So speech, in a way, becomes irrelevant: truth, and not eloquence alone, must

For any one of us, if he reflect, might see things in a different light and have something to add, be it right or wrong.'[151]

One said, 'I think we should send messengers to all the other animal kinds sharing the news and asking them to send delegates and orators to aid us in the contest that we've entered. For every kind has its special virtues, its insights and discernment, its own kind of eloquence, argument, thought, and explanation. With enough helpers there might be hope of success and a chance to carry the day, for God helps whom He will and succours the God-fearing.'

The assembly agreed that this was sound, practical advice. So they sent six of their number to each of the six kinds of animals (for the seventh were already present, the beasts and cattle). One messenger went to the beasts of prey, one to the birds of prey, one to the fowl, one to the swarming creatures, one to the crawling creatures, and one to the aquatic animals.

Chapter 11
The Message Goes Out

Reaching Abū'l-Ḥārith the lion, king of the beasts of prey,[152] the messenger told him the news, how the delegates of beasts and cattle had gone to law with the human spokesmen before the King of the

prevail. Within the fiction, however, the problem of persuasion is resolved by the call for reinforcements. New delegates will complement and broaden the diverse viewpoints of the animals already present.

151 Diverse perspectives, rightly used, give wisdom, the animals suggest — a striking contrast with the narrow mindedness of human counsels, where each disputant sees things only from his own angle, so that diverse perspectives yield only the sort of dissension that the Ikhwān have already pilloried in human divergences of opinion. Consultation, as the text suggests, was a Muslim political ideal, harking back to the Arab tribal councils and commended by theorists as an antidote to less open and more authoritarian procedures. According to a hadith, a properly qualified decisor (*mujtahid*), using his own judgement in unresolved matters of practice is rewarded by heaven even if his ruling is erroneous; he earns a double reward if he decides rightly. See J. Schacht and D. B. McDonald, 'Idjtihād', *EI2*, vol. 3, p. 1026; J. Schacht, 'Khaṭa', *EI2*, vol. 4, p. 1101.

152 Isidore is among the many who call the lion the king of the animals, *Etymologies* 12.2.3–6. Cf. *Pañcatantra* I.14–15, ed. Olivelle, pp. 62–65. The Ikhwān, dividing the cares of rule, confine the lion's rule to the beasts of prey.

Jinn and had called on all other animal kinds for help. 'They sent me to ask you to send back with me a spokesman from the ranks of the beasts of prey to represent the members of his kind and argue for them when his turn comes to address the court.'

'What do the humans claim? What is their brief against the beasts and cattle?' the king asked the messenger.

'They claim', said the messenger, 'that we are their slaves and chattels, and that they are our masters and the masters of every other animal on the face of the earth.'

'How', roared the lion, 'do they boast themselves worthy to rule over us? Are they stronger or braver? Do they charge more boldly or lunge more fiercely? Do they bound more powerfully or take hold more tightly? Are they doughtier in battle, attacking, toppling, or standing firm? If they brag of any such powers, I'll call up my troops and rout them in a single charge. I'll send them flying in all directions!'

'Well,' said the messenger, 'some humans do boast of such qualities. But they also have arts and inventions, techniques and devices. They make sharp, pointed weapons like swords, spears, darts, lances, knives, bows and arrows, and shields. They protect themselves against the claws and teeth of beasts of prey by making padded clothing and breastplates, helmets, armour, and coats of mail, which the teeth of carnivores cannot pierce and even the sharpest claws cannot penetrate. Besides, they have ways of catching predators and other wild beasts — buried traps, pits camouflaged with earth and grass, gins and snares, nooses, toils, and other devices that wild animals would not detect and so cannot avoid or escape once fallen foul of them.[153]

---

153 Galen writes of man in *De Usu Partium*:

> ... he is an intelligent animal and alone, of all creatures on earth, godlike — in place of any and every defensive weapon Nature gave hands, instruments necessary for every art and useful in peace no less than in war. Hence he did not need horns as a natural endowment, since, whenever he desired, he could grasp in his hand a weapon better than a horn; for certainly swords and spears are larger weapons than horns and better suited for inflicting wounds. Neither did he need hoofs, for clubs and rocks can crush more forcibly than any hoof. . . . But, you say, a lion is swifter than a man. Well, what then? With his skilful hands he has tamed the horse, an animal swifter than a lion, and, using a horse, he both escapes and pursues the lion, from his lofty seat striking down at him below. Surely, then, man is not naked, vulnerable, defenceless, or unshod, but, whenever he wishes, he may have

'Still, the decision in the dispute before the King of the Jinn rests on none of these things, but only on arguments and evidence clearly set forth and fluently expressed, preponderance of intellect, and subtlety of discernment.'

Having heard the messenger's report as well as that statement, the lion thought for a time and then gave his order. A herald issued the summons, and before the king his forces gathered: every sort of predator and untamed carnivore — tigers, cheetahs, bears, jackals, wolves, foxes, wild cats, hyenas, all sorts of apes and weasels — in short, every meat-eating beast with claws or fangs.

When all were assembled before their king, he told them the news the messenger had brought and said, 'Which of you will go to represent our kind? We promise him whatever prize or mark of favour he desires if he makes our case and prevails in the dispute.'

For a while the beasts of prey were silent, wondering if any of them were fit for such a business. Then the tiger said, 'You are our king and master. We are your flock,[154] your subjects and troops. A king should consult with those who have insight and expertise about a subject and

> a corselet of iron (an implement harder to damage than any kind of skin), and sandals, weapons, and vestments of all sorts at his disposal. . . . With these hands of his, a man weaves himself a cloak and fashions hunting-nets, fish-nets and traps, and fine-meshed bird-nets, so that he is lord not only of animals upon the earth, but of those in the sea and the air also. But, being also a peaceful and social animal, with his hands he writes laws for himself, raises altars and statues to the gods, builds ships, makes flutes, lyres, knives, fire-tongs, and all the instruments of the arts, and in his writings leaves behind him commentaries on the theories of them. Even now, thanks to writings set down by the hand, it is yet possible for you to converse with Plato, Aristotle, Hippocrates, and the other Ancients.' (*De Usu Partium* I.2, tr. May, pp. 68–69).

But as Galen adds, 'it is not, as Anaxagoras says, because he has hands that man is the most intelligent, but, as Aristotle says, because he is the most intelligent that he has hands.' See Prologue of the Ikhwān, note 19 above. Cf. *Pañcatantra* I.75, ed. Olivelle, p. 83.

154 The image may seem an odd one for predators, but it calls attention to a key thesis of the Ikhwān. The idea of a ruler as shepherd and his subjects as his flock is developed in Plato (*Republic* I.342–343) and in the pastoral imagery of both Testaments, notably, for instance, in Psalm 23. The relation may be read as exploitative or nurturant. Hence Socrates' difference with Thrasymachus. The more cynical classical authors think of a herd rather than a flock. The Ikhwān side with Plato.

then command and forbid accordingly, ordering things as he ought; and the subjects must hear and obey. For a king is to his subjects as a head is to its body; the subjects are the limbs and organs. When each plays his part, things are ordered aptly and well for the sound working of the whole and the welfare of all.'

'What are the special roles and terms by which you say a king and his subjects are bound?' the lion asked the tiger. 'Will you spell them out for us?'[155]

'Certainly', said the tiger. 'A king must be acute, cultured, understanding, courageous, just, compassionate, high-minded, sympathetic, resolute, stern, deliberate, thoughtful, and insightful.[156] Beyond that, he must be kindly to his subjects, forces, and vassals, tender as a father is to his little children, and as firm in protecting their interests. The subjects, troops, and vassals, for their part, must render unquestioning obedience and devotion to their king and loyalty to his supporters. Each subject should make known any skills or strengths he has to offer. Then the king will know the character and capabilities of each and can place each in the post where he is most able, and employ him where he is best suited to serve.'[157]

155 The organic state of the Ikhwān does not warrant absolute power. To them no creaturely power is unconditioned or unconditional. But conditional rule, we note, is the core idea of constitutionalism. Absolute authority is largely a modern notion, linked to the rise of the sovereign secular state. A feudal state — with its vassals, troops, and supporters — inevitably harbours multiple authorities, much to the consternation of early statists. In feudalism, a monarch's vassals are quite literally his constituents, a fact that both he and they can never, in practice, forget. In a state founded on religious claims, only God is absolute. But, as T. S. Eliot knew well, between the idea and the reality falls the shadow: clerics in such a state are the natural exponents — or critics — of its authority. They may curb its excesses. But establishment puts them at risk of co-optation by state power, security renders them subject to decadence and complacency, and the high claims of their spiritual authority tempt them sorely to abuse the powers reserved to them.

156 For the qualifications of the ideal ruler, see Abraham Melamed, *The Philosopher King in Mediaeval and Renaissance Jewish Political Thought* (Albany, NY: SUNY Press, 2003); pp. 13–21 deal with the Greek and Islamic sources, followed up in the ensuing pages.

157 In court, then, a meritocracy is envisioned to perform the work of government. Again the Ikhwān echo Plato's thought, that each member of a society should serve where he is best suited (*Republic* II.370–371) — and not just where he is, say, best connected. Plato's modest but still revolutionary proposal takes on

'What you say is true and well put', said the lion. 'Bless you as a wise counsellor to your king, his peers, and the offspring of his race. What help, then, can you offer in this case to which we are called and in which our aid is sought?'

'May your Majesty's star rise and his hand be victorious', said the tiger. 'If force and power to strike and overwhelm with fierce lunges or a penchant for hatred, rancour, and wrath will help, I'm the one for it.'[158]

'No,' said the king, 'none of the qualities you mention will win the day in this matter.'

The cheetah said, 'If springing, bounding, seizing, and holding are needed, I'm the one for it.'

'No', said the king.

The wolf said, 'If bold raids and daring assaults are called for, I'm the one.'

'No', said the king.

The fox said, 'If wiles and ruses, sly tricks and dodges, twists and deceptions will help, then I'm the one.'

'No', said the king.

The weasel said, 'If the mission will succeed by stealthy spying and plundering, I'm the one.'

'I'm afraid not', said the king.

The ape said, 'If impudence, mimicry, tomfoolery and play, or dancing to the beat of a drum or tambourine will help, I'm the one for it.'

'No', said the king.

The cat said, 'If fawning, begging, and stand-offishness will help, I'm the one.'

'No', said the king.

The dog said, 'If I can help by wagging my tail and barking or by keeping watch, tracking, or howling, then I'm the one.'

The king said, 'No.'

---

some prominence in Galen's summary of the *Republic*, well known in Arabic. Averroes focuses on it with fascination in his commentary, ed. and tr. E. I. J. Rosenthal (Cambridge: CUP, 1966), pp. 113–114

158 Pliny (*Natural History* VIII.25) and Isidore (*Etymologies* 12.2.7) both report the great speed of the tiger.

The hyena said, 'If digging up graves and dragging off corpses, or taking down hounds and horses, or bad breath will help, I'm the one.'[159]

'No', said the king.

The rat said, 'If looting and destruction, gnawing and shredding, pilfering and damaging could help, I'm the one.'

'No', said the king. 'Nothing you've mentioned will help.'

Turning to the tiger, the lion, said, 'The traits, temperaments, and natures that these parties have claimed for themselves would be useful only to human kings' forces and to human rulers, commanders, generals, military officers, and war leaders. They are the ones who need such powers most and are most suited for them. For such men may have human shapes and bodies, but their souls are the souls of savage beasts.[160] Still, the learned assemblies of scholars, jurists, and philosophers — persons of wisdom, science, understanding, insight, discernment, and reflection — have characters and dispositions like the angels who dwell in the heavens and govern the spheres, the hosts of the Lord of the universe. Who, then, do you think most fit to represent our community?'

'What you say is true, your Majesty', said the tiger. 'But I'm afraid the scholars, jurists, and judges of mankind have left the path you call angelic for more demonic ways. They vie for rule and sway and quarrel with rancour, hatred, and ill will. They dispute with ugly screaming and shouting. You can see them in the courts of law showing the same

---

159 The hyena's bad breath is a reminder of the tale of 'The Innocent Camel' in *Kalīla wa-Dimna*. See *Pañcatantra* I.365–395, ed. Olivelle, pp. 178–187. There, the crow, wolf, and jackal all volunteer to be eaten by the starving lion, so as to deceive the camel into making the same offer and free the lion of his promise of friendship to the camel, allowing him to eat the foolish dromedary and share the meat with them. The crow's sly offer is declined, since he is too small. The wolf is excused, since his meat is deadly. The jackal is turned down because his bad breath suggests that his flesh is putrid. But the camel's offer, to his dismay and the delight of the plotters, is accepted. Here, the hyena takes the place of the jackal.

160 The charge that animals are savage is turned back upon humans: animals don't wantonly slay their own kind or kill at all except for food and in self-defence. For a modern critique of the expressive force and descriptive weaknesses of the notion of animal savagery, see Mary Midgley, 'The Concept of Beastliness', *Philosophy*, 48 (1973).

malice and aggressiveness that you've described.[161] They've abandoned all justice, fairness, and courtesy.'[162]

'True', said the king. 'But a royal envoy must be calm and shrewd, upright, high-minded, disinterested, and fair. Whom, then, do you think we should send as our delegate and spokesman? Is there no one among all those present fit for this mission?'

Chapter 12
The Traits of a Good Envoy

'Can you explain, your Majesty,' the tiger asked, 'just what qualities are called for in an emissary?'

'Yes', said the king of the carnivores. 'First, he must be a person of intelligence and character, well spoken, eloquent, and articulate, able to remember what he hears, and cautious in what he answers. He must be loyal, faithful, true to his word, circumspect, and discreet, adding nothing to his message but what he sees is in the sender's interest. He must not be grasping or avaricious. For a greedy person who meets with generosity from his hosts may shift his loyalties and betray the sender, adopting the new country for the good life he enjoys there, the blandishments and gratifications he finds. Rather, he must be faithful to his sender, his brethren, countrymen, and kind, deliver his message, and return promptly to those who sent him with a full report from start to finish of what passed on his mission, omitting nothing for fear of causing displeasure. For clarity is the whole duty of a messenger.'

'Well,' the lion asked the tiger, 'which of all these animals do you find apt to the task?'

'Who but the good and virtuous Kalīla, brother of Dimna?' said the tiger.[163]

---

161 Ghazālī judged most of the doctors of religion (*'ulamā'*) in his day more worldly than godly. Plato denounced philosophers yet more sweepingly, even as he reasoned that they (if genuinely wise) are the rightful kings; see Plato, *Republic* I.473–496.

162 Courtesy — culture (*adab*) — in the tiger's list of royal traits, is a secular virtue; cf. the Greek *paideia*. See also Goodman, *Islamic Humanism*, pp. 83–84, 101–113, etc.

163 The original Kalīla was virtuous, although Dimna, his brother was cunning but hardly good. The Persian author, Rūzbih, known in Arabic as Ibn al-Muqaffa',

produced the book *Kalīla wa-Dimna*, based on a sixth-century Pahlavi translation of the second-century BCE Sanskrit fables of Bidpai. The Sanskrit text, the *Pañcatantra*, is edited and translated by Patrick Olivelle as *Five Discourses on Worldly Wisdom* by Vishnu Sharman (New York: NYU Press, 2006). Ibn al-Muqaffa''s Arabic fables were translated into Syriac, Hebrew, Farsi, and Turkish. The Farsi version, then translated into French, was used by La Fontaine in preparing the second edition of his *Fables*. African versions of the Arabic appear to have influenced Joel Chandler Harris' Uncle Remus stories, and a Spanish version from the Arabic was prepared (ca. 1251) in the translation school at Toledo sponsored by Alfonso X of Castile, known as The Scholar (El Sabio). This was the first lengthy prose work to appear in the Spanish vernacular. John of Capua, a Christian convert from Judaism, made a Latin version of the Hebrew translation (prepared in the early thirteenth century by one Rabbi Joel). The Latin was widely read and translated into most European languages. Sir Thomas North made an English version from it in 1569 or 1570. See *La version arabe de Kalīlah et Dimnah*, ed. Louis Cheikho (Beirut: Catholic University Press, 1905), based on a manuscript dated 1539, and collated with a Beirut edition of 1888. See also *The Fables of Kalilah and Dimna*, tr. S. S. Jallad (London: Melisende, 2002). The Ikhwān tip their hats to Ibn al-Muqaffa' as their predecessor in Aesopian satire. Part of what they owe to him is their tone, and the conceit of a court of animals and their kings and courtiers. They take their pen name from an epithet given to a body of animals mentioned in the 'Tale of the Ring-Dove'. Ibn al-Muqaffa' was a disciple of the Umayyad author of the earliest Arabic prose works. He himself set the patterns of the Persian mode in court literature for Arabic writers, fusing the two senses of *adab*, courtesy and literary urbanity, in a single medium of polite letters, the literature of the 'secretarial school'. It is doubtful that Ibn al-Muqaffa' was a whole-hearted Muslim. The fact that he was executed makes the tribute to him by the Ikhwān, by casting Kalīla as a paragon of urbanity, all the more telling. We have already cited van Gelder's finding that animals do not regularly speak in Arabic literature before the appearance of *Kalīla and Dimna*. The same author notes (p. 330) that 'more or less fully developed Arabic debates apparently exist only from about the middle of the ninth century', although the genre flourishes after about the year 1000. In literary debates, he writes, there are typically two or more adversaries speaking in turn before some arbiter or umpire, each vying for recognition of their superiority. The arguments swing between rhetoric and reason, and the speakers often open their remarks with a proem, a convention observed by most of the animal and human speakers in our fable. Ancestral to the debate genre, which often became a playful literary exercise, are the panegyrics, boasts, and lampoons of the pre-Islamic poets. Van Gelder notes the contest between spring and autumn attributed to al-Jāḥiẓ (d. 868) but probably written by a Persian around 1000. A lost debate between the cosmetics civet and musk may well be by Jāḥiẓ, however. Jāḥiẓ's essay 'On Singing-Girls', ed. and tr. A. F. L. Beeston (Warminster: Aris and Phillips, 1980), takes the form of a semi-ironic defence of an art widely regarded as improper by more purist and puritanically minded Muslims. Among the topics contested in the epistles of Jāḥiẓ are: the merits of winter versus summer, belly versus back, blacks versus whites, and (in the *Book of Animals*) the relative merits of dogs, cocks, sheep, goats, etc. The Ikhwān emulate this sort of by-play, and echo the

'What do you say to what he says of you?' the lion asked the jackal.

'God requite him', said the jackal, 'and favour his watering hole! He spoke as befits his grace and generosity.'

'So you will go as our spokesman?' asked the king. 'You'll be well rewarded if you return successful.'

'Your Majesty, I hear and obey', said the jackal. 'But I don't see how I'll manage with all the enemies I have there of our own kind.'

'What enemies have you there of your own kind?' asked the lion.

'Dogs, your Majesty', said the jackal.

'Indeed', said the king. 'What of them?'

'Well,' said the jackal, 'have they not sheltered with humans and turned ally to them against all beasts of prey?'

'What induced them to do that?' asked the king. 'What came over them to make them leave their own kind and side with others who are not like them against their own?'

No one knew but the bear. He said, 'I have some idea of what moved them to do this.'

'Tell us,' said the king, 'so that we too may know the explanation.'

'I shall, your Majesty', said the bear. 'Dogs were drawn to the precincts and abodes of men simply by their kindred nature and character. With men they found food and drink that they relish and crave — and a greedy, covetous, ignoble, stingy nature like their own. The base qualities they found in men are all but unknown among carnivores. For dogs eat putrid meat from the carcasses of slaughtered animals, dried, stewed, roasted, salted or fresh, good or bad. They eat fruit, vegetables, bread, milk (sweet or sour), cheese, butter, syrup, oil, candy, honey, porridge, pickles, and every other sort of food that humans eat, which most carnivores would not eat and do not know. They are so greedy, gluttonous, and mean that they cannot allow a wild beast into a town or a village, lest it compete with them for something there. So if a fox or jackal happens to go into a village at night to steal a hen, a cock, or

premise of Jāḥiẓ's essay 'On Lads and Lasses', that boy-lovers do not share the tastes of those who prefer girls (van Gelder, pp. 333–334). But in the present *risāla* of the Ikhwān, the animals are not mere objects of praise. For the most part they speak up for themselves. After all, the stakes are higher for them than they are, say, for civet and musk.

a cat, or even drag off some discarded carcass or scrap of meat from a dead animal, or a shrivelled piece of fruit, just see how the dogs set upon him, chase him, and drive him out! They are so wretched, lowly, abject, beggarly, and covetous that when they see a human being, man, woman, or child, holding a roll, or a scrap of bread in his hand, or a date, or any morsel, they beg for it and follow him about, wagging their tails, bobbing their heads, gazing up into his eyes, until the person feels embarrassed and throws it to them. Then see how they run for it and quickly snatch it, lest another reach it first. All these low qualities are found in humans and dogs. So it was their kindred nature and character that led dogs to leave their own kind and shelter with men, as their allies against the hunting animals, who were of their own race.'

'Besides dogs,' asked the king, 'who else lodges with men?'

'Cats, among others', said the bear.

'Why did the cats seek shelter with humans?' asked the king.

'For the same reason', answered the bear, ' — a character like that of man. For cats too are greedy and gluttonous, avid for the same foods and drinks as the dogs crave.'

'What sort of life have they with men?' asked the king.

'Somewhat better than dogs. For cats are allowed into their houses. They sleep in people's chairs and under their covers, come to the table, and are given food and drink by their masters. Sometimes, if they get the chance, they steal a morsel from the master. But dogs aren't allowed into men's homes or onto their seats. That's why there's such fierce envy and enmity between cats and dogs. When a dog sees a cat coming out of a man's house, he attacks as though wanting to catch her, tear her to bits, and devour her. And when a cat sees a dog, she bristles, arches, and spits in his face. All this is done out of hostility, rancour, and jealousy arising from the rivalry of cats and dogs for human favour.'

'Do you know of any other hunting animal who has taken shelter among men?' the lion asked the bear.

'Mice and rats enter human dwellings, houses, shops, and storerooms, but by stealth, not as companions.'

'Then what makes them do it?'

'An appetite for the variety of human foods and drinks.'

'What other hunting animals enter human houses?'

'Weasels, as robbers, to ferret things out and steal them away.'

'Who else?'

'No one else but captives like apes and cheetahs,[164] which they take by force.'

'How long', asked the king, 'have dogs and cats lived among men?'

'Since the sons of Cain joined forces against the sons of Abel', the bear replied.

'Tell us how that came about.'

'When Cain killed his brother Abel,[165] the sons of Abel sought to avenge their father. They made war on the sons of Cain, and the two sides slaughtered each other. But Cain's family defeated Abel's, put them to flight, and plundered their wealth, including their sheep and

---

164 The cheetah (*fahd*, cognate with the Latin '*pardus*'), *Acinonyx jubatus*, confounded with the panther or leopard since ancient times, is distinctive in form and habit. Cheetahs have a dog-like cranium and teeth; their claws are non-retractile. Unlike the leopard (*nimr*, Panthera pardus), lion (*asad*, Panthera leo), and tiger (*babr*, again Panthera leo — for lions and tigers can be interbred), cheetahs do not tear and rend their prey. So Sharīʿa law permits their use in the hunt. DNA analysis by Stephen J. O'Brien traces cheetahs to an origin in North America, where the extinct ancestors of today's species diverged from a stock common to the puma and jaguar six to eight million years ago. Cheetahs returned to the Old World by the Bering land bridge some three million years ago. They died out in the Western hemisphere and gradually migrated to their present diminished and diminishing habitats in Asia. Using their great stride to run down rather than stalk their prey, cheetahs achieve speeds of 60 mph or more. Normally nocturnal hunters, cheetahs were long noted for their daytime drowsiness but prized for their speed and grace and domesticated for hunting as early as 3000 BCE, as shown by the image of a leashed, hooded cheetah on a Sumerian royal seal. In his article 'Fahd', *EI2*, vol. 2, p.738, F. Viré vividly describes how cheetahs were captured and trained to mount and dismount the crupper of their master's horse in the opulent hunts of which Arab and other eastern princes were enamoured. Each new generation was taken in the wild, since the cheetahs did not breed in captivity.

165 The Ikhwān supply the names of Cain and Abel, who are not named when the Qur'an (5:27–31) tells their story and reports God's sentence: whoever slays a soul, save to avenge another soul or for corruption on earth, is as if he had slain all mankind; and whoso saves a life is as if he had saved all mankind (5:32). The trope is Mishnaic (Sanhedrin 4.5), from the instructions to a witness in a capital case, although the Qur'an adds the exceptions and drops the biblical proof-text: 'the bloods of thy brother cry out to me from the ground' (Genesis 4:10) — the use of the plural affording the spring for the rabbis' inference that Cain shed not only Abel's blood but that of all the progeny he might have fathered.

cattle, camels, horses, and mules. Grown rich, they began giving parties and feasts, for which they slaughtered many beasts, throwing the heads, shanks, and entrails about their towns and settlements. The dogs and cats, transported at the sight of such abundance and luxury, left their own kind and went over to man.[166] They have remained man's allies ever since.'

When the lion had heard the bear's account of these traits, he said, 'There is no power and no strength but in God,[167] sublime and exalted. *His we are, and to Him do we return.*'[168]

Again and again he repeated the phrase, until the bear said, 'What troubles you, good king? Why are you so disheartened by the parting of dogs and cats from their kind?'[169]

'It's not for the loss of them', said the king. 'But the wise say that nothing is more dangerous to a king or more harmful to him and his subjects than deserters from his ranks. When a vassal turns renegade he betrays his king's secrets, his habits, methods, and blind spots. Defectors make known to the enemy who is trustworthy in the king's army and which of his subjects is a traitor. They point out hidden paths and divulge the subtle tactics a king uses. All this is ruinous to kings and their forces. May God not bless dogs and cats!'

'Your Majesty,' said the bear, 'God has already answered your prayer and done as you ask. He has taken the blessing from their strain and transferred it to sheep.'

'How so?' asked the king.

'Why, because a single bitch is mounted by many males and suffers violent strain and stress, pushing and pulling. Finally, she gives birth

---

166 The bear's account anticipates the findings of today's ethologists, who believe that dogs essentially domesticated themselves, drawn to human habitations by the abundance of waste meat.

167 The phrase is a well-known hadith, echoing Qur'an 18:39 and 2:165.

168 *We will surely test you with something of fear and hunger, loss of goods, and lives, and fruits. But give the news to those who steadfastly endure, who say when stricken by misfortune, 'God's we are and to Him do we return', that their Lord's blessings and mercy are upon them — and they are right!* Qur'an 2:155–156.

169 Edward Lane's *The Manners and Customs of the Modern Egyptians* (London: Everyman, 1963), pp. 333–334, amply illustrates how pregnant with connotations fixed pious phrases can be. Here, as the bear senses, the lion expresses consternation in language commended by the Qur'an.

to eight pups or more. Yet you do not see dogs in town or country in such herds as the sheep in the country, even though countless sheep are slaughtered daily in city and village, and sheep bear only one or two lambs a year. The reason is the harm so often suffered by young dogs and cats, even before they're weaned. The highly disparate foods they eat make them vulnerable to a great many illnesses that we hunting animals never suffer.'

At that the lion said to Kalīla, 'Go with Godspeed to the court of the King. Convey to him the message I have given you.'

Chapter 13

When the messenger reached the Simurgh, king of the birds,[170] that

170 The Simurgh, a mighty bird of Persian myth, nests on a peak in the Elburz mountains, the chain grazing the sky that separates the central plateau of Persia from the Caspian depression. Although never seen by human eyes, he darkens the heavens with his wings. His feathers have magical healing powers, a power preserved from the ancient Avestan myths where the Simurgh first takes flight. For rescuing and raising the exposed infant Zāl, the father of Rustam, the great hero of Firdawsī's *Shahnameh*, he is hailed as 'King of Birds' (Shah Murgh), 'heaven-blessed with strength and wisdom, help of those in need, benefactor of the worthy and comfort of the afflicted'. The Simurgh bears Rustam to a distant tree from whose branches he fashions the arrow with which he slays Isfandiyār. See Appendix C and Edward G. Browne, *A Literary History of Persia*, vol. 1, p. 121; F. C. de Blois, 'Sīmurgh', *EI2*, vol. 9, p. 615; Olga M. Davidson, *Poet and Hero in the Persian Book of Kings* (Ithaca, NY: Cornell University Press, 1994), pp. 4, 23. The mythical raptor of the Avesta was fused in legend with the phoenix and the divine and royal bird Garuda, who carries Vishnu in Hindu myth. The shifting identities respond to the demands of diverse narratives. In the Sanskrit *Pañcatantra*, birds bring a complaint to Garuda, but in the Old Syriac version, Garuda has become the Simurgh. In Ibn al-Muqaffa''s Arabic rendering, the bird is the eagle/phoenix. Tha'labī calls it a phoenix (*'anqā'*) when describing pre-Muslim beliefs. In the *Risālat al-ṭayr*, dubiously ascribed to Aḥmad al-Ghazālī or Muḥammad al-Ghazālī, the birds of the allegory embark on a quest for the Simurgh, emblematic of the Sufi search for God. 'Aṭṭār elaborates on the theme in his Persian poem *Manṭiq al-ṭayr*, the *Discourse of the Birds*. The Simurgh, 'from which souls emanate,' Henry Corbin writes, 'is also a figure of Gabriel the Archangel, Active Intelligence and Holy Spirit' — the fount of revelation; *Avicenna and the Visionary Recital*, tr. W. R. Trask (London: Routledge and Kegan Paul, 1960), pp. 182–183; cf. pp. 198–203. Suhrawardī expands on the symbolism of the Simurgh as an emblem of the Active Intellect, who brings down inspiration from his nest atop the mythical Mount Qāf: 'All are full of him, but he is empty of all. All knowledge emanates and derives from his shrill cry'; Suhrawardī, *The Philosophical Allegories and Mystical Treatises*, ed. and tr.

king commanded a crier to summon all species of birds from land and sea, mountain, and plain. They came in numbers God alone could count. The king told them the tidings the messenger had brought, how the animals were gathering before the King of the Jinn to contest the human claim to them as slaves and servants.

Then the Simurgh said to the peacock, his vizier, 'Which of the eloquent, talking birds is best suited for us to dispatch as our delegate in the dispute with the humans?'

'A great many are suitable', replied the peacock.

'Name them for me, that I may know which ones they are.'

'There's the scouting hoopoe, the muezzin cock, the homing pigeon and the calling partridge, the singing pheasant and the preaching lark, the miming bulbul and the building swallow, the soothsaying raven, the watchful crane, the cheery sandpiper, the saucy sparrow, the green woodpecker, the mournful ring-dove,[171] the journeying wood-pigeon, the Meccan turtle-dove, the mountain finch, the Persian starling, the quail of the plains and the stork in his ramparts,[172] the magpie of the garden, the duck of Kaskar, the heron of the shore and his brother Abū Timar, the meadowlark from the dell, the cormorant from the sea, the ostrich of the desert, and that fluent songster the nightingale.'

'Point them out to me,' said the Simurgh to the peacock, 'so I may see them one by one, study each, learn his qualities, and decide if he's suited to this mission.'

Wheeler M. Thackston (Costa Mesa, CA: Mazda, 1999), p. 92. With Suhrawardī, the hoopoe, too, is an emissary of emanation, moulting to be reborn as the next Simurgh, with the humbler fowl's new status foreshadowed in the hoopoe's scouting for King Solomon. See Chapters 8 and 36 below and above. For the Simurgh's later linkage to Shi'i imams, see Corbin, *En Islam iranien: Aspects spirituels et philosophiques* (Paris: Gallimard, 1971), vol. 2, p. 231.

171 The ring-dove was thought, as late as the beginnings of the twentieth century, simply to express emotion in its cooing, often answered by a neighbouring ring-dove. The behaviour was in fact, as Hartshorne puts it, 'a startlingly clear case' of territoriality: the ring-dove's mournful tones are declaring territory, and the answering bird's 'counter-singing' makes a corresponding claim nearby. See *Born to Sing*, pp. 69–70.

172 The stork, according to tradition, fortifies its nest — building it in a high place — to protect its young. See Abū Ḥayyān al-Tawḥīdī, 'The Zoological Chapter', tr. L. Kopf, *Osiris*, 12 (1956), § 158; for storks and cranes, cf. Isidore, *Etymologies* 12.7.14–17.

'Surely, your Majesty. The scouting hoopoe, friend of Solomon son of David, is that personage standing in the particoloured, patched, and foul cloak with the hood pulled over his head, bobbing as if bowing and bending in prayer.[173] He commands good and forbids evil. It is he who told Solomon: "*I apprehend what you do not, and bring you news from Sheba, sure. I have found a woman ruling them, blessed with all things, and she has a splendid throne. She and her folk bow to the sun instead of God. Satan has made their doings seem fair to them and turned them from the true path. For they are misguided in not bowing to God who reveals what is hidden in heaven and on earth and knoweth what you conceal or reveal...*"[174]

'The cock who summons to prayer is that figure, perched on the wall, with the red beard, the crenellated crown, and the red eyes, his wings outspread and tail raised up like a banner. He is zealous and generous, highly devoted to God's orisons. For he knows the hours of prayer and wakes the neighbourhood to remind them tunefully that dawn has come.[175] In his daybreak call to prayer he says:

---

173 Solomon relied on a hoopoe to scout water for his forces, using its fabled powers to see water through the earth. In one legend, the bird invites the king and his host to a feast on an island and then throws a single locust into the sea, saying, 'Now eat, prophet of God. If there is not meat enough, there's still plenty of sauce!' Solomon is said to have laughed for a year. Another tale, embroidered on a Qur'anic frame (cf. Chapter 8 above), has Solomon riding his magic carpet with the hoopoe as his guide. Flying off to scout, the bird meets another hoopoe from Yemen, introduces himself as the hoopoe of Solomon, king of men and jinn, and learns from the Yemeni bird of the Queen of Sheba, whose splendid court and mighty forces he flies on to see. It was then that Solomon missed his hoopoe (Qur'an 27:20). The raven, sent to search for him, according to legend, meets the returning bird, whose feathers Solomon is ready to pluck out for insolence, when the hoopoe reminds him that even the prophet-king will soon stand before God, 'between heaven and hell'. He then reports what he has seen in the land of Sheba. See al-Kisā'ī, *Qiṣaṣ al-anbiyā'*, tr. Thackston, p. 313. A member of the order Scansores, the hoopoe (*hudhud*) is prized in Muslim bird-lore for its faithfulness — feeding its parents in their old age and seeking no new mate when widowed. Its tufted crest is the bird's reward for shrouding and bearing its dead mother's body. The nodding of the bird's crest suggested worshipful genuflections, and its patchy coat was a mourning cloak or Sufi garb. The foul smell results from nesting in dung.

174 Qur'an 27:22–25.

175 The cock is nature's muezzin. Muslim law permits the killing of both cocks and fleas but forbids their being reviled since the former awaken the faithful and the

How long, neighbours, will you sleep!
Remember God, ye mindless of death and decay,
Heedless of hell and careless of paradise,
Thankless of God's good!
Oh, that creatures had not been created —
Or, once created, would that they knew why!

'The partridge, herald of the heath, is the one standing on that rise, with the white cheeks and speckled wings. His back is stooped from long bowing and prostration. He is blessed with many offspring, and gives glad tidings in his crier's call. In springtime he says, "Thanks make grace last, scorn looses retributions." And also in the spring he sings this song:

Praise God, be He extolled,
For His bounties all-embracing.
Spring has scattered winter's cold;
The year, its course retracing.
Every honest deed that's done,
All that's generous and right,
Means the doer's meed is won,
Day squared once more with night![176]

'And he prays, "O Lord, preserve me from the mischief of jackals, birds of prey, and human hunters — and from doctors and the cravings of their patients."

'Circling there in the air is the well-guided homing pigeon. He carries letters and flies on missions to far-off lands. As he flies forth and returns, he coos:

Ah for the grief of parted brothers,
The yearning of true friends —
Lord, lead us to our home![177]

---

latter once roused a prophet from sleep. The Ikhwān see the cock as warning of the inexorable passage of time, against which only penitence can stand.

176 The partridge speaks for an eschatology of works rather than sheer predestination, supporting his Muʿtazilite leanings by appeal to the symmetry of the seasons, emblems and instruments of God's justice.

177 The homing pigeon's song echoes the language of the Ikhwān's pen name.

'The warbling pheasant is that one, strutting daintily in the gardens, among the trees and fragrant plantings. He makes music with his melodious calls and his lovely and diverse intonations. In his elegies and admonitions, this is what he sings:

Waster of life in your building,
Garden digger and tree planter,
Castle builder of the land,
You there, on your covered dais,
Heedless of the turn of time
Beware! Do not be lulled
By the respite grace affords you.
Remember, in your gardens,
That death will take you downward,
To a place of worms and serpents,
When your pleasures here have ended.

'The preaching lark is that one in the dusty cap. He soars high in the air at midday, over meadows and fields of grain, as a preacher mounts his pulpit.[178] He sings in varied and delightful melodies. This is his homily and reminder:

Where are the shrewd and the willing,
Men of commerce and eager for profit,
Who would plant the earth's wastes for a harvest
Where each grain yields seven thousand per cent?[179]

178 The lark's soaring flight and delivery of its song from the heights suggest pulpit oratory to the Ikhwān, since sermons in the mosque are delivered from a high rostrum, the *minbar*, often beautifully carved and decorated and mounted by stairs. The lark's song is a homily on the fruits of the fields he surveys. The conceit of life's harvest is highly developed in monotheistic homilies. Cf. Baḥyā ibn Paqūda, *Kitāb al-Hidāya ilā farā'iḍ al-qulūb*, II.5, ed. A. S. Yahuda (Leiden: Brill, 1942), p. 119. Where the pheasant berated the folly of development (cf. Saadiah, *The Book of Critically Selected Beliefs and Convictions*, X.10, tr. Rosenblatt, pp. 383–385), the lark proposes a more profitable investment of energies.

179 Qur'an 2:261: *Those who spend their wealth in God's way are like a grain that sprouts seven ears, each bearing a hundred kernels.* The Ikhwān promise a seventy-fold yield, seven thousand per cent; the Qur'an holds out a seven-hundred-fold yield on one's seed corn.

A favour like that, from a Lord all-forgiving
Should be weighed well by all who have sense.

'"Pay Him his due at the harvest and don't start the day chuckling over the charity you withhold, pleased that no wretch will call to share your yield. One who sows goodness will reap in sheaves on the morrow. Plant merit, and you'll gather its fruit in time to come.

'"For this world is as a sown field. Those who work it and win the hereafter are as tillers of the soil. Their deeds are the seeds and trees, and death is the reaper who harvests the fruit. The grave is the threshing floor, and Resurrection Day is the winnowing season. The folk of the Garden are the wheat and fruit. Those of the Fire are the worthless chaff and dead wood. Sorting *fair from foul, God stacks the foul one on the next. He piles them up and casts them into hell. . .*[180] *But God will save those who sheltered in their Refuge. No ill shall touch them, and they shall not sorrow.*"[181]

'The bulbul is the mimic over there, perched on that branch, with the small body and swift movements, the white cheeks, and frequent turns left and right. He sings clearly and expressively with many melodies. He visits humans in their gardens and mingles with them in their abodes. Often he answers them in their own speech and echoes their singing. When they dally forgetfully he admonishes them:

Lord, Lord! Are you still playing —
As if laughter had no measure.
Lord, Lord! You should be praying,
Not panting for more pleasure!

Weren't you born to die?
And weren't you bred to rot?
Won't all you build and garner
Run to ruin when you're not?

Indeed, are you still playing?
Tomorrow you must die,

180 Qur'an 8:37; for the fate of the dead wood, see the Sermon on the Mount, Matthew 7:19.

181 Qur'an 39:61; cf. 5:69, and Revelation 21:4.

And lie in dust and ashes,
And never have known why.

'"*Ah no, but you shall learn*[182] O son of Adam, *Have you not seen what thy Lord did with the folk of the elephant? Did he not upset what they had devised, send flying flocks against them, to pelt them with shards of brick and leave them like cropped stubble?*"[183] Then he prays, "O Lord, guard me from greedy boys and the nasty neighbourhood cats, Most Gracious, Most Merciful God."

'The soothsaying raven is that figure clad in black.[184] He is wakeful and watchful and at daybreak accosts revellers in their haunts. He can follow a trail and is a great flyer, a redoubtable traveller in many lands. A seer of the future, he cautions against heedlessness. This is the warning he croaks:

Watch out! Watch out!
Take care! Take care!
Look out for ruin,
Villain! Lecher!
Greedy worldling!

Run, where?
Hide, where?

182 Qur'an 102:3.

183 Qur'an 105:1–4. According to Muslim tradition, in the year of Muhammad's birth (560), Abraha, the Abyssinian ruler of Yemen, marched against Mecca, presumably in support of Justinian's long-standing war against the Iranian empire of Anushirwan. Mecca's pagan defenders despaired at the advance of the host, with its awe-inspiring elephant, but the aggressors were beaten off. Muhammad, decades later, appealing for Meccan support, reminded the Meccans how God had come to their aid. The birds proudly quote the brief sura in full, since it credits their support in Mecca's salvation.

184 The raven (*ghurāb*, cognate with the Latin '*corvus*'), ominous by its colour, becomes a soothsayer, by transference of the omen to the bird as speaker — as in Edgar Allen Poe's poem 'The Raven'; cf. Isidore, *Etymologies* 12.7.44, 76. The crows that gathered as scavengers when tribes broke camp were emblems to the early Arab poets of the melancholy of parting; see Ilse Lichtenstadter, 'Das Nasīb der altarabischen Qasīde', *Islamica*, 5 (1931), p. 36. Jāḥiz, the worldly-wise essayist and satirist, lampooned this sort of augury or pathetic fallacy as a superstition fostered by the word '*ightirāb*' ('estrangement').

From judgement?[185]
Only in prayer!

The Lord of the skies
May save you.
He can spare you —
If He please.

'There's the building swallow[186] sailing through the air, a blithe flyer with stubby legs and full wings. He's mankind's neighbour and broods his young amongst their homes. Profuse in his praises at dawn, morning, and evening, he pours forth prayer and petitions for pardon.[187] He travels far, summering in warm climes and wintering in cool. Here is his paean and prayer:

Praise the Creator of wilds and seas,
Who brings on the night and the day.
The wayfarer's Friend,
Guard of families and hearths,
Who raised up the great peaks,
Makes the broad rivers flow,
— And metes out our weal and our woe.

'He also says:

Through the world we have flown,
Having all its creatures known,
And turn now with coming morn
To the land where we were born,

185 Qur'an 75:10 pictures sinners seeking a hiding place on Judgement Day.

186 Those who minimize animal intelligence stress that the birds build only in a fixed form. Those who stress animal ingenuity note that swallows' nests vary to fit their corner. Since the issue is the degree to which animal intelligence is mechanical, awareness and responsiveness are critical, and the restiveness of cocks and cranes become virtues and key arguing points.

187 For living creatures' implicit praises, see Ginzberg, *Legends of the Jews*, tr. Henrietta Szold, 7 vols. (Philadelphia: Jewish Publication Society, 1909–1938, repr., 2003), vol. 1, pp. 42–46.

Thanking God, our souls repaired —
For His is all that we have shared.

'The watchful crane is that person, standing up in the sand, with the long neck, long legs, short tail, and wide wing-span — the one who's taking flight! He whistles as he stands two watches in the night,[188] and this is his song of praise:

Praised be He who yoked two lights in heaven,
And freed two seas on earth.
Lord of two easts and wests.
Maker of the airy and earthbound kinds.
Our Guide on life's two roads,
Who makes all things in pairs.[189]

'The dusty sand-grouse lives in moors and deserts. He travels far by night and day to find a river watering place. God's name and praise are often in his mouth as he sets out and returns at dawn and evening. This is the song he sings:

Praise God who made the vaulted skies
And the wide earth spread below,
The zodiac signs that turn and rise,
And the spheres that wheel and flow.

He caused the wandering stars to shine.
Auspicious clouds He raises.
He sends the winds that whirl and whine.
The thunder chants His praises.

---

188 For the crane's watches by night, see Tawḥīdī, 'The Zoological Chapter', §§108, 144.

189 See Qur'an 43:12. God gives mates to all His creatures. The cranes' double line is their V-formation, forming a single flight wing that reduces the birds' fatigue. There are two easts and wests (Qur'an 55:17), since the sun rises at different points in winter and summer. The lights subservient to God are, of course, the sun and moon (Qur'an 7:54). For the loosing of two seas, see Qur'an 55:19; the two are sweet water and salt, which meet but do not fuse (Qur'an 25:53). In Arabic, any large body of water and even a large perennial river can be called a sea (*baḥr*). For life's two roads, high and low, see Qur'an 90:10–20. Sand cranes, we observe, pair-bond by walking in step with their mate.

Lord of lightnings' flashing streaks,
And oceans' swollen might,
Founder of mountains' towering peaks,
Who governs time, and day, and night.

Beasts and plants, all things alive,
He made — wastes, seas, the dark, and day.
Dry, withered bones He will revive
From death, destruction, and decay.

Praise Him whose praise eludes all tongues,
Whose essence beggars all depiction,
Whose being transcends being's highest rungs,
Whose Godhead is beyond description.[190]

'The sandpiper, harbinger of good fortune, is that one on the sand-bar, with the white cheeks and the long legs. Quick-witted and light-hearted, in the dark of night he reminds his fellow birds when they grow forgetful of God's tenderness and blessings. This is his song of praise:

Ah Thou who makest the dawn's bright ray,
To cleave the sky with light,
And the winds of each land to blow in their way,
Flinging the clouds in flight.
Torrents and streams run swift with Thy rain,
Feeding the grass and the trees,
Bringing forth fruit, and golden grain,
And granting the bird race ease.
Thy bounty sustains their life in the air —
Fellow birds, be mindful of the good Lord's ample care!

'The nightingale of many melodies is that one, perched on a branch of that tree. His body is small, his movements sprightly, his music delightful. This is the song he trills:

190 In the metaphysics of Plotinus, the One (that is, God) transcends being itself, since being is definite, or determinate and thus limited, whereas the absolute One is infinite, the Source of being, but itself beyond definition or description.

O manifest Giver, circumspect in Thy giving,
Unique and alone, unto Thee be all thanks,
Whose manifold bounties to all of the living
Overflow as great rivers spill over their banks.[191]

Ah, the life that was mine in a time I once knew —
Breezy meadows and gardens, I perched on a bough,
Leafy trees bearing fruit, every colour and hue —
Were my brethren to aid me, I should sing of them now.'[192]

Said the Simurgh to the peacock, 'Which of these do you think most fit for us to send as our delegate in the dispute with the humans?'

'Any one of them would do', said the peacock. 'All are eloquent speakers and songsters, but the nightingale is the most eloquent and expressive, the finest and most tuneful singer.' So the Simurgh sent the nightingale on his mission.[193]

Chapter 14

When the messenger reached the king of the swarming creatures, the bee,[194] and made his report, the king gave orders to his herald, who

191 Emanation, called '*fayḍ*' ('flowing forth') in Arabic, is the shedding of unity, beauty, being, and truth from God's oneness, as light flows from the sun or water wells up from a spring, in the imagery favoured by Neoplatonic philosophers.

192 The nightingale's song evokes the paradisiacal pleasure garden on which Eden was figured. The secular and the otherworldly play hide-and-seek with one another here, as symbol and object. See Goodman, *Islamic Humanism*, Chapter 1.

193 Song here ranks higher than speech, as its emotive powers urge. For they are rooted in the very plan of the cosmos and thus, as it were, echo the music of the spheres. Voiceless creatures, as the cricket explains, are not unfairly deprived. For they are given all and only the gifts requisite to their station. But their silence can never rival the nightingale's song.

194 The bees in our fable have a king rather than a queen. The error can be traced to Aristotle, who raises many questions about apian procreation, although he could hardly have expected his tentative speculations here to become the fixed opinion of so many later readers. Some writers, he notes, call the hive leader the mother and view the drones as male and workers as female. But Aristotle has his doubts, since the workers are armed with a sting, and he thinks defensive

summoned the insects. Before him gathered wasps, bees, flies, gnats, mosquitoes, beetles, scarabs, and locusts — all the small-bodied, winged animals without feathers, bones, wool, hair, or fleece. None of them lives a full year, except the bees. The rest perish in the extreme heat of summer or the extreme winter cold.

Having told them the news, the king said, 'Which of you will go to represent our community in the dispute with the humans?'

'What makes humans boast that they are our betters?' asked the throng.

'Their huge bodies and enormous frame, their power to dominate and prevail by force', said the messenger.

'We will go', said the chief of the wasps.

'We will go', said the chief of the flies.

'We will go', said the chief of the mosquitoes.

'We will go', said the chief of the gnats.

'We will go', said the chief of the locusts.

But the king said, 'Why do I see every band of you so eager to rush into this mission without thinking things through and appraising the situation?'

'Trust in God's help,' they all buzzed together, 'and success and victory are assured. We have long experience with tyrannous kings among vanished nations in ages gone by.'

'How so?' asked the king, 'Tell me how that was.'

'Your Majesty,' said a gnat, 'didn't the slightest and frailest of us slay Nimrod, the greatest of all human kings, the most arrogant, powerful, and despotic of them all?'[195]

---

weapons unlikely in females. To be fair, he also doubts that the workers are male, since they care for the young. See Aristotle, *Historia Animalium* V.21; *Generatione Animalium* III.10; cf. Pliny, *Natural History* XI.18.56–57; Robert Mayhew, *The Female in Aristotle's Biology: Reason or Rationalization* (Chicago: University of Chicago Press, 2004), pp. 19–26.

195 Nimrod's persecution of Abraham is recounted in Targum Jonathan at Genesis 15:7 and Baba Bathra 91a; cf. Maimonides, *Guide* III.29. The Qur'an (2:258, 29:24) echoes the story, and Muslim legend elaborates, as recorded in Ṭabarī's *Commentary on the Qur'an* and at the start of the Antar romance. In al-Kisā'ī's *Qiṣaṣ al-anbiyā'*, Nimrod is warned by his idol that he will lose his kingdom unless he accepts Abraham's Lord. He responds by offering seven hundred bulls, sheep, and cows to the idol; tr. Thackston, p. 133. Failing to slay Abraham by casting

'True', said the king.

'Is it not also true', said the wasps, 'that when one of the tribe of Adam is clad in armour from head to toe, grasping his sword, lance, dirk, and arrows, and one of us advances and pricks him with a stinger no bigger than a needle's point, he's completely distracted from all he so fiercely purposed and resolved to do. His skin is inflamed, the whole limb swells up until he can hardly grip his sword or dirk?'[196]

'Yes', said the king.

'Isn't it true, your Majesty,' said the flies, 'that the mightiest, most august and exalted human king, seated on his throne, surrounded by chamberlains, all solicitous that nothing unpleasant or annoying come near him, cannot keep one of us from flying out of his kitchen or privy and lighting on his throne, to pester him by dragging our filthy feet and wings across his royal robes and face?'

'It is', said the king.

'Isn't it true', said the mosquito, 'that when a human sits in his chair or rests on his couch or divan, surrounded by screens, netting, and curtains, and one of us gets into his clothing and bites him, disturbing his repose, he snatches at us but only slaps his own neck and cheeks, and we flit away.'

'All true, fellow insects', said the king. 'But at the court of the King of the Jinn none of the tactics you mention would work. Only justice,

---

him into the fire, which the angel Gabriel stripped of its heat, Nimrod built the Tower of Babel, hoping to confront Abraham's God. The tower fell, but Nimrod, undeterred, sought to fly to heaven in a chest borne by four great eagles. He fell to earth, causing mountains to shake with a violence thought to be alluded to at Qur'an 14:46: They laid their plots, but God knew their scheme, though it was a plot that would move mountains. Even after his great fall Nimrod sought to make war against God, but Abraham's army divided Nimrod's forces, and they fell into confusion by the division of their languages. They were finally discomfited by swarms of gnats, one of whom entered the tyrant's ear or nostril, penetrated his brain and there grew prodigiously, causing such excruciating pain that the wicked king had his head beaten with mallets for relief — according to some authors, for 400 years, a span equal to his tyrannous reign. The Ikhwān seem happy to have the gnat dispatch the tyrant more expeditiously, but the insects relish the irony that inspires the story, the harshest despot falling to the tiniest insect, according to God's plan. The story reflects the Midrash, where a gnat slays Titus; Giṭṭin 56b, Genesis Rabbah 10:7. See Georges Vajda, 'Bukht-naṣ(ṣ)ar', *EI2*, vol. 1, p. 1297. The steady refrain 'How was that?' echoes the *Pañcatantra*.

196 Cf. Montaigne, *Apology for Raymond Sebond*, in *Complete Essays*, p. 349.

dispassion, courtesy, keen thinking and discernment, clear reasoning, and lucid arguments can win the day. Do any of you have these?'

For a time the assembly fell silent, pondering the king's words. Then he said, 'With God's help and at God's pleasure, I appoint myself. For I am better spoken than the rest of you.'

'God favour your mission', said the whole assembly together. 'God aid you and grant you triumph over your foes and adversaries and all who wish you ill.'

The wise bee bade farewell and, after provisioning for the journey,[197] set out. He travelled until he reached the Kingdom of the Jinn, and presented himself at court along with the other animals who were assembling there.

Chapter 15

When the messenger reached the griffin,[198] king of the birds of prey, and made known his news, the herald gave summons and before the king gathered all manner of hunting birds — eagles, hawks, falcons, kites, vultures, owls, and parrots — every bird with talons and a hooked beak, all that eat meat.[199] The king told them what the messenger had reported, how the animals were gathering before the King of the Jinn

197 As a bee would, since the bees, inspired by God, are far more provident than their fellow insects.

198 The griffin is 'an animal with feathers and four feet, a kind of wild beast that breeds in the Hyperborean mountains. Griffins are lions through the torso but have wings and faces like eagles.' Isidore, *Etymologies* 12.2.17. In mediaeval bestiaries the griffin often symbolized of the quest for union with God.

199 Aristotle makes all birds with hooked talons carnivores; *Historia Animalium* VIII.3. He mentions the parrot's hooked claws and remarks that wine makes the bird 'saucier than ever' but does not directly class it as a carnivore; ibid. VIII.12.597b27–29. He does say that no bird with hooked talons lives in flocks (I.1.488a3–5), a claim untrue of parrots and their kin; cf. *De Partibus Animalium* III.1.662b. The ritual classification of owls and parrots was disputed in Islam. Long claws and a stout, hooked beak lend parrots a superficial resemblance to birds of prey, but the organs are prehensile. Parrots use them with dexterity, but their diet is vegetarian. The Ikhwān may be serving the needs of their tale in making parrots carnivores, since that gives the parrot a prominent place among the animal delegates. The Ikhwān seem here to play down the reliance on carrion of many of the meat-eating birds, although they speak favourably of

for the suit against mankind. Then said he to his vizier, the rhinoceros,[200] 'Are any of the raptors you see here suited for us to send to represent all his fellows in this contest with the sons of Adam?'

'None is right for this mission but the owl', said the vizier.

'Why so?' asked the king.

'Because', said the vizier, 'all other birds of prey shun and fear men. They don't understand human speech and would not do well in mingling with men and trading arguments with them. But the owl is their neighbour. He lives in their desolate dwellings, decayed buildings, and deserted castles. Having studied mankind's ancient ruins, he has learned the lessons of ages past.[201] His piety, humility, austerity, asceticism, and self-mortification, moreover, are unique. He fasts by day and weeps and worships by night. Often he cautions mankind and calls them to reflect with his threnodies for bygone kings and vanished nations, declaiming stately elegies:[202]

> Where have your cohorts departed?
> It is long since these halls heard their tread.
> The hoards they amassed stand unguarded;

---

the work of insects as scavengers and voice approval of the putative scavenging of carnivorous animals in prehistoric times.

200 The 'Second Voyage of Sindbad' in the *Thousand and One Nights* makes it clear why the rhinoceros is the griffin's vizier. Sindbad tells of an island where there is 'a kind of wild beast called rhinoceros that feeds like a steer or buffalo but is a huge brute, with a body bigger than a camel's. It feeds on leaves and twigs and has a great, thick horn, ten cubits long, in the middle of its head, within which, when it is split, is found the likeness of a man. Voyagers, pilgrims, and travellers declare that this beast, the karkadan, will carry off a great elephant on its horn and graze about the island and the seashore, paying it no notice, until the elephant dies and its fat, melting in the sun, runs down into the rhinoceros's eyes and blinds him, making him lie down on the shore. Then a roc comes and carries off the rhinoceros and the beast, still impaled on its horn, to feed its young.' The rhinoceros, in effect, is the griffin's hunting partner — and thus, in the fable, his vizier. Isidore too reports that a rhinoceros can impale an elephant; *Etymologies* 12.2.12.

201 The owl's wisdom reflects his mournful acquaintance with human history, gained through long sojourn among the ruins that bear witness to the vanity of human ambitions. Isidore, *Etymologies* 12.7.38–42, speaks of the keening and moaning of the owl. The motif is ancient. Thus Psalm 102:7: 'I am like a pelican in the desert, an owl among the ruins.'

202 Kalonymos reduces the owl's elegies to simple rebukes of human sinfulness.

Forlorn, for their masters are fled.
Seek well for them. What do you find
Of the men who once ruled in these lands?
Broken graves, rotting bones left behind,
And the desolate trace of the dead!

'He also says:

Speak, house of evil omen!
Where are your men and women?
Why have they journeyed on?
But the house stood dark in silence.
For it could not say in answer,
"It is not that we have vanished,
But you, in fact, have tarried
Where we could not linger on."

'And sometimes he says:

"Answer, ruin," I said, "and tell me
What my loved ones once did here."
"Just a few days did they sojourn,
And then they travelled on."
"Where, then, did they rest?" I cried.
"Where shall I seek them now?"
"In their graves," the ruin answered,
"Faced — by God! — with all they've done."

'Or he says:

I have seen the halls of time,
And down them people passing,
My folk, great and small together,
Through the passageway to death,
Once they entered none returned.
Those who dallied could not stay —

So I knew there is no exit
From the ceaseless march of death.

'And he says:

Sleep comes to the carefree;
I feel not its lull.
My pillow knows best of my anguish.
It is grief, not a sickness,
Pounds within, low and dull,
And looms, gripping my heart where I languish.
Where are the monarchs of old
Who ranged from Udhayb to Murād . . .[203]
The lands of Khawarnaq, Sadīr, and Bāriq.
And the turreted towers of Shaddād?[204]
Life was good there,

---

203 MS Atif Efendi 1681 continues: 'What hope have I if the halls of Muḥarriq are ruined / And after the fall of Iyād.'

204 In the *Thousand and One Nights*, 'Abdallāh ibn Abū Kilāba, hunting for a lost camel, stumbles on a vast palace blazing with jewels, and he loads his beast with treasure. Summoned to the court of Mu'āwiya, he tells of his find but is not credited until the learned Ka'b al-Aḥbār identifies the site as the lost city of 'Irām, built by Shaddād, son of 'Ād, a mighty king, whose palace was meant to rival paradise, as described in ancient books. Three hundred years in the building, the palace was filled with tribute from royal vassals. Just to move into this magnificent seat, Shaddād and his huge retinue journeyed for twenty years. But God sent a rushing sound from the heavens, destroying them all, a fate alluded to with frustrating brevity in the Qur'an (69:6–7). According to the legend, not one of Shaddād's court lived to see his great citadel. Even the road to it was destroyed, and the city will remain desolate until Judgement Day. See al-Kisā'ī, *Qiṣaṣ al-anbiyā'*, tr. Thackston, p. 109. In folklore, the monitory message of the Qur'anic archaeology is overturned by the subtext: glittering visions of untold wealth of lost provenance, buried and only waiting to be chanced upon. See Ibn Khaldūn, *Muqaddimah*, Introduction, tr. F. Rosenthal, vol. 1, p. 26. Aristotle notes that one does not, in the proper sense, *deliberate* about finding treasure; see *Nicomachaean Ethics* III.3.1112a28. Ibn Khaldūn expands on the point, expressing his distaste not only for substituting romantic tales for sober historical narratives but also for misguided and impractical life-plans, in a chapter headed 'Trying to make money from buried and other treasures is not a natural way of making a living', 5.4, tr. Rosenthal, vol. 2, pp. 319–326.

In a king's bower.
With tent posts secure,
Firm as any man's power —
But storm winds swept the air,
And, as if at their call, all was gone in a day,
And I saw all must pass that is fair
And all that delights must decay.[205]

'He also recites, "*There's many a garden and spring that they've left behind, many a sown field, noble site and pleasance where once they made merry. So it was. Now We've left them to others, and heaven and earth shed no tears for them; they were given no respite.*"'[206]

Said the griffin to the owl, 'What say you to what the rhinoceros has told us?'

'What he says is true,' said the owl, 'but I cannot go.'

'Why not?' asked the griffin.

'The reason', said the owl, 'is that the tribe of Adam loathe me. They find the sight of me ominous.[207] They hate me, even though I've done

---

205 The verses are adapted from the *Mufaḍḍaliyyāt* of the long lived pre-Islamic poet al-Aswad ibn Yaʿfūr (late sixth century); see C. Pellat, 'Aswad b. Yaʿfūr', *EI2*, vol. 1, p. 728. Called 'al-Aʿshā' for his night blindness, he struck sombre chords in laments for lost youth and the approach of death. In the owl's lament, the wording and line order of al-Aʿshā's famous poem are altered, as Andras Hamori notes: 'The first two lines correspond to the text in the *Mufaḍḍaliyyāt*, but after that there is quite a bit of skipping around.' The Ikhwān have also cast a mantle over the poet's intent, making death an encounter for which only piety can prepare one. For the elegiac themes of Jāhiliyya poetry and their classical and mediaeval parallels, see C. H. Becker, 'Ubi sunt qui ante nos in mundo fuere', in *Islamstudien* (Leipzig: Quelle & Mayer, 1924), vol. 1, pp. 501–519. Although Kalonymos does not attempt to render the owl's re-mastered elegies in his Hebrew translation, Judah Halevi does adapt such themes in his Hebrew laments.

206 Qur'an 44:25–27.

207 The owl's abode reflects old Arab beliefs that dead souls in avian form haunt their tombs crying for vengeance. For the Ikhwān, the owl, as an archaeological bird, fuses the elegiac mood of pre-Islamic poetry, musing on the vagaries of fate and death, with monitory Islamic meditations on the vicissitudes wrought by time, read as signs of life's evanescence and the urgency of resort to God. These themes link with the Qur'anic archaeology, where the ruins of vanished civilizations warn of the judgements meted out as history unfolds:

> *Have they not travelled the land and seen what the outcome was for those who came before them? Their power was mightier than theirs. They*

them no wrong and caused them no harm. So how will they take it if they see me appearing against them in this dispute? A dispute is a kind of conflict. Conflict breeds enmity; and enmity, warfare, which lays waste to lands and destroys their people.'

'Well,' said the griffin to the owl, 'who do you think suitable?'

'Of all the birds of prey,' answered the owl, 'human kings most love hawks, falcons, and their kin. They prize and honour them, bear them on their hands, and stroke them with their sleeves. It would be politic for the king to send one of them.'

The griffin turned to the assembly and said, 'You have heard what the owl has said. What do you think?'

'What the owl says is true,' said the falcon, 'but the honour men show us comes not from any friendship or warmth between us, nor any understanding they have of us or refinement they find in us. They're just the parasites who take our prizes. It's sheer greed and gluttony on their part, and love of sport, thrill, and waste,[208] heedless of their duty to make ready for the hereafter, obey God, and be mindful what they will be asked on Judgement Day.'

'Who would you consider most apt for this mission?' the griffin asked.

---

made their mark on the land, they settled it more fully than they. The messengers who came to them gave them clear warnings. God was not unjust with them. It was they who wronged themselves! (Qur'an 30:9.) *Look at the outcome of their deceit. We annihilated them, and all their folk together. There are their homes, in ruins, for the wrongs that they have done. There's a portent in that for folk who are aware.* (Qur'an 27:51–52).

208 Falconry (*bayzara*), practised by Arabs from pre-Islamic times, became a prime secular pursuit of Muslim caliphs, sultans, and nobles. Like the cheetah hunt, hawking was an extravagant enterprise, employing numerous keepers and trainers. Hawking preserves used large tracts of land, so the sport was inherently wasteful. One prince was said to have bankrupted himself by his devotion to the aerial hunt. Hunters, the animals complain, greedily deprive their birds of the prey they have taken, a decadent act, since princes hardly need such tiny morsels. Hawking cultivated military virtues in a peaceful pursuit, but horsemanship and the frisson of the kill were autonomous secular values kept alive by the hunt and celebrated in its ancillary art and literature. Falconry persists among nomadic and rural populations in the Middle East, an index, F. Viré argues, of the economic importance of the sport as a source of employment in mediaeval times; see 'Bayzara', *EI2*, vol. 1, p. 1152. For the survival of secular values and pagan practices in the sport, see R. B. Serjeant, *South Arabian Hunt* (London: Luzac, 1974); Goodman, *Islamic Humanism*, pp. 54–55, 67–68.

'I think a parrot would do best', said the falcon. 'All humans love him, kings and commoners, men, women, and children, wise and foolish alike. He chatters with them and they chatter back and hear just what they've said as he mocks their every word.'[209]

'What do you say to what the falcon says of you?' the griffin asked.

'His account is true', said the parrot. 'With God's help, and aided by His power, I shall go, a faithful and willing delegate of our kind. But I'll need help from the king and from everyone here.'

'How can we help?' asked the griffin.

'By praying to God for His succour and sustenance.'

The king then prayed for God's help and support, and all present responded 'Amen'.

But the owl said, 'Your Majesty, unless your prayer is accepted, it's wasted effort and trouble. For to pray is to pollinate. Only when it's heard does prayer bear fruit. For that, certain conditions must be met.'[210]

'What conditions are needed for a prayer to be acceptable?' asked the king.

'There must be purity of intent and sincerity of heart like those that spring from real need; and fasting, worship, charity, sacrifice, piety, and decency must precede a behest.'[211]

The assembly responded. 'You have spoken rightly and justly, as befits a wise and reverent servant of God.'

---

209 Parrots were long thought not to mimic in the wild, but only because parrots in flocks are in constant communication with each other. Parrots as pets respond to those who keep them. See Hartshorne, *Born to Sing*, pp. 63–64, 67, 76.

210 The owl's reasoning here, like his earlier argument classing disputes as a type of conflict, uses a strikingly explicit syllogistic form, echoing the style of early Islamic philosophy. The art of syllogistics was not inborn but learned. Early Arabic theology generally relies on hypothetical reasoning like that of the Stoics. The categorical syllogism, using class logic, was preferred in philosophy, since it could cover whole universes of discourse — a coverage that Stoics had thought specious. Here, the Ikhwān mingle arguments from analogy (canonical in Islamic legal reasoning) with causal principles ('conflict breeds enmity [. . . and] leads to warfare') and categorical premises. Although not always sensitive to the demands of logic for quantification, the Ikhwān are careful to omit no link in the chain of predications. Kindī shows similar caution in his use of syllogistic.

211 The Ikhwān here speak through the wise owl against mere mechanical performance of the obligations of ritual worship, and in praise of sincerity and the moral purity without which prayer is mere verbiage, undeserving of God's regard. Compare the text at Chapter 37, p. 282 below.

The griffin then addressed all the flocked birds of prey: 'You see, fellow raptors,' he said, 'how pervasive is man's oppression and how widespread are his trespasses against animals, if their repercussions have come all the way to our habitations, even though we avoid humans and shun their abodes. I myself, despite my great strength, my massive frame, and swift flight, left the realm of men and fled to mountain-tops and islands in the sea. Even my friend the rhinoceros has retreated to the deserts and wastes far from the realms of men, seeking relief from their evil. Yet still we are not clear of them. They drag us into their quarrels, wrangles, and disputes. Any one of us, if we liked, could carry off hordes of them every day, and we would have them in our power. But it is not for free spirits like us to behave as they do, repay evil for evil, or sink to the level of their foul ways. We should just leave them alone and keep our distance, leave them to their Lord, mind our own business and look after our interests, seeking heart's ease here, and repose in the hereafter.'[212]

The griffin concluded, 'How many ships tossed by the tempest on the fathomless deep have I led back on course! How many shipwrecked and drowning men have I brought safe to islands or shores, only to please my Lord and give thanks for the blessing of my massive frame and huge body, to show due gratitude for His bounty toward me. *For He is our meed and faithful Protector.*'[213]

Chapter 16

When the messenger reached the sea-serpent, king of the aquatic animals, and told him the news, the king's herald issued the summons,

---

212 The owl praises sincerity; cf. Chapter 35, p. 272–273 below. Prayer is worthless without honesty, decency, and charity: the worth of worship cannot be cut off from moral and spiritual values. The griffin boldly rejects retributivism, invoking the ultimate standard of God's judgement in behalf of an ethic of toleration: great and noble souls will simply leave the misguided in the toils of their disputes and delusions — a sound, Epicurean expedient, if one is safe from the harm that misguided souls can wreak. But the royal bird's withdrawal is from human evil, not from humanity. So he hastens to cite his help of those in distress, as befits his Godgiven power and awareness.

213 Qur'an 3:173.

and to him thronged every kind of water animal — turtles, sea-serpents, crocodiles, swordfish, dolphins, whales, fish, crabs, frogs — all animals with shells or scales, some seven hundred kinds, of diverse colours and forms.

The king then told the news the messenger had brought and asked the emissary, 'On what account do the sons of Adam vaunt themselves over others? Is it their size or might or strength to crush and conquer? If their boast is any of these, I'll go there and with one blast of breath send them all sprawling, and with the next, suck them up and swallow them one and all!'

'The sons of Adam boast of none of these things,' said the messenger, 'but of the pre-eminence of their minds, their varied sciences, marvellous culture, ingenious inventions, and elegant arts, their thought and discernment, insight, and penetration.'

Said the sea-serpent, 'Tell me a little about these, so that I may understand man.'

'I shall, your Majesty. You know, of course, that the sons of Adam have the skill and knowledge to dive into the depths of the dark, swelling, and surging sea and bring back pearls and coral. In the same way, by science and technique, they can scale the peaks of the loftiest mountains to capture hawks and eagles.[214] And with the same sagacity and cunning they fashion wagons of wood and yoke them to the chests and shoulders of oxen who must bear their heavy loads and transport them from east to west, across deserts and wastes. They make boats and ships to bear their goods and freight across the sea to far off lands. Their science and devices let them penetrate caves in mountainsides and dig pits in the hills, mine into the depths of the earth to extract precious minerals — gold, silver, iron, and copper. By their knowledge and art, if one of them comes to the sea-shore or a

214 Another example of human overreaching, reflected in the angels' complaint at the creation of Adam, Qur'an 2:30. In the *qiṣaṣ* literature, the animals share in such concerns: 'Before God created Adam, the animals could speak. The eagle would come to the fish in the sea and tell it what was on land, and the fish would relate what was in the sea. When God created Adam, the eagle came to the fish and said, "Today God created a creature, and I have seen something this day that will bring me down from my aerie and take you up from the sea."' Thaʿlabī, *'Arā'is al-majālis fī qiṣaṣ al-anbiyā'*, tr. William Brinner as *Lives of the Prophets* (Leiden: Brill, 2002), p. 47.

sand-bar or ford and sets up a talisman, effigy, or icon, ten thousand of our sea-serpents, crocodiles, and swordfish cannot pass or come near. But have no fear, your Majesty, for at the court of the King of Jinn only justice and fairness prevail. Clear argument alone can win the day, not force or power, craft or deceit.'

Having heard the messenger, the sea-serpent said to the ranks of his subjects about him, 'Now what do you think and what do you say? Which of you will go to dispute with the humans as delegate of all his brethren and the sons of his kind?'

The dolphin, rescuer of castaways, said, 'The whale is the fittest of all water animals for this task, being the largest, the most massive, the handsomest, whitest and cleanest, sleekest and swiftest, the strongest swimmer, and the most numerous and prolific. For seas, rivers, streams, springs, shallows, brooks, and ditches are filled with his kind, large and small.[215] Besides, whales are well thought of among men because a whale once sheltered one of their prophets, gave him refuge in its belly and returned him to safety. And humans also believe and affirm that the earth rests on a whale's back.'

'What do you think of the dolphin's suggestion?' the sea-serpent asked the whale.

'All that he says is true', answered the whale. 'But I can't see how I could go there and address them without feet to walk on or an articulate tongue to speak with, let alone the ability to live out of water for even an hour. I think the turtle would be better for the job. He can hold up out of water and forage on dry land as well as live in the ocean. He breathes as well in air as he does in water, and he has a strong body

215 There are, in fact, freshwater cetaceans — the freshwater dolphin and the bouto of the new world, for example. But the Ikhwān seem to see in such creatures an analogue of their own status, as fish out of water, like these air-breathing 'fish'. For they too, they claim, are far more prevalent and ubiquitous than those who hunt them may suppose. In a later essay they write the following: 'Know, dear brother… that we have brethren and friends scattered everywhere among the virtuous and great souled. Some of them are the children of kings and princes, viziers, ministers of state and chancery officials; some, the sons of nobles, lords, merchants, and planters. Some are the sons of clerics and men of letters, jurists and religionists, or of artisans, officials and peace keepers [. . .]. *Rasā'il*, Epistle 48, vol. 4, p. 165, repeated at vol. 4, p. 188.

and a hard back. He has good limbs, and is wise and grave, patient when annoyed and able to bear a load.'[216]

'What do you think?' asked the sea-serpent of the turtle. 'The whale nominates you.'

'What he says is true,' said the turtle, 'but I'm not well suited for this mission. I walk slowly, and it's a long way. I'm not much of a talker. I'm mute in fact. I think the crab is more fit than I. He has many legs and can walk well and run swiftly. He has sharp claws, stout limbs, and a powerful bite; and he has spines as well as pincers with lots of teeth, and a hard back like a warrior in armour.

'What do you think of the turtle's suggestion?' said the sea-serpent to the crab.

'What he says is true. But I don't see how I can go there with my monstrous, twisted form. I'm afraid I'd be a laughing stock.'

'How so?' asked the sea-serpent.

'Well, they'll see a headless animal with his eyes on his shoulders, his mouth in his chest, and his jaw cleft at the sides, an animal with eight bent, crooked feet, who walks sideways as though his back were made of lead.'[217]

'True', said the sea-serpent. 'So who is best suited for this mission?'

'The crocodile, I suppose', said the crab. 'His legs are strong, and his body long. He's a great walker and runs swiftly. He has a capacious mouth, a good-sized tongue and plenty of teeth, a powerful body, and a fearsome aspect. He can lie in wait, intent on his quarry, and then plunge right after it.'

'What do you say?' said the sea-serpent to the crocodile.

'These things are true,' said the crocodile, 'but I fear I'm not fit for the job. I'm short tempered and irascible, pugnacious, mercurial, and treacherous.'

'Besides,' said the messenger, 'we won't win there by brute force

---

216 See Pliny, *Natural History* IX.12.37–38.

217 Aristotle remarks on the eyes and gait of the crab but does not see the creature as deformed; *Historia Animalium* IV.3.527b. He does, however, find the lobster oddly shaped, since his claws are asymmetrical, 'as a matter of chance. . . owing to their imperfect formation and to their not using them for their natural purpose but for locomotion'; *De Partibus Animalium* IV.8.683a30–35; cf. Pliny, *Natural History* IX.51.97–98.

but only by tact and dignity, insight and discernment, eloquence and clarity, justice and dispassion of address.'

'I was given none of those qualities', said the crocodile. 'But I think the frog might do. He's mild, grave, patient — and pious, for he often sings God's praises in the night and at broad day and daybreak too. He offers worship and prayer at dawn and evening. He enters the dwellings of men and earned credit with the Israelites twice: once when Nimrod cast Abraham, the friend of God, peace be upon him, into the fire and the frog brought water in his mouth and poured it on the fire to quench it,[218] and again when he helped Moses son of Amram against Pharaoh and his host.[219] Besides, he's eloquent, a great talker, always singing hymns and psalms of praise and exaltation. He's one of those animals who live both on land and in the water, so he can walk as well as he swims. His head is round, and his face is not buried in his body. His eyes sparkle. He sits up straight with his arms and forepaws extended. He hops and leaps and bounds right into the homes of men. He's not afraid of them, and they do not fear him.'

The sea-serpent turned to the frog. 'What say you to the crocodile's suggestion?'

'All he says is true', said the frog. 'I shall go to represent our brethren and all aquatic animals. But I'd like you to beseech God's aid and succour with a prayer deserving of answer.'[220]

So the king said a prayer for the frog, and all present said, 'Amen, may God speed and prosper this mission.' They bade farewell to the frog, and he set out, travelling until he came to the court of the King of the Jinn.

---

218 Thaʿlabī relates that all the animals except the gecko helped put out the fire in which Nimrod meant to burn Abraham.

219 See Exodus 8:2–13; Qur'an 7:133.

220 In the manuscripts, the sea-serpent asks 'What will allow our supplications to be heard?' and refers readers to the answer already given by the owl to the same question.

Chapter 17
The Dragon: His Compassion for All Crawling Creatures

When the messenger reached the dragon,[221] king of the crawling animals,[222] and told him the news, the dragon had his crier issue a summons, and all the kinds of crawling creatures gathered around him — snakes, vipers, scorpions large and small, earwigs, lizards, geckos, chameleons, salamanders, beetles, roaches, spiders, grasshoppers, fleas, lice, ants, ticks, and crickets, every sort of worm that breeds in rotting matter or crawls on the leaves of trees, or genders in kernels of grain or in the heart of trees or the bowels of larger animals — termites, borers, and creatures that breed in dung or mud, vinegar, snow, or fruit,[223] those that creep in caves or burrow in dark depths. All gathered before their king in numbers known but to God, who created, formed, and sustains them, and *who knows their every lair and refuge.*[224]

When their king beheld them in all their fantastic diversity of forms and shapes, he was transfixed with amazement. Surveying them, he

221 Isidore names the dragon as the greatest of all serpents, or of all land animals (*Etymologies* 12.4.4): 'It is often drawn out of its caves and soars aloft, agitating the air. It has a small mouth and narrow pipes through which it breathes and flickers its tongue. Its strength is not in its teeth but in its tail, and its harm is more in the lashing of its tail than with its jaws.' Isidore's dragon needs no poison, given its size and powers of constriction. The Ikhwān picture the mighty reptile quite differently.

222 The taxonomy of the Ikhwān is rough by modern standards — quite biblical, in fact. There are crawling and swarming creatures rather than reptiles and insects, and since insects crawl, many of our classificatory lines are crossed. Lévi-Strauss observes that traditional taxonomies can be quite precise, but they use their own criteria of relevance; *The Savage Mind*, tr. John and Doreen Weightman (Chicago: University of Chicago Press, 1966), pp. 35–74. Falconry affords a case in point: Arabs classified as suitable for training only birds with a black or yellow iris, a traditional sign of keen vision. Modern ornithology similarly classes 'dark eyed birds' as falcons. But such congruence depends on a parity or parallel of interests. In grouping animals as beasts, predators, fowl, birds of prey, aquatic, crawling, and swarming creatures, the dominant interest of the Ikhwān is in habitat, as befits their ecological perspective. Morphology is of secondary interest to them, since form is in any case (divinely) adapted to function and milieu.

223 See Chapter 7 above.

224 Qur'an 11:6. Human activities may affect all creatures, although theirs need not affect man: far from existing for man's sake, many animals dwell in places known but to God.

saw that they were the most numerous of animals, yet the smallest, weakest, and frailest, the least resourceful, sensitive, and aware. The dragon long pondered their lot. Then he said to the viper, his vizier, 'Do you see anyone among all these hordes suitable for us to send as our spokesman in this dispute? Most of them are deaf, dumb, and blind. They have no hands, feet, wings, beaks, or claws; no feathers, hair, wool, fleece, or scales on their bodies. Most of them are naked and unshod, feeble, flaccid, wretched, and poor, lacking all art and strength.'

The dragon was touched with pity for his subjects, and his heart went out to them in compassion, sympathy, mercy, and solicitude. His eyes filled with tears of sorrow, and he looked upward to heaven and cried out, 'Creator of all creatures, who spreads before them ample sustenance and directs all things, Most Merciful, who hears, sees, and knows all hidden and secret things from Your exalted heights — You make them and guide them, create and sustain them, give them life and cause them to die — be Thou our guardian and protector, our help and sustainer, guiding us and leading us, greatest in mercy.'

Then with clear voices they all cried out together, 'Amen, Amen, O Lord of the universe.'

Chapter 18
The Cricket's Wise Homily

When the cricket saw how troubled the dragon was, how solicitous and concerned he was for his subject hosts and vassals, the members of his kind, he mounted a nearby wall, set his fiddle strings in motion, piped on his pipes and began to sing sweet songs and melodies celebrating God and proclaiming His oneness:[225]

---

225 It is not unimportant to the Ikhwān that the cricket voices his thoughts in song and accompanies himself with his natural instrument. The authors believe that melody moves the soul by its natural affinities to the measures on which nature at large is built. Harmony moves us upward spiritually, although music, as Plato had urged, can also be abused, when made the mere plaything of the passions. Cf. Owen Wright, 'Music and Musicology in the *Rasā'il Ikhwān al-Ṣafā*', in

Hallelujah, praise God, our help,
And give thanks for His plenteous blessings,
For His bounties never cease:

Praised be God,
Our Judge, most loving and good,
One and peerless,
Hallowed and lauded,
Lord of all angels,
Spirit, eternal and living,
Glorious and glorified,
Known by awesome names,
Giver of portents and proof,[226]
Who was before time, before space,
Before all things that there are,
With no air above or water below.
Robed in light,
Unique and alone,
His mystery impenetrable —
When the heavens were not yet built

And the earth not yet spread out,
He judged and determined,
Allotted as He would.
He willed and created pure light
From no prior matter,
Or precedent form,
He simply said "Be!" And it was.[227]
He is the Active Intellect,[228]

Nader El-Bizri, ed., *The Ikhwān al-Ṣafā' and their 'Rasā'il'*, pp. 216–220, 227–229, 239–241, 244–246. See Prologue of the Ikhwān, note 72 above.

226 Each verse of the Qur'an is called a portent (*āyah*), and the Book itself, *Burhān*, or 'Proof'.

227 See Qur'an 2:117. The cricket rejects Platonic notions that the Forms that give pattern to the world are in any way independent of God.

228 The Active Intellect, mentioned in Aristotle's *De Anima* (III.5) and *Eudemian Ethics* (VII.4.1248a17–29), becomes in Neoplatonism the divine mind in which the Forms find a home, and from which Forms flow to all things, imparting the definiteness that the being of particulars requires. As '*dator formarum*', the

Possessed of knowledge and secrets,
Creating not from loneliness in His solitude
Nor out of any need at all,
But acting as He would
And ruling as He pleased,
With none to stay His judgement,
Or gainsay His sovereign decree,
For He is swift at reckoning.[229]

'Your Majesty,' said the cricket, 'you are kind and merciful, full of compassion for these throngs, your subjects, but don't be saddened by the tiny, frail bodies you see, or disheartened by their nakedness, poverty, and small device. For God who created and sustains them is all merciful and all kind. He loves and cares for them more than a loving mother and loving father do for their children. For when the Creator formed the animals with all their diverse forms and varied shapes, he gave them their ranks and stations. Some are great bodied and powerful; some, small, weak, and helpless. But all were treated equably in the giving of generous gifts, the organs and implements by

Active Intellect stands at the interface of the divine and natural worlds. Many Muslim philosophers give it command of the sphere of the moon. The cricket retains Alexander of Aphrodisias' Aristotelian identification of the Active Intellect with God. Kalonymos, in introducing his Hebrew translation, finds our fable's central theme in the thesis that all human powers spring from the Active Intellect, although many are shared with other living beings.

229 The cricket's song ends with a Qur'anic echo (2:198, 3:17, 199, 5:6, etc.). It affirms *creatio ex nihilo* and the associated doctrine of divine voluntarism. God acts and creates by grace, not necessity. So emanation does not entail eternalism. The cricket's voluntarism sets up the theodicy that answers his king's concern: God fashioned the crawling creatures at His pleasure, giving each its measure of grace. Birds and insects praise God in their songs. But the design of every creature is implicit praise, evidence of God's beneficent plan. Since praise of God is the object of creation, each creature's nature and actions give meaning to its existence. Man need not witness all these silent praises. For they are addressed to God. Nor does human praise alone have worth. In the Hebrew liturgy, the *Nishmat* prayer presses the same broad theme: man could not adequately praise God unless he had the wings of the eagle, the fleetness of the hind, etc. So one calls upon all his organs — the body's design — to join in with his paean.

which all might obtain what is good for them and protect themselves from injury. So all were sufficed.'[230]

'God gave the elephant his great bulk and mighty frame, the long, strong tusks he uses to defend himself from harm, and the long trunk he uses to grasp what is useful to him. But He also gave the tiny, frail gnat two delicate wings matched to his size, the power to fly swiftly and escape harm, and his own tiny proboscis, to take in nourishment. So the great and small are put on equal footing by the gifts they use to obtain what is good for them and avoid what is harmful. In the same way, the Creator who formed and shaped these poor, frail bands of yours, that seem to you so naked, unshod, and deficient, made them fruitful. For when their Creator formed them as He did and as you

230 God's gift of equality regards opportunity. For God, as Galen stresses, suits the anatomy of every species to its temper, and *vice versa*. 'A pious person,' Judah Halevi writes, 'firmly convinced of God's justice, cloaks and screens himself from the losses and woes that occur in this world, in his spiritual assurance that the Creator is just, sustaining and guiding all living things with a wisdom whose detailed workings are beyond us, but grasped general terms in the consummate mastery of their construction and the marvellous and awesome traits that bespeak the will and intent of a wise and knowing Power, who afforded the least and the greatest of His creatures all the inner and outward senses and organs they need, tools apt to the spirit of each: He made the hare and the stag timid and gave them the limbs for flight; He made the predators bold and gave them the limbs they need to seize and grip. If one reflects on how useful organs are and how well-matched to the spirit of each kind, one will see a just and judicious system that leaves no room to doubt the justice of its Maker. If any fiendish fancy finds it wrong for the hare to be fed to the predator, or the fly to the spider, reason replies with a rebuke: "How can you call the All-Wise unfair, when I'm already convinced of His justice and His having no need to do wrong? If predators hunted flies, or spiders, hares at hazard, I'd call it proof that chance rules. But I see that a wise and just ruler formed the lion's hunting tools and gave him his boldness and strength, fangs and claws — and formed the spider as well, inspiring the tactics she uses and the instinct to weave her web, without any instruction, and gave her the requisite tools for her art, and the flies as the food that sustains her, just as many of the fish in the sea are provided as food for other fish. So, should I see this as anything but the work of a wisdom beyond me, deferring to Him who is called the Rock whose work is perfect (Deuteronomy 32:4)? Just as Nahum of Gimzo was said to have done, whatever befell him, one whose spirit is solid here will always say 'This too is for the best' (Ta'anit 21b, Sanhedrin 108b). His life will be steadily sunny, and he'll bear hardships with ease."' *Kuzari*, 3.11, ed. David Baneth (Jerusalem: Magnes Press, 1977), pp. 101–102. The translation here is Goodman's; cf. tr. H. Hirschfeld (New York: Schocken, 1964), pp. 148–150.

see them now, He gave each ample means to secure its interests — to pursue the beneficial and guard against harm.[231]

'Study them, your Majesty, consider and reflect on their lives. The smallest, frailest, and least resourceful of them, you'll see, have the sprightliest bodies and steadiest spirits. They are less alarmed in escaping harm, calmer and less agitated in pursuing their livelihood and seeking their interests, and less demanding than larger, more powerful, more resourceful animals. If you study the case, you'll find that the larger, more powerfully built animals defend themselves from pain and injury by sheer force and brute power — as do carnivores, elephants, buffaloes, and other animals with massive frames and great strength. Others protect themselves by flight and swift running, as do gazelles, rabbits, and others, like wild asses, for example.[232] Others take to the air, like the birds. Still others plunge into the water and swim, as do the aquatic animals. Some seek safety by burrowing in the ground, hiding in holes and tunnels, like ants and mice, as God tells us in the story of the ant, where He said, '*Ants, get into your dwellings, lest Solomon and his troops trample you unawares.*'[233] Some, God clothes in heavy armour, like turtles, crabs, snails, and shell fish. Others, like hedgehogs, defend themselves by rolling up in a ball and tucking their heads under their tails.

231 Pursuit of the beneficial and avoidance harm are the aims of all living beings. As the Stoics reason, attraction and aversion in turn ground all value notions. The scheme is preserved down to the moral psychology of Spinoza, the utilitarians, and beyond.

232 See Galen, *De Usu Partium* I.2, 'the body is the instrument of the soul, so animals differ greatly in their parts, because their souls differ too. Some animals are bold, others timid, some wild, others tame. Some belong, so to speak, to a state, and work together for it; others are unsociable, as it were. In each case the body is adapted to the character and powers of the soul. The horse is given strong hoofs and adorned with a mane, for truly he is a swift, proud animal and not faint-hearted. The strength of the fierce and fearless lion, however, lies in his teeth and claws. Likewise with the bull and boar: the one has horns as its natural weapons, the other tusks. But since deer and hares are timid animals, their bodies are fleet, but completely unarmed and defenceless. For speed, I think, suits the timid; weapons are for the brave. Thus nature did not arm the one at all or strip the other.' Tr. after May, p. 67.

233 Qur'an 27:18; see note 123 above. The tale of Solomon's conversation with the ant is set down *in extenso* in al-Thaʿlabī, *'Arā'is al-majālis*, tr. W. Brinner, p. 498.

'There's great variety in the means by which animals seek their livelihood and well-being. Some, like hawks and eagles, rely on their keen vision and powerful flight.[234] Others, like ants, dung-beetles, and scarabs, have a powerful sense of smell. Others are led to their needs by their sense of hearing, as are the vultures. And some are guided by their sense of taste, as are fish and other aquatic animals. When the All-Wise Creator deprived this company of yours, who are so small, weak, frail, and artless, of these tools and organs, and denied them any great skill in their use, this was an act of grace. He spared them the trouble of seeking and the need of fleeing, placing them where they were hidden and protected, in holes, or plants, or the bowels of larger animals, or in clay or dung. He surrounded them with the nutriments they need and the materials they require, and He gave them the power of suction, to draw in liquids to nourish, sustain, and strengthen their bodies, making it unnecessary for them to pursue or to flee from anything.[235] So He did not create them with feet for walking, hands for grasping, a mouth to open, or teeth for chewing — no gullet for swallowing, no crop to collect food, no gizzard, stomach, or rumen in which to digest it, no bowels or intestines for thickening, no liver to cleanse the blood, no spleen to draw off the thick wastes of the chyme, and no gall-bladder to draw off the thin, no kidneys or bladder to drain the urine, no veins for blood to flow and pulse through, no nerves from the brain for sensation. No chronic disease touches them, and the pain of illness is unknown to them. They need no drugs, cures, or treatments. They are free of all the hurts that afflict larger, stronger, stouter animals. So praise the wise Creator who gave them all they need and spared them toil and trouble. For praise is His due, and thanks and lauds for His plenteous gifts, His abundant, unfailing bounties.'

'Bless you!' said the dragon, king of the crawling creatures, when the cricket had finished his speech. 'Well said! What a splendid orator

234 Modern optical experiments confirm that the vision of these soaring raptors is many times stronger than man's. Even worms and grubs, in the account of the Ikhwān, are generously cared for by God. Each species receives what suffices, not just for its needs but for its advantage.

235 A scholium here reads: 'Such are the worms and wormlike creatures.' Isidore writes: 'The weevil [*gurgulio*, literally, 'gullet'] is so named because it is almost nothing but a throat.' *Etymologies* 12.8.17.

God made you! How eloquent! How thoroughly has He schooled you! How compellingly you make your case! Praised be God for making a member of our kind so wise and virtuous and so cogent a pleader. You must make the journey', the dragon said, 'as spokesman of us all in the case against humankind.'

'At his Majesty's command and in faithful service to my brethren,' said the cricket, 'I obey.'

At that the snake said, 'Don't mention there that you represent serpents and snakes.'

'Why not?' asked the cricket.

'Because there's an inveterate hatred, a grudge nursed from time immemorial between snakes and the Adamites. Many men even criticize their Lord, often asking why he created snakes, since there's no value or good in us but only harm, and thus no wisdom in our creation.'[236]

'Why do they say that?' asked the cricket.

'Because of the poison in our fangs. They say it's of no use except for killing and destroying living things. That shows how ignorant they are of the nature things and of what is useful or harmful.

'To be sure,' the snake continued, 'God has made mankind suffer through these poisons. He has visited chastisement on them by this means.[237] God even made it necessary for some human kings to hide our poisons under the stones of their signet rings against need. In fact, if these critics considered the conditions in which all creatures live, and the vicissitudes to which they are subject, this would be clear to them; they would see how very useful is the venom in the fangs of vipers[238] and would not ask why God created it and what good it is. If

236 The lost *Kitāb al-Sirr* of Ibn Karrām asks: 'What good is it for God to create snakes, scorpions, and mice but then order that they be slain?' The passage is preserved in Ibn al-Dāʿī al-Rāzī's (twelfth century) *Kitāb Tabṣīrāt al-ʿawāmm fī maʿarifat maqālat al-anām* (Tehran: Matba'a-i Majlis, 1934); and see J. van Ess, 'Ibn ar-Rewandi, or the Making of an Image', *al-Abhath*, 27 (1978/1979), p. 7; Eric Ormsby, *Theodicy In Islamic Thought*, pp. 144–145.

237 In Zoroastrian belief, all creatures play a part in combating Ahriman. See also Louis Ginzberg, *The Legends of the Jews*, tr. Henrietta Szold, vol. 5, p. 60, note 191; cf. Lactantius, *The Divine Institutes* VII.4, ed. Mary Francis MacDonald (Washington, DC: Catholic University Press, 1964).

238 Galen expatiates on the medicinal virtues of vipers; *On Simples*, 11. Paul of Aegina writes: 'Dioscorides recommends vipers, having their head and tail cut off, and the entrails taken out, boiled with oil, wine, a little salts and dill, for

they understood, they would not speak so, finding fault with the rule on which their Lord devised His Creation.'[239]

Said the cricket, 'Can you tell us about this, wise one, so that we may better understand?'

'Certainly, eloquent speaker', said the snake. 'When the wise Creator formed those creatures you spoke of, and endowed each kind, as you

---

nervous affections and scrofula. He gives no credit, however, to the vulgar belief of his time, that living upon vipers prolonged life, or that they prevented lice from forming on the body.... The Arabians display much more credulity than Dioscorides, in describing the medicinal virtues of vipers, ascribing to them wonderful powers, not only of preserving life, but even of restoring youth. See in particular Avicenna, *Canon*, and Rhases [Rāzī] (*Cont.* 1 ult. 1, 731 [that is, the *Continens Liber* = the *Ḥāwī*]).' The Muslim medical authors seem here to follow Galen, who 'gives a very lengthened disquisition on the medicinal virtues of vipers.' Paul of Aegina, *The Seven Books*, tr. Adams, vol. 3, pp. 120–121.

239 In the printed editions, the speech continues: 'Besides, although God created the poison in our spittle to destroy living things, He also made our flesh an antidote to these poisons.' It goes on by having the serpent explain: 'For the ancient physicians found in our flesh a capacity to counteract our poisons, and used that flesh as an ingredient in their antidote. But most people do not appreciate this.' Both theodicy and science in the Middle Ages urged that every poison has its antidote — just as the Ikhwān press the point that every beast is vulnerable, every created power vincible by some other, perhaps seemingly insignificant power. Antidotes today are still prepared using materials derived from venomous serpents, since most anti-toxins are too complex chemically to be synthesized artificially. Internal immunities often protect venomous creatures from the action of their own poison — notably, in the case of neurotoxins. Modern antivenins, consisting primarily of antibodies against venoms, are produced by injecting a laboratory animal such as a horse or sheep with venom to induce a reaction product effective against that specific poison. Antidotes typically act through their close chemical complementarity to the venom whose action they block. One contemporary antivenin technician reports being bitten by venomous snakes some 170 times, but he has made it a practice to inject himself directly with the venom of the serpents he handles. Starting in 1948 with small doses of cobra venom, he gradually increased the quantity to a full lethal dose and diversified the types. In 2007, he reached age 95. His story recalls the close of 'Terence, This Is Stupid Stuff' in A. E. Housman's *A Shropshire Lad*: 'There was a king reigned in the East: / There, when kings will sit to feast, / They get their fill before they think / With poisoned meat and poisoned drink. / He gathered all that springs to birth / From the many-venomed earth; / First a little, thence to more. / He sampled all her killing store: / And easy, smiling, seasoned sound, / Sate the king when healths went round. / They put arsenic in his meat / And stared aghast to watch him eat; / They poured strychnine in his cup / And shook to see him drink it up: / They shook, they stared as white's their shirt: / Them it was their poison hurt. / — I tell the tale that I heard told. / Mithridates, he died old.'

told us, with implements and organs to obtain all their needs and protect themselves from harm, He gave some a hot stomach, others a rumen, and some a paunch for digesting their food after chewing it well, so as to nourish them. Snakes were given no hot stomach, rumen, or paunch, or even molars to chew their meat. Instead, God set burning poison in our fangs to prepare the meat we eat.[240] So, when a snake seizes an animal's body and sinks his fangs into it, he pumps in his venom to reduce it instantly, so it can be gobbled up and swallowed at once, and digested. Had this poison not been created for snakes and had we not been given our nutriment, we would have died of starvation or injury. Every one of us would have perished, and our kind would be extinct.'[241]

'Goodness', said the cricket. 'I see how venom is useful to snakes, but what good are snakes to other animals? What wisdom or worth is there in their creation and existence on earth among the crawling creatures?'

'They serve the same purpose as predators do among wild and domestic beasts, the same purpose as sea-serpents in the sea — or swordfish, or crocodiles — or hawks and eagles and other birds of prey.'[242]

240 One seventeenth-century copyist objects, noting in the margin of his manuscript that a snake will not die just because its fangs are removed, discrediting the claim that venom is necessary to ophidian digestion. He might have mentioned also that many a snake is venomless.

241 The argument is neat, but circular. It loses its force unless it is assumed that all species ought to exist. But the question at issue is whether serpents ought to exist. Perhaps the intent is to lead the reader to adopt the perspective of another species than one's own.

242 Here the serpent broadens his case to allude to the ecological advantages of death. Sexual reproduction, individuality, and death are all parts of a system no element of which would exist without the rest. The Ikhwān have already suggested that death, at times, may aid those who suffer or face intolerable risks. The point is directed over the animals' heads to a human audience, arguing in effect that mere physical survival is not the highest value. There are circumstances that can make death welcome. For the Ikhwān, as in the Qur'an, the values that transcend sheer survival are linked with promises of immortality. Beyond that thought, resignation, acceptance of God's plan, can also regard death as a good. The same alienation from degrading aspects of this life that prompts a quest for values beyond survival also yields world weariness, *taedium vitae*, which may find expression as an acceptance of the wisdom of death in the divine or natural scheme. Baḥyā ibn Paqūda finds in death a mark of God's wisdom in the world, albeit one not obvious to His creatures; *Al-Hidāya ilā farā'iḍ al-qulūb*, II.3, ed.

'Spell that out a little further for me', said the cricket.

'Certainly', said the snake. 'When God first brought all creatures into being, gave them their origin, by His power ordering all things according to His will, He made some dependent on others for their sustenance. He made some the means and instrumentality of others' survival — all for the common good. Granted, what benefits some may harm others. But the harm was not His primary intention. He foresaw what was to be, yet knowing of this harm did not keep Him from creating these dangerous creatures. For He saw that the benefits they would confer were more general; the good they would do would outweigh the harm.

'To illustrate: when God created the sun and moon and the other stars of the firmament, He made the sun the lamp of the world and the light of life, a cause of all generation through its heat. He made its role in the world like that of the heart in the body. Just as the heart spreads the bodily heat to all the extremities, giving life and health to the whole body, so the sun gives life and health to all, and its benefit is universal.[243] Some loss or injury may result to a given animal or plant. But that is offset by the general benefit to the well-being of all. In the same way, Saturn, Jupiter, Mars, and all the other stars in the spheres were created for the good of the world and the general benefit they afford, even though their influences may at times bring dire excesses of heat or cold.[244] Likewise with the rain: God sends it to give life to the earth and sustenance to His creatures — animal, vegetable, and mineral — even though floods may destroy or damage some animals or plants or ruin the homes of some who are helpless.

'The same holds true with snakes and beasts of prey, sea-serpents, crocodiles, and all crawling and swarming creatures — scorpions, locusts, and all the creatures that God forms from mouldering, corrupting matter. They come to be to cleanse the air, lest it grow polluted with the putrescent vapours that rise from such matter,

---

Yahuda, p. 100, line 4 (tr. M. Mansoor, p. 156), citing Genesis 1:31, Ecclesiastes 4:2, as rabbinically interpreted.

243 The analogy comes from the Stoics.

244 The planets and stars link the spiritual with the physical world, governing nature through their influences. The word 'influence', originally an astrological term, is the name for the intellectual connection between the physical and the non-physical.

corrupting the atmosphere and causing plague and the loss of all animals at a stroke.[245]

'To explain: worms, flies, gnats, and dung-beetles are not found in dry goods stores, carpenters' shops, or at blacksmiths' forges, but mostly in butcher shops, butteries, and dairies, or at the fishmonger's, if not in manure. When God forms them out of such putrefactions, they absorb the rotting matter by feeding and nourishing themselves on it, and the air is purified. These tiny animals are eaten in turn, and provide nourishment to larger ones, all by the wisdom of the Creator who creates nothing useless and does nothing in vain.

'But those who don't recognize these blessings may criticize their Lord, asking why He created such beings and what good they are. This is simply captious ignorance, incomprehension of the laws of God's handiwork and the canons of its rule. Some thoughtless humans, I've heard, even claim that providence does not reach below the sphere of the moon.[246] But if they reflected and studied the way things work, they

245 Predators are necessary, the Ikhwān argue, ecologically, to allow the recycling of biomass. Without them, putrescence would take on catastrophic proportions, the food-chain pressing all in one direction, creating pollution that would render life ultimately impossible. The Ikhwān did not know that 'putrescence' is itself critical to the food cycle, otherwise their argument might have been made even stronger. For not only predators and scavengers are ecologically necessary but so are decomposers, nitrogen fixers, etc. In evolutionary terms, not only would life have been snuffed out if these (seemingly menial) functions were not performed, but in fact, a complex and stable system of life forms would never have emerged.

246 The standard Peripatetic view, voiced, for instance, in Alexander of Aphrodisias' critique of Stoicism, was that providence extends to the celestial bodies, since their motions are perfect, their matter uncompounded, their lives eternal. For the spheres, being animated and intelligent, were seen as divine. But providence did not reach sublunary individuals as such, subject to change and privation. Only the species in the sublunary world, not the individuals, were so graced. For natural species were the locus of the unchanging Forms. God's unconcern for particulars, it was argued, does not derogate from His perfection: a gentleman pays no mind to the affairs of the cats in his house, went the riposte — and, in the same way, it is no discredit to God that He pays no mind to mortals. Monotheists were scandalized at such dismissals of special providence, and Maimonides countered Alexander's arguments by reminding Aristotelians that (by their own account) only particulars exist. If providence below the sphere of the moon reaches classes, Maimonides argued, then it does reach individuals, even on Peripatetic premises. The Ikhwān rely on astral influences to translate general goodness into terms of concrete particularity: the forms imparted to

would clearly see and understand that God's providence encompasses all creatures, great and small, and they would not utter such slanderous lies. That is all I have to say. May God Almighty have mercy on us all.'

Chapter 19
The Court in Session

The next day, when the animal delegates had arrived from all their distant lands and the King of the Jinn had taken his seat, a herald announced, 'Hear ye, hear ye! Let all who have grievance or suit attend. For the King is seated in judgement.'

Present were the jinni judges, jurists, and justices, jurymen, and sages, as well as the parties: human and animal delegates who had come from every quarter. Ranged in rows before the King, they hailed him with wishes of long life and felicity. The King gazed left and right. Beholding the immense diversity of shapes and forms, colours, sounds, and songs before him, for some time he was overcome with wonder. Then, turning to one of the wise jinni philosophers, he said, 'Look at these marvellous creatures, handiwork of the All-Merciful.'

'I see them, your Majesty', came the reply. 'I see them with the eyes of my head, but in my heart I behold their Creator. Your Majesty is amazed at them, and I am amazed at the wisdom of the Creator who formed and fashioned them, raised and reared them, who gave them being, and preserves and provides for them still, *who knows their every lair and refuge.*[247] All this, writ plain in His Book, with nothing left out or forgotten but each detail clear and precise.[248] Hidden from sight by veils of light and far beyond reach of thought and fancy, He made

all species by the Active Intellect (and manifested in their organs, habits, and strategies) are vehicles of divine providence over particulars.

247 Qur'an 11:6. Cf. Job 38–40.

248 Divine omniscience and human destiny are both associated with the Book and the celestial Preserved Tablet (*al-Lawḥ al-maḥfūẓ*). The Book is at times synonymous with revelation and law, but it also refers to God's plan, the universal pattern of all that is, the source of the Forms through which nature is governed. See Oliver Leaman, 'Preserved Tablet', in *The Qur'an: An Encyclopedia* (London: Routledge, 2006).

his works manifest, expressing and revealing what was concealed in His inviolable fastness,[249] so that eyes might apprehend and need no further proof or argument.[250]

'Know, wise Majesty, that the forms and shapes, figures and types you see in the corporeal world, the world of bodies and physical appearances, are but copies, spectres, idols, imitations of the Forms in the world of spirits. The Forms *there* are luminous and clear; these are dark and opaque. The relationship of these to those others is like that of pictures painted on boards or the surface of walls to the forms of living beings of flesh and blood, skin and bone. For the Forms in the realm of spirits cause motion, but these are what they move, and lesser forms are silent and still. Forms here are objects of the senses, but *those* are objects of thought. They endure, but the rest perish and fade.'[251]

---

249 A hadith widely circulated and admired, especially among Sufis, despite the doubts of hadith scholars as to its provenance, ascribes to God the words: 'I was a hidden treasure, and I wished to be known, so I created all creatures, that I might be known'; see William Chittick, *The Sufi Path of Knowledge* (Albany, NY: SUNY Press, 1989), p. 131.

250 Qur'an 6:59: *His are the keys of the unseen, which He alone knows. He knows what is on land and sea. No leaf falls but He knows it; not a grain in the dark of the earth, no thing fresh or dry but is in His clear Book.* Qur'an 10:61: *Nothing about you, no recitation of yours, no act that you do but We witness it. When you go forward with it, not the weight of an atom on earth or in heaven escapes thy Lord, nor anything greater or less, but is in His clear Book.* As the Ikhwān gloss the verses, the Qur'an intends not some divine memorandum book, as if God might forget a detail of things if He lacked a written reminder, but rather an affirmation of the plainness and evidence of God's handiwork, God's clear hallmark in nature. The conceit of God's being veiled by light is ancient. It is well rooted in the philosophic repertoire and in the symbolic vocabulary of scriptural monotheism. Psalm 93 presents God as robed in majesty. For, mere human notions of majesty do not reach the Absolute but only point in the direction of God's transcendence. Aristotle argues that some truths are missed by their very manifestness, as light (proverbially) is of no use to the bat; *Metaphysics* II.1.993b10–11: 'as the eyes of bats are to the blaze of day, so is reason in our soul to the things that are by nature most evident of all.' The Stoics favoured a phrase that Sufis later repeated widely: 'One does not use a candle to seek the sun.' Ghazālī's *Mishkāt al-anwār*, develops an elaborate schematism of veils of light, citing the hadith: 'God has seventy veils of light and darkness; were He to lift them, the glory of His face would consume all who saw Him'; see note 318 below. Given the transcendence of the God of monotheism, His hallmarks in nature are crucial evidence of His unseen glory; thus Psalm 19 complements Psalm 93, making the heavens witnesses to the work of the unseen God.

251 Cf. Qur'an 28:88: *All things perish except His face.* Linking evanescent nature and its eternal Creator in the jinni philosopher's appeal to divine design are the

The jinni sage then rose and declaimed, 'Praised be God, Creator of all creatures, Giver of being to all that is, first Author and Deviser of all that is made, who governs all times, ages, and moments, Architect of space and the dimensions, who regulates the spheres and sends forth the angels, who raises up the heavens as their dwelling place and spreads forth the level earth beneath the storeyed skies, who formed all creatures, with all their varied hues, traits, and tongues, who gives them countless gifts and bounties, their Author and Creator, Guide and Master of their fate, Bestower of life and death. Glory and exaltation to Him who is at once near and far, near to the solitude of those who call upon Him, far from the reach of the grasping senses. The tongues of those who would limn His true attributes weary in the attempt, and the minds of the discerning fall into confusion at the thought of His glory, His majesty, His awesome dominion, and the clarity of His signs and proofs. No power of mind can apprehend Him, and no power of speech can describe Him. He is God, unique and triumphant, august and much-forgiving, who created jinn before Adam, from the flame of the simoom, airy spirits, and ethereal phantoms, swiftly moving with wondrous forms, floating with ease, freely through the air, by God's providence and grace.

'He it was who made every sort of creature — jinn, humans, angels, animals of every kind. He ordered them by ranks and classes, at His pleasure, some as the highest of the high — the cherubim and His pure servants, formed from the light of His throne and charged with bearing it; some as the lowest of the low — rebel demons and their kin, infidels, idolaters, and hypocrites, jinni and human alike. But some are intermediate: His upright servants, male and female, who are Muslims and believers. Praised, then, be God who graced us with faith and led us to Islam, making us his vice-regents on earth, as He stated, *that I may observe how you act.*[252] And praised be God who by His grace favoured our king with clemency, learning, justice, and equity. Hear the King now and obey if you are wise. That is all. God's forgiveness on me and upon all of you.'[253]

---

pure and ideal archetypes by which God created, that is the Platonic Forms; see Plato, *Republic* VI.507–VII.521.

252 Qur'an 10:14.

253 Echoing Plato's creation story in the *Timaeus*, the philosophical jinni ascribes the origin of all things to God's temporal instantiation of the eternal Forms. God's act is immanent, although He Himself remains transcendent. Hence His

Chapter 20

When the jinni sage had finished speaking, the King surveyed the body of humans standing before him, about seventy men in all, of diverse forms, garbs, tongues, and colours, and seeing among them a man of middling stature, even build, handsome form, and well-cut figure, a man with fine features, a clear complexion, and a cheerful face, lively and pleasant, he turned to his vizier and asked, 'Who is that, and where is he from?'

'He is a man from Iran-Shahr', came the reply — meaning Iraq.[254]

'Tell him to speak', said the King.

The Iraqi complied. 'Praised be God, Sovereign of the universe,' he began, 'hope of those who fear Him and foe to none but the wicked. God bless Muhammad and all his House together. Praised be God, one and unique, alone, ever-abiding, all-merciful, and all-bountiful, full of majesty and beneficence, who was before all time, space, and substance, before all beings that are, who then created *ex nihilo*, bringing forth from His hidden fastness a brilliant light, and from the light a lambent flame and a churning sea. He mingled fire with water and there arose

---

propinquity and distance: He is near in the bestowal of the Forms that impart reality and intelligibility to all things in nature. Yet He transcends all that He generates. Since God acts and creates through the Forms, the jinni philosopher argues, providence extends to 'all creatures, great and small'. So it is arbitrary of Aristotelians to halt providence at the sphere of the moon, confining it to the world's 'principal parts'. The Peripatetic and Neoplatonic philosophers held it arbitrary to have God's act begin abruptly at a particular moment in time. Is it not equally arbitrary, the Ikhwān imply, for God's governance to stop short of all that He creates? Moreover, if grace and providence apply to all creatures, then even malefactors, miscreants, and devils have their place in God's scheme. Relying on God's compassion, the argument stops just a step away from Origen's inference that even these wicked individuals, after many cycles of purgation, may be forgiven; see *De Principiis*, tr. G. W. Butterworth (New York: Harper and Row, 1966), p. 57, with note.

254 The reference is to western Iran, the so-called 'Irāq 'Ajamī, that is Persian Iraq, as distinguished from Iraq proper, that is, Mesopotamia. From Sāsānian times Persians called this region Iran-Shahr. See E. Yarshater, ed., *Encyclopaedia Iranica*, 'Ērān, Ērānšahr' and 'Ērāq-e 'Ajam(ī)' (Boston: Routledge and Kegan Paul, 1985–). In our text, the area is feistily given its Iranian name — reflecting the outlook of the Shu'ūbiyya. Today, the delegate would probably be called Iranian; his references to Iranian kings testify to his loyalties. The Ikhwān, however, call him an Iraqi, and seem to include all of Iraq within his homeland. They identify as Persian only the Khurāsānian who speaks at this chapter's end.

a rosy smoke and curdled foam. From the smoke he made the vaulted heavens, and from the foam the outstretched earth. He anchored it with towering mountains, and dredged the swelling seas. He sent scouring winds in all directions, raising vapours from the sea and plumes of dust from land, blending these into clouds and mists to be driven by winds over desert and plain and there send down the blessed rain. He thus caused grass to grow for us and plants to flourish to refresh us and our cattle.[255]

'Praised be God *who from water formed a man and gave him issue and kin*,[256] who formed *from it a spouse, that they might live together*,[257] and *from them sowed a multitude of men and women*,[258] blessing their seed and subjecting to them all that is on land and sea *to enjoy for a time*[259] *— after which you die, to be raised up again on Resurrection Day*.[260]

'Praised be God, who preferred us to so many of His creatures, chose us for the most central of lands as our home,[261] gave us the balmiest air and richest soil, the most plenteous of rivers and trees. His are the praise, the thanks, and the glory for favouring us with keen spirits, clear minds, and towering intellects. We have sounded the deepest sciences

255 The spokesman passes insensibly from acknowledging God's bounty to the presumption that man was indeed its sole ultimate object.

256 Qur'an 25:54.

257 Qur'an 7:189; in the verse God creates man, that is, Adam, from a single soul, and from that soul (the 'it' of the verse), creates Eve, as his mate.

258 Qur'an 4:1. This verse begins with the same language as 7:189 but does not continue with the line '*that they might live together*'. The Ikhwān conjoin the verses, either relying on memory or simply joining passages that seem naturally to link with one another.

259 Qur'an 16:80. The verse in full may support the animals' case: *God it is who made you homes to dwell in, from the hides of cattle, houses easy to manage on days when ye strike or pitch camp, and from their wool, fleece, and hair, rich furnishings to enjoy for a time.* Human hegemony is not absolute or eternal. It is a gift, conditional and transitory.

260 Qur'an 23:15–16.

261 William Lethaby, in *Architecture, Mysticism and Myth*, cites many versions of the geography that renders, say, Paris, London, Boston, etc., the world's hub. Ancient Persia, China, Japan, and India, made similar claims. Delphi, Moriah, Ararat, and others have been called the omphalos, or navel of the world, its foundation stone, well-spring, tent post of the sky, etc. Mystic architecture, Lethaby argues, often projects a *templum* orienting the precincts of the heavens, not just enclosing space but aligning the cosmos and signalling the centrality of a regime. The pyramids, Stonehenge, the Ka'ba at Mecca, and Buddhist stupas or pagodas all exercise similar functions.

and devised new arts, settled new lands, dug channels, planted trees, built buildings, and founded states and societies. We were vouchsafed the gift of prophecy and leadership. For Noah was one of us, as was the sublime Idrīs, and Abraham, God's friend.

'Of our number too were virtuous kings[262] like the celebrated Afrīdūn, the invincible Manūjahr, Darius al-Bahmānī,[263] Ardashīr son of Bābakān the Persian, Bahrām, Anūshirwān, Buzurgmihr son of Baḥtikān, the Sāsānian kings,[264] and the Samānids,[265] who dredged rivers for irrigation, planted trees, built cities and villages, and established the order of the realm — throne, administration, army, and subjects.[266] So we are the heart of mankind, mankind is the heart of the animals, animals are the heart of all that grows, and growing things are the heart of the elements. We, then, are the heart of hearts. But God's is

262 For these figures, see Appendix C.

263 The Ikhwān voice their pride in Darius' achievements, treating Iraq as part of the Iranian heartland.

264 The Sāsānid monarchs, who ruled Iran from 224 until their defeat by the armies of Islam in 651, were celebrated in Persian legend and in the epics that formed the basis for Firdawsī's *Shahnameh*, completed not long after the *Rasā'il*. Tha'labī appropriates these Iranian traditions in his *'Arā'is al-majālis*, tr. W. Brinner; see, e.g., pp. 410, 608, 609. For the history of the dynasty, see M. Morony, 'Sāsānids', *EI2*, vol. 9, p. 70–83.

265 Established in Transoxiana in the early ninth century and expanding to Khurāsān, the Sāmānid dynasty, sprung from Persian land owners Islamized only a century earlier, gained significant power around 900 and established their capital at Bukhara. There, its ministries ran an orderly administration that gathered rich proceeds from the agricultural oases of Soghdia, Farghāna, and Khurāsān, and from the slave trade out of Inner Asia. Praised for their mild rule and moderate taxation, the Sāmānids held the marches against pagan tribes from the steppes, relying on Turkic slave guards, who as a result gained significant power in their own right. The dynasty was overthrown at the start of the new millennium, just as Avicenna, the son of a Sāmānid governor, came of age.

266 The Iranian order is made a paradigm of national and civil life here, much as Aristotle elevates the Greek *polis*. The speaker's pride may be warranted, but his chauvinism is meant to be noticed. Despite its virtues, the national, hierarchical mode of governance was not ideal from all standpoints. Aristotle saw it as illiberal — although he, for his part, was all too ready to accept the exploitation of slaves and subordination of women and the 'lower' orders, without which the liberty and the leisure he prized seemed to him unattainable. He also glossed over the erosion of civil liberties and deliberative engagement of the citizenry in imperial Athens and the further diminution of both liberties and participatory activity under the rule of Alexander.

the praise, His are the glory and thanks.[267] Unto Him do all return once they grow old and die. I have said my say. I appeal to God for mercy on myself and on you.'

The King asked the jinni sages who were present what they had to say about this human's remarks and the distinctions of which he had boasted. All agreed that everything the man had said was true, except the jinni savant who was known as the hard-headed and outspoken one. He was not afraid to correct anyone's errors or slips and rebut his mistakes or misstatements. He said, 'This learned body should know that the human from Iraq has omitted capital, crucial matters from his speech.'

'What might they be?' asked the King.

'He did not say, "On our account the Flood was sent, drowning all animals and plants on the face of the earth", or "In our land human discord arose, confusion of mind and heart in a babble of misunderstanding." Nor did he say: "Nimrod the Tyrant was one of us", or boast, "We cast Abraham into the flames." Nor did he state: "Nebuchadnezzar, who destroyed the Temple, burnt the Torah, slew the seed of Solomon and the House of Israel, and drove the House of Adnān[268] from the banks of the Euphrates to the plains of the Ḥijāz, that bloodthirsty rebel and tyrant, was one of us."'

'How could he report such things?', asked the King. 'They all count not for him but against him.'

'It is not proper in law and equity', said the forthright jinni, 'to count and vaunt one's virtues but omit one's failings without even trying to repent or excuse them.'

Surveying the group again, the King saw a man with a lean, brown body, a long beard, and a great mane of hair. He was wrapped in a

---

267 The spokesman caps his boasts with a shallow obeisance to God for making his people the best of all creatures. The Ikhwān relish the irony, evidently finding hierarchical patterns somewhat distasteful when shifted from heavenly or earthly rule to the relations of races or species — especially when the temporal fortunes of wealth and warfare are treated as if they were permanent products of absolute desert. The Ikhwān do not hold all creatures equal. Yet all are recipients of grace. So no one has grounds for chauvinism — or hegemony, except as and as long as God allows.

268 See Chapter 8, note 134 above.

red waist-cloth tied about his middle. 'Who is that over there?' asked the King.

'A man from India,' came the reply, 'from the isle of Ceylon.'

'Command him to speak', said the King.

The vizier did so, and the man spoke: 'Praise be to God, one and unique, alone and impassive, ageless and ever-enduring, who was before all places, ages and times, before every being and substance. He then raised up a swirling sea of light, compounded the spheres from it and set them spinning.[269] He formed the stars in their courses, allotted the zodiac signs and let each one rise in its turn. He spread out the earth and settled it, marked out the climes, dredged the seas, caused rivers to flow and anchored the mountains, spread wide the deserts and wastes. He brought forth plants and gave being to animals. He favoured us with the most central of lands, the most even in climate, where night and day are balanced, winter and summer tempered, neither too hot nor too cold. He made the soil of our land the richest in minerals, its trees the finest, its plants the most medicinal,[270] its animals — elephantine! Our trees are teak; our reeds are cane; our grass, bamboo; our pebbles, jacinths and chrysolites. Here was the place God gave his origin to Adam, the forefather of all human beings, peace be upon him — and the point of origin for all other animals too. For they all came to life at the equator.[271]

'God, blessed and exalted be He, singled us out for yet more blessings. He sent prophets to our land and made most of our people sages — like the Buddha, the Brahmins,[272] Bilawhar, and Budasf.[273] He favoured us

269 Again, the Ikhwān speak through a quasi-transparent persona: compounded spheres are not 'simple substances' — so they are created, not eternal, and their parts need not have been joined as they are — so their natures are not unconditioned. The motion of the spheres too is a mark of their mutability. The spheres are no more indestructible than they are uncreated. For no compound endures forever, and nothing that changes lacks an origin.

270 Paul of Aegina describes many medicinal plants as having an Indian origin.

271 The equable balance of celestial influences made the equator, in theory, the most temperate clime. The idea that this climate fosters an ideal mix of the elements aids the Ikhwān in naturalizing the act of creation; cf. Ibn Ṭufayl, *Ḥayy ibn Yaqẓān*, tr. Goodman, pp. 103–105.

272 For Muslim knowledge of Buddhism and the Brahmins see Shahrastānī, *Kitāb al-Milal wa'l-niḥal*, pp. 444–446; B. Carra de Vaux, 'Budd', *EI2*, vol. 1, p. 1283; G. Monnot, 'Sumaniyya', *EI2*, vol. 9, p. 869.

273 Bilawhar and Budasf feature in Greek, Manichaean, Hebrew, and Arabic tales.

with the subtlest of sciences — astrology, sorcery, incantations, augury, conjuring, and divination. He made the folk of our land the swiftest of men, the nimblest and most daring of acrobats, the most fearless of the turns of fate, the most scornful of death. That is what I have to say. God grant forgiveness to me and to you.'

Said the outspoken jinni, 'Had you finished your speech, you would have said, "We are also plagued with burning the bodies of our dead,[274] worship of idols, images, and apes, and the many offspring of our fornication, the blackening of our faces, and the eating of betel nuts."'

The King then scanned the group and noticed another man. Studying him, he saw that he was tall and wore a yellow robe. In his hand was a scroll that he pored over, murmuring and swaying to and fro.[275] Said the King to his vizier, 'Who is that?'

'A man from Syria, a Hebrew of the House of Israel', he replied.

'Command him to speak', said the King.

'Praised be God, one and eternal, living and abiding, powerful and wise,' said the Jew, 'who was in all ages past, with none else beside Him. He then made a beginning, creating radiant light, and from the light a white-hot fire and a churning, watery sea. He mingled these and out of the mix came smoke and foam. He said to the smoke, 'Be the sky'; and to the foam, 'Be the earth.' He formed and fashioned the heavens, finishing them in two days. In two more days He spread forth the earth, and in the many storeys of heaven and earth formed all manner of creatures — angels, jinn, humans, birds, and wild beasts, in two days.

Bilawhar was a wandering ascetic to whom Budasf, a world-weary prince, turns for guidance. For the parables from this sequence used by the Ikhwān, see Rūzbihān al-Baqlī, *Le livre de Bilawhar et Budasf selon la version arabe ismaelienne*, ed. and tr. D. Gimaret (Paris: Droz, 1971), pp. 36–37.

274 A more spiritual reading is given to this practice in Chapter 39.

275 Bernard Septimus, a friend and colleague from Harvard, tells us that this is the earliest reference he knows to the Jewish practice of 'shukeling', or rocking, in prayer. Midrashically, it is said that the worshipper is alternately drawn by the light of the sacred texts and repelled by the intensity of their heat. The practice, Septimus writes, may be influenced by Ezekiel 1:14 ('rushing forward and back'), as applied to exegetical boldness in Chapter 1 of *Sefer Yetzirah* (The Book of Creation) and taken up in the kabbalistic sources.

Then, on the seventh day, He settled on His throne.[276] As the elect of all His creatures, He chose Adam,[277] the father of mankind; and of his seed, Noah; of his, Abraham, God's Beloved; and of his, Israel. From his descendants, God chose Moses, son of Amram. God spoke with him, rescued him, and gave him the signs of the hand and the rod.[278] He gave him the Torah and the books of the prophets, and cleft the sea for him. He drowned Pharaoh, his foe, and all of his host, sent down manna and quails to Israel in the desert, made them kings, and gave them a dominion granted to none else in the world. I have finished my say. God grant pardon to me and to you.'

Said the outspoken jinni, 'You neglected or forgot or to say, "He made us *apes and pigs, worshippers of false gods*,[279] stricken with *abasement and misery by God's wrath*.[280] *That is their shame here*

---

276 Creatures are given their habitats in the many-tiered cosmos. The Sabbath celebrates the act of creation, in keeping with the dictum of Genesis 2:1–3 and Exodus 20:8–11. Maimonides interprets God's being settled on His throne (see Psalms 93:2, etc.) as a reference to the ontic primacy of the ground of being; *Guide* I.11.

277 The word the Ikhwān choose here to express God's election, '*iṣṭafā*', is of the same root as that of their own epithet, 'al-Ṣafā''. It is also the root of a favourite epithet of Muhammad, 'Muṣṭafā', meaning God's 'chosen one'.

278 The rod is the staff God changed to a serpent as a sign for Moses (Exodus 4:2–4, 17; Qur'an 7:107). In Exodus 4:7 and Qur'an 7:108, Moses draws a gleaming white hand from his bosom, another sign of his mission.

279 Qur'an 5:60. Verses 57–59 warn Muslims not to befriend other People of the Book, since these recipients of scripture mock the faithful, their call to prayer, and their worship. Jews are accursed, transformed into apes and swine, objects of God's wrath for their idolatry, unbelief, and sin. In rejecting Muhammad's mission, they have said, in effect, that God's hand is fettered, and thus have been made powerless themselves. Some modernist Muslims seek to soften the impact of this Qur'anic obloquy by linking its bitterness to the heat of Muhammad's polemic against the Jews of his time, for rejecting his mission. Kalonymos drops the abusive 'apes and pigs' but sustains the intent of the outspoken jinni's rebuke by dwelling on the golden calf and other instances of prophetically condemned backsliding for which traditional Jews in the Middle Ages acknowledged an abiding sense of communal guilt. In place of the charge that Jews are abased for disobedience, Kalonymos has the 'reprover', as he calls the outspoken jinni, charge that God has punished Israel by making the lesser child greater, a reference to the worldly ascendance of the seed of Ishmael.

280 Qur'an 2:61, where Moses rebukes the Israelites for demanding fresh vegetables. The verse charges Jews with disbelief in God's revelations and with the sin of slaying His prophets.

below, and theirs is a great chastisement in the hereafter[281] *— requital for their deeds.*"'[282]

Again scanning the throng, the King saw a man clad in a woollen robe, bound at the waist with a leather belt. He had a censer in his hand that he swung to and fro, spreading incense smoke as he sonorously chanted the words he was reciting. 'And who is that?' asked the King.

'A Syrian man', was the reply, 'of the House of Christ.'

'Let him speak', said the King.

Said the Syrian, 'Praise be to God, one, unique, alone, and eternal. He was in the beginning without any peer, without number or measure. Then He kindled the lamps, lit the lights, made spirits appear, formed spectres, framed solids, compounded bodies, set the spheres turning, gave the angels their charge. He finished the broad earth and the heavens, raised the towering mountains, sank the churning seas, spread out the deserts and plains, a haven for animals and seed-bed for plants.

'Praised be God, who from a virgin maid took on human flesh, joined with that body the substance of divinity, sustained by the Holy Ghost, and through it performed wonders, reviving the House of Israel from the death of sin, making us his followers and disciples, priests and monks, the meek of the earth. He put kindness, compassion, and monasticism into our hearts. For all this, His are the praise and the thanks. We have other merits, which I pass over. God grant pardon to me and to you.'

Said the outspoken jinni, 'Say also "We don't tend our flocks as we ought, and we've turned infidel and said 'He's one of a trio'! We've worshipped the cross, eaten swine's flesh in sacrifice,[283] and uttered lies and calumnies about God."'

281 Qur'an 5:33. The outspoken jinni makes free with his text here. The punishments cited in the verse are execution, crucifixion, amputation, and banishment, not for Israelites but for those who do battle with God.

282 Qur'an 56:24. According to Islamic tradition, the Jews perverted their scriptures and played false to their God and their law, charges in part reflecting the strictures of Israelite prophets, whose mantle Muhammad assumed. The claim that Jews were abased as God's punishment for retaining their faith originates in Christian polemic.

283 See note 71 above.

The King next looked at a man standing nearby. Studying him, he saw a deep brown, lean figure clad in two garments, the waist wrap and shoulder wrap of a *ḥajjī*,[284] kneeling and bowing, intoning from the Qur'an and imploring the mercies of the All-Compassionate.

'Who is that?' asked the King.

'A man from Tihāma, a Qurashī.'[285]

'Let him speak', said the King.

Said the man of Quraysh, 'Praise be to God, one and unique, alone and impassive, unbegetting, unbegotten, and peerless.[286] He is the first and the last, manifest and hidden — first without beginning, last without end, manifest to all in His rule, hidden in all things, in His knowledge and pleasure, the puissant sway of His will. Great is He and clear is His proof, who was before time, before place, before any substance and all things that are, who *then said to it "Be!"* — and it was,[287] who formed, fashioned, ordered, and guided.[288] He raised up the heavens and *built the vault of the skies, balanced and shaped them, made them dark by night, and brought them the dawn. He spread out the earth and brought forth its water and pasturage, raised up its*

---

284 The Muslim is fittingly clad in pilgrim's garb, as ordained in the hadith: 'If one has two garments, let him wear a waist wrap and shoulder wrap.' A modern-day handbook of Islamic practice, lays out the details: a *ḥajjī* 'assumes the pilgrim's sacred robe, which is called *iḥrām*. This garment consists of two seamless wrappers, one being wrapped round the waist, and the other thrown loosely over the shoulder, the head being left uncovered. Sandals may also be worn, but not shoes or boots. After he has assumed the pilgrim's garb he must not anoint his head, shave any part of his body, pare his nails, nor wear any other garment than the *iḥrām*.' Thomas Hughes, *A Dictionary of Islam* (repr., Lahore: Premier Book House, 1965), p. 156.

285 Tihāma is the coastal lowland of southwest Arabia. A Qurashī belongs to the Arab tribe of Quraysh (the Shark tribe). Muhammad was born into a cadet branch of the tribe. Prosperous and fairly prestigious before the rise of Islam, the Quraysh came to be thought of as the noblest of Arab blood by association with the Prophet.

286 The Qurashī's monotheism is more radical and militant than the Christian's. The formulaic 'unbegetting, unbegotten, and without peer' is a standard Islamic response to trinitarianism, echoing the briefest sura in the Qur'an, 112: *Say: 'He is God, one alone, God inviolate, unbegetting and unbegotten. He has no peer.'*

287 Qur'an 2:117, 3:47, 19:35, 40:68; cf. Qur'an 6:73, 16:40, 36:82. At 3:59, the reference is to Adam: *God formed him of earth and then said to him 'Be!', and he was.*

288 The Qurashī echoes the language of Qur'an 87:2–3.

mountains, a comfort for you and your cattle.[289] *There was no god beside Him, or each would have made off with what he had created, or perhaps one would have overcome the other! — exalted be God above their aspersions*[290] and the lies of those who assign Him any peer. They are strayed far indeed and most plainly lost![291]

'*He it was who sent His messenger with guidance and the true faith, to triumph over every creed, despite the pagans.*[292] God bless and keep him and all his House, and all His upright creatures, faithful men, and women, in heaven and on earth.[293] May He in His mercy place us and you among them, for *He is the most merciful of all who show mercy.*[294] Praised be He who chose us for the best of all faiths, made us the folk of the Qur'an, taught us to read its rule, to fast in Ramadan, to circle the sacred precinct, the Corner where the Black Stone is enshrined, and site of Abraham's Stone.[295] He ennobled us with the Night of Power,[296]

289 Qur'an 79:27–33.

290 Qur'an 23:91. The Mu'tazilite commentator al-Zamakhsharī explains the verse, saying: 'each would have made off with what he had created, so that each god could keep what he had created and have it all to himself. You've surely seen kings who vie for supremacy with one another, as earthly kings do. But here you never see the effects of such a struggle. So you know that He alone is God, sovereign over all.' The argument, parallel to Aristotle's case that there is but one world, is echoed in the *kalām* polemic against dualism. It persists in Spinoza's proof that there is just one self-sufficient substance, since plurality would involve limitation and hence restrict God's self-sufficiency; see *Ethics*, Part I, Propositions 1–8.

291 Cf. Qur'an 4:119.

292 Qur'an 9:33.

293 The beginning of this sentence follows a conventional Islamic formula; the end, rather unconventionally, extends the same blessing that is prayed for in behalf of the Prophet and his House to all righteous creatures of good faith, be they Muslim or non-Muslim.

294 Qur'an 12:64.

295 The Corner (*Rukn*) is the site of the Black Stone in the Ka'ba. The Stone of Abraham (called *maqām* in Arabic) is the place where the Patriarch stood when completing the construction of the Ka'ba. The stone is said to bear his footprint. See Qur'an 2:125, 3:97.

296 The Muslim delegate lapses into rhymed prose (*saj'*), an ancient device of Arabic rhetoric much used in the Qur'an and similar in impact to the use of alliteration in English. The Night of Power was the occasion of the Qur'an's revelation in the month of Ramadan. In commemoration of that momentous event, the faithful fast in Ramadan during the daylight hours and devote themselves to religious devotions, spiritual exercises, and prayer. See Qur'an 2:183–187. Sura

Mount Arafat,[297] our alms tax, ablutions, devotions, mosques, festivals, rostra, sermons — the law and lore of our faith, our knowledge of the ways of the prophets and the lives of the great teachers and masters.[298]

'He gave us tidings of the first and last generations, the reckoning of the Day of Judgement, and the reward promised to prophets, martyrs, and godly folk[299] of heaven and earth for ever and ay. Praised be God, Lord of the universe, and blessings upon Muhammad, Seal of the Prophets and chief of God's messengers.[300] We have many other merits

---

97 preserves the memory of that first revelation of the Qur'an: *We revealed it on the Night of Power. If only you knew what the Night of Power is like. The Night of Power is better than a thousand months. On that night the angels and the Spirit descend, by leave of their Lord, with all His commands. Peace, then, until break of day.*

297 Pilgrims hear a sermon when they stop on the plain beside Mount Arafat, about 13 miles east of Mecca, on the ninth day of the *ḥajj*. In one Islamic legend, Arafat was the site at which Adam and Eve, who had become far separated from one another at the fall, met and recognized one another (*taʿārafa*). The halt at Arafat was a vital part of the ceremonies practised in connection with the trade fairs and religious practices of pre-Islamic Arabia. Ritually it is the core element of the Islamic pilgrimage and a *sine qua non* in the performance of the obligations of the *ḥajj*. In the ritual of standing at Arafat, scholars see a parallel to the stance of the Israelites at Sinai, waiting in purity and patience to accept God's commands.

298 The Muslim spokesman touches on the Five Pillars of Islam: (1) *shahāda* — witness to God's unity and the authenticity and authority of Muhammad's prophetic mission; (2) *ṣalāt* — worship in the stipulated manner at the five daily times assigned to prayer; (3) *zakāt* — the alms tax, a specific annual obligation; (4) *ṣawm* — the fast of Ramadan; and (5) *ḥajj* — the pilgrimage to Mecca, where the 'sacred precinct' of the Kaʿba is circled. The *ḥajj* is incumbent at least once in a lifetime on all Muslims able to achieve it. These foundations of Islam, along with other institutions like those the Qurashī cites, give the religion its distinctive cultural flavour.

299 The godly folk here (*ṣāliḥīn*) are the saintly. An Islamic saint, or *walī*, is a person known for exemplary piety and spiritual insight, often thought to be graced with the power to perform miracles (*karāmāt*, as distinguished from prophetic evidentiary miracles, or *muʿjizāt*). Early theories of sainthood, or *wilāya*, differ as to whether this state is won through spiritual perfection or simply bestowed by God as an act of grace. Opinions also differed over whether a saint is known to others or even to himself. See Abū Bakr al-Kalābādhī, *Kitāb al-Taʿarruf li-madhhab ahl al-taṣawwuf*, tr. Arberry as *The Doctrine of the Ṣūfīs* (repr., New York: CUP, 1989), pp. 57–66. The most extensive reflection on saints and sainthood in early Islam was al-Ḥakīm al-Tirmidhī's *Kitāb Khatm al-awliyā'* (Beirut: Catholic University Press, 1965).

300 Kalonymos plays down the praises that the Qurashī heaps on Muhammad.

that would take far too long to expound. I seek God's forgiveness for myself and for you.'

Said the outspoken jinni, 'Say also, "Then, after the death of our Prophet, we rebelled, forsook and spurned his faith. Hypocrites and doubters, we slew our finest, most virtuous leaders, seeking the world through the faith."'[301]

---

301 The Arabs of Arabia saw their pacts with Muhammad as tribal arrangements that expired on his death. The first caliph or successor, Abū Bakr, used his forces to subdue the fractious tribes. Quelling their secession and aligning their forces under the banner of Islam, he launched the Islamic conquests of the seventh century. The early resistance to Muhammad's message by the chief men of the Quraysh at Mecca branded them as non-believers and doubters; the hesitancies of many early converts marked them as hypocrites. A pall is cast over the early years of Islam by the slayings of the second caliph, 'Umar (at the hands of a Persian slave), the third, 'Uthmān (at the instance of rivals), the fourth, 'Alī (by a partisan fanatic), both of 'Alī's sons, Ḥasan and Ḥusayn, the latter in an abortive campaign against Yazīd (successor to the fifth caliph, the former governor of Syria, Mu'āwiya) — not to mention the battle against 'Alī joined by 'Ā'isha and several prominent followers. See Bernard Lewis, *The Arabs in History* (New York: Harper, 1960), pp. 60–63; Carl Brockelmann, *History of the Islamic Peoples*, tr. Joel Carmichael and Moshe Perlmann (New York: Capricorn, 1960; first German edition, 1939), pp. 64–67; Philip K. Hitti, *History of the Arabs — from the Earliest Times to the Present* (London: Macmillan, 1956), pp. 178–182; and see L. Veccia Vagilieri, "Alī', and W. Montgomery Watt, "Ā'isha', in *EI2*, vol. 1, pp. 307–308, 381–386. Muslim sources tend to shift the blame in these early struggles away from the Prophet's house. 'Alī, Ḥasan, and Ḥusayn become saints and martyrs, and the onus shifts more fully to the shoulders of the Meccan aristocratic party of 'Uthmān and Mu'āwiya. The outspoken jinni calls the slain leaders imams, rightful caliphs. Mu'āwiya's Umayyad dynasty is traditionally blamed for worldliness in lifestyle and in policy. The Qurashī delegate shares in the blame. Quest for wealth and station through the abuse or exploitation of the faith continue throughout Muslim history to vex Islamic moralists. The Shi'i tilt of the Ikhwān shows through in the outspoken jinni's censure. But it seems important to the authors not to sully their own confession with the worldliness they find in other versions of the Shi'i outlook. As they write: 'There is one group who have made their Shi'ism a source of income for themselves, like professional mourners and story tellers. They know nothing more of Shi'ism than denigrating (the first three caliphs), cursing, defaming, insulting and weeping' (*Rasā'il*, vol. 4, pp.147–148). Taqī al-Dīn al-Maqrīzī (1364–1442) blames compromises with secular authority dating back to the times of the Prophet himself for the historic loss of ground by spiritual to worldly authority in Islamic history; see his *Kitāb al-Nizā' wa'l-takhāṣum* (Cairo: Dār al-Ma'ārif, 1988), tr. C. E. Bosworth as *The Book of Contention and Strife Concerning the Relations between the Banū Umayya and the Banū Hāshim* (Manchester: University of Manchester Press, 1980). Kalonymos stresses the outspoken jinni's charge that Muslims have

Scanning the crowd again, the King saw a fair-skinned man with a band about his head standing in a small arena, with an astronomical instrument in his hands.[302] 'Who is this?' the King asked.

'A Byzantine from Greece.'

'Let him speak.'

'Praise be to God,' the Greek began, 'one, unique, alone, eternal, everlasting, and impassive, who was before matter, with its form and dimensions, as unity precedes the numbers even and odd, without equal or opposite.[303]

'Praised be God who in bounty and grace caused the Active Intellect to flow forth from His goodness, source of science and mysteries, light of lights, and element of all spirits.[304]

---

forsaken the hereafter for the here and now, underscoring the rebuke with the charge that they flout God's prohibitions of pork and wine drinking.

302 The instrument, perhaps an astrolabe, symbolizes science but also judicial astrology. Alchemy and astrology were humanistic disciplines par excellence, since they sought to master fate and control nature — a quest in tension with the pietistic side of the ideals of the Ikhwān.

303 The Greeks are admired for their rational sciences, and mathematics is the first subject in the *Rasā'il*, with arithmetic, its first branch, occupying the first *risāla*. Plato's *Republic* (VII.525) treats the study of number, and unity in particular, as drawing the mind away from nature's diversity and toward the divine unity of the Forms. Proclus opens his commentary on Euclid's *Elements* by commending Plato's pathway via the idea of unity toward the Divine; see Proclus, *A Commentary on the First Book of Euclid's 'Elements'*, tr. Glenn Morrow (Princeton: Princeton University Press, 1970), pp. 3, 70; cf. Proclus' *The Elements of Theology*, ed. and tr. Dodds (Oxford: OUP, 1963), pp. 2–7, Props. 1–6; and his *Commentary on 'Alcibiades I'*, tr. W. O'Neill (The Hague: M. Nijhoff, 1965), pp. 1–8. Seeking God through philosophy, the Ikhwān find a gateway in arithmetic, above all in the concept of unity. They see the Greek approach as an opening to the universal truth, that all diversity and change derives ultimately from God's perfect unity. However, the risk of the Greek approach, from their standpoint, is that it may seem to derive the world from God by necessity, as numbers flow from unity, or theorems from axioms in geometry.

304 The Active Intellect is distinct from God here, reflecting the desire of Greek Neoplatonists to protect the transcendence of the One by delegating all engagement with diversity and change to lesser hypostases. But since the manifestations emanating from the One are neither identical with it nor wholly separate from it, these philosophers felt able to have their cake and eat it, too: to engage God in the world without compromising God's ultimate transcendence. The Ikhwān speak of the Active Intellect as the element of all spirits, using the word 'element' (*'unṣur*) to echo the terminology characteristic of Greek philosophy in its Arabic recension. The Active Intellect is the source of all sciences, giving form, that is, conceptual content, to the mind, and raising it

'Praised be God who produced Mind from His light, and from its substance caused the celestial Universal Soul to flow forth, endowed with the power of movement, the source of life and all blessings.[305]

'Praised be God who from the power of the Soul brought forth the elements with matter and essence.[306]

'Praised be God who formed bodies with dimensions, measure, place, and time. Praised be He who compounded[307] the spheres and planets and entrusted their courses to spirits and souls, angels with form and figure, powers of speech, and thought, who gave the heavenly

---

from potential to actual understanding. It reveals mysteries too. For mystic enlightenment is the highest phase in the mind's attainment of Form. It is the Light of lights, as the Giver of Forms — the objective Forms that make things what they are, and the subjective forms of the ideas we command when we understand things. It is the element of all spirits, since it is the source of the universal Soul, which in turn is the source of life in all living beings. Scriptural monotheists in the Neoplatonic tradition fuse the imagery of the Psalms (36:10) — 'In Thy light do we see light' with Aristotle's thought that the Active Intellect is the condition of understanding, as light is of seeing; *De Anima* III.5.

305 The metaphysics encapsulated here is treated as a Greek religion, since it was meant to explain the structure of reality and the aim of life. The imagery, like the ontology, is Neoplatonic: God, the primal Unity, is the Well-Spring of Light, overflowing with intelligence, that gives rise in turn (albeit not in time) to the life principle, the Universal Soul. Emanation here is the inevitable expression of the ontic pregnancy of the Infinite, so it is called *production*, not creation. The language of flowing forth and of radiant light, put into the Greek's mouth by the Ikhwān, is meant to give emphasis to emanation's mechanical, even logical necessity as distinguished from the free act of creation ascribed to God's grace in scriptural monotheism. Nous or Intelligence, the God of Aristotle, was demoted by Plotinus from the supreme rank among the gods, since intelligence is not the highest of things; see *Enneads* VI.9.2 ; ibid. I.7.1, 8.2; ibid. V.1.5; cf. Aristotle, *Nicomachaean Ethics* VI.7.1141a21. God is perfect unity. But Nous, the mind, is a 'one-many' — it lacks the primal unity of the Form of the Good, since it houses (and is identical with) the Forms of Plato, which are, as Aristotle noted, many in one way and diverse in another. Plotinus says, moreover, that reasoning is both the same as and different from its object. Soul, Psyche, the World Soul, that is, marks a definite entry into the realm of diversity and becoming. That seems clear to Neoplatonists from the discursive character of the human thought process. Soul's power of movement is in fact the power to impart movement. For it animates all living beings.

306 In Neoplatonic philosophy, the World Soul produces nature by giving rise to time, since Psyche, by contrast with the pure and timeless intuitions of the Active Intellect, must think discursively.

307 The celestial bodies are again conceded to be composites.

bodies their rotary motion[308] and spherical shapes, as lights of the gloom and orient lamps at every horizon.

'Praised be God who constituted the natures that underlie being and made them the basis of plants, animals, humans, and jinn.[309] He brought forth the plants and made them the foodstuff that nourishes animals and from the sea's depths and the peaks of mountains brings forth the mineral substances with their many uses.[310]

'Praised be God who favoured us with an excellence beyond so many of His servants and graced our land with its ample, fertile, and fruitful country-side. He made us natural rulers, for our virtues, our attainments, and our just way of life, our overwhelming intelligence, keen discernment, and deep understanding, our many sciences and wonderful arts — medicine, geometry, astronomy. He taught us how the spheres are framed, and showed us the uses of animals, minerals, and plants. He gave us the sciences of measurement and movement, the instruments of astronomy, and talismans, and taught us mathematics and logic, physics and metaphysics. His are the praise, the glory, and thanks for all these lavish gifts. We have other distinctions besides, too many to mention. I seek pardon in God for myself and for you.'[311]

Said the outspoken jinni, 'Where did you get these sciences and the wisdom you brag of? Didn't you take some from the Israelites in

---

308 The heavenly bodies must be intelligently steered. For their revolutions involve a constant change of direction. The minds entrusted with this governance are no longer the gods of pagan mythology but angels and spirits. The celestial bodies they animate light up every horizon: their lamps illuminate the heavens and guide wayfarers and navigators; their spirits are endowed not only with thought but with speech, so they can transmit revelations, as suggested in philosophers' identification of the Active Intellect with the angel Gabriel, who revealed the Qur'an to Muhammad.

309 Fire, water, earth, and air are arrayed in layers, each with its proper denizens.

310 The Greek, like earlier speakers, leaps to anthropocentric conclusions. He reads the benefits derived from plants and minerals, as their *raison d'être*, since the lower must exist for the sake of the higher.

311 The same pride that leads the humans to see themselves as the pinnacle of creation tempts each race to assign the highest worth to the attainments with which its most outstanding contributors have been favoured. The self-effacing formula that concludes this and other speeches by the humans bears a touch of dramatic irony, when pronounced on the heels of so many boasts framed in accents of appreciation.

Ptolemy's time, and some from the scholars of Egypt in the days of Themistius, transplant them to your own lands, and then take credit for them?'[312]

Said the King to the Greek, 'What do you say to this?'

'He is right', said the Greek. 'We did take most of our sciences from other nations, just as they have taken most of theirs from us. For men do adopt the sciences from one another.[313] Otherwise, where would

312 The antiquity of Middle Eastern civilization gave currency to the claim that Greek sciences rested on Hebrew, Egyptian, and other ancient foundations. Fārābī, for one, speaks of the return of the sciences, via Greece, to their birthplace in Mesopotamia; see *Fī taḥṣīl al-ṣaʿāda* I.4.53, tr. Muhsin Mahdi as *Alfarabi's Philosophy of Plato and Aristotle* (Ithaca, NY: Cornell University Press, 1969), p. 43. Ptolemy here is Ptolemy Soter, founder of the Hellenistic dynasty in Egypt that bore his name. He was patron to Theophrastus' student Demetrius of Phalerum, whom he commissioned in 294 BCE to found the Museum in his show-place city, Alexandria. The period cited, then, is the Hellenistic period, for which, see Moses Hadas, *Hellenistic Culture Fusion and Diffusion* (New York: Columbia University Press, 1959). Themistius, a pagan philosopher, statesman, and commentator on Aristotle, taught at Constantinople. His harmonization of Plato and Aristotle, and of pagan and Christian ideas helped fashion the tradition of Neoplatonic Aristotelianism that became the philosophic heritage of the Islamic Middle East. It is not clear just which Egyptian thinkers the outspoken jinni has in mind. Philo lived in Egypt and Plotinus came from there, but they would not normally have been called Egyptians.

313 The Ikhwān eschew a chauvinistic reading of claims about cultural borrowings, pleading instead for a cosmopolitan appreciation of the sciences and arts. Cf. Kindī: 'Truth demands that we blame no one who has afforded us even a slight and trivial benefit. All the more must we thank those who are in some major way responsible for real, weighty, and significant benefits. Even if they missed some portion of the truth, they were our allies and partners, aiding us with the fruits of their thinking, which opened up avenues and gave us tools that allowed us access to much that they themselves failed fully to apprehend. . . . Had they never lived, the basic truths that we have used in reaching the hidden objects of our quest would never have been gathered for us, no matter how hard we worked in our own era. For they were put together aeons ago, year by year, down to our own time, through intensive inquiry, and only by hard work and dedication to the task. It would not have been possible to bring together such a body of knowledge in one man's lifetime, even were it long, no matter how probing his investigations, no matter how subtle his thinking or how diligent his efforts — nor even in many lifetimes.' Al-Kindī, 'On First Philosophy', in *Rasāʾil falsafiyya*, ed. M. Abū Riḍā (Cairo: Dār al-ʿArabī, 1950–1953), p. 102; the translation here is Goodman's; see al-Kindī's *Metaphysics*, tr. Alfred Ivry (Albany, NY: SUNY Press, 1974), p. 57, and the excellent commentary, ad loc.; cf. Aristotle, *Metaphysics* II.1.993b11–14.

the Persians have gotten astronomy and cosmology and the use of astronomical instruments, if not from the people of India? Where would the Israelites have learned magic, sorcery, and spells, talisman making and divination, if Solomon son of David, peace be upon him, had not taken this lore from the treasuries of the kings of the nations he conquered, translated it into the Hebrew tongue, and brought it to the land of Syria, to his kingdom in Palestine? Some, of course, was Israel's legacy from the books of their prophets, to whom God had sent angels bearing inspiration and revelation from the highest throng of the denizens of heaven, the lords of the spheres, the hosts of the world's Sovereign.'

Said the King to the jinni philosopher, 'What do you answer to this?'

'It is true', he replied. 'The sciences flourish in one nation as opposed to another only for a time. If one people acquires prophecy or royal dominion, it rules over the rest, adopts their virtues, sciences, and books, and brings them to the land of the victors, who claim them as their own.'[314]

The King next cast his glance upon a powerfully built, finely dressed man gazing towards the welkin, his eyes following the sun's course across the sky.

'Who is that?' he asked.

'A man of Khurāsān,' the vizier answered, 'from the land of Marw Shāhān.'[315]

'Command him to speak.'

---

314 For the recurrent cycles of the rise and fall in philosophy and allied branches of learning, see al-Fārābī, *Kitāb Iḥṣā' al-ʿulūm*, tr. John L. Longeway as *The Book of Al Farabi on the Origin of the Sciences*, http://uwp.edu/~longeway/Al%20 Farabi.htm; Muhsin Mahdi, *Alfarabi and the Foundation of Islamic Political Philosophy* (Chicago: University of Chicago Press, 2001), pp. 234–235.

315 Khurāsān, the great eastern land southeast of the Caspian and northeast of Fārs (Persia proper) stretched towards the Oxus River (see Appendix B). The 'word picture' the Ikhwān paint evokes the image of the Khurāsānian troops who came to form the military backbone of the Islamic empire. Merv Shāhijān (Royal Marw) lay south southwest of Bukhara, about 500 miles east of the Caspian on the Murghab river in today's Turkmenistan. Even in pre-Islamic times, the city, commanding Persia's north-eastern frontier, was long the seat of the Shah's satraps and his garrisons against tribal forces from the Central Asian steppes. Its fertile oasis was notorious for a humid, unwholesome climate and endemic diseases, not least the filarial Guinea worm (possibly identical with the biblical

'Praised be God,' said the Khurāsānian, 'one and alone, great and exalted, awesome and terrible, invincible and triumphant, author of mighty acts. There is no god but He! Destiny is His, whose attributes the most fluent tongue cannot describe, and whose essence the deepest thinkers cannot grasp. Minds are confounded by His awful majesty, even those with vision and insightful hearts.[316] He is lofty and low, indwelling, yet manifest in glory, *unseen but seeing, gracious, and aware.*[317] Veiled by light[318] before the making of day and of night, He rules the encircling spheres and raised the high heavens in all their vastness.

'His is the praise, who formed creatures of all kinds — angels, jinn, humans, and demons — double-winged, triple-, and quadruple-, two-legged and four-legged, those that crawl on their bellies or dive or glide through the air.[319] He divided His creatures into species and individuals, and the sons of Adam into peoples and tribes of diverse colours, tongues, abodes, places, and times, meting out His gifts and blessings and parcelling out the bounties of His grace.

'Praised be God for favours granted and means afforded, for blessings given and promised. Praised be He who chose and favoured us. For He made our land fullest of all in cities, markets, villages, fields, citadels, castles, rivers, trees, mountains, minerals, animals, plants, men, and women. Our women are strong as men; our men, as camels; our camels, as mighty mountains!

'Praised be God who chose us and commended us by his prophets' tongues for our stalwart strength, our fierce and warlike nature, our

---

'fiery serpent' of Numbers 21:6). Yet Marw lay on the famous Silk Road and was a centre of silk making — hence the delegate's rich apparel.

316 The Khurāsānian echoes the language of Qur'an 29:38.

317 Qur'an 6:103.

318 Thus the hadith, 'His veil is light'; Wensinck, *Concordance*, vol. 1, p. 424; cf. Qur'an 42:51. 'God has seventy thousand veils of light and darkness. Were He to withdraw their curtain, the splendours of His face would surely consume all who saw Him.' Ghazālī, *Mishkāt al-anwār*, tr. W. H. T. Gairdner as *The Niche for Lights* (Lahore: Ashraf, 1952), p. 77; tr. Buchman as *The Niche of Lights* (Provo: Brigham Young University, 1998), p. 1.

319 Qur'an 21:82 tells of the demons subdued by God's favour to Solomon's service: some dived for him and did other work. Traditional Qur'an commentaries have it that the diving was for pearls.

love of the faith and devotion to its messengers. For He said, through Muhammad, Seal of the Prophets: "*We are strong, fierce and warlike. But command is thine, so consider what thou wilt command*",[320] and *tell the laggard Arabs: "You will face a fierce and warlike people"*,[321] and, *Then will God bring a people He will love and who will love Him.*[322] And the Prophet, peace be upon Him, said, "If faith hung from the Pleiades, the sons of Persia would surely reach it",[323] and, "Blessings on my brethren of Persia, who will come at the end of time and love black more than white and believe in me and my truth."[324]

'Praised be God who chose us for faith and certitude, to strive for the last of days and make ready for the Resurrection. Some of us recite the Torah, grasping but little of it yet believing in Moses. Others read the Gospels and can make out not a word of it yet believe in Christ and accept his truth. Some of us recite the Qur'an and chant it without fathoming its meaning, yet we believe in God's elect, Muhammad. We accept his truth and cleave to him. We wear black and cry out for vengeance for Ḥusayn. We rail against the outrages of the sons of Marwān,[325] who wickedly rose against God and broke faith with His

320 The boast is quoted from the menaces made by the Queen of Sheba's counsellors as to their own forces, Qur'an 27:33. By the authority of a hadith, the Khurāsānian applies the words to his own people.

321 Qur'an 48:16. At Qur'an 17:5, Nebuchadnezzar's forces are called God's servants, following Jeremiah's treatment of the Babylonian monarch as God's instrument of judgement (Jeremiah 25:9, 27:6, 43:10). At Isaiah 47, Babylon's downfall is laid to the Babylonians' presumption that they were raised up for any purpose beyond service as God's scourge.

322 Qur'an 5:54 intimates that God will shift His favour to another people if the Arabs prove unfaithful. The Khurāsānian, in Shuʿūbī tones, identifies with those successors.

323 See *Ṣaḥīḥ Muslim* Book 31, hadiths 6177 and 6178.

324 Black banners from Khurāsān, in some partisan hadiths, are harbingers of the reign of truth. They were the ensigns of the ʿAbbāsids, whose revolution began in Khurāsān. See Elton L. Daniel, *The Political and Social History of Khurasan under Abbasid Rule 747–820* (Minneapolis: Bibliotheca Islamica, 1979), pp. 25–72.

325 The sons of Marwān are widely execrated by the Shiʿa. As caliph, ʿAlī confronted as a rebel the Syrian governor Muʿāwiya, of the House of Marwān, at the battle of Ṣiffīn in Iraq (657). Despite attempts at mediation, ʿAlī's cause was frustrated, and he died at the hands of an assassin in 661. Shiʿi loathing for Marwānids redoubled when Muʿāwiya's son Yazīd assumed the caliphate as the second Umayyad ruler and slew the third Shiʿi Imam, ʿAlī's second son, Ḥusayn, the grandson of Muhammad, at Karbala' in 680. Ḥusayn's martyrdom is commemorated annually in passion plays known as *taʿziyya*. Ritualized grieving for the slain

Law. Our hope is that the long awaited imam of Muhammad's house, will appear in our land.[326] For his name and fame are great among us. Praised be God for all that he gave and vouchsafed us, His blessings and benefactions. I have said my say. God pardon me and you.'

When the Persian had finished speaking, the King looked at the sages round about him and asked, 'What do you think of these remarks?'

The chief philosopher replied, 'What he says is true, so far as it goes. But he might have mentioned their rude natures and foul tongues, how they couple with boys and marry their mothers, worship fire, and bow to the sun instead of the All-Merciful.'[327]

---

imams took on eschatological dimensions in Shi'i spirituality. Muhammad, on coming to Medina and seeking Jewish followers, had ordained a fast on the tenth of Muḥarram, modelling it on the Day of Atonement (Leviticus 16:29), as testified by the name "Āshūrā", a reference to the tenth day of the month. The Prophet made this fast optional when his relations with the Jewish populace of Medina became strained. Shi'is, however, commemorate the martyrdom of Ḥusayn on the tenth of Muḥarram. Reflecting on the voluntary nature of the fast and the redemptive echoes that its observances preserve, Mahmoud Ayoub writes: 'It is clear... that sorrow and weeping for the martyrdom of Imam Ḥusayn and the suffering of the Holy Family became a source of salvation for those who chose to participate in this unending flow of tears. For human beings this is a choice which they could make or refuse, thereby choosing salvation or judgement. The rest of Creation, however, is by divine decree the stage, as it were, upon which this drama of martyrdom is forever enacted.' Mahmoud Ayoub, *Redemptive Suffering in Islam: A Study of the Devotional Aspects of 'Āshūrā' in Twelver Shi'ism* (The Hague: Mouton, 1978), p. 147. And see R. Le Tourneau, 'al-Ḥusayn', *EI2*, vol. 3, pp. 606–607; P. Marçais, "Āshūrā", *EI2*, vol. 1, p. 705; and M. Plessner, 'Muḥarram', *EI2*, vol. 7, p. 464.

326 The Shi'i speaker awaits an 'Alid Imam who is 'occulted', reigning but hidden, yet fated to emerge and resume his rightful dominion. That subversive hope often intensified and was itself intensified in turn by Sunni appeals to the legitimacy of de facto authority. The mildly satiric treatment that the Ikhwān give the thick-skulled and barely acculturated Khurāsānian suggests that they are not readily pigeon-holed as mere propagandists of a particular Shi'i sect — at least, not one that avidly awaits a particular occulted imam.

327 The calumnies heaped so off-handedly on the Persians reflect anti-Shi'i canards and anti-Persian reactions to the Shu'ūbiyya. No ignominy was too foul for use in such polemics. But the charges are old. Sextus Empiricus writes: 'amongst the Persians it is the habit to indulge in intercourse with males, but amongst the Romans it is unlawful . . . intercourse with a mother is forbidden in our country, in Persia it is the general custom.' *Outlines of Pyrrhonism*, tr. R. G. Bury (Cambridge, MA: Harvard University Press, 1933), vol. 1, p. 152. J. S. Slotkin sought to give colour to such allegations in 'On a Possible Lack of Incest Regulations in Old Iran', *American Anthropologist*, 49 (1947), pp. 612–617. Ward

Chapter 21
Description of the Lion — His Character and Exploits, the Praiseworthy Qualities and Failings that Distinguish Him among Wild Predators

On the third day, the delegates of the two parties appeared again as appointed and took their places as before. Scanning the throng, the King saw the jackal standing next to the ass, looking askance and turning this way and that, quizzically, as though afraid of a dog. Said the King, speaking through an interpreter, 'Who art thou?'

'I am the delegate of the predators', the jackal replied.

'Who sent you here?'

'Our king.'

'Who is he?'

'Abū'l-Ḥārith, the lion.'

'Where does he shelter, and in what sort of land does he dwell?'

'In the jungles, savannahs, and canyons.'

'Who are his subjects?'

'The beasts of the wild, and the cattle, and sheep.'

'Who are his troops and vassals?'

'Leopards, cheetahs, wolves, jackals, foxes, wild cats — all predators with fang or claw.'

'Describe his form and character for us, and his treatment of his subjects and forces.'

'I shall, your Majesty. He is the largest of predators and the mightiest in frame, the strongest, fiercest, most terrible and majestic. His chest is broad, his waist narrow, his haunches shapely, his head massive, his face round, his brow ample. His jaw is square, his nostrils flared.

H. Goodenough, in 'Comments on the Question of Incestuous Marriages in Old Iran', *American Anthropologist*, 51 (1949), pp. 326–328, pp. 326–328, citing the work of other scholars, remarks that 'nearly all the classical sources, of which Slotkin makes so much, are merely restatements of a Greek ethnocentric legend about Persian morals'. While there is some evidence of ritual royal incest and allied practices in Iran, as in other highly stratified societies, Goodenough seems just in his conclusion, 'that the practice was limited, was contrary to popular mores, and, of course, does not survive among modern Parsees, who object to the idea that it was ever advocated by Zoroastrians. . . . Slotkin's thesis that we have here a serious challenge to the concept of the "universality" of incest taboos is without adequate support.'

His paws are stout; his fangs and claws, strong as iron.[328] His eyes flash like lightning. His voice is deep, and his roar mighty. His shanks are like granite, his heart bold, his aspect terrible. He fears no one. Water buffaloes and elephants do not alarm him, nor do crocodiles, or even men, with all their powers to do injury — not even armed horsemen with weapons that can pierce a coat of mail. He is doughty and steadfast. Whatever he undertakes, he sees to it himself and asks no help from his forces or vassals. But he is generous. When he's taken a prize, he eats his share and leaves the rest liberally to his followers and dependents. He disdains worldly things and will attack neither woman nor child — nor orphan.[329] For his nature is noble. If he sees a light far off, he approaches through the dark of night and stands at a distance, his ferocity lulled and savagery gentled. If he hears a sweet melody he draws near and settles down peacefully. He fears nothing, and no creature can harm him but the tiny ant, which is given power over him and his cubs, as the gnat over the elephant and water buffalo, and the power of the fly over the mightiest of human tyrants.'[330]

'How does your king treat his subjects?'

'Most fairly, justly, and well, as I will explain later on, God willing.'

---

328 Isidore locates the lion's pertinacity in his head, his strength in his chest, his courage, in his front and tail; *Etymologies* 12.2.3–6.

329 The lion heeds the Biblical and Islamic norm of showing kindness to orphans and chivalry to the helpless. Pliny reports that an angry lion will attack men but not women, spares those who lie prone before it, and will attack children only if desperately hungry; *Natural History* VIII.17–21; Isidore, *Etymologies* 12.2.6: 'With humans, the nature of lions is such that, unless hurt, they are unlikely to grow angry. Their tender-heartedness is manifest from continual examples. For they spare those who lie prone, allow captives whom they meet to return home, and never kill a human except in great hunger.' A once-popular doggerel began: 'The most chivalrous fish in the ocean/ With a manner both gracious and mild/ Tho' his name may be dark is the man-eating shark/ Who will eat neither woman nor child . . . ' Montaigne tells of a tiger that refused to devour a kid because it was 'his friend and his guest'. *Complete Essays*, II.12, p. 353.

330 The balance of nature reflects divine justice. Every creature, as we have seen repeatedly, is overmatched by some other; cf. Isidore, *Etymologies* 12.4.6–7, where even the deadly basilisk fears its mortal enemy, the weasel, since 'the Creator of Nature sets forth nothing without its remedy'. See Chapter 14, note 195 above.

Chapter 22
Description of the Griffin and the Flora and Fauna of His Island Home

The King then scanned the parties in attendance and saw the parrot perched on a tree limb nearby, watching and studying all who spoke and mimicking their words and their speeches.

'Who are you?' said the King.

'The delegate of the birds of prey.'

'Who sent you?'

'Our king.'

'Who is he?'

'The griffin.'

'In what land does he shelter?'

'In the peaks of the towering mountains on an island in the Green Sea seldom reached by sea-faring ships or any mortal.'

'Describe that island for us.'

'Surely, your Majesty. Its soil is good, its climate even. It lies on the equator and has sweet water in springs and streams, many great, branching teak trees that rise high in the air. The reeds in its thickets are cane, the grass is bamboo. The beasts are elephants, water buffaloes, pigs, and many other kinds known but to God.'[331]

'Describe for us this griffin's form, his character and manner of life.'

'I shall. He is the greatest of birds in size, the mightiest in frame, and the strongest in flight. He has a huge head and a mighty beak, strong as a cast-iron pickaxe. His sharp, hooked talons are like iron grapnels; his vast wings, when he spreads them, like two sails of a sea-going ship. His tail, in proportion, is like the pavilion of Nimrod the Tyrant.[332] When he swoops from the sky, the mountains quake as his mighty legs touch down, at the great surges of air stirred by the

331 The parrot echoes the claims of his human predecessors: animals, too, are blessed with bounteous, paradisiacal lands. A parrot, of course, would freely repeat arguments he has heard.

332 According to legend, Nimrod ordered his master builder, Terah, Abraham's father and the son of Nahor, to build him a splendid home. The resulting palace was 1,000 square cubits, with walls of pearl, a floor of silver, a roof of sandalwood, and portals of ivory. Rivers of milk and honey flowed within, and in every chamber hung the tyrant's portrait. Terah was rewarded with the post of vizier; see al-Kisāʾī, *Qiṣaṣ al-anbiyāʾ*, tr. Thackston, p. 131–132.

beating of his wings. He sweeps elephants and buffaloes from the earth in mid-flight, like a kite snatching mice from the earth.'

'And what manner of life does he lead?'

'The best and most just, as I'll mention anon.'

Chapter 23

Description of the Dragon and Sea-Serpent — Their Wondrous Forms and Fearsome Aspect

The King then heard a melodious buzzing from a crevice in a nearby wall. It warbled and hummed, never still or silent for a moment. Looking, he saw it was the cricket, standing and moving his wings lightly and swiftly with a tuneful hum like a tiny violin string.

'Who are you?' the King said.

'The delegate of the crawling creatures.'

'Who sent you?'

'Our king.'

'Who is he?'

'The dragon.'

'What manner of land does he live in?'

'In the peaks of lofty mountains, above the sphere of mild air, in the frigid sphere of frost, higher than clouds or mists can rise, where no rain falls, no plants grow, and no beasts can survive the bitter chill of the Zamharīr.'[333]

'Who are his troops and vassals?'

'The snakes and scorpions and all crawling creatures.'

'And where do they live?'

'On earth. Everywhere there are nations of them, multitudes none can count but God, who made and formed them *and knows their every lair and refuge.*'[334]

---

333 The bitterly cold Zamharīr lies between the fresh air of the *nasīm* and the heat of the *athīr*, or aether, fired by the sphere of the moon. It is in the Zamharīr that thunder originates, when hot, rising vapours burst its moist envelope. Lightning results when water vapour contacts the fiery upper region. See Nasr, *Islamic Cosmological Doctrines*, p. 85.

334 Qur'an 11:6.

'Why does the dragon fly so far from the ranks of his followers and the children of his kind?'

'He seeks relief in the cold of the Zamharīr from the heat of the searing venom that he bears in his jaws and that blazes in his body.'[335]

'Describe his form for us, his character, and manner of life.'

'His form is like that of the sea-serpent, and so are his traits and his life.'

'Who then will tell of the sea-serpent?'

'The delegate of the aquatic animals.'

'Who is he?'

'That one, perched on a piece of wood.'

The King looked and saw the frog mounted on a piece of wood by the sea-shore nearby. The frog was croaking his songs of thanks and praise, his lauds, exaltations, and hallels, known but to the angels, pure and exalted.

'Who are you?' asked the King.

'Spokesman of the water animals.'

'Who sent you?'

'Our king.'

'Who is he?'

'The sea-serpent.'

'What sort of land does he live in?'

'In the depths of the sea, where the waves clash, the birthplace of mists and dense clouds.'

'Who are his troops and vassals?'

'The crocodiles, swordfish, and dolphins, the crabs, and all manner of aquatic creatures, their number known to God alone, who created and sustains them.'

'Describe the form and character of the sea-serpent for us, and his manner of life.'

'I shall, your Majesty. He's a huge animal of wondrous form, great length, enormous girth, dread aspect, and awesome repute. All marine animals fear him and flee before his vast power and strength. When

335 Warmth was the digestive principle and venom was a digestive juice. In Isidore's bestiary, cold is what makes the serpent's venom so deadly; Isidore, *Etymologies* 12.4.39–40.

he moves, the sea itself rocks with his swift swimming. His head is immense, his eyes flashing, his teeth numerous, his mouth and gullet tremendous. He swallows countless hordes of sea creatures each day, and when his belly is full and he finds it hard to digest them, he arches and bends like a bow, supporting himself on his head and tail, and raises his mid-parts out of the water into the air, gleaming like a rainbow in the sunlight, huffing and puffing about, sunning himself to aid his digestion. But sometimes, in this posture, he swoons, and the rising mists lift him up from below and bear him through the air to dry land, where he dies, and the beasts feed on his hulk for days — or he is borne to the shores of the land of Gog and Magog,[336] who live beyond the great barrier, two nations of human form but savage spirit, who know neither order nor government and have no commerce or trade, industry or craft, ploughing or sowing, but only hunting and fishing, plundering, raiding, and eating one another.

'Know, your Majesty, that all marine animals flee in terror before the sea-serpent. But he fears nothing, save only a tiny beast resembling a mosquito, which he cannot harm and against whose sting he is defenceless. Once it stings him, its poison percolates through his body and he dies. Then all the sea animals gather to gorge on his carcass for days. For small beasts do feed on the larger when they can. The same is true with birds: sparrows, larks, swallows, and their ilk eat grasshoppers, ants, gnats, flies, and the like. Then sparrow-hawks and falcons and their kind hunt and devour the sparrows and larks. Hawks and eagles hunt and eat these in turn. But when large animals die, they are eaten by the smallest — ants, flies, and worms.[337]

'Such too is the life of humans. They eat the flesh of kids and lambs, sheep, cows, birds, and the rest. But when they die, they are consumed in their coffins and graves by worms, ants, and flies.

---

336 Gog and Magog are malefactors of yore, against whom Dhū'l-Qarnayn (identified with Alexander) built an iron barrier. It is said that at the apocalypse these two monstrous races will break through and wreak havoc before the final judgement; see Qur'an 18:93–97, 21:95–96; cf. Ezekiel 38:2–3, 38:14–18, 39:1, 39:11; Revelation 20:8. For the pertinent Islamic lore, see E. van Donzel and Claudia Ott, 'Yadjūdj wa-Madjūdj', *EI2*, vol. 11, p. 231–234.

337 See Montaigne, *Apology for Raymond Sebond*, in *Complete Essays*, II, 12, p. 338.

'Now smaller animals devour larger ones; now the larger eat the smaller. So the wisest human naturalists say that in the rot of one thing is the bloom of another.[338] God said, *These are the days whose revolutions I bring about among men.*[339] *None grasps this but the learned.*[340]

'We have heard, Majesty, that these humans claim to be our masters and aver that we and all other animals are their slaves. Don't they consider the give and take in animals' lives that I've described? Are they any different in this way from the rest of us? They can be eaters or eaten. So what do the Adamites have to boast of over us and all other animals? Their fate is like ours. As it is said "Their works bear their signet signs."[341] All of them are formed of earth,[342] *and thither is their destiny.*'[343]

338 Cf. Aristotle, *Metaphysics* III.4.1000b9–12; Pseudo-Aristotle, *On Melissus, Xenophanes, and Gorgias* 2.975a25–29; Anaximander, apud Simplicius, on the *Physics* 24.17, also in G. S. Kirk, J. E. Raven, and M. Schofield, *The Presocratic Philosophers* (2nd ed., Cambridge: CUP, 1984), § 110, p. 117.

339 Qur'an 3:140. See Chapter 5, note 61 above. The Ikhwān are clearly revolutionaries. They reject and abhor the ʿAbbāsid regime. It was partly on this basis that Abbas Hamdani, citing the discussion (in Epistle 48) of the secret meetings and revolutionary methods envisioned by the Ikhwān (see *Rasā'il*, vol. 4, pp. 148, 187–190), assigned an early date to the *Rasā'il*, seeing the work as a manifesto of the Fāṭimid revolution of 909, and pegging the composition of the essays just prior to that event. This early dating, however, required him to mark as interpolations the passages that refer to later events. See his 'Religious Tolerance in the *Rasā'il Ikhwān al-Ṣafā*", in Langermann and Stern, *Adaptations and Innovations*, pp. 137–138; Hamdani, 'The Arrangement of the *Rasā'il Ikhwān al-Ṣafā'* and the Problem of Interpolations', *Journal of Semitic Studies*, 29 (1984), pp. 97–110, updated in Nader El-Bizri, ed., *The Ikhwān al-Ṣafā' and their 'Rasā'il'*, pp. 83–100; and his 'Brethren of Purity, a Secret Society for the Establishment of the Fāṭimid Caliphate: New Evidence for the Early Dating of their Encyclopaedia', in *L'Egypte Fatimide: son art et son histoire*, ed. Marianne Barrucand (Paris: Presses Universitaires de Paris–Sorbonne, 1999), pp. 73–82. It is not necessary, however, to discard the evidence of Tawḥīdī and press for an early date to recognize that the Ikhwān, like Plato, hoped for a better basis for human political organization than they saw around them and, again, like Plato, did what they could to foster such a change.

340 Qur'an 29:43.

341 See Job 37:7: 'By every man's hand is it sealed, that each may know his deeds'; cf. Genesis 38:6–26. The Hebrew liturgy of Rosh ha-Shanah, in the *Unetaneh Tokef*, poetically describing the Book of Life, echoes Job: 'And the signet sign of every man is there.'

342 See Genesis 2:7, 3:19; Psalms 103:14, 104:29; Ecclesiastes 3:20, 12:7.

343 Qur'an 5:18. The frog takes the words to trace man's end to the earth (cf. Genesis

'You must know, wise Majesty,' said the frog, 'that when the sea-serpent heard the human claim that animals are slaves to men and that they are our masters, he was astounded at their making so false an aspersion. He said, "How utterly senseless these humans are! How utterly insolent and vain! How outrageously blind to any canon of reason! How could all wild beasts and carnivores, all birds of prey, dragons, sea-serpents, swordfish, and crocodiles be their slaves, created for their sake?[344] Don't they reflect and consider? If the beasts of prey were to unite and come out of the forests and wastes to attack them, and the birds of prey were to swoop down on them from the air, and the dragons to fall upon them from their mountain peaks, and the sea-serpents and crocodiles to issue from the sea and assail them in concert, would even one human survive?[345] Indeed, if these animals mingled with them in their dwelling places and abodes, would life be quite so good for humans? Could they even survive? They don't consider what a blessing it was to them that God kept these creatures far from their habitations, lest humans be harmed by them. They're simply misled by the fact that harmless animals are their prisoners, beasts that are not fierce or violent and have no sting or device. These they torment with the most grievous tortures night and day. Only this led them to make this false and unfounded claim."'[346]

Chapter 24

The King then scanned the assembly of men standing before him, some seventy in all, of diverse colours, descriptions, costumes, and garbs, and said to them, 'You have heard what the animals say. So consider and reflect on it.' Then he said to them, 'Who is your king?'

3:19), although the verse is normally be read as affirming that God is the final refuge and judge.

344 If the human case hinges on presumed primacy in the food-chain, other animals too fill such a niche. But in fact, as the animals stress, the food-chain is cyclical and has no true head. If the appeal is to sheer force, humans forget the vulnerability of all creatures.

345 Cf. Montaigne, *Apology for Raymond Sebond*, in *Complete Essays*, II, 12, p. 339.

346 The humans confound might with right.

'We have many kings', they replied.

'Where are their domains?'

'In diverse lands,[347] each in his own state with his own troops and subjects.'

'Wherefore and why', asked the King, 'do all these animal groups have a single king for each kind, despite their great numbers, and you humans have many kings, despite your small numbers?'

The Iraqi spokesman replied, 'Your Majesty, I'll tell you how it is that human kings are many when humans are so few, and animal kings are few although the animals are many.'

'Tell us then', said the King.

'It's because the ends of humans are many. Their inclinations vary. Their conditions are diverse. So men need many kings;[348] not so with other animals. Also, it matters that animal kings win their title by dint of their physical strength alone, great bodies and powerful frames. With human kings it's often just the opposite. The king may be the smallest, frailest, and most delicate of all. All that is asked of human kings is good government, just rule, care for their subjects, minding the welfare and good order of the troops and seeing to their needs. For the subjects of human kings and their forces and vassals vary by class and type. Some bear arms, and the king uses them to combat his enemies and all who threaten his realm — rebels, recusants, brigands and bandits, mobs, and rabble — all who would foment rebellion, civil strife, or disorder in the land.

---

347 Even here there are hints of usurpation, since each animal kind has its own proper habitat.

348 'Each type of ignorant polity has a variety of quite distinct subtypes, some vicious in the extreme, others only slightly harmful, and highly beneficial for its leading people. For souls respond to polities much as bodies of diverse temperaments respond to the seasons: some bodies and temperaments do well in the autumn, others in summer, others find winter most conducive and agreeable, others still, far prefer the spring. Likewise with souls and polities, only bodies are far more limited than ways of life. For in patterns of living there are virtually infinite combinations of natural, chosen, and chance factors, and many people who find themselves in a given life-pattern can be rather miserable without realizing it. But someone who is ill or suffers from a bad constitution can hardly remain unaware of it, nor will one who examines him.' Al-Fārābī, *Fuṣūl al-madanī*, § 87, ed. and tr. D. M. Dunlop as *Aphorisms of the Statesman* (Cambridge: CUP, 1961), pp. 162, (trans.) 70–71; the translation here is Goodman's.

'Other subjects are clerks and administrators, treasurers, heads of ministries, and tax agents, through whom the king gathers funds and the stores and supplies for his forces, as well as whatever clothing, furnishings, and provisions he needs.

'Still others are propertied settlers — landlords, planters, farmers, stock-breeders. The economy of the land depends upon these, and all people count on them for their livelihood.

'Others are judges, jurists, and clerics, who uphold the faith and religious law. For a kingdom needs a faith and religious law to protect its subjects, govern them, and see that their affairs justly and rightly ordered.

'Others are merchants, tradesmen, artisans, and their aides in the diverse crafts, trades, and industries of town and village. Without these and their cooperation life would be lacking and a good life would be impossible.

'Others are servants, attendants, maids, stewards, bailiffs, runners, emissaries, intelligence agents, favourites, and the like, needed by kings to enhance their lives.

'All the classes I've mentioned need a king to oversee their work, look after their welfare, and adjudicate among them.

'With all this diversity, humans need many rulers. In every land or state a king arises to order its affairs and those of all its people, as I've said. One person can't manage all these responsibilities. For there are seven climes on earth, and each clime has many lands. Each land has many cities. And every city teems with people — God alone knows how many! — who differ in language, mores, beliefs, ways of thought and practice, values and temperaments.

'So God's wisdom and providence find many human kings needful. All are God's vice-regents on earth, set by Him to reign over His lands and charged to care for His creatures, to govern and guide their affairs, preserve civil order among them, promote their welfare, curb injustice and aid its victims, render fair and impartial judgement, ordain what He has commanded, prohibit what He has forbidden, and emulate Him in their rule and direction. For God rules the universe. He governs all creatures from the highest of the high to the lowest of the low. He is their Preserver and Creator, Provider and Originator, who will resurrect them as and how He pleases. *For He is not to be asked of what he does. Rather they will be asked.*[349] I have said my say and beseech God's mercy on myself and on you.'

Chapter 25
The Virtues of the Bee — His Marvellous Life and Economy and the Special Gifts that Set Him Apart from All Other Insects

When the human delegate had finished speaking, the King scanned the motley throng of animals assembled before him and heard a whizzing, buzzing sound. It came from Yaʿsūb, prince and leader of the bees, stock still in mid-air, moving his wings swiftly with a hum that sang like the highest note of tiny lute. He was praising, sanctifying, and celebrating God.

'Who are you?' asked the King.

'I am the delegate of the swarming creatures and their prince.'

'How is it that you came yourself and did not send one of your subjects or soldiery as an emissary, like the other animals?'

'It was because of my tender feelings of compassion and concern for them. I feared some harm, ill, or misfortune might befall one of them.'

'Why are you so sensitive compared to all the other animal kings?'

'Only because my Lord favoured me with gifts of His bounty, grace, and immense generosity, beyond my accounting.'

'Mention a few of those gifts, and explain, so that we may hear and understand.'

'I shall, your Majesty. Among God's special blessings on me and my fathers and grandfathers were his gifts of royal rule and prophecy, which He made our heritage, from our fathers and forefathers and our legacy to our offspring and posterity, to be passed down from generation to generation until the Day of Judgement — two splendid gifts that most creatures, jinni, animal, or human, are denied.

'Among our special blessings and gifts from our Lord is the skill God inspired in us and the artistry He taught us to use in making our dwellings, building our homes, and gathering our stores.[350] Another

349 Qur'an 21:23; cf. Job 9:12.

350 When Muslim philosophers call bees, ants, and other social insects divinely

privilege is God's license to feed on every kind of flower and fruit. Another, that God made the capital store that flows from our bellies a sweet, delicious liquor in which there is healing for mankind. There's proof of what I say in God's words: *Thy Lord inspired the bee saying, "Make thy home in the mountains, in trees and trellises. Eat of all the fruits and take the ways that thy Lord hath eased for thee." From their bellies flows a liquor of diverse hues in which there is healing for mankind.*[351]

'Among our special gifts and blessings from our Lord are the form and frame He gave us, our fair mores, and the admirable conduct of our lives, truly a lesson for those with hearts to understand, a portent

---

inspired, the claims is no mere metaphorical extravagance. Animal instincts anchor the more general pattern of inspiration that emanationists see behind all cognition. This theme connects the scientific commitments of these philosophers with the language of scripture. Galen's experiments showed that certain animal behaviours are innate. Like the Stoics, he saw such behaviours as gifts of providence; *De Locis Affectis*, in *Opera Omnia*, ed. Kühn. Avicenna, in the same tradition, ascribes instincts to *ilhām*, inspiration. The innate capacity of animals to discriminate 'intentions', the practical import of appearances, was a paradigm case. Avicenna writes: 'We need to investigate and consider carefully how the intentions [*maʿānī*] of sensory things are grasped when one perceives the forms of those objects, since no such thing is perceived by the senses, and many of these objects of perception are not immediately harmful or beneficial. We say that this involves an evaluation of the aspect of a thing [*wahm al-wujūh*], part of the general inspiration emanating to all things by God's grace. An example is the way a newborn babe clings to the breast, or how a baby learning to get up and stand will grab hold of something when he starts to fall, or the way he immediately blinks if something potentially harmful flies toward his eyes, before understanding what is harmful or what to do about it — showing that this is instinctual and involuntary. Animals, too, have an inborn inspiration. The cause is their soul's steady attachment to her underlying source, which is never broken like some linkage that may hold or fail to hold, say, in the growth of reason or grasp of a true idea. Everything, in fact, comes from this source. But these inspirations enable evaluation of the significance, helpful or harmful, that lies unseen in the objects of perception: any sheep is wary of a wolf, even if it has not seen it before and has suffered no harm from it; many animals are wary of a lion; and other fowl are wary of birds of prey — the weaker ones give them a wide berth, without any experience of them.' Avicenna, *Kitāb al-Shifāʾ*, ed. Fazlur Rahman as *Avicenna's 'De Anima'* (London: OUP, 1959), pp. 183–184. The translation here is Goodman's; cf. *Liber de Anima*, 4.3, ed. S. van Riet as *Avicenna Latinus* (Leiden: Brill, 1968–1972), vol. 2, p. 37; *Liber de Anima*, 5.1, ed. S. van Riet, vol. 2, p. 73; see also Robert J. Richards, *Darwin and the Emergence of Evolutionary Theories of Mind and Behavior* (Chicago: University of Chicago Press, 1987), pp. 20–21.

351 Qur'an 16:68–70.

for all with eyes to see.[352] For God, in his wisdom, gave us an intricate and ingenious body and a wondrous form. Our bodies are segmented in three articulated parts: the mid-part, squarish or cube-like; the hind part, tapered and turned; and our heads, rounded and flat. Mounted on our mid-section are four legs and two hands, all fitted to the sides of a hexagon inscribed in a circle. With these we can support ourselves standing, sitting, alighting, and ascending, and can base our homes and hives on regular hexagons, so as to keep out the air that might harm our offspring or spoil the liquid stores that are our provisions and treasure.[353]

'With these four legs and two hands we gather the nectar and resinous fluids from the leaves of trees and from their blossoms and fruit, to build our homes and dwellings.

'On our shoulders God placed four wings of silky tissue, so we can fly freely through the air, borne upward by their use. He made our hindquarters tapered and hollow, air-filled, to balance our head's weight in flight. He gave us a sting sharp as a thorn, our weapon to menace our foes and drive off those who seek to harm us.[354] He made

---

352 See Qur'an 3:13, 39:21, 79:26.

353 Darwin writes, 'with respect to the combs of the hive bee; here again we must look to some faculty or means by which they make their hexagonal cells, without indeed we view these instincts as mere machines. At present such a faculty is quite unknown: Mr Waterhouse supposes that several bees are led by their instinct to excavate a mass of wax to a certain thinness, and that the result of this is that hexagons necessarily remain. Whether this or some other theory be true, some such means they must possess. They abound, however, with true instincts, which are the most wonderful that are known . . . If we knew the instinct of all the bees, which ever had existed, it is not improbable that we should have instincts of every degree of complexity, from actions as simple as a bird making a nest, and rearing her young, to the wonderful architecture and government of the hive bee.' From the 'Essay' of 1844, expanded by Darwin from the notes he wrote in 1842 while editing the zoology and writing the geology of the voyage of the *Beagle*. Darwin quoted the 'Essay' in his 1858 paper for the Linnaean Society announcing the theory of evolution. The piece was known to his son Francis by 1887, who published it in 1909, along with the 1842 sketch found among Darwin's papers in 1896, under the title *The Foundations of the Origin of Species*. The passage quoted here is from *The Works of Darwin*, ed. Barrett and Freeman, vol. 10, p. 95; cf. *The Origin of the Species*, in *The Works of Darwin*, ed. Barrett and Freeman, vol. 15, pp. 162–169.

354 Cf. Aristotle, *De Partibus Animalium* II.9.655b, III.1.661b; *Historia Animalium* IV.7.532a.

our neck slight, so we can easily turn our heads from side to side. He made our heads round and broad, with eyes on each side that gleam like a pair of sparkling mirrors. These He gave us as sense organs, to perceive visible things — colours and shapes — in light or darkness.

'On our heads, like horns, He set two tiny, delicate parts for tactile perception, apprehending soft and hard, rough and smooth, moist and dry. He opened two tiny nares for us, our organ for scenting fragrant odours. And He opened our mouths to taste and recognize the pleasant flavours of the foods we eat and liquids we drink. He formed the double-edged proboscis we use to gather delicate nectars from the fruit of trees and the blossoms of plants.

'In our bowels, God placed the power to take in and hold, treat, concoct, and cure those nectars, transforming them to delicious honey, a sweet, pure, and nourishing drink for ourselves and our young, to store and to keep us through the winter, just as He placed in the udders of cattle the power of concocting which transforms blood to *pure milk, delicious to drink.*[355]

'God has so lavished his gifts and blessings on me that I can hardly list them and adequately thank Him in the praises, hallels, lauds, and paeans by which I exalt my Lord daily and into the night. So I give thanks by the care I give my subjects, my vassals and troops, and the rearing of my offspring. For to my subjects I am like the head in the body, and they are the limbs and organs. Neither lives or prospers without the other.[356] I am their ransom in many a crucial matter. For

355 Qur'an 16:66: *Truly there is a lesson for you in the cattle: We give you drink from their bellies, between the dung and blood, pure milk delicious to drink.*

356 Thomas Hobbes, too, makes the life of the bee a political model. Although irrational, he argues, bees 'nevertheless live in good order and government, for their common benefit, and are so free from sedition and war amongst themselves, that for peace, profit, and defence nothing more can be imaginable.' Among bees 'there is no question of precedence in their own species, nor strife about honour or acknowledgment of one another's wisdom, as there is among men; from whence arise envy and hatred of one towards another, and from thence, sedition and war.' Bees 'aim every one at peace and food common to them all; men aim at dominion, superiority, and private wealth, which are distinct in every man, and breed contention'; and 'having not learning enough to espy, or to think they espy, any defect in the government', bees are contented. Lacking speech, they are 'unable to instigate one another to faction', yet 'have no conception of right and wrong, but only of pleasure and pain, and therefore also no censure

I care about them and feel for them. That is why I've come in person as emissary, spokesman, and delegate of my subjects and troops.'

When Ya'sūb had finished speaking, the King exclaimed, 'How amply God has blessed you with eloquent speech and how well has He instructed you in wisdom! What an enlightened ruler and leader He made you! What favour has He shown your subjects by making you their king, and how well has He has taught you as His subject, to appreciate the gifts of your Lord!'

Then the King inquired, 'In what land do you dwell?'

'In the mountains, hill-tops, and wooded glens. Some of us are neighbours to the Adamites in their dwelling places and domains.

'What kind of life have you with them? How do you keep safe from them?'

'Those who live far from human haunts and habitations are mostly unharmed by them. But sometimes they come looking for us and face us with harm. If they overpower us, they wreck our dwellings and burn our homes. They don't balk at killing us and our young, taking our stock and stores. They divide it up among themselves and leave nothing for us.'

'How do you put up with them? How do you bear such oppression from them?' asked the King.

'Patience can be a hateful durance. But discretion is the better part of valour. If we break away and fly far from the Adamites, they follow, trying to lure us back with all sorts of tricks, drum-beats, tambourines, flutes, and fancy presents of treacle and cream. So we come back and make up with them. We're good natured and have peace in our breasts and little rancour or spite — and reconciliation is good.[357] But with all that, these humans are not content. They even claim us as slaves and

---

of one another, nor of their commander, as long as they are themselves at ease.' Such concord, Hobbes argues, is 'the work of God by the way of nature; but concord amongst men is artificial, and by way of covenant.' Thomas Hobbes, *The Elements of Law, Natural and Politic,* I, 19.5, ed. J. C. A. Gaskin (Oxford: OUP, 1994), pp. 105–106. Hobbes' concerns with sedition, dissension, and dissent, do not correspond squarely with the political values of the Ikhwān, which are focused less on fear of anarchy than on the ideal of a ruler's political responsibility for (albeit not *to*) his subjects.

357 In the Dār Ṣādir printed edition, the bee continues: 'Our hearts hold God's inspiration and so have no place for malice or spite. Those are opposites to

make themselves out our lords and masters, with no evidence or proof beyond slander and lies. *God protect us from what you say*!'[358]

Chapter 26
The Superb Obedience of the Jinn to their Leaders and King

Ya'sūb then asked the King of the Jinn, 'How well do the jinn obey their chiefs and kings?'

'They are the most obedient of subjects, utterly steadfast in fulfilling our commands and prohibitions.'

'Would your Majesty be so gracious as to tell us something of this?'

'Certainly', he replied. 'You must know, then, that there are good and bad jinn, both Muslims and unbelievers, some pure and some profligate, just as there are among humans. The better jinn show indescribable loyalty to their leaders and kings, far beyond anything known to mortals of Adamite race. They follow their kings as the stars in the heavens follow that greatest of luminaries, the sun. For the sun in the celestial sphere is like a king, and the other stars are like his vassals, troops, and subjects. Mars serves, as it were, as his general; Jupiter as judge, Saturn as treasurer; Mercury as minister, Venus as consort. The moon is crown prince. The other stars are his troops, vassals, and subjects.[359] For all are yoked to the sphere of the sun, and move with

---

inspiration and cannot share its place. Since God chose us as his good intimates and gave us His revelation, it ill became us to be sinners and wrongdoers.'

358 Qur'an 12:18.

359 For the Ikhwān, the heavenly bodies are, as it were, the organs of the macrocosm (*Rasā'il*, vol. 2, p. 248; ibid., vol. 4, p. 427). The sun, with its heat, is the heart of the organism, much as man is the heart of terrestrial creation. As God's caliph, or vice-regent in the governance of the world, the sun plays a critical role in embryology. Its affinities in the human body are with the mouth. The moon relates closely to the navel. Her influences affect the rhythms of the menstrual cycle. Saturn's influence, necessary but often malign, maintains the nexus of form with matter. In anatomy, Saturn corresponds to the spleen; its black bile gives cohesion to the body, promotes coagulation of the blood, cools the body, and calms the mind. But it is also responsible for depression (melancholy). Its organs are those of excretion, and its affinities are with lead among the minerals, and with black and purple among the colours. It may bring poverty, misery, fatigue, or illness, and even paralysis and death. Jupiter is more benign. Like the pagan god of justice and hospitality, whose name the planet preserves in Western

it as they rise and set, pause, conjoin, or diverge — without deviation, never transgressing the pattern laid out for them, their courses never unwonted as they rise and set, ascend and descend. Never are they seen to change or show disaffection.'[360]

astronomy, it promotes order in the world. It keeps the four elements in balance, assigning their natures, and in that sense their very being. Its humour is sanguine, thus 'jovial', imparting bodily and psychic good humour. The Ikhwān picture Jupiter in a judge's mitre, adjudicating amongst the opposing natural tendencies of the elements. Its colour is green; its minerals, gemstones including rock crystal, coral, and pearls. Its organs are the eyes, and, in the ascendant, it oversees the birth of prophets and lawgivers. Mars is malign, linked to the gall-bladder. Its humour is bilious, and it prompts war, dissension, cruelty, strife, murder, and sacrilege. God allows strife so as to set apart good from evil and bring out the best in his creatures. So Mars marshals the birth of aggressive souls: heroes and champions, warriors, sultans. In the heavens, as already mentioned, Mars is the general, as it were, commanding the caliph's forces. Its influence affects anything combustible. Its minerals are iron and other materials of war. In the hereafter, Mars superintends the torment of errant souls. Venus, a beneficent star, aids the world's good order, bestowing beauty, luminosity, and the love of all things fine. A source of joy to all creatures, she gives plants their equipoise and blossoms their brilliance. She fosters friendship, desire, and love, centring her action on the breast. She favours the colour blue and promotes honour, courage, and nobility. Overseeing the birth of women and especially song-girls, she is the songstress of the caliph's court; her affinity is with scented trees, flowers, and jewels. Mercury is the sun's chief minister. Associated with the Active Intellect, Mercury is charged with governance of the world, overseeing angels, humans, jinn, demons, and spirits. It imparts consciousness, intelligence, understanding, discernment, science, prophecy, and inspiration. Its action centres on the brain, the imagination, and the ears, but its special organ is the tongue. The angels it sends earthward oversee the birth of secretaries and ministers of state, governors, and all perceptive or insightful persons. As the source of their Forms, it presides over all animals, vegetables, and minerals, especially the liveliest of living beings and the most iridescent of minerals.

360 The Ikhwān see a higher freedom in the invariance of the celestial bodies' movements, which sublunary natures may approximate but cannot perfect. Aristotle provides the underlying argument in the *Metaphysics* (XII.10.1075a12–25) when he wonders whether the good, or the highest good, is immanent in nature or 'apart and by itself'. 'Probably in both ways,' he says, 'for the good in an army lies both in its order and in its commander — but particularly in the latter, since he is not the product of the order, but it depends on him. . . . The world is not such that one thing is unrelated to another. Rather, everything is interconnected, since all things are ordered to one end. But it is like a household, where the free men are least free to do as they like, but everything or almost everything they do is determined by the interests of the household, whereas the slaves and the animals do little with a view to the common good and mostly live at random, each on his own.' Slaves and animals serve the

Said Yaʿsūb to the King of the Jinn, 'Where do the stars get such good order and discipline, such fine obedience and steadfast allegiance to their king?'

'From the angels, the hosts of the All-Merciful.'

'How would you describe the obedience of the angels to the Lord of the universe?'

'It's like the obedience of the five senses to the rational soul.'

'Explain this a bit more.'

'Surely. You see, O wise one, that in apprehending their objects and reporting what they perceive to the rational soul, the five senses need neither command nor prohibition, neither promise nor threat. Rather, whenever the rational soul is interested in some sensory thing, the senses immediately and unhesitatingly represent that object. Just so do the angels obey the Lord of all worlds. They don't balk at God's orders but do just as they're told by their Commander-in-Chief, the King of kings and Lord of lords, Ruler of the universe, Creator of all, the fairest of judges and most merciful of the compassionate.[361]

'Even evil, misbelieving, and iniquitous jinn are more obedient to their leaders and more steadfast in loyalty to their kings than wicked, depraved, or sinful humans.[362] The splendid obedience shown by the demons and rebellious jinn to Solomon, peace be upon him, proves

---

common good only insofar as they are put to use, on Aristotle's account. But free men order their own lives in behalf of that higher end. So, although it is they who act freely, most of what they do is laid out for them by their roles and the higher interests they know they must serve. The jinn, as natural forms and forces operative in the world, like the minds that steer the celestial bodies, act with steady invariance, understanding, as it were, the roles they must play in sustaining the good ends served by maintenance of the world's order. Their freedom is obedience to God's command.

361 A scholium preserved in the Dār Ṣādir edition quotes the Qur'an here (21:22): *If there were in heaven or earth any god besides God, both would have been ruined. Praised, then, be the Lord of both worlds!* The scholiast seems anxious to counter any doubts of God's sovereignty raised by Neoplatonic efforts to smooth the transition between God and nature by delegating divine authority and power to intellectual hypostases and celestial bodies.

362 The invariance of the observed courses of the heavenly bodies was early interpreted as visible evidence of their divinity. The Ikhwān, as monotheists, ascribe the steady pattern to what they term metaphorically the strict obedience of the lesser celestial beings to the sun, their leader, the sun being the visible paradigm of the invisible but absolute subordination of all things to God. Their

this. For when they were in his thrall and he set them to onerous and exhausting tasks, *they made whatever he wished — palaces, statues, basins like cisterns, and mountainous cauldrons.*[363]

'Another sign of how well the jinn obey their leaders is what certain humans have found in traversing waste and desert places: if one descends into a wadi where he fears bewitchment by the jinn, and he hears their cries and clamour all about, he has but to call on their leaders and kings for protection and recite a verse or a word from the Qur'an, the Torah, or the Gospels, seeking in it protection from them and from any harm or hindrance wrought by them, and they will not disturb him as long as he remains in that place.

'So well do the jinn obey their chiefs that if some rebel jinni troubles an Adamite with madness, terror, confusion, or panic, and a human enchanter calls for help from the leader of that jinni's tribe, or from their king or his forces, they throng and rally around, doing just as they are commanded and forbidden with that person.

'Another mark of the discipline of the jinn, showing how sensitive they are, and how responsive to an appeal, is the way that a band of jinn responded to Muhammad, peace be upon him, when they came upon him and found him reciting the Qur'an. They stood nearby listening intently and then acknowledged him *and went off to caution their folk,*[364] as is told in some twenty verses of the Qur'an.[365]

'These verses and this evidence all show how well the jinn obey, how readily, willingly, and swiftly they comply and hearken to any who call on them and seek their help, for good or ill.

'But the nature and temper of humans are quite the opposite. Their obedience to their chiefs and monarchs is mainly hypocrisy and dissembling, gulling and grasping for stipends, payments, rewards, vestments, and prizes. If they don't get what they're after, they come out in open defiance and rebellion, shed their outward allegiance, secede

---

emanationist rationalization of angelology is the justification for the ostensible digression from the primary issue of the essay.

363 Qur'an 34:13.

364 Qur'an 46:29.

365 Qur'an 72:1–19, the introductory *basmala*, invoking God, is counted as the twentieth verse.

from the commonwealth, and bring dissension, civil war, bloodshed, and destruction to the land.

'Their treatment of their prophets and the apostles of their Lord is no different. Now they reject their call with denials of obvious truths and disavowals of unimpeachable proofs,[366] demanding miracles of them out of sheer perversity.[367] Now they humour them, but remain hypocritical, dubious, incredulous, sceptical, deceitful, perfidious, false — secretly faithless. All this is due to their flawed nature, hostility, and insensitivity, their vicious character, bad morals, and wicked ways. They are hugely rude and blind of heart. But on top of all this, they're not satisfied until they claim, without proof or argument, that they are lords and others are their slaves!'

The assembled humans were surprised on seeing how long the King of the Jinn spoke with Yaʿsūb, the delegate of the swarming creatures, and openly voiced their disapproval: 'The King has granted a privileged role in this council to the royal emissary of the insects, Yaʿsūb, that he did not give to the spokesman of any of the other parties.'

A jinni sage replied, 'Don't be so surprised or displeased. Yaʿsūb may be small in size, tiny to look at. His body may be frail, but he makes huge good sense. He's solid and substantial, keen spirited and most worthy, graced with mastery, and adept in his art. He is the chief of all insect chiefs, their spokesman, king, and prophet. Kings converse with their peers, who have leadership and authority in common with them, even if they differ in outward appearance and manner of rule. But don't imagine that the wise and just King of the Jinn is biased in favour of one party over another, swayed by some whim or affinity, or for any other reason or cause.'

When the jinni was finished, the King surveyed the throng before him and said, 'You have heard, assembled humans, the tenor of these animals' complaints against you on grounds of oppression and injustice. We have heard your claim that they are your slaves and chattels, which

366 Prophecy, after all, is a poetic expression of philosophical truths. See al-Fārābī, *Ārā'* 17.2, ed. Walzer, pp. 218–281; *Fuṣūl*, 52, ed. Dunlop, Arabic pp. 135–136, English p. 49.

367 Muhammad rejected calls for miracles in proof of his mission, proclaiming each verse of the Qur'an itself a miracle; each verse, accordingly, is called a portent, *āya*.

they deny and repudiate. We have sought your proof and evidence. You have presented your brief, and we have heard their response. Have you anything to add beyond what you said yesterday?

Chapter 27

A delegate from the rulers of Byzantium rose and said: 'Praise be to God, gracious, bountiful, kindly and good, clement and forgiving, who created man and inspired him with science and clarity, showed him the pathways of evidence and proof, gave him dignity and dominion, taught him how times change and ages pass, who set animals and plants in his service, and instructed him in the uses of the minerals and elements.

'Indeed, your Majesty, we have many laudable qualities and manifold attainments that confirm the truth of what we say.'

'What are they?' asked the King.

'Our many sciences and forms of knowledge, our subtle discernment and fine reasoning and rule, our marvellous capacity for managing our lives and collaborating in arts, industries, commerce, and trade, and in dealing with this world and the next.[368] All this confirms our claim that we are their masters and they are our slaves.'

Said the King to the animals thronged before him, 'What do you answer to their assertions and to the evidence they adduce in support of their claims of ownership and mastery?'

The assembly fell silent for a time, considering the virtues and gifts that the human claimed God had lavished on the Adamites, distinguishing them from all other animals. Then the bee spoke, rising as an orator with these words of praise, 'Praised be God, one and unique, Creator of the heavens and of all creatures, who orders the seasons and causes the rains to fall as blessings, the grass to grow in desert places, and flowers to emerge from plants, who allots provender and sustenance to all. We praise Him when we rise at dawn and adore Him when we retire at evening with the prayers and salutations we

368 The Byzantine spokesman seems to fall into the trap of thinking that even religion is a matter of trade with the divine; cf. Plato, *Euthyphro* 14; *Republic* II.362.

have been taught, as He says, *There is no thing that does not sing His praises, but you comprehend not their praise.*[369]

'Wise and just Majesty, this human claims that they have sciences and forms of knowledge, thought and judgement, skill in governance and management that show them to be our masters and us to be their slaves. Had they considered our natures and studied our lives, they would have seen clearly from how we manage our affairs and co-operate to secure our interests that we, too, have knowledge and understanding, awareness, discernment, thought, judgement, and governance, subtler, wiser, and finer than theirs.

'Take the social organization of bees in their hamlets — how we make ourselves a monarch, who takes on vassals, troops, and subjects, ruling and caring for them as his flock, and how we make our homes in hexagonal cells joined together like tiny tubes turned on a lathe.[370] Consider too how we organize our porters, chamberlains, guards, and inspectors,[371] how we go out to forage on spring days and moonlit nights in summer and gather wax from the tree leaves with our legs and honey with our lips from the blossoms of plants, how we store it in certain cells and seal their heads like jugs stoppered at the mouth with paper, how we lay our eggs in other cells to brood and hatch, how we lodge in others and sleep there through the days of winter cold, wind, and rain,[372] feeding on the honey we've stored away, we and our offspring, day by day, neither squandering nor stinting,[373] until winter is past and spring arrives, the grass sprouts, the weather improves, plants emerge, and flowers bloom. Then we go out to pasture again, as in the last year. Such are our lives, untutored, untaught, even by our mothers and fathers, but instructed by God, through the gift of divine

---

369 Qur'an 17:44.

370 Bees 'live in apartments and construct their homes with indescribable skill; they make their honeycombs from various flowers, build wax cells and renew their citadel with countless offspring; they have armies and kings, wage battle, flee smoke, and are roused by any disturbance.' Isidore, *Etymologies* 12.8.1; cf. Pliny, *Natural History* XI.15.45.

371 Ibid. XI.10.20–26.

372 Ibid. XI.5.13–14.

373 Ibid. XI.7.17.

inspiration, by His grace and bounty upon us. Praise be to God, *the fairest of creators, and greatest in mercy*![374]

'Further, your Majesty, humans should know the life of the ants,[375] how they build towns underground, houses and chambers, tunnels and passages, galleries, and multi-storeyed, sloping apartments, some filled with grain, stores, and foodstuffs for the winter, cached in sheltered cellars with sloping entrances that draw off the water lest it reach the grain — and if a bit does get wet, how they spread it out to dry on sunny days — how they cut wheat grains in half, and husk barley, beans, and lentils, knowing that these will not sprout once cut up.[376] See how they work through the summer, day and night, building their homes and gathering their stores, how they search one day to the left of their village, one day to the right, coming and going like veritable caravans. If one of them goes out and finds something she can't carry, she takes a sample and goes back to the rest with the news, and whenever another meets her, it smells what she has and knows what she has found. Then see them all on the trail to the site, how they throng about and carry it off, guarding it as they struggle to drag it along as a team.

'Should they find one of their number slack in her efforts or lax in contributing her fair share to their joint labour, all join in killing her and cast her aside, as a lesson to the rest.

'So, were this human to study the life of the ants and consider their ways, he would find that they have science, understanding, discernment, awareness, knowledge, governance, and an ordered

---

374 Qur'an 23:16; 12:64.

375 'Look at the ant, lazy-bones! Study her life and grow wise. With no taskmaster, overseer, or foreman she readies her stores in the summer and gathers her food at the harvest. How long, lazy-bones, will you lie there? When will you wake up from your sleep? Just a bit more sleep, a bit more slumber, a bit more hugging yourself in your bed, and want will be there like a brigand; poverty, like an armed man!' Proverbs 6:6–11, translated after the Jewish Publication Society version in the *Hebrew–English Tanakh* (Philadelphia: JPS, 1999).

376 In a typically fanciful etymology, Isidore writes: 'The ant [*formica*] is so named because it carries bits of grain [*fert micas farris*]. It has great shrewdness, for it provides for the future and prepares in the summer what it consumes through the winter; at the harvest it chooses wheat and does not touch barley. When it rains on the ant's grain, the ant sets it out to dry.' *Etymologies* 12.3.9; cf. Montaigne, *Apology for Raymond Sebond*, in *Complete Essays*, II, 12, p. 347.

polity, just as humans do, and he would not boast of superiority on that score.

'Again, your Majesty, he should consider the life of the locusts, how they fatten by grazing through the spring and then seek good soft soil to dig in and alight there and burrow with their feet and mandibles, insert their tails, lay their eggs, cover them up, and fly off. They live on just a few days, and when the time comes to die they're eaten by birds, or blown away to perish in the heat or cold, or are lost in the wind, the hail, or rain.

'But when the year comes full circle and spring returns with its mild weather and fine air, tiny worms emerge from those buried eggs and crawl over the surface of the earth. They feed on grass and herbage, sprout wings, and take flight. They eat the leaves of trees and fatten and lay, just as in the last year. This is the steady pattern of their lives, laid out for them by the All-Knowing and Majestic. So this human should see that they too have knowledge and discernment.

'The same is true, your Majesty, of the silkworm, who lives in mountain tree-tops. Sated and fattened with grazing through the spring, these worms in the foliage spin a sort of nest or wrapper about themselves from the gossamer thread of their spittle. Here they sleep a set number of days and when they wake lay their eggs in the cocoon they've spun around themselves. They bore through it and emerge, sealing the opening behind them. Sprouting wings, they fly off, to be eaten by birds or die in the heat, or the cold, or the rain. But their eggs remain in those coverts through summer, autumn, and winter, shielded from heat and cold, wind, and rain, until the year is full and spring has come. The eggs have brooded in their cases, and from the openings emerge what look like tiny worms that creep out in the tree-tops on a certain day. Once they have fed, fattened, and had their fill, they too spin about themselves with their saliva, the same as last year. This is their life, allotted by God, majestic and aware, *who gave all things their natures and led* all to what is useful and helpful to them.[377]

---

377 The bee quotes the words ascribed to Moses in the Qur'an (20:50), in support of the view that providence acts through the steady patterns of nature, contrary to the doctrine of the occasionalist *kalām*, which denies fixed natures resident in things.

'The same could also be learned from the wasps, yellow, red, or black. They too build homes and dwellings, theirs in rafters, on walls, or, like beehives, in the tree branches. They too lay eggs and brood and hatch them. But they don't gather food for the winter or store anything for the morrow. They feed day by day while the season holds, and when they sense changing weather and the onset of winter, they retreat to caves and other hidden, protected places. Some enter cracks in the wall or other sheltered hiding places. There they fall into a deathlike sleep. All through the winter they remain, suffering neither the harsh cold nor the wind and rain. Then, when winter ends and spring comes and the season is equable and the weather fair, God breathes the spirit of life into their bodies and they revive. They build their houses, lay their eggs and brood them, and the young emerge once more, the same as last year. This is their regular pattern of life, allotted to them by a wise and majestic God.

'All these swarming and creeping kinds lay eggs, brood them, and raise their young with sage intelligence, care, and concern, tender, gentle, and compassionate. They do not ask for honour or respect, recompense or thanks from their offspring. But most humans want reverence and recognition, requital from their children — if not a reward for raising them. Is that manly virtue?[378] Where is the noble liberality of free, high-minded, generous, and magnanimous spirits? What have these humans to boast of over us?

'As for fleas, gnats, worms, flies, and others of their ilk,' said the delegate of the bees, 'they don't lay eggs and brood them or bear young and nurse them, nor do they rear their offspring, build houses, store food, or build a nest. They fritter away their lives in prodigal pleasures, heedless of the cold, wind, and rain of winter and the changes of season that others must face.

'When the weather changes, their carefree life is put out of joint. The elements shift their balance, and they give up their souls to a new generation, resigned to die, sure that God will revive them and return them next year to life, just as He *raised them up* to life at the first.[379]

378 In traditional Arabic texts, both Jewish and Muslim, parental concern is a manly trait. Nurture is not exclusively feminine.

379 At Qur'an 36:79 God teaches Muhammad to argue that to resurrect the dead

They utter no such denial as humans did, saying: *"Shall we, then, return in the grave? Shall we, once we are rotted bones? Surely that would be a sorry return!" — But there will be just one blast.*[380]

'If this human considered the transformations I've cited, your Majesty, the metamorphoses these swarming and creeping creatures go through, he would understand and see clearly that they have knowledge and discernment, awareness, discrimination, judgement, thought, ideas, polity, and a social order, all by God's providence. He would not boast that the traits he cited make them our masters and us their slaves. I have said my say. God grant pardon to me and to you.'

Chapter 28

When the wise bee had finished, the King of the Jinn said to him: 'Bless you! What a learned philosopher God has made you, how eloquent a speaker, how lucid in your exposition!' Then the King said, 'You have heard, assembled humans, what the bee has said. You understand his answer. Have you anything to add?'

Another human rose, a Bedouin, who said, 'Yes, your Majesty. We have many fine points and worthy qualities which show that we are the masters and they are our slaves.'

'Very well, then', said the King, 'name some of them.'

'Our delightful lives and elegant ways of living, our fine foods, of every type and flavour, our delicious drinks — God alone knows how many. These animals have no share in all this. They're kept well away from such things. Our food is the flesh of fruits; they get the rind, the pits, and the stem. We enjoy the heart of the grain; they get the chaff, bran, and straw. We have the oil and juice; they get the lees and the dregs. Besides, our foods are artfully prepared — all sorts of breads, rolls, cakes, biscuits, and pastries of semolina, sweets of all sorts. We

---

will not be hard for God, who raised up mankind to life in the beginning. Gnats and the others are fearless, being confident of the resurrection of their kind, since they were raised up at the start from inanimate matter. The gnats seem not to distinguish individual resurrection from the continuance of their kind.

380 Qur'an 79:10–13; we translate in keeping with *Tanwīr al-miqbās min tafsīr Ibn ʿAbbās*.

have confections — savoury dumplings, sweetmeats, pickles, stews, casseroles of meat stewed in milk, sugar, and corn-starch, fritters, and nougat.

'We have all kinds of drinks, good pure wine of grapes and dates, sweet and dry, juleps, fizzy drinks, barley-water, and milk of all sorts — sweet and sour, whey, buttermilk, butter and cheese, curds, and all that is made from milk — all sorts of cooked dishes, dainties, delicacies, appetizing specialities — again, in limitless variety.

'We have salons and entertainments, fun, joy and delight, weddings, banquets, dancing, stories and occasions for laughter, celebrations, receptions, honours, and testimonials. We have vestments and robes of honour, turbans, and all sorts of other garments, bracelets, bangles, anklets, raised seats and sunken cups, rich cushions and ample rugs, paired divans facing each other, soft pillows, and countless other such comforts.[381]

'Of all this, too, they are deprived. Their food is crude, coarse, dry, and tasteless. It has no sweetness or richness in it. That shows how little they can enjoy it. But that is the mark of slaves, and our fine foods and drinks are the meed of masters, the prerogatives of the noble and free. All this shows that we are their masters and they are our chattels and slaves. I have said my say. God forgive me and you.

Chapter 29

The delegate of the birds then spoke, the nightingale, rising from his perch on a tree branch: 'Praised be God, one and alone, unique and impassive, ever-abiding and eternal, without peer or offspring, but the Creator and Former of all, Cause of all beings, Ground of all becoming, of all that grows or stands inert, Author of all Creation, who composed the passions and engendered all joys and delights as He chose and pleased.

'Noble Majesty, this human boasts of their fine foods and delicious drinks, little knowing that all these are chastisements, sources of trouble and painful affliction.'

381 This paragraph is not represented in the manuscripts collated for this translation or in the Dār Ṣādir text. It is attested only in Dieterici's version, but we have included it here, since the nightingale cites and responds to it in his reply.

'How so?' asked the King. 'Explain this to us.'

'Certainly. The point is that they gather and prepare these things by the toil of their bodies and torment of their souls, the exhaustion of their spirits and sweat of their brows, to the infinite detriment of their strength and health. The pleasure or profit in eating such things is outweighed by the endless ploughing, sowing, and clearing of land, diverting rivers, digging canals, damming flood channels, fashioning ponds, setting up water-wheels, dredging, irrigating, watching crops, weeding, harvesting, hauling, gathering, threshing, winnowing, measuring, distributing, weighing, milling, kneading, baking, building ovens and tending pots, gathering firewood, thorns, dung, and kindling, feeding fires and suffering their smoke, building shops, haggling with butchers, and chaffering with grocers. They toil and moil to eke out a living in pennies, schooled in crafts and trades that weary the body and labours that degrade the soul — reckoning, trading, coming and going on distant journeys in search of their wants and needs, hoarding, and engrossing while suffering all the austerities of a niggardly miser.

'If all this getting and spending is licit, that's still a heavy price to pay. But if their gains are improper or their spending not godly, there's woe and retribution besides.[382]

'We, however, are far removed from all this. Our food and nutriment are what spring up for us from the ground at the rain from the sky — all sorts of fresh, green vegetables, leafy and tender, grasses and herbs, and fine kernels of grain wrapped in their husks and ears, all sorts of fruits of diverse forms, foods of varied scent and savour, fresh green leaves, flowers, and fragrant plants from the meadow. These the earth brings forth for us season by season, year after year, without toil to our bodies, trouble to our souls, or strain to our spirits. We need no such labour as ploughing nor such trouble as watering. We need no sowing, reaping, threshing, milling, baking, cooking, or roasting. That's the mark of our freedom and nobility.

'Besides, when we've eaten our daily food we leave over what we don't need. We needn't store or preserve it, guard or protect it, or hoard

382 Here a copyist, as reflected in the Dār Ṣādir text, interjects: 'But food and clothing are also needs, just as much as death and an accounting for one's deeds!'

it for the future. For we fear no robbers or brigands but sleep where we are in our homelands. Our nests have no high walls, nor any door, bolt or lock. We're safe, secure, unshrinking, and at ease — clear marks of the noble and free. They're far from enjoying such peace of mind.

'Beyond that, for every pleasure they name from all their foods and drinks there's a price to pay in sufferings, afflictions from which we are free — all kinds of illnesses, chronic and wasting diseases, burning fevers — hectic, alternate, tertian, and quartan[383] — dyspepsia, vomiting, diarrhoea, colic, gout, pleurisy, plague, jaundice, dropsy, ulcers, consumption, leprosy, apoplexy, ophthalmia, night-blindness, kidney stones, small-pox, warts, abscesses, scrofula, measles, sores, and swellings of all sorts.[384] These demand all kinds of harrowing treatments — cautery, lancing, inhalants, bleeding, suppositories, foul, loathsome laxatives, harsh diets, neglect of the appetites so rooted in their natures, and all sorts of like torments and chastisements, mortifying to body, spirit, and soul.

'All these ills beset you humans because you rebelled against your Lord, spurned the obedience due Him, and ignored His charge.[385] We're far above all this. So how can you claim to be masters and call us your slaves — if not by brazen impudence and shameless arrogance!'

Said the human, 'Illness strikes you animals too, the same as us. It doesn't discriminate between us.'

---

383 Fever was defined by the fourth-century Roman author Palladius as 'abnormal heat that begins in the heart and spreads throughout the body via the arteries, noticeably harming the bodily functions'. To explain fevers as an excess of bodily heat was no mere tautology, since heat was critical to life and arose as a basic property of one of the four elements at the root of the humoral system. Still, the ancient medical writers recognized that fever could be a symptom rather than a disease in its own right. See Galen, *Therapeutica ad Glauconem* I, in *Opera Omnia*, ed. C. G. Kühn.

384 For the Galenic background, see the works collected in *Galen on Food and Diet*, ed. and tr. Mark Grant (London: Routledge, 2000); and Paul of Aegina, *The Seven Books*, vol. 1, pp. 106–108. Among the sources cited in the commentary: Hippocrates, *De Dieta*; Galen, *De Alimentorum Facultatibus*; as well as Dioscorides, Oribasius, Aetius, Psellus, Rāzī, Avicenna, and Averroes.

385 The animals moralize illness. God's neglected charge here is perhaps not the prohibition of the forbidden fruit, as in Chapter 32, but nature's counsel of moderation. Plato argues that a life of luxury creates or aggravates the need for physicians, whereas the wholesome society and the temperate individual have little need of them; Plato, *Republic* II.373; ibid. III.405–408.

The bird answered: 'These maladies afflict only those of us who mix with you — doves,[386] cocks, chickens, dogs, cats, hunting birds, cattle, and sheep — or those imprisoned by you and kept from freely seeking our own good as we see it.[387] When we're left to ourselves, to do as we like and pursue our own interests, under our own recognizance, using our own discipline and direction, we're rarely stricken by illness, agony, or pain. For we eat and drink only when we need to, only in due measure, one comestible at a time,[388] just enough to still the pangs of hunger. Then we rest or sleep, calm ourselves, and avoid too much stirring or lying too long in the hot sun or chill shade. Nor do we settle in lands inhospitable to our natures or eat foodstuffs unsuited to our constitutions.

'But the animals that mingle with you — dogs and cats, and those you have interned, like sheep and cattle — are kept from seeking their own good as they see it and when called for by the instincts implanted in their natures. They are fed and watered at unsuitable times, not at their own desire, or when so dreadfully hungry or thirsty that they take in more than they need. They're not allowed to rest and slow down enough but pressed to exhaustion in service. That's why they succumb to some of the diseases that afflict you.

'Likewise with the ailments and ills of your children. Your pregnant women and wet nurses tend to eat and drink greedily, like gluttons. They stuff themselves with unwholesome foods and drinks — the very ones you boast of. That causes crude, uneven mixing of the

---

386 The dove, as Isidore writes, 'loves human society; it is always a pleasant inhabitant of a house. Doves are tame birds, comfortable in large groups of humans, and without bile. The ancients called them lovebirds because they often come to nest and show their love with a kiss.' *Etymologies* 12.7.61–62.

387 Liberals deem the individual the best judge of his own interest, a principle rooted in the naturalism of the Epicureans. The Ikhwān would qualify this view, asking greater openness to the teachings of prophets and sages. But those teachings, the Ikhwān reason, are themselves clear truths, obscured only by prejudice and convention. So, inspired wisdom does not conflict with the pursuit of our interests but supports it. Using the language of Islamic jurisprudence, the nightingale makes individual judgement (*ra'y*) a good guide to those interests (*maṣāliḥ*). The animals are free to follow such counsels since they are not recipients of special revelation and are not bound by a particular juridical tradition.

388 As Adams remarks in his commentary to Paul of Aegina's *The Seven Books*, 'Horace agrees with Galen and our author in condemning the mixture of various articles of food'. See *The Seven Books*, vol. 1, p. 108.

conflicting natures in their bodies, and the foetuses are affected in the womb; or the babes' bodies are affected by bad milk that brings on disease and debility — crippling, palsy, paralysis, malformations, deformity, and disfigurement.[389]

'The many diseases and disabilities I mentioned that chronically afflict you, and the untimely deaths that result, the violent struggles, the grief and sorrow that follow, the mourning, weeping, wailing, and affliction, are all punishments to chastise your souls — results of your bad actions and unwholesome choices, from which we are spared.[390]

'Another thing counts against you, O human, which you ought to consider.'

'What is that?'

'Your finest food, tastiest liquor, and best medicine is honey,[391] the spittle of bees. It comes not from you but from an insect. The milk, butter, cheese, whey, and other foods you boast of eating and drinking come not from you but from animals. You eat fruit, cereals, and grains, as we do, fresh or dry. So how can you brag that you are our betters? Our forefathers shared these equally with yours in the days when we all lived in that garden in the East, atop that mountain. We all once ate of those fruits without toil or trouble, strain or strife, rivalry or rancour. There was no envy, engrossing or hoarding, no coveting, avarice, fear, alarm, anxiety, or sorrow[392] — until that pair spurned their Lord's good counsel, deceived by the words of their foe. They rebelled against their Lord and were expelled, naked, banished, cast

---

389 For the classical and medieval views on the ill effects of bad diet among nursing mothers and wet nurses, see Avner Giladi, *Infants, Parents, and Wet Nurses: Medieval Islamic Views on Breastfeeding and their Social Implications* (Leiden: Brill, 1999); and J. Lascaratos and E. Poulakou-Bebelokou, on Oribasius, the fourth-century Byzantine physician, in *Journal of Pediatric Gastroenterology and Nutrition*, 36 (2003), pp. 186–189; cf. *Galen on Food and Diet*, tr. Grant, p. 164.

390 In mediaeval medicine all disease was distemper, that is, an imbalance of the bodily humours. Improper diet was the chief imputed cause.

391 Honey was widely thought of as medicinal, claims attested as early as Hippocrates and Democritus. See Paul of Aegina, *The Seven Books*, vol. 1, pp. 178–179.

392 'With any ill, where the cause is not known the cure will not be found. So we must analyse what sorrow is and what its causes are, so that its remedies may be readily found and easily effected. We say, then, that sorrow is psychological suffering arising when something loved is lost or something desired eludes us.' Kindī, *Essay on How to Banish Sorrow*; tr. here is Goodman's.

down from the mountain's top to its foot. Fallen there into a desolate waste, without water, trees, or shelter, they remained hungry and naked, rueing their fate and the joys they had lost.

'It was then that God's mercy reached out to them and He relented, sending an angel to teach them how to plough, sow, reap, thresh, mill, and bake, and how to make clothes from the herbs of the earth — cotton, flax, and hemp — with labours, toils, struggles, hardships, and sufferings numberless but to God, of which hardships we mention only the merest fraction.[393]

'When the two reproduced, their offspring multiplied and spread over the earth, land and sea, mountain and plain. They usurped the habitats of other animal kinds that lived on earth, wrested from them their ancestral lands, took from them what they would, captured those they could, and put the rest to flight, or hunted them down. At last the oppression grew so outrageous that it reached its present extreme of vainglory, belligerence, emulousness, and aggression.

'As for the gatherings you mention, the entertainments, parties, salons, the joyous levees and happy celebrations — the weddings, feasts, and dances, your stories, your times to laugh, your receptions and testimonials, your glories and honours, adornments and embellishments — the bracelets, bangles, anklets, and the like, which we have not — all the joy and gladness you derive from these are offset by all sorts of painful consequences, afflictions and chastisements, from which we are immune.

'The weddings give way to bereavements, the celebrations to wakes, the song and merriment to wailing and mourning, the laughter to tears,

393 Industry and agriculture reflect man's fallen state; freedom from toil and concern for the morrow belongs to the animals — a romantic distortion, since industry, agriculture, and commerce create leisure on a scale unknown in other species. Prejudice against 'artisanship' as illiberal and dehumanizing is embedded in the thought of Plato and Aristotle; see Plato, *Laws* VII.846–849; Aristotle, *Politics* I.13.1260a36–1260b1; ibid. III.5.1277b34–1278a14; ibid. VII.9.1329a26–29; ibid. VII.12.1331a19–35. 'No man can practise virtue', Aristotle writes (*Politics* III.5.1278a20), 'who is living the life of a mechanic or a labourer'. The Ikhwān resist disparagement of true arts, but here allow the animals to deploy similar attitudes against human pretensions of gentility. Even here, though, they skirt the dichotomy of labour and leisure, linking both to man's fallen state.

the joy and gladness to sorrow and grief.[394] You leave your parties and your lofty, well-lit halls perforce, for dark graves and narrow coffins. Your broad court-yards are replaced by dark dungeons and gloomy keeps. Your lively dancing done, you face whips, the scourge and the lash, your bangles and bracelets turned shackles, fetters, and chains, your praises and honours are now shame, humiliation, and disgrace — an evil for every good, a torment for every pleasure. For every joy, a heart-break, care, calamity, or sorrow — all foreign to us. But all these are the marks of wretched slaves.

'You have your assembly-rooms, halls, court-yards, and squares. But we revel in the broad expanse of open air, in lush meadows by the river-bank or sea-shore. We sail over gardens and tree-tops, soar over mountains, roam and alight where we like in God's ample land, eating of the provender God gives us, without trouble or toil — all manner of grains and fruits — drinking from rivers and pools without hindrance or let. We need no rope, bucket, or jug, no water-skin like those you struggle with carrying water. We have no need to treat and purvey it, buy it or sell it, haggle over its price, exhausting the body, troubling the soul, grieving the heart, and wearying the spirit. All these are the marks of miserable slaves. So what makes you so sure that you are the masters and we are the slaves?'

Said the King to the spokesman of humans, 'You have heard this answer. Have you anything to add?'

'Yes. We have many more achievements and distinctions that mark us as the masters and them as our slaves.'

'What are they? State them.'

Chapter 30

A man from Syria,[395] a Hebrew, rose and said, 'Praised be God, Lord of all worlds fate of the faithful and foe to none but the wicked. *God*

394 Happiness, as the human conceives it, means giving hostages to fortune; hence the classic Stoic reminders that all joys have their counterparts in grief.

395 The speaker here is a Hebrew from Palestine, which the Ikhwān treat as part of Syria, as many mediaeval geographers do.

chose Adam, Noah, the House of Abraham, and the House of Amram above all the world, each from the seed of the last. God hears and knows.[396] It was He who favoured us with prophecy and inspiration, graced us with miracles and revealed books, the unshakeable verses that bear His divers permissions and prohibitions, His statutes and laws, commands and interdictions, His dreadful threats and His promises of delight, His praises and exaltations, remonstrance, memorial and lore, parables, lessons and legends, accounts of the first and the last, of Judgement Day, and the lovely gardens He promised us. He graced us too with ablutions, purifications, fasts, worship, charity and alms, festivals, convocations, and attendance at houses of worship — mosques, churches, or synagogues, sanctified houses of God. We have pulpits, sermons, calls to prayer, church-bells,[397] convocations, holy places, ritual observances, ceremonies, and the like.[398] All these are marks of God's grace that you lack. They show that we are the masters and you are our slaves.'

Said the delegate of the birds, 'Had you reflected on the matter, O human, and given it serious thought, you'd have realized that all these things count against you, not in your favour.'

'How so?' asked the King. 'Explain this to us.'

'Because all these are penalties, chastisements to expiate sin and atone for wrong-doing, or to restrain you from foul, shameful doings, as God said, *Prayer bars what is shameful and foul*[399] and *Good deeds dispel ill. This a reminder to the mindful.*[400] And the Prophet said 'Fast

396 Qur'an 3:33–34. The Ikhwān seem to sense no irony in the Hebrew spokesman's citing a Qur'anic verse to support Israel's chosenness.

397 Dieterici's printed text adds 'shofars and trumpets'.

398 The Hebrew speaks for humankind at large, alluding to the religious institutions of all peoples.

399 Qur'an 29:45.

400 Qur'an 11:114. In full, the verse reads: *Fix your worship at both ends of the day and at the approaches of night. Good deeds dispel ill. A reminder to the mindful.* The verse is the key proof-text for the five daily times of prayer canonical in Islam. As the King Fahd Qur'an commentary explains, the two ends of the day mark the morning and afternoon prayers: 'The morning prayer is the *Fajr*, after the light is up but before sunrise. We thus get up betimes and begin the day with the remembrance of Allah and our duty to Him. The early afternoon prayer, *Ẓuhr*, is immediately after noon: we are in the midst of our daily life, and again we remember Allah' — although, other scholars take the latter end of the day

and be pure.'[401] If you, the human race, did not keep these pillars of piety you could be beheaded.[402] So it's only from fear of the sword that you heed them. But we are free of sin and evil, indecency and disgrace. We don't need the rituals you boast of.

'Besides, you must know, O human, that God sent His prophets and messengers only to miscreant peoples and the ignorant masses, who assign His divinity to others or deny His sovereignty, dispute His oneness, presume other gods,[403] twist His laws, defy His commands, shirk obedience, slight His bounty, fail to acknowledge Him, and forget His covenant and trust. They stray and lead others astray, seducing good people from the Straight Path. But we are clear of all these things. We submit to our Lord, acknowledge Him and humbly believe in Him, proclaiming His oneness without cavil or doubt.

'You must know, O human, that prophets and emissaries are physicians and astrologers of the soul. No one but the sick needs a

---

to be late afternoon or evening. The approaches of night are traditionally taken to be three: 'The late afternoon prayer, *'Aṣr*, can be one of these three, and the evening prayer, *Maghrib*, just after sunset, can be the second. The early night prayer, *'Ishā*, at supper time, when the glow of sunset is disappearing, would be the third of the "approaches of the night," when we commit ourselves to Allah before sleep.'

401 This hadith is not found in the standard collections, but there are others of similar sense: 'Abdallah ibn 'Amr reported that God's messenger said: "Fasting and the Qur'an intercede for a man. Fasting declares, 'O my Lord, I have kept him from his food and his passions by day, so accept my intercession for him.' The Qur'an says, 'I have kept him from sleep by night, so accept my intercession for him.' And their intercession is accepted."' *Mishkāt al-maṣābīḥ* VII, I, 3, ed. Robson (Lahore: M. Ashraf, 1975), vol. 1, p. 418.

402 The bird echoes the language of Qur'an 8:12.

403 The Dār Ṣādir edition continues here with an apparent interpolation by a scholiast: 'Thus your saying: *God is one of three* [Qur'an 5:73], *Uzayr is the son of God . . . the Christ is the son of God* [Qur'an 9:30], and saying that God almighty has the form of a beardless youth with cropped curly locks — and other such extravagant drivel.' Uzayr, mentioned only this once in the Qur'an, is usually identified with the biblical Ezra by traditional Muslim commentators. Ṭabarī knew that Jews had not made Ezra a son of God and saved the passage by pronouncing that only one Jew (Phineas) had done so. Ibn Ḥazm assumed that the Qur'an referred to a small group of Jews in the distant past. Qurṭubī read the verse as a reference only to the Jews' extreme admiration for the learned. Earlier commentators of a more midrashic bent explain the verse as a reference to Ezra's miraculous recovery of the Torah. Other commentators make Ezra the perverter of the biblical text or its message, presumably playing on his role as the scribe of the Torah and founding figure of biblical Judaism.

doctor, and no one needs an astrologer but the hapless, wretched, and forlorn.

'Ablutions and purifications, you must know, O human, were imposed on you only because of the concomitants of sex and coupling — your unbridled lewdness and lust, your lechery, sodomy, whoredom, lesbianism — not to mention your fetid armpits and foul breath, your profuse, stinking perspiration, worked up night and day — morning, evening, noon, and dawn.[404] All this is foreign to us. We are roused to mount but once a year, and not with overmastering passion or at pleasure's call but for the survival of our race.[405]

'As for worship and fasts, these were imposed on you only to atone for your backbiting, gossip, slander, and foul language, your trifling, frivolity, and folly.[406] We're free of all that. It's far beneath us. So, fasting and set forms of worship and prayer were not mandated for us.

'Charity and alms taxes were laid upon you only because you pile up a surfeit of wealth by fair means or foul, robbery, thuggery, larceny, light weights and false measures. You collect and hoard goods but stint with your obligations. You're niggardly and selfish, denying others their due. You gather what you do not eat and store what you do not need.[407]

---

404 Four times of day are covered, suggesting that the five daily prayers and their ablutions are needed for each.

405 Pliny reports that wolves breed only during twelve days of the year; Pliny, *Natural History* VIII.34; cf. Isidore, *Etymologies* 12.2.23–24. Modern biologists note: 'The female rat is in heat for a few hours every 4 days, the cow has recurrent periods lasting about 24 hours every 18–21 days, and the female dog is in estrus for 6 to 12 days about every 6 months. Female rabbits and ferrets will usually breed at any time.' Storer and Usinger, *General Zoology*, p. 584.

406 The language echoes Qur'an 57:20 and 68:11. A scholiast continues in MS Feyzullah 2130: 'The prophets, peace be upon them, dosed you with these therapies. For you are ill with disobedience. Your souls are surfeited with the food of sin and the drink of slander and backbiting, which is devouring the flesh of your brethren [cf. Qur'an 49:12]. So the Law commands abstention from the food of sin, and abstention is fasting. For abstention is the root of all therapies, and the belly is the root of all illness. Seeing your lives and your disobedience to God, night and day, how you eat up sins and doubts and drink in false notions about Him, the prophets prescribed a variety of exercises for you, to purge you of these unwholesome foodstuffs. These therapies are the five daily prayers. For a physician prescribes specific exercises and paces on the ground to make food weigh lighter when it lies thick on the stomach after heavy meals at night.'

407 The Dār Ṣādir printed edition continues: 'You *treasure up silver and gold and spend it not in God's path, wherefore herald their painful chastisement!* (Qur'an

'As for the clear, sure verses of revelation that you cite, laying down in statutes and laws what is allowed and forbidden — all that is just to teach you, since you're so blind of heart,[408] backward, and ignorant of what is beneficial or hurtful. You need teachers and trainers, admonishers and exhorters, just because you're so thoughtless and heedless. But we are inspired innately, directly by God, with all we need know, without messenger go-between or summons from beyond the veil, as God said: *Thy Lord inspired the bee to make his home in the mountains, in trees and trellises,*[409] and *Each knows His worship and praise,*[410] and *So God sent a raven to probe in the earth, to show him how to hide his brother's corse, and he said, "Alas, would I were like that raven and could hide my brother's corse." Thus did he become penitent*[411] — regretting his ignorance, but not his error and sin!

'You say you have festivals, convocations, attendance at houses of worship, and we have none. But we don't need them. All places are our temples. All quarters are the *qibla* we face in prayer. Wherever we turn, *there is God's face.*[412] Every day is a day of festival and assembly for us. Our every movement is worship and praise. So we need none of the things that you boast of.'

When the spokesman of the birds and had finished, the King turned to the human delegation and said, 'You have heard and understood what the bird has said. Have you anything to add? If so, please lay it out plainly.'

9:34). If you spent your surplus on the poor and helpless among you there would be no mandated alms tax or duty of charity. But we are far removed from all this. We care for our kind and do not begrudge them any bit of provender we find. Nor do we store more than we need but fly out lean and hungry each day, trusting in God, and return sated and plump, singing His praise.' The added passage echoes Jesus' homily of the birds in the Sermon on the Mount, Matthew 6:26: 'Consider the birds of the air. They sow not, neither do they reap, nor gather into barns. Yet thy heavenly Father feedeth them.' Cf. Qur'an 29:60: *How many are the beasts that carry not their own provender. God provides for them and you. He hears and knows.*

408 Echoing Qur'an 22:46.

409 Qur'an 16:68.

410 Qur'an 24:41: *Do you not see that God is praised by all in heaven and on earth — the birds arrayed in flight? Each knows His worship and praise.*

411 Qur'an 5:31. The reference, Qur'anically, is to Cain's discovery of repentence after slaying Abel.

412 Qur'an 2:115: *Unto God belong the East and the West. Whithersoever you turn, there is God's face. God is everywhere and all-knowing.*

Chapter 31

At that, the Iraqi rose and said, 'Praised be God, Creator of all, sustainer and lavish giver, who ennobled and blessed us, bore us over land and sea and favoured us so greatly over many others of His creation. Your Majesty, we do have further distinctions, gifts, and marks of favour and honour which show that we are their masters and they, our slaves. These include our fine clothing, the elegant garments that cover our nakedness, our deep cushions, lush coverlets, and rich comforters, our exquisite trappings of silk and fancywork, our silk-worsted, raw silk, and damask,[413] our cotton, linen, sable, miniver,[414] and all manner of furs — our coverings, hangings, leather mats, bolsters, carpets, felts, brocades, and the like. All these luxurious gifts confirm that we are their masters and they are our slaves. Their coarse clothing and rough hides, foul coverings and unconcealed nakedness show that they are our slaves and that we are their masters and owners, who can treat them as our property and use them as masters treat chattels.'

When the Iraqi had finished, the King looked at the bands of animals before him and said, 'What say you to these statements and boasts at your expense?'

Chapter 32

The delegate of the beasts of prey, Kalīla, brother of Dimna, then rose and said, 'Praised be God Almighty, all-knowing, Creator of mountains and hills, who raises up plants and trees in the forests and jungles and gives them as provender to wild beasts and cattle. Exalted and wise, He created the bold and fierce beasts of prey, relentless and daring, with powerful paws, sharp claws, adamant fangs, gaping jaws, long leaps and swift lunges, who roam the gloomy night seeking prey. He it was who gave us our sustenance, the bodies of men and flesh of cattle,

413 Silken fabrics are generally forbidden in Islam, especially for men, as being excessively luxurious; see Goodman, *Islamic Humanism*, pp. 43–44.

414 The soft, smooth grey fur of the miniver is still used in European court dress.

provision for the nonce,[415] decreeing thereafter death and destruction, decay for us all.[416] His is the praise for the gifts that He gave — for all that He ordained, to be enjoyed or endured.'

The predators' spokesman then turned to the throng of jinni sages and animal delegates and said, 'Has this sage body ever seen, have you, assembled speakers, ever heard of anyone more thoughtless, more obdurately oblivious than this human?'

'How so?' asked the assembly.

'Why, he cited among their merits this and that article of fine clothing and soft covering. Tell me, human, would you have any of the things you boast of had you not taken them from others, from other animals, by force?'

'When was that?' asked the human.

'Is there anything', the jackal continued, 'softer for you to wear or more luxuriant to deck yourselves out in than garments of silk or brocade?'[417]

'No indeed.'

'Aren't these made from the spittle of worms? They're hardly offspring of Adam? They belong to the crawling creatures! They spin their gossamer threads about themselves to make a nest to sleep in. It's *their* shelter and coverlet, a refuge from heat and cold, wind, and rain, and all the daily accidents and incidents of time. But you come along and wrest it from them, seize it as your ill-gotten plunder. But God punishes you for it! He tasks you with unwinding, spinning and weaving it, sewing, cleaning, cutting, embroidering, and all the other

---

415 The speaker seems to expect carnivores one day to revert to a vegetarian diet, as if taking literally Isaiah 11:7: 'The cow and the bear shall graze, and their young lie down together, and the lion shall eat straw like the ox.'

416 Paul Ramsey argues, in *Fabricated Man*, that monotheistic religions are ever mindful of death and decay and the fragility of material things — insights held constant by the thought of God's constancy. Threats of earthly death and destruction, accordingly, should not bias or distort moral judgements.

417 Compare Shakespeare's turn on this ancient trope: 'Is man no more than this? Consider him well. Thou owest the worm no silk, the beast no hide, the sheep no wool, the cat no perfume. Ha! Here's three on's are sophisticated; thou art the thing itself; unaccommodated man is no more but such a poor, bare, forked animal as thou art. Off, off you lendings! Come; unbutton here.' *King Lear*, 3.4.105 (references are to act, scene, and line).

labours and troubles you inflict on yourselves to improve it, mend, buy and sell it, and store it, distracting your hearts, fatiguing your bodies, and distressing your souls, never allowing yourselves a moment's rest, peace and quiet, or surcease.

'You do the same with the fleece you take from sheep and the hides from beasts, the wool and hair of carnivores, and the feathers of birds.[418] You seize them by force and strip them from their rightful owner wrongly and unjustly, and put them on without any right to them. Then you shamelessly boast that they make you better than we, unthinking that if these things were something to boast of, we'd have more grounds for pride than you, since God caused them to grow on our backs and made them our clothing, carpet, and cushion, our cover and ornament — a mark of His favour to us, His kindness, compassion, mercy and grace upon us, and His tenderness toward our little ones and our young.

'For when one of our number is born he already has a skin well suited to him, with hair or wool, fleece or scales, all fashioned by Him as our clothing, wrap, cover, and adornment, in just the right size for his body and the bulk of each individual's frame. We don't need to labour and tax ourselves with combing, carding, spinning, weaving, cutting, and sewing as you do, exhausting and abusing yourselves, without let until you die. All this is your punishment for the sin of your two ancestors, who strayed and rebelled, heedless of their Lord's command.'

Said the King to the spokesman of the beasts of prey, 'How was it at the start, when Adam was first created? Tell us about that.'

'Certainly, gentle Majesty. When God created Adam and his mate, He gave them all they needed to survive and sustain their lives as

418 'Nature appears to have created all other things, though she asks a cruel price for all her generous gifts, making it hardly possible to judge whether she has been more a kind parent to man or more a harsh stepmother. First of all, man alone of all her creatures she drapes in borrowed clothes. To others she assigns a variety of coverings — shells, bark, spines, hides, fur, bristles, hair, down, feathers, scales, fleeces. Even the trees she protects against cold and heat with bark, sometimes in two layers. Man alone, on the day of his birth she casts away naked on the naked ground, to burst at once into wailing and weeping.' Pliny, *Natural History* VII.2, tr. after Rackham, vol. 2, p. 507; and *The Elder Pliny on the Human Animal: 'Natural History Book VII'*, ed. and tr. Mary Beagon (Oxford: OUP, 2005), p. 59.

individuals — provender, nutriment, cover, clothing, just as He did for all other animals in that garden atop the mountain on the equator in the East. Having created them naked, He caused long hair to grow from their heads, falling in thick profusion on all sides, down to their feet, black and soft as the loveliest tresses that ever graced a virgin. He raised them up as a pair of budding youths, the finest in form of any of the animals there. This hair, a garment to them both, covering their nakedness, served as their coat, carpet, cloak, and defence against cold and heat.

'They used to walk in that garden, gathering its varied fruits, eating of them and nourished by them. They strolled its lush meads among the blooming flowers, savouring the pleasant breezes and fragrant plants in joy and delight, contented and at ease, unburdened in body and untroubled of soul. They were forbidden to overstep their station and take what was not theirs before its time. But they flouted their Lord's command, seduced by the words of their foe. They took the forbidden fruit and lost their high rank. Their hair parted, and their nakedness was exposed. Banished and exiled, cast down and abased, they were punished, now having to provide for themselves what they needed to live in this world.'[419]

When the carnivore sage had reached this point, the human spokesman said, 'You predators would be better off keeping silent and not speaking for shame.'

'Why so?' asked Kalīla.

'Because, of all the parties gathered here, none is wickeder than you, O predators. None is more heartless, useless or noxious, none is more ravenous or bloodthirsty!'

'How is that?'

'Why you predators prey upon cattle and sheep with your sharp claws. You rend their skins, break their bones, drink their blood, rip up their bellies without mercy, without a thought or care for them.'

Said the delegate of the carnivores, 'We learned this from you. We modelled our actions on your treatment of these beasts.'[420]

---

419 The text continues, 'As the spokesman for the birds stated in a previous chapter [Chapter 29] and as the wise jinni mentioned in a similar chapter [Chapter 8].'

420 Milton too, midrashically, ascribes the struggle among animals to the fall of

'How so?' the man replied.

'Why, before the creation of your father Adam and his children, we carnivores did no such thing. We didn't hunt living beasts. There were plenty of carcasses, and the animals that died by nature each day were plenty for us to feed on. We had no need to hunt the living or risk stalking, attacking, and battling them, wrestling with fate. Lions, leopards, cheetahs, wolves, and other carnivores did not take on elephants, buffaloes, or swine, as long as we could find plenty of corpses to sustain us — except in dire need. For we do pity them, as any creature would.

'But when you humans came, you rounded up the sheep, cows, camels, horses, mules, and asses, and corralled them. Not one was left in the wilds and wastes or forests. We meat-eaters were left without carrion and had to start hunting living beasts.[421] But this was permitted to us, just as you, in an emergency, may eat an animal that has died of natural causes.[422]

'You say we are cruel and ruthless, but we don't see these beasts complaining of us as they do of your tyranny, excess, and oppression. You say that we seize them with our claws and fangs, tear their skin, rip open their bellies, break their bones, drink their blood, and eat their flesh. But so do you, and far worse. You slaughter them with sharp knives, flay them, gut them, and break their bones with cleavers, axes, and the cooking fire and roasting heat.

'We harm other animals, you say. That is so. But if you gave thought you would see and admit that all this is minor, trivial alongside the wrong and harm and oppression you work on them, as the delegate of the beasts made clear in his opening statement.

'Still, your harm to one another is much greater. You attack each other with strokes of the sword and thrusts of the dagger, shocks of

---

man: 'Beast now with beast gan war, and fowl with fowl, / and fish with fish; to graze the herb all leaving, / Devoured each other.' *Paradise Lost*, Book 10, lines 710–712.

421 Lucan's poem the *Pharsalia* (I.371–374) would have it that tigers were first blooded on slaughtered cattle and have ravened after flesh ever since.

422 This is according to Muslim dietary law. Thus Aḥmad ibn Naqīb al-Miṣrī writes, 'If compelled to eat of an animal not properly slaughtered, one may eat as needed to preserve one's life.' *'Umdat al-sālik*, ed. N. Keller (Beltsville, MD: Amana, 1994), p. 363.

the lance, and blows of the mace, whip, and scourge. You lop off hands and feet, lock each other in dungeons, rob and steal, thieve and cheat, dupe and defraud one another in your dealings. You collude, slander, deceive, and assault each other in all kinds of ways. We carnivores don't use tricks like yours on the beasts or on each other. All this is unknown to us.

'You say we're of small use to others. Had you reflected, you'd have seen how clearly useful we are to you. You use our hides, hair, wool, and fleece. You use the birds of prey you've pressed into service to hunt for you. But tell us, O human, what good are you to any animal besides yourselves? The harm you do is plain enough. You rival us in slaughtering these animals and eating their flesh. You use our hides and hair, but you're stingy with the corpses of your own kind. You bury them underground, so no one gets any use out of you dead or alive![423]

'You say that we beasts of prey attack other animals, seize and slay them. But we took up that practice only when we saw the sons of Adam doing them same to each other since the days of Cain and Abel. Down to our own time we've seen killing and maiming, warfare and combat, from the days of Rustam and Isfandiyār, Jamshīd[424] and Ḍaḥḥāk, Tubbaʿ[425] and Afrīdūn, Siyāwush and Manūjahr, Darius[426] and Alexander, Nebuchadnezzar and the House of David, Bahrām[427] and the House of ʿAdnān,[428] Constantine and the folk of Greece, ʿUmar[429]

423 If man is indeed the acme of creation, he need not be useful to other creatures. But if man's primacy is in question, his value to others must be weighed — if not as nature's steward, then as her exploiter and food for worms.

424 For these figures, see Appendix C.

425 The first Tubbaʿ, a South Arabian ruler of the early fourth century, subdued the realms of the Sabaeans and Ḥaḍramawt. A century later, the most famous of his dynasty expanded the empire into central Arabia. Legends coalescing around his name ascribed to him feats probably influenced by the Alexander romance. See A. F. L. Beeston, 'Tubbaʿ', *EI2*, vol. 10, p. 575.

426 See note 263 above.

427 See note 91 above.

428 See note 137 above.

429 Both the Dār Ṣādir and the Dieterici texts have "Uthmān' here, reflecting an evident effort to avoid disparagement of the early caliph ʿUmar, who is specified in all the manuscripts. The sources used by these print editors have substituted the name of a caliph often disliked in Shiʿi histories.

and Yazdijird, the ʿAbbāsids[430] and Marwānids,[431] and the rest, down to this day.[432] Every year, every month, every day, and every minute we see men at one another's throats and witness the countless, measureless evils that result, even now — the killing, maiming, and plundering.

'Yet now you come and lord it over us and try to shame us beasts of prey as the worst creatures on earth! Aren't you embarrassed to make so false and outrageous a charge, when anyone can see that we predators only do what you humans daily do to each other?'

Then the delegate of the carnivores said to the human spokesman, 'Had you humans considered the lives of predators and studied their behaviour, you would realize and admit that we're purer and better than you.'

'Is that so?' said the human. 'Can you prove it?'

'Of course! Aren't the best of you your ascetics and holy men — monks, rabbis, mendicants?'[433]

---

430 The ʿAbbāsid dynasty, caliphs from the time of their revolution in 750 until the Mongol conquest of Baghdad in 1258, are no favourites of the Ikhwān, as we've seen from the outset of their narrative. Their reign at Baghdad was largely titular after 945, when their Būyid military commanders seized effectual control of the caliphate. Compare the warmer mention of the Sāmānids in Chapter 20, pp. 202–203 above.

431 The Umayyad dynasty had two branches, Sufyānid line of Muʿāwiya, the son of Abū Sufyān, who was succeeded by his son and grandson; and the Marwānid line of Muʿāwiya's second cousin, which reigned from 684 until overthrown by the ʿAbbāsid revolution in 750. The Ikhwān have little sympathy for the Umayyads, typically branded as Arab hegemonists in Muslim and especially in Shiʿi texts.

432 The Ikhwān do not exempt from their condemnation of human destructiveness even the great parties to religious/national wars whose partisans remained active and powerful in their own time. They look askance at still active and popular movements, as they do at those safely behind them in deep antiquity. Their cosmopolitan stance reflects a Stoic (originally Cynic) heritage. But the condemnation of sectarian causes as unworthy of bloodshed is Epicurean in flavour and smacks of the cynicism of Muḥammad ibn Zakariyāʾ al-Rāzī, who regards all claims to special revelation as impostures that promote only bloodshed. The Ikhwān do not follow Rāzī into levelling so extreme and categorical a charge, but they, like Rāzī , bear poignant witness to the same cataclysms that prompted distaste or even horror among their Hellenistic predecessors of quite widely varying outlooks.

433 The Ikhwān, like the animals, respect asceticism. Self-denial and turning away from all things but God had a well developed Hindu and Christian history; and, as Andras Hamori shows, pre-Islamic poetry held up an ascetic outlook as a judicious response to the vanities of earthly life; see A. Hamori, 'Ascetic Poetry

'Yes.'

'And when one of you reaches the peak of probity and piety doesn't he remove himself from your midst and flee your society? Doesn't he shelter in the hills and mountains, or the bosoms of valleys, by the seashore, or in the forest — the haunts of wild beasts? He mingles with us beasts of prey in our own realms and shelters at our side, unharmed by any of us?'[434]

(*zuhdiyyāt*)', in *The Cambridge History of Arabic Literature: 'Abbasid Belles-Lettres*, ed. J. Ashtiany et al. (New York: CUP, 1990), pp. 265–266; G. Gobillot, 'al-Zuhd', *EI2*, vol. 11, pp. 559–562; and P. F. Kennedy, 'Zuhdiyyāt', *EI2*, vol. 11, pp. 562–564. Basra, the home of the Ikhwān, had seen an efflorescence of ascetic devotional schools in the eighth century, each centred on a female spiritual guide known for her abstemious and scrupulous practice of the religious law. Often living in seclusion and abjuring family ties, these women, filled with ritualized dread of God's wrath, devoted themselves to mourning and tears over human sinfulness. See Abū 'Abd al-Rahmān al-Sulamī, *Dhikr al-niswa al-muta'abbidāt al-Sūfiyyāt* (*Early Sufi Women*), ed. and tr. R. Cornell (Louisville, KY: Fons Vitae, 1999), pp. 60–61. Successors to the early ascetic movements were the bands who called themselves 'Blameworthy' (*malāmatiyya*), and held that rigorous self-scrutiny and spiritual progress were possible only if an adept remained anonymous and shunned dramatic ascetic displays. These pietists held 'inwardly' to the Sharī'a but sought to curb their pride and subdue the ego by drawing censure upon themselves. Mainstream Sufis rejected what they saw as the *malāmatī* obsession with the ego and pursued more intellectual substance than they found in the earlier ascetic tradition. See S. Sviri, 'Hakim Tirmidhi and the Malamati Movement in Early Sufism', in *The Heritage of Sufism*, ed. L. Lewisohn (Oxford: Oneworld, 1999), vol. 1, pp. 605–607; see also Ḥujwīrī, *Kashf al-maḥjūb*, tr. R. A. Nicholson (London: Luzac, 1967), Chapter 6 'On Blame', pp. 62–69, esp. p. 62: 'The followers of Truth [*ahl-i ḥaqq*] are distinguished by their being objects of vulgar blame . . . Such is the ordinance of God, that He causes those who discourse of Him to be blamed by the whole world, but preserves their hearts from being occupied by the world's blame.' The mature Sufi tradition grew out of the teachings of early masters like al-Muḥāsibī, al-Bisṭāmī, Sahl al-Tustarī, and al-Junayd. The Ikhwān favour the more intellectual trend. Zuhd is prominent in tenth-century Iraqi Christian ethics and pietism. The Christian writer Yaḥyā ibn 'Adī celebrates it as a virtue of the pious, defining it as 'paying little mind to the higher social orders, thinking little of kings and their kingdoms or the wealthy and their wealth. This trait of character is to be highly esteemed. But it is for scholars, monks, religious leaders, orators, preachers, and whoever arouses in people an appetite for eternal life.' *Tahdhīb al-akhlāq*; tr. after Griffith, p. 63.

434 Rami ben Ḥama in the Talmud (Sanhedrin 38b) proposes that a wild beast has no power over a man unless the man appears to it as a wild beast. His proof-text is the verse (Psalms 49:13) comparing a man without honour to beasts that perish: *nimshal ka-v'hemot nidmu* — which Ben Ḥama playfully takes as if it read 'when he is like a beast, he will perish'.

'Yes, just as you say.'

'Well, if beasts of prey are not your betters, why do the best of you lodge with us and the most saintly of you live with us?[435] The best consort with the best, not the worst, so they flee from you; and you shun them in turn. This shows that we predators are good, not the wickedest of God's creatures, as you claim. What you said is a false and wicked calumny.

'Another sign that we predators are virtuous, and not as you claim, comes from the practice of your own human tyrants. When they mistrust virtuous and honest members of your kind and throw them to the beasts of prey, if we don't eat them it's because we know that they're good.[436] For it takes the good to know the good, as the poet said:

> The searcher knows another of his kind,
> Though all men else to him are blind.

---

435 The eremitic Desert Fathers of Eastern Christianity retreated to barren wastes so as to devote themselves to prayer and spiritual exercises. Removed from human society, these anchorites were pictured as living among the wild beasts, and hagiography typifies them as befriended by fierce animals. In legend, Paul of Thebes, like Elijah, was fed by a raven who brought him bread each day. St Jerome aided a lion with a wounded paw. As a result, the lion became his identifying attribute in countless paintings. An account of Abū Sa'īd ibn Abū al-Khayr's saintly life relates that a traveller lost in the desert hailed him: '"O shaykh, help me, for God's sake. I am a man of Nishapūr . . . The caravan has departed, and I do not know the way."' As the traveller told his story, the shaykh 'lowered his head for a moment. When he looked up, he took me by the hand, and I saw a lion emerge out of the desert. The lion came up to him, bowed, and stood before him in attendance. He put his mouth to the lion's ear and whispered something. Then he seated me on the lion's back and, fixing my hands on the beast's mane, said to me "Grip the lion's belly firmly with your legs. . . . When it stops, dismount and walk in whatever direction it faces."' M. Monawwar, *Asrār al-tawḥīd fī Manāqib Abū Sa'īd*, tr. John O'Kane as *The Secrets of God's Mystical Oneness* (Costa Mesa, CA: Mazda, 1992), p. 145; a more cynical version is found in Ibn al-Muqaffa'. In the *ta'ziyya* passion plays of Shi'i Islam, the lion is often called from his lair by Ḥusayn, to acknowledge the sanctity of the soon-to-be-martyred grandson of the Prophet.

436 Montaigne retells the story of Androcles and the lion in his *Apology for Raymond Sebond* (in *Complete Essays*, II, 12, pp. 350–351), giving his source as Apion, who claimed to have witnessed the dramatic denouement in the arena, which George Bernard Shaw later set on the stage.

'You should know, O human, that carnivores can be good or bad. But even the bad ones devour only wicked men, as God said *We subject the unjust to one another, just as they deserve.*[437] I have had my say. God grant pardon to me and to you.'

When the delegate of the predators had finished speaking, a jinni sage said, 'True it is, as he says, that the good flee from the wicked and befriend the good, even among those not of their kind. The evil hate the good as well, and shun them. They seek out their own evil sort. Were it not that most humans are evil, the best of them would not flee their presence for mountains, forests, and the haunts of savage beasts that are not of their kind and not like them in form or nature but only in character, probity, and innocence.'

All answered, 'The sage is right in what he says, relates, and states.'

The humans were shaken on hearing this and bowed their heads in shame, mortified at the censure and rebuke they had heard. The session drew to an end, and the herald cried: 'Repair to your lodgings, our honoured guests; and, God willing, return safe and sound in the morning.'

Chapter 33

On the morrow the King held court again, and all the parties attended in due rank and order. The King turned his gaze toward the body of humans and said, 'You have heard yesterday's exchanges and the response to your claims. Have you anything further beyond what you've already said?'

At that point the Persian delegate rose and said, 'Yes, most just Majesty. We have further merits, distinctions aplenty, that show the truth of our assertions and claims.'

'Well,' said the King, 'tell us somewhat about that.'

'Know, your Majesty, that we have kings, princes, caliphs, sultans, chiefs, viziers, clerks, prefects, ministers, legates, chamberlains, notables, nobles, privy councillors, and adjutants. We also have merchants,

437 Qur'an 6:129. The animals adapt a Qur'anic reference to the wages of sin, originally a part of Muhammad's theodicy. Kalīla's claim, smacking of Mu'tazilite thinking, that only the wicked suffer, is a risky assumption at best.

artisans, growers, and animal husbandmen. There are builders, landowners, the worthy and wealthy, the doughty and refined. We have cultured, learned, pious, and virtuous people, eloquent speakers, orators, poets, theologians, reciters of scripture, tellers of tales and purveyors of lore, narrators of traditions, scholars, jurists, judges, magistrates, and ecstatics. Among us too there are philosophers, geometers, astronomers, naturalists, physicians, diviners, soothsayers, sorcerers and enchanters, interpreters of dreams, alchemists and talisman makers, astrologers, and many other sorts, too numerous to mention. All these classes and ranks of men have their own ways, their own tempers, natures, and characters, their own fine points, virtues, merits, and distinctions, their own beliefs and laudable schools, metiers, arts and sciences, manifold and diverse. All these are ours alone. These animals lack them completely. This shows that we are their masters and they are our slaves.'

Chapter 34

When the human delegate had finished his speech, the parrot spoke up and said, 'Praised be God who created the outspread heavens and the broad earth, the towering mountains and swelling seas, the deserts and wastes, scouring winds, dizzying clouds, and torrential rains, the plants and trees, and the pure hearted birds, each schooled in His worship and praise.

'This human, you know,' the parrot continued, 'has only listed the classes of men and catalogued their types. Had he given thought, sagacious Majesty, and fairly considered the great variety of birds of all types and species, he would have realized how numerous they are and how few and slight by comparison are the kinds of men.[438] But look at the other side, Mr Man. For every fair and worthy type you mentioned there are sordid, unsavoury types that we are free of.

'You have pharaohs, nimrods, tyrants, and miscreants, profligates, wantons, pagans, libertines, hypocrites, scoffers, apostates, traitors,

---

438 A note in the text recalls the variety of birds reviewed by the Simurgh in Chapter 13.

recusants, and renegades.[439] You have highwaymen, brigands, vagrants and low-lifes, ruffians, swindlers, and double-dealers. You have charlatans, despots, and overreachers, apostates, defamers, backbiters and talebearers, fault-finders, impostors, villains , and time-servers. You have panders, effeminates, lechers, wantons, catamites, whores, and sodomites. You have confidence men, artful dodgers, and body-snatchers. And you have fools, boors, numbskulls, dimwits, and other like types — all sorts of the most shameful character, the most vicious nature, the foulest deeds, and basest lives. We are far above all this. Yet we share in most of your good points, your fair and laudable customs and equable ways.

'You boasted first of your kings and leaders, with their vassals, troops, and subjects. Don't you know that the bee society and ant society, the society of beasts of prey, and that of the birds, all have leaders, troops, vassals, and subjects? And our leaders and kings are more statesmanlike than yours, and serve more faithfully the needs of their flocks than human kings — they are kinder, and more considerate and compassionate. Most human kings and leaders pay no heed to the interests of their subjects, troops, and vassals, unless to get some benefit or protection from them for themselves or some favourite or other, near or far. They give no thought or care whatever to anyone else's interests, no matter how close or remote. That is not the way of intelligent kings or virtuous leaders who are statesmanlike and compassionate. In fact, one mark and test of leadership and statesmanship is a king or leader's kindness and compassion for his flock. He has fellow feeling and concern for his troops and supporters, modelling himself on the ways of God, the King of kings and Chief of all chiefs, who is most merciful and compassionate, generous, tender and kindly toward His creatures, whoever they be.

'The monarchs of animal kinds, however, outshine human kings and leaders in emulating God's ways. The king of the bees looks to the interest of his subjects, troops, and vassals and seeks their well-being. He does not serve his own private whims or even the caprices of his people, but acts in their interest and protects them from harm,

439 The renegades here are *Khawārij*, that is, Khārijites, violent *takfīrī*s, sectarians who damn as unbelievers and apostates all who fail to follow their own faction.

favouring not even one who supports his own wishes but acting solely in compassion and concern, kindness, and affection for his subjects, troops and supporters. So do the king of the ants and the king of the cranes, who oversees their flight, and the king of the sand-grouse, who leads their flight and alighting. The same with all other animals who have leaders and rulers. They seek no recompense or requital from their subjects for their rule, just as they seek no reward, recompense, return, or show of filial gratitude from their offspring, as Adamites do. For, every animal that leaps and mounts, conceives, bears, nurses, and rears its young, and every kind that mounts, lays, broods, tends, and minds chicks or hatchlings, we find, seeks no reward, recognition, or recompense from its offspring but raises its young and cares for them kindly, tenderly, gently, compassionately, on the model of God, who created His creatures, raised, nurtured, and looked after them kindly and generously, asking nothing in return and seeking no reward or requital.

'Were it not for the ignoble nature of humans, their base characters, crooked lives, vicious mores, vile doings, foul acts, ugly, misguided, and depraved customs, and rank ingratitude, God would not have commanded them: *Show gratitude to Me and toward your parents, for unto Me shall ye come in the end.*[440] He gave no such command to us and our offspring. For we show no such disrespect or thanklessness. Command and prohibition, promise and threat are addressed solely to you, the human race, not to us. For you are creatures of mischief. Conflict, deceit, and disobedience are ingrained in you. You are more fit for slavery than we! We are more worthy of freedom. So how can you claim to be our masters and to own us as your slaves, if not by sheer effrontery, outrageous lies, and calumnies?'

When the parrot had finished, the jinni sages and philosophers said, 'He has spoken truly in all that he states and relates.'

Again the assembled humans were chagrined and hung their heads in shame, crushed by the indictment directed at them.

440 Qur'an 31:14: *We charged man as to his parents, since his mother bore him in travail and weaned him at two years: show gratitude to Me and to your parents, for unto Me shall ye come in the end.*

But at this point in the parrot's discourse, the King said to the chief of the jinni philosophers, 'Who are these kings that this speaker has mentioned and lauded so highly, describing their deep compassion and concern for their subjects, their kindness and affection toward their forces and vassals, and how well they treat them? Tell me what he really means and what he is hinting or suggesting.'

Chapter 35

'I shall, felicitous Majesty, as your obedient servant. The word "king" [*malik*], you know, derives from "angel" [*malak*]. And kings' names are taken from those of angels. For there is no animal kind, no species or individual among them, great or small, that does not have a band of angels charged by God with overseeing its growth, preservation, and welfare, at every stage. Every class of angels has its chief to look after it. And these chiefs are kinder, gentler, and more compassionate than mothers toward their tiny sons or infant daughters.'

Said the King to the sage, 'Where do the angels get this kindness, mercy, tenderness, grace, and compassion of theirs?'

'From God's mercy and compassion on His creation, from His kindness and love. All the mercy and tenderness of parents — fathers and mothers — and the angels themselves, all the grace and goodness of creatures toward one another is but the thousandth part of God's mercy and kindness toward His creation, His grace and beneficence upon his creatures.[441]

'One mark of the soundness of what I say and the truth of my account is that when He first created them and gave them their start, when He fashioned, finished, and reared them up, their Lord entrusted

441 Playing on the words for 'king' and 'angel' the Ikhwān lay out a view not only of providence but of legitimate royal rule. Mortal kings should emulate God's governance. But even animal paragons fall short of the ideal. Nature's real kings are the angelic Forms, the intellects that govern each species. The influential Akbarian school founded by Ibn 'Arabī similarly traces emanation to God's (hypostatic) mercy (*raḥma*); see Ibn 'Arabī, *al-Futūḥāt al-Makkiyya* (*Meccan Revelations*), cited in William Chittick, *The Sufi Path of Knowledge*, pp. 130–132; Ibn 'Arabī, *Fuṣūṣ al-ḥikam*, ed. A. Afifi (Cairo: Dār al-Kitāb al-Arabī, 1946), p. 50.

their care to angels, the purest of His creatures, and made them in turn compassionate, noble, and pure. He formed them with all sorts of useful appurtenances and advantages, marvellous anatomical pathways, elegant forms, keen and subtle senses, inspiring them to avoid the harmful and seek the beneficial.[442] He set night and day in their service — sun, moon, and stars serving at His command.[443] He ordered their lives in winter and summer, on land and sea, mountain and plain. He made foodstuffs for them from trees and plants, their delight for the

442 The Stoic philosophers held that providence inspires all creatures naturally to pursue what is good for them and avoid what is harmful; see Diogenes Laertius, *Lives of the Eminent Philosophers*, 7.85–86, ed. and tr. R. D. Hicks (Cambridge: Harvard University Press, 1965; first printed, 1925) vol. 2, pp. 192–195; Galen, *De Usu Partium* I.5, tr. May, pp. 70–71. See also the passage from Galen's lost work *Peri Ethon* (On Dispositions) preserved in Arabic by al-Marwazī (twelfth century) from the translation of Ḥunayn ibn Isḥāq , in S. M. Stern, 'Some Fragments of Galen's *On Dispositions* in Arabic', *Classical Quarterly*, 6 (1956), pp. 91–101.

443 Cf. Qur'an 14:33 and 31:20. The Ikhwān link the subordination of celestial beings to God's command to another Qur'anic theme dear to their hearts, God's adaptation of nature to creaturely needs. For the prostration of the stars (Qur'an 55:5–6), see Kindī, 'Essay on the Prostration of the Outermost Sphere and its Obedience to God', in Kindī's *Rasā'il falsafiyya*, ed. Abū Riḍā, pp. 245–246. Kindī writes: 'Many Arabic words have multiple meanings; some even denote opposites . . . "*Sujūd*" in Arabic signifies prostration, kneeling, and pressing hands to the ground. But it is also a term for obedience without actual bowing, kneeling, or pressing of the palms. In a general sense, outside the context of worship, "*sujūd*" means obedience. As Nābigha al-Dhubyānī says: "Ghassan bows down to him, in hopes of bounty. / So do the Turks, and the champion and troops of Persia." Bowing here means fealty. It cannot refer to prostration as in prayer. For they remain standing even as they "bow", showing that their "bowing" is constant, unlike that of worship. Here it can only mean subordination. The notion of obedience can entail a shift from privation to realization — as one says of a growing plant that it is "behaving"! Thus, the poet says: "The very herbs of the garden yield to her" — that is, they bear fruit, grow, and fill in. Or, as he also says: "Stormy Arcturus and Virgo obey him" — that is, the storms are in his control, they shift from potency to act, from want to realization. Obedience in Arabic can also mean observance of a command in things that are not deficient and do not shift from privation to realization. In that case obedience just means following a command, voluntarily. For free choice pertains to perfect souls, that is, rational ones.' In citing Nābigha and Imru' al-Qays, Kindī uses Mu'tazilite exegetical technique to support a Neoplatonic reading of the Qur'an. Cf. Richard Walzer, *Greek into Arabic* (Oxford: B. Cassirer, 1962), pp. 182–183, 196–198; and see the Mu'tazilite exegete Zamakhsharī at Qur'an 33:72. The translation here from al-Kindī is Goodman's.

nonce.[444] *He lavished blessings upon you, seen and unseen,*[445] so manifold that if you tried to count them, you would find them numberless. All this manifests and proves God's great mercy, compassion, and grace on His creation.'

Said the King, 'Who is the chief angel charged with the care and welfare of the children of Adam?'

'That', said the sage, 'is the universal human rational Soul, vice-regent of God on His earth.[446] She it was who was linked to Adam's body when he was formed from earth, *and the angels all bowed down to him together.*[447] These angels are the animal soul, directed by the rational.[448] The universal rational Soul is still in Adam's seed, just as the corporeal form of Adam's body survives in his seed. In the pattern laid down by this Soul they grow, develop and thrive; through it they are rewarded or punished, to it they return, and with it they will be raised on Judgement Day, when by it they enter paradise and with it — the rational Soul, vice-regent of God on His earth — they rise to the realm of the spheres.'[449]

Then the King inquired, 'Why are angels and souls invisible?'

'Because they are luminous, diaphanous, spiritual substances

444 Cf. Qur'an 2:36, 7:24.

445 Qur'an 31:20.

446 The analogy of macrocosm to microcosm (see Epistles 26 and 34), as Seyyed Hossein Nasr explains, is a key notion for the Ikhwān 'in showing the unicity of Nature and in demonstrating the inward relation between man and Nature'. The study of nature serves for them, as the present essay shows, 'as a support for spiritual realization', even as the study of man deepens our understanding 'of the inner aspects of Nature'. The Ikhwān, Nasr explains, compare the transcendent world of the Forms to the universal man, and the sublunary world to the particular man. But each human being 'is created between the Universal and particular man and takes part in the nature of each'. Thus, 'particular man is created from Universal Man just as in the creation of the world the sublunary region is generated from the heavens and is always passive and obedient with respect to them'. Nasr, *Islamic Cosmological Doctrines*, pp. 66–68.

447 Qur'an 15:30.

448 God's vice-regent, or caliph, on earth, strikingly, is the human rational Soul. Aristotle's animal soul is the life principle; Plato's spirited soul is here identified with Iblīs, that is, Satan who refused to bow down, thus rationalizing the traditional demonology. The fused vegetative and appetitive souls are unmentioned here. Souls are feminine by grammatical (and mythological) convention.

449 Immortality here is spiritual rather than bodily, ultimately won, as in Plato, when intelligence is disencumbered of the body.

without colour or mass. They escape the bodily senses like scent, taste, and touch, but are seen by a subtle sight like that of prophets and messengers — and heard by such as well. For these men of chaste soul have roused themselves from the sleep of neglect and the slumber of folly. Freed from the tyranny of sin, they have cleansed their souls and are reborn sanctified. Becoming akin to the souls of angels, they see them and hear their discourse, take up their message and inspiration and pass it on to their fellow mortals in their diverse tongues, being embodied and corporeal like them.'[450]

Chapter 36

Said the parrot, 'As to your statement, O human, that you have artisans and masters of diverse crafts, that does not set you apart from the rest of us. Several kinds of birds and crawling and swarming creatures share with you in this. Bees are insects, but they make their cells and build dwellings more aptly and skilfully than your artisans, better and more ingeniously than your builders and architects. They build their homes as round, multi-storeyed hives that look like stacked shields, just by setting one chamber atop another. With their consummate wisdom, craftsmanship, and builder's art, they form each apartment as a perfect equilateral and equi-angular hexagon. They need no compass to guide them, no straight-edge to rule, or plumb line to drop, nor any angle to try their corners, as human builders do.

'Bees go out to forage and gather wax from the leaves of trees and plants on their legs and nectar from the blossoms of plants and trees with their probosces. They need no basket, pouch, or peck to collect it, nor any tool or utensil to ladle it out, as your builders need their tools and implements — their hoe, shovel, spade, bucket, and the like.

---

450 Plato, too, uses Empedocles' notion that knowledge is of like by like as a tag on which to hang his concept that only by an eternal, Form-like soul can we know Forms (here, angels). The Ikhwān, like Fārābī, elaborate the Platonic and Aristotelian counsel that prophecy must accommodate its audience. Purity here is the epithet the Ikhwān adopt as their own. As the context shows, they mean not just formal sincerity (truth to one's intent) but candid insight, inquiry, and commitment, and nobility of spirit and aspiration.

'The same is true of the spider. She is of the crawling creatures, yet in weaving her web and setting out her net she is more dextrous and ingenious than any of your weavers. For she spins as she weaves her web, first a single thread from one wall to another or from one branch to the next, from tree to tree or bank to bank of a stream, not walking on water but sailing across through the air. Then she treads on the thread she has stretched out and makes the warp of her web, straight lines like the taut guy-ropes of a tent. Next she weaves upon those in a circling pattern, leaving in the centre a small open ring where she sits, waiting to snare flies. All this she does without distaff, spindle, wheel, comb, loom, or any other tool or implement used by your weavers or spinners, who depend on the familiar tools of their craft.[451]

'Silkworms, again of the crawling creatures, are more highly skilled in their art and wiser than your artisans. When sated with feeding they find a place in the trees, shrubs, and thorns, and from their saliva spin fine, glossy, strong, threads that they entwine about themselves in a tough pouch-like nest to guard against heat and cold, wind and rain. Then they sleep for a definite time — all this untaught by a master, untrained by fathers or mothers, but inspired by God, instructed directly by Him, and all without need of a distaff, spindle, needle, or scissors, like those that your tailors, menders, and weavers require.

'Likewise the swallow, a bird, builds a home for himself and his young, out of mud, a cradle hung high in the air, under the eaves, needing no ladder to reach it, no hod to carry his clay, no post to support it, nor any tool or implement whatever.[452]

'So too the termites, who are of the crawling creatures. They build roofs of pure clay over their heads, like vaulted galleries. This they do without digging up the ground or moistening their clay, or even drawing water. Tell us, then, O philosophers and sages, where do they

451 Spiders 'spin a long thread from their small body and tend their webs continually, never ceasing work on them, ever suspended in their handiwork'; Isidore, *Etymologies* 12.5.2.

452 A glossator adds the following (as reflected in the Arabic manuscripts): 'And when her young are blind she brings a certain grass called *māmīzān* from the mud, and rubs their eyes with it to treat their vision. All this is learned from God, not man. You need teachers and instructors to master the simplest arts and humblest crafts and can do nothing on your own without extensive training.'

get that clay? Where do they gather it, and how do they carry it — if you know?

'In the same way, all sorts of birds and beasts build their homes, nests, or bowers, and rear their young. You will find them more ingenious and skilled, more knowing than humans. The ostrich, for example, a cross between a bird and a beast, treats her chicks thus: having collected twenty or thirty or forty of her eggs, she divides them into three groups. One third she covers with earth, one third she leaves in the sun, and one third she broods. When her chicks emerge, she breaks the eggs that were in the sun and lets the chicks drink the fluid the sun has made runny and liquid within. When the chicks are stronger and sturdier, she unearths the buried eggs and pokes holes in them. Ants, flies, and worms, crawling and swarming creatures gather, and she feeds her chicks on these until they can forage and fend for themselves.[453]

'Tell us, then, O human, which of your women takes such care in raising her children? Without a midwife to help with the delivery when they go into labour, draw out the newborn, and cut the umbilical cord, or a nurse to show them how to suckle, swaddle, and anoint the babe, put kohl on its eyes and put it to sleep, your women would have not the faintest idea how to do this.

'The same is true of your children. So ignorant and backward are they at birth that they have no notion of what's good for them. They don't know how to take care of themselves or stay out of trouble until they're over four years old, or seven, or ten, or twenty! Every day they need new knowledge and fresh training to the end of their lives. But our young, as soon as they issue from the womb, egg, or hive,

453 Cf. Lamentations 4:8; Isidore, *Etymologies* 12.7.20. Ostriches incubate eggs that are not their own and may roll extras out of the nest — perhaps prompting the ancient story that they feed their young on eggs of their own. The book of Job (39:13–18) remarks that an ostrich treats her young as though they were not her own, perhaps by expecting the hatchlings to forage for themselves. Like the Bible, the Ikhwān are not judgemental about such behaviours; these too are facets of God's providence in nature. As Marvin Pope comments on the Job passage, 'The seeming stupidity of this creature proves the wisdom and providential care of its Creator'; see Pope's commentary in the Anchor Bible: Job (Garden City, NY: Doubleday, 1973), pp. 308–309. Cf. the Stoic account of instinct: von Arnim, ed., *SVF*, pp. 724–725, apud Plutarch and Origen.

are ready taught, inspired, aware of their interests and of what their welfare requires. They need no instruction by fathers or mothers. With the chicks of hens, quail, partridges, mountain quail, and the like, for instance, you'll find that as soon as they hatch they immediately start racing around, pecking for grain, and running from anyone who chases them, so fast that they rarely get caught — all without direction by fathers or mothers but by God's inspiration and guidance. This is a mark of God's mercy toward His creation, His kindness, bounty, and grace. For in birds of this sort, unlike other birds — doves, sparrows, and such — the male does not help the female brood and rear the young. So God gives them many chicks and makes them self-reliant, not needing nurture by fathers or mothers — milk to drink, or the cracking of seeds, or provision of food, as the young of other sorts of birds and beasts require. All this is by God's providence, glorified and sanctified be He, His concern in caring for these animals, as already mentioned.

'So tell us now, O human, who stands higher in God's eyes, those He cares for more amply and over whom His providence is fuller, or somebody else?[454] Praised, then, be God, the compassionate Creator, who shows His creatures grace, caring, and love. We praise and exalt Him when we rise with the dawn; and we go to our rest chanting hallels and paeans by day and by night. For His are the praise, the thanks and lauds, the meed and thanksgiving, the All-Gracious, All-Wise, the best of creators.

'You mentioned that you have poets, orators, theologians, and such. But if you could follow the discourse of the birds,[455] the anthems

454 Humans are highly dependent, especially at birth. But culture steps between nature and need. The Ikhwān score a point for the animals here: humans rely on personal and collaborative efforts. But animal instincts, a gift of providence, typify the pietist ideal of *tawakkul*, utter reliance on God. The argument rests on the sophists' dichotomy of art and nature. But culture too is part of nature and is itself, as the Ikhwān hold, a gift of grace.

455 The 'discourse of the birds' (*manṭiq al-ṭayr*) is a Qur'anic phrase (27:16). The biblical Solomon could discourse *of* the birds (1 Kings 5:13, MT), but midrashic fancy has him talking *with* the birds. Taking flight from that fancy is 'Aṭṭār's allegory, translated by A. Darbandi and D. Davis as *The Conference of the Birds* (New York: Penguin, 1984). The birds speak again in many a mediaeval and renaissance narrative.

of the swarming creatures, the hymns of the crawling creatures, the hosannas of the beasts, the meditative murmur of the cricket, entreaty of the frog, admonitions of the bulbul, homilies of the larks, the sand-grouse's lauds and the cranes' celebration, the cock's call to worship, the poetry doves utter in their cooing and the soothsaying ravens in their croaking,[456] what the swallows describe and the hoopoe reports,[457] what the ant tells and the bee relates, what the flies portend and the owl cautions, and all the other animals with voice or buzz or roar, you would know, O human race, you would realize that among these throngs are orators and eloquent speakers, theologians, preachers, admonishers, and diviners, just as there are among the sons of Adam. So why do you brag of your orators, poets, and the like at our expense?

'There's ample argument and proof of what I say in God's words in the Qur'an: *There is not a thing that does not praise and exalt Him, but you understand not their praises.*[458] God calls you dim and benighted when he says *you understand not.* He connects us with insight, good sense, and awareness when He says, *Each knows His worship and praise.*[459] And again: "*Are they alike who know and who*

---

456 For the raven as a bird of omen, see note 184 above.

457 For the hoopoe's report, see Chapters 8 and 13 below and above.

458 Qur'an 17:44. Augustine recalls in his *Confessions* (9.10.25), sharing a similar thought with his dying mother as they stood at a window in the Roman port of Ostia, 'We were then saying: if to any the tumult of the flesh were hushed, hushed the images of earth, and waters, and air, hushed also the poles of heaven, and the very soul were hushed to herself, and by not thinking on self surmount self, hushed all dreams and imaginary revelations, every tongue and every sign, and whatsoever exists only in becoming, since if any could hear, all these say "We made not ourselves, but He made us that abideth forever" — if, then, having uttered this, they too should be hushed, having roused only our ears to Him who made them, and He alone speak, not by them, but by Himself, that we may hear His Word, not through any tongue of flesh, nor Angel's voice, nor sound of thunder, nor in the dark riddle of a similitude, but might hear Whom in these things we love, might hear His Very Self without these (as we two now strained ourselves, and in swift thought touched on that Eternal Wisdom which abideth over all) — could this be continued on, and other visions far unlike be withdrawn, and this one ravish, and absorb, and wrap up its beholder amid these inward joys, so that life might be for ever like that one moment of understanding which now we sighed after; were not this, 'Enter into thy Master's joy'?' Tr. after E. B. Pusey (1838).

459 Qur'an 24:41.

know not?"[460] — a rhetorical question expressing dismay. For anyone with any sense knows that ignorance is no equal of insight in the eyes of God or man.

'So what have you to vaunt over us, O humans, that makes you our masters and us your slaves — even with all your distinctions — beyond sheer slander and lies?

'You tell of the astrologers and sorcerers among you. You should know that they scratch out a living by their trickery, dodges, and deceptions. But these fool only vulgar ignoramuses, women, youngsters, and dolts — although that seems to be lost on you and on many bright and cultured people. One such diviner will forecast the future, announce things unknown, events of which he has no actual knowledge, no clear evidence or warrant. He'll say that in such and such a month and such and such a year, in such and such a land, such and such an event will occur. But he has no idea what will happen in his own land, to his own people, in his own neighbourhood. He has not the faintest notion even of what will befall him personally, how his fortunes will fare, what will become of his children, his servants, or anyone close to him. He keeps his conjectures to matters unknown, in some far away place and distant time, so as not to run foul of experience that might shed light on the truth or falsity of his pretensions and deceptions.

'Besides, you should know, O human, that no one is fooled by an astrologer but the most despotic and outrageous human tyrants, your pharaohs and nimrods, who are seduced by transitory passions and thoughtless of their eternal abode and their fate in the hereafter. They learn nothing from the lessons of the past and are blind to the sealed doom that awaits them. Such were Nimrod the Tyrant, and 'Ād, and *Pharaoh of the Tent-Pegs, who overstepped in the land and filled it with much corruption.*[461] They slew infants at the word of astrologers who

---

460 Qur'an 39:9: *Is one who worships humbly in the watches of the night, bowing and standing, wary of the hereafter, hopeful of God's mercy — are they alike who know and who know not?*

461 Qur'an 89:10–12. Muhammad's first audience, Robert Irwin remarks, well knew the legends underlying the Qur'an's allusions: 'Ad, Thamood, and the Pharaoh of the tent-pegs were part of the mythology of pre-Islamic Arabia, one of the many ancient Arabian myths commemorating lost peoples who were damned because they rejected the messages of God's prophets.' See Robert Irwin, *Islamic Art in Context: Art, Architecture, and the Literary World* (New York: Prentice Hall, 1997), p. 32. Qur'anic references, as we observed in note 101 above, make

knew not the Maker and Ruler of the stars. They held to the delusion that events on earth are governed by the seven planets and twelve signs of the zodiac, not knowing Him who rules them all from on high,[462] their Creator, Author of their form and composition,[463] who sends them in their courses, and holds them continually, moment to moment, under the sway of his will and command.

'Nimrod the Tyrant was told by his astrologers that a child would be born in his realm in a certain year, according to the astral signs, who would grow up, win great power, and abolish idolatry.[464] So he asked them, "In what family will it occur, on what day will he be born, where will he grow up?" They had no idea. But his ministers and courtiers advised him to slay every infant born in that year, to ensure that the intended victim would be among them. They assumed this was possible, knowing nothing of the past and uncomprehending that destiny is sealed and fate inexorable. He did as they urged. But God spared Abraham, his beloved, from their snare and saved him from their scheme.

'Pharaoh did the same to the Israelites when his astrologers foretold the birth of Moses son of Amram. But God rescued His Interlocutor from their net and foiled the plot they'd devised, showing *Pharaoh, Haman, and all their host what they had sought to forfend.*

'The edict of the stars always follows this pattern and plan. So astrology is no help in overcoming God's ruling and decree. Astrologers' words only throw you humans into deeper confusion and uglier outrages. You don't reflect or consider or rouse yourselves

---

Pharaoh an archetype of the insolent and hardened tyrant. Josef Horowitz thought the epithet 'of the Tent-Pegs' might refer to his building activity — the pyramids of Egypt, conflated with the Tower of Babel in Qur'an 28:38. For the Ikhwān, as in the scriptures they follow, corruption is moral pollution; but physical pollution is also a moral evil, emblematic of overreaching.

462 Tyrants' desperate gambles to seize and hold power make them easy prey to astrological delusions. The observation seems as true today as it was a millennium ago.

463 Since the composition of the celestial bodies shows that they are created, not eternal or self-sufficient, they are hardly capable of rule. The Ikhwān reject the pagan notion that the stars control destiny. Knowledge of the unknown (*ghayb*) does not come from divination. It belongs to God; see Nasr, *Islamic Cosmological Doctrines*, p. 82.

464 Qur'an 2:258, 21:51–70, 26:69–104, 37:83–99.

from your torpor. Yet now you come and boast of being our betters because you have astrologers, physicians, geometers, scholars, and so-called philosophers!'

Chapter 37

When the parrot had reached this point in his speech, the King said to the delegate of the birds of prey, 'Tell me, what good is foreknowledge? What help is it? What use is there in all that is foretold by the masters of the many divining arts — the soothsaying, astrology, omens, sortilege, geomancy, palm reading, and like ways of seeking signs of impending disaster and the changes brought by the days, years, and seasons — if one cannot prevent or forestall them?'[465]

'Indeed,' said the parrot, 'it is possible to avoid and guard against such misfortunes, but not in the ways sought by astrologers and other such folk.'

'How then? By what means are such protection and safeguards to be sought?'

'By taking refuge in the Lord of the stars, who created and controls them.'

'How does one take refuge in Him?'

'By keeping the practices ordained in God's laws, the rules revealed in scripture — prayer, lamentation, self-abasement, fasting, worship, charity, sacrifices in houses of worship[466] — pure hearts and candid

465 The same objection was raised to the Stoic teaching that caring gods must warn us of their intent: how does that square with the Stoic belief that destiny is implacable? The Stoics answered that portents serve a moral purpose. Thus, with Caesar's unheeded warnings to beware the Ides of March: 'These portents were given by the immortal gods to Caesar that he might foresee his death, not that he might forfend it'; Cicero, *De Divinatione* I.52.119; cf. ibid. II.10. 25. The Ikhwān hold that one may yet side-step an inexorable blow; and further, even where that is impossible, a transtemporal, spiritual escape remains possible.

466 So the Ikhwān do find portents in the stars: as intermediary causes of terrestrial events, executing God's plan, the stars do yield signs of things to come. The outcomes remain inevitable — but repentance, prayer, and charity (as in the Hebrew liturgy) allow escape from their ill effects. Fatalism, then, (passivity in the face of human helplessness) is not the proper response to astral determinism: human choices can place one's fate under God's protection. For the value of works of piety in averting of the ill effects of God's decree, see the *Unetaneh*

intent, calling on God to guard us and avert such disasters from us, if He please, or give them a favourable and salutary outcome. For the signs of astrology and divination only foretell the acts of the Lord of the stars, who created and rules them and who gave them their form and their courses. To seek help from the Lord of the stars, the Power beyond the spheres and above the stars, is better, more fitting and proper, than invoking the will of some star to ward off the fixed outcomes of astral events — intersections, revolutions, the dawn of new years and months, and conjunctions and oppositions marking nativities.'

'But if these norms and laws are observed as you say, and supplications are duly made,' asked the King, 'does God call off events known to be inevitable?'

'What is known to be so must be so.[467] But God may spare one the event's ill effects, or turn it to one's benefit and welfare — or set one in the bourne of His peace.'

'How does that happen?' asked the King. 'Explain that to me.'

'Certainly, your Majesty. When Nimrod the Tyrant was told by his astrologers of the conjunction that presaged the birth of an infant who would overthrow his idolatrous faith, wasn't it Abraham, friend of the All-Merciful, who was meant?'

'Yes.'

'Didn't Nimrod fear the downfall of his faith and flock, his realm and his forces?'

'Yes.'

'Had Nimrod implored the Lord and Creator of the stars to change this disaster to his flock and forces into something good and beneficial, wouldn't God, exalted and glorified be He, have acceded and welcomed

---

Tokef in the Ro'sh ha-Shanah liturgy: one averts *ro'a ha-gezerah*, that is, 'the ill of the decree', not 'the evil decree', as the phrase is too often translated.

467 The Ikhwān do not use Fārābī's trenchant refutation of the specious appeal from a fact's givenness to its necessity; see al-Fārābī, *Commentary on Aristotle's 'De Interpretatione'*, ed. Kutsch and Marrow (Beirut: Catholic University Press, 1960), Chapter 9. Fārābī showed that while a true proposition necessarily implies the corresponding state of affairs, it does not imply the necessity of that state of affairs. The necessity does not shift from the relation of entailment to the state of affairs; see Goodman, 'Al-Fārābī's Modalities', *Iyyun*, 23 (1972); and cf. Gilbert Ryle, 'It Was to Be', in *Dilemmas* (Cambridge: CUP, 1954), pp. 15–35.

him into the fold of Abraham's faith, along with his forces and flock?[468] Wouldn't that have been a great good, a great benefit for them?'

'Certainly.'

'Likewise with Pharaoh. When his astrologers foretold the birth of Moses son of Amram, had he beseeched his Lord to make Moses a blessing and a solace to him and embraced the faith of Moses, would not that have been a great help to him and his people and followers — as it was for Pharaoh's wife and the man closest to him, the noblest Egyptian, whom God cited and praised in the Qur'an, saying, *A man who had faith in the household of Pharaoh, but concealed his faith, said, "Will you slay a man for saying, 'My Lord is God'"* all the way to *So God saved him from the evil they plotted against him, which only recoiled on Pharaoh's folk.*[469]

'And didn't Jonah's hearers, when they feared impending doom, call on their Lord, Sovereign of the stars, their Creator and Ruler, and wasn't their chastisement therefore averted?[470]

'So you can see clearly the benefits of astrology and foreknowledge of events. One can take precautions against them, avoid their ill

468 Here Islamic triumphalism and the sympathy of the Ikhwān for a fellow Mesopotamian — should he but shed his pagan tyranny — may trump their historical sense. If the great civilizations of Babylonia and Egypt were to turn monotheistic in time, they seem to wonder, why didn't they turn earlier? Only intransigence seems to them to be the answer. For the astrologers' warnings to Nimrod, see al-Kisā'ī, *Qiṣaṣ al-anbiyā'*, tr. Thackston, p. 137.

469 Qur'an 40:28–45. More fully (23–39): *We sent Moses with our signs and clear charge to Pharaoh, Haman, and Korah. But they said, 'A lying sorcerer!' When he brought them Our Truth, they said 'Slay the sons of his fellow believers! But let the females live.'* Yet miscreants' plots only go astray. *Pharaoh said 'I'll slay Moses. Let him call on his Lord. I fear he'll change your faith or spread rot in the land.' Moses said, 'I do seek refuge in my Lord and thine from all who are haughty and believe not in the Day of Reckoning.' A man who had faith within the House of Pharaoh but concealed his faith said, 'Will you slay a man for saying, "My Lord is God", one who has brought you clear proofs from your Lord? If he be a liar, his lie is his. But if he be truthful, some of what he warns of will strike you. God does not guide an arrant liar. People, the realm is yours today, the land is yours. But who will stand against God's wrath if it come?'* The Qur'an goes on to survey similar warnings to the generation of the Flood, 'Ād and Thamūd, the Egyptians warned by Joseph, and again the subjects of Pharaoh. Only through submission (*islām*) can one take refuge in God.

470 Cf. Qur'an 10:98; 37:139–148. God relented from punishing Nineveh when its people heeded Jonah's warnings and repented; see Jonah 1:1, 3:1–10.

effects, or seek to turn their outcome to the good. That is why Moses counselled the Israelites, "When you fear hard times — strife, dearth, drought, inflation, the triumph of foes, the reign of the evil, and the calamities that befall the good, return to God in humility and prayer, and uphold the ways of the Torah — prayer, charity, repentance, weeping, and sacrifices. When God knows that your hearts are pure and your intentions sincere, He will spare you what you would forfend and annul what you dread, the fate you seek to avoid." Such was the counsel of all prophets and messengers of God from Adam, mankind's progenitor, down to the elect master of the prophets, Muhammad ibn ʿAbd Allah.

'That is how one should use the determinations of the stars and the foreknowledge their signs afford us of our fortunes and the shifts of destiny — not as they're used today by astrologers and those taken in by their words, who pick out a particular ascendant and seek its protection from the larger effects of astral influences. How can a general effect be blocked by reliance on a mere part of the system? And how can one turn to the sphere for protection from Him who rules it? Better to turn to the Lord of the spheres for protection from them, like Jonah's folk, or the faithful hearers of Ṣāliḥ[471] or Shuʿayb?[472]

'In the same way one should use medicines and treatments of disease, turning first to God with prayer and entreaties, imploring His aid to remove an illness, hoping that He will act (just as I said regarding the decree of the stars), removing the illness, protecting us from it, and our restoring health, as God made clear through his beloved Abraham, who said, "*He who created me will guide me. He who gives me food and drink will heal me when I fall ill.*" Nor should one resort to prescriptions of doctors deficient in their art, ignorant of nature's laws or unmindful of nature's Lord and His grace on His handiwork.[473]

471 Ṣāliḥ was the warner of Thamūd; most rejected his mission and were destroyed but those who heeded his warnings were spared; Qur'an 7:73–79. Cf. al-Kisāʾī, *Qiṣaṣ al-anbiyāʾ*, tr. Thackston, pp. 117–128.

472 Shuʿayb, identified with Jethro/Reuel, was the warner of his people, the Midianites; Qur'an 7:88–93.

473 Qur'an 26:78–80. Just as we rely on food when hungry, so it is not impious to use medicines when we are ill. The Ikhwān do not reject medical help, as some do who carry pietism to an extreme. The Ikhwān see physicians as a last rather than

'But most people, you find, scurry to the doctor at the first sign of illness but turn to God only if treatment is protracted and the medicine prescribed unavailing. When they've given up hope of a medical cure, they pray desperately, perhaps writing on scraps of paper to stick up on the walls of mosques, churches, or synagogues. They pray privately or make public penitential vows, saying "God have mercy on a troubled supplicant" — as He did in celebrated cases. This is the reward they expect for thieving or robbing or some such crime! Had they turned to God to start with and called on Him inwardly,[474] not just publicly, it would have been well for them, far better than their public protestations and acts of penance.

'This is how one should use the determinations of the stars, to avert injury and disaster and forearm against astral influences and the events they presage, not as astrologers do, choosing particular ascendants to counteract the stars' general determinations, brought on by the rising combinations of stars, the dawn of new years, months, conjunctions and oppositions, and not by choosing times propitious for prayers to be answered — but by seeking forgiveness and asking God to annul or deflect, according to His will, what inspires fear or dread.

'Thus, it is said, a king was told by his astrologers that at a certain time an event would occur that meant destruction for some of the populace of his city. He asked how and in what way this would happen, and they had no inkling of the details but said the force would be irresistible. The king asked when the disaster would occur, and they told him, this year, on such and such a month and day. The king sought advice on how the calamity could be avoided, and God-fearing divines counselled him that he and all his people must evacuate the city and

a first resort, in recognition of God's power over nature. But divine power acts through the Forms and forces that render science possible. The good physician knows the laws of nature and sees medicines as part of God's grace. Cf. Baḥyā ibn Paqūda, *Kitāb al-Hidāya ilā farā'iḍ al-qulūb*, IV.3, ed. A. S. Yahuda, p. 190; and see Lenn Goodman, 'Baḥyā and Maimonides on the Worth of Medicine', in *Maimonides and His Heritage*, ed. I. Dobbs-Weinstein, L. Goodman, and J. Grady (Albany, NY: SUNY Press, 2009), pp. 61–93.

474 Conscience would demand moral uprightness, a more prudent course than the nefarious doings presumed to have brought illness upon the sufferers. The Ikhwān, perhaps following their penchant for Muʿtazilite theodicy, seem too ready to blame the victim. In their defence, one might suspect that they have a particular, perhaps notorious, case in mind.

beg God to spare them the dread fate the astrologers had foretold. The king followed their advice and left the city, most of the people going with him. They spent the night praying for God to spare them what they feared.[475]

'Some stayed behind, unimpressed by the astrologers' warnings and what the rest dreaded and sought to avoid. But that night came a torrential rain and a vast flood. The city was built at the mouth of the wadi.[476] So those who stayed that night perished, but those who left and spent the night in the desert were saved.

'Just so are some preserved and others stricken. Even to those who do not actually escape an inexorable disaster, God still grants a favourable outcome, if they turn to Him in prayer, charity, worship, and fasting, as He did with Noah's people: those who believed, He granted a good outcome and saved, as God states in the Qur'an: *We saved him and those with him in the ark, and drowned those who gave the lie to his signs. They were a blind folk.*[477]

'As for your so-called philosophers, logicians, and disputers, they count against you, not in your favour.'

'How so?' the human demanded.

'Because they are the ones who lead you off the straight and narrow path and cause you to stray from the high-road of faith and the laws of religion, with their many disputes and conflicting opinions, doctrines, and schools. Some hold the eternity of the world, or of matter, or form. Some affirm two causes, others three, or four, five, six, or seven.[478] Some

475 For the story of people who left their homes in fear of death, see Khāzin al-Baghdādī, *Lubab al-ta'wīl fī ma'ānī al-tanzīl* (Beirut: Dār al-Ma'rifa li'l-Ṭibā'a wa'l-Nashr, 1970–1979), vol. 1, p. 189. The commentators link this story with Qur'an 2:243 and 2:259.

476 Petra, among other cities, was so sited. The location was dangerous, but also well supplied with water in its desert setting, from the winter torrents characteristic of desert wadis. Such locations are salubrious if well regulated, but fatal if dealt with negligently.

477 Qur'an 7:64.

478 Strict Platonists and Aristotelians regard Form as eternal. Many philosophers thought matter was eternal. God's act, on their account, was *formatio mundi*, giving order to nature but not creating from nothing. Rāzī held such a view, and indeed assumed five eternal things: God, time, space, matter, and the World Soul. We do not know who opted for higher numbers of eternals. The remark may be sheer hyperbolic disparagement of the philosophers' habit of positing

speak of an Author and his work.[479] Some say the world is infinite, others finite. Some uphold resurrection, others reject it. Some support prophetic revelation, others dispute it. Some are sceptics or doubters, or merely confused. Others proclaim their reliance on reason and proof.[480] Still others depend on authority or unquestioning faith in the rival dogmas and conflicting opinions by which the Children of Adam are simply perplexed and befuddled, and set at odds with one another.[481] But we are all of one school. We follow one path and have but one Lord, who has no peer, and to whom we assign none. We praise Him when we wake, and sanctify Him when we retire. We harbour no malice or ill will toward anyone, and boast ourselves better than no one in God's creation. For we are content with the lot God affords us. We humbly accept His decree, not asking the why, how, and wherefore of His acts and His governance, as human beings do, who cavil at the judgements of their Lord and the rulings by which He governs His handiwork.

'You boast of your geometers and surveyors. I'll say they busy themselves with proofs too subtle to follow and theorems too remote to conceive — that only distract one from the sciences one really needs. And, as if their ignorance were not enough, they pile up superfluities: one tries to measure distant bodies, find the height of mountain peaks and the depth of the sea-floor, to anatomize the deserts and wastes, discover the composition of the spheres, the centres of weights and the like, yet he does not know the make up of his own body or its true dimensions — the length of his own bowels and intestines, the capacity

---

entities to meet the needs of their cosmological systems and metaphysical schematisms.

479 By speaking of an Author, these speculative cosmogonists seem to play down the idea of absolute creation, making God responsible for the world, perhaps eternally, but avoiding saying that it had an origin.

480 That is, in opposition to the sceptics just mentioned. See Saadiah's introduction to *Kitāb al-Mukhtar fi'l-āmānāt wa'l- 'i'tiqādāt.*

481 Reliance on dogmatic authority was a routine charge against the Ismailis; see Ghazālī, *Munqidh*, tr. Watt, pp. 43–54; and *Faḍā'iḥ al-bāṭiniyya*, ed. A.-R. Badawi (Cairo: Dār al-Qawmiyya, 1964). Sceptics capitalize on the failure of all others, whom they call dogmatists, to agree on a criterion. Muslims call the Qur'an their criterion (*fayṣal*). The animals are as bemused or amused by diversity within Islam as by all other divergences in human opinion.

of his own chest, heart, lungs, or brain, the fashioning of his stomach and bones, or how his joints are knit together — or other such things that he would more readily discover and grasp, since they're closer to hand, more relevant and useful to study, and more conducive to knowing the Lord and Creator who fashioned and formed him.[482] But such a one, with his ignorance of all these things, often neglects even to study God's Book and to seek to fathom the laws of His religion, the pathways of His faith, and the duties of the life He prescribes — not content with ignoring and flouting them.

'You boast of your physicians and healers. I'll say you need them! And so you will, as long as your bellies are so ample, your appetites so noxious, your souls so gluttonous, your foods so conflicting, spawning all kinds of chronic diseases, painful sicknesses, and wasting ailments. All this is what drives you to the doctor's door.[483] For no one is seen at the physician or pharmacist's but one who is sick, ill, in poor health, just as no one is seen in the astrologer's doorway but one who is wretched, miserable, or afraid. And the astrologer only compounds his misfortune. He takes his coin but can't advance good fortune or put off trouble. He just offers flowery phrases, guesswork, and unfounded conjectures. Your so-called physicians do just the same. They aggravate the illness and make the disease more painful with the harsh diets they prescribe. Often the things they forbid would cure the patient if taken,

---

482 In the Feyzullah 2130 manuscript, the text continues: 'As the Prophet said (peace be upon him), He who knows himself knows his Lord.' This famous hadith is one of several Islamic variants of the Delphic maxim, *gnôthi seauton*. Originally taken as an admonition to recognize one's mortality, the maxim was reinterpreted by Socrates in light of his discovery of human subjecthood and pure understanding, to mean that he who knows himself discovers a divine being within. Wherever Neoplatonism was given a Shiʿi or Sufi cast, the linkage of creature to Creator opened up epistemological possibilities widely explored by mystics and philosophers including such notable figures as Suhrawardī, Ibn ʿArabī, and Mullā Ṣadrā. The central idea was that self-knowledge leads on to knowledge of God. Here, however, following hints found in Kindī and echoed in Isaac Israeli, the maxim is taken as an encouragement of anatomical studies. Baḥyā ibn Paqūda reads Job 19:26 in that vein. See Alexander Altmann 'The Delphic Maxim in Mediaeval Islam and Judaism', in *Studies in Religious Philosophy and Mysticism* (Ithaca, NY: Cornell University Press, 1969), pp. 1–40, esp. pp. 23–25.

483 In the Dār Ṣādir edition, the text continues: 'Rightly did the poet say: "No doctor with all his drugs and pills / Can purge you of your moral ills."'

although they prohibit and bar them, and if the patient were simply left in nature's care, his recovery would be faster and his cure fuller. So your boasts about your physicians, O human, like those about your astrologers, count against you, not in your favour.

'But we need no physicians or astrologers. We eat only what we need day by day, one food and flavour at a time. So we're not stricken by the mob of diseases and ills that afflict you. We don't need physicians, draughts, theriac,[484] and the whole pharmacopoeia that you use. Our condition bespeaks freedom, quality, and nobility more clearly than yours. Yours looks more like the misery and abasement of slaves. So how can you say that you are masters and we slaves, without proof or argument beyond pure calumny and slander?

'As for your merchants and the landlords and builders you boast of, they're nothing to brag about. They live lives lower than miserable slaves or helpless beggars. You see them all day long, distracted of heart, spent of body and mind, troubled of soul and tortured of spirit, putting up buildings they'll never live in, planting crops they will not reap, gathering harvests they will not eat. Through the cycles of life they go, breaking up graves,[485] astute so far as this world goes, but obtuse about the next. Such a person gathers dirhams, dinars, and goods, too tight to spend on himself. Then he leaves it all to his wife's husband, his son's wife, his daughter's husband, or someone he's never met. You see them toiling for others, without repose until they die.[486]

484 Theriac, a legendary blend of viper's flesh, opium, and many other ingredients, was used at first against snake-bite but later thought of (given its presumed powerful effects) as a kind of panacea. The Arabic name is borrowed from the Greek for a bestiary. Theriac was said to have been developed by Mithridates, King of Pontus, who experimented with it on his slaves. His medical notes were said to have fallen into Roman hands on his defeat, and his name survives as the label of a legendary panacea. Nero's physician perfected a theriac of sixty-four ingredients. Marcus Aurelius took it regularly, a hygienic counterpart to his Stoic tactics for coping with the court life trenchantly captured in the line that so affected Matthew Arnold: 'Even in a palace a good life is possible.' A. E. Housman's poem 'Terence, This is Stupid Stuff', in its final lines, projects a kinder, wiser Mithridates.

485 Farmers plant and builders lay foundations over the graves of their predecessors — a fitting commentary on the evanescence of human projects; John Donne echoes the thought in 'The Relique': 'When my grave is broke up againe / Some second ghest to entertaine . . . '

486 Cf. Ecclesiastes 2:4–23: 'I made me great works, built me houses, planted me

'Your merchants gather goods by fair means or foul. They build shops and stores and fill them with goods, hoarding and crowding themselves, their neighbours and brethren.[487] They deprive the poor, the orphaned, and the wretched of their rights,[488] not spending what they've amassed in godly ways — until they lose it all in a fire or flood, or by theft, or confiscation by a despotic government, or highwaymen or the like. Then the merchant is left with his misery and grief, inflicted by his own hand. He has given no alms tax or charity, befriended no orphan, extended no kindness to the helpless. So he has no bonds of kinship or friendship to call on, and he is unready for resurrection and ill prepared for the hereafter.

'You say there are gentlefolk, virtuous people among you. But if they had the virtue you speak of, how could they enjoy life when they see their hapless neighbours, orphans, their brethren's offspring, helpless members of their own kind, starving, naked, wasted by disease, paralysed, cast out on the road, begging a morsel of them, or a rag for raiment, without even turning toward them or pitying them, or giving them a thought? What kind of virtue is that? What sort of nobility? How can they take joy in that sort of life, unless they're *like cattle but further astray*?[489]

---

vineyards. I made me gardens and orchards, and planted trees in them bearing all manner of fruits. I made me pools to water a flourishing forest of trees. . . . All that my eyes asked I denied them not, and no object of joy did I keep from my heart. For I was pleased with all my work, and that was the meed of my labours. But looking again at all that my labours had wrought, all was worthless, a will-o'the-wisp, profitless under the sun. . . . And I hated all the work I had done under the sun, that I would leave to another man who would come after me. Who knows whether he'd be foolish or wise, he'd own what I'd worked for. . . . For what has a man from all his labour and heart's striving, all his toil under the sun, since all his days are ache and anguish, and even by night his heart knows no rest. This too is pointless.' The Ikhwān distance themselves from the urban and agrarian projects long known in Iraq. Saadiah, a generation before in Baghdad, glosses Ecclesiastes (5:8) as warning that a landowner is slave to his land; he reads Job as complaining (3:14) that even kings build only ruins; Saadiah, *Kitāb al-Mukhtār fī'l-āmānāt wa'l-iʿtiqādāt*, ed. J. Kafih (Jerusalem: Sura, 1970), X.10.

487 Kindī's worldly collector, on the island in his parable, 'must settle into a cramped, narrow, hard, and rough spot.' See Prologue of the Ikhwān, note 29 above.

488 As in the Hebrew concept of charity as (*tzedakah*) justice, the welfare of the poor is a matter of right, not just freely conferred (or withheld) benevolence.

489 Qur'an 7:179.

'As for the clerks, treasurers, and ministers of state you mentioned and bragged about, how is it even decent to boast of them? They're your worst villains. Aren't they the ones who set the worst example, who hatch vicious, avaricious schemes that no one else would even dream of, using their subtle minds and their cunning to get what they covet,[490] with devious plots, smooth tongues, and the deadly rhetoric of their writs? Such a man may write to a brother and colleague in flowery, deceitfully honeyed language, all in rhyme, hoping to dazzle him, while behind this veil of words he's seeking to destroy him, plotting to strip him of his perquisites, or work his downfall by framing him, to have his property confiscated, or forging lies to get it for himself.

'Your scripture reciters and the devout that you count as the best among you, whose prayers you hope will be answered and whose intercession you rely on with your Lord — why they're just the ones who have gulled you with outward shows of piety, humility, self-abasement — trimming their beards, cropping their sleeves, buckling on a belt and trousers, wearing coarse wool, or hair, or patched cloaks, keeping long bouts of silence and following endless rules, while forsaking all interest in the faith, neglecting study of the laws and usages of religion, and of moral and spiritual improvement.[491]

490 I.e., perverting their divinely given gifts.

491 Several groups and fashions are targeted here. The antinomian Qalandar movement was found across the Persian, Turkish, Indian, and Arab lands. Wandering bands of mendicants, dressed in deliberately provocative garments and startling head-gear, marked their identities with shaved beards, and often shaved eyebrows and hair as well, breaching social norms and flouting the sunna of the Prophet, who said, 'Do the opposite of what the pagans do. Keep the beard and cut the moustache short' (*Ṣaḥīḥ Bukhārī* Book 72, hadith 780). The parrot's mention of trousers and belt likely alludes to Turkish Qalandarīs. The early history of the movement, like that of other antinomian or anarchically inclined sects is murky. But the picture becomes clearer with the emergence of distinct institutional and doctrinal elaborations in the thirteenth century; see Ahmet Karamustafa, *God's Unruly Friends: Dervish Groups in the Later Middle Period, 1200–1550* (Salt Lake City: University of Utah Press, 1994), pp. 51–63. Along with Qalandarī practices, the parrot points to the woollen or patched frocks of Sufis, which are also affected by would-be Sufis. In his handbook on Sufism, Ḥujwīrī writes a chapter about these cloaks and cites works by himself and others on the topic. He says that 'the wearing of a *muraqqa'a* ['patched frock'] is the badge of aspirants to Ṣūfism', but he insists that inner devotion is the true cloak for the real Sufi; see Ḥujwīrī, *Kashf al-maḥjūb*, tr. Nicholson, pp. 45–57.Criticism of pseudo-Sufism came from both within the tradition and without. Al-Muḥāsibī developed an elaborate Sufi psychology around the

'They grow so obsessed with the mindless tally of their bows and prostrations that you can see the marks on their brows and the calluses on their knees.[492] They neglect food and drink, making their brains dry and dull, their lips fleshy, their bodies gaunt. They grow pale and stooped, their hearts full of rancour and spite toward anyone unlike them.[493] Their souls are sullen within and full of resentment toward God: 'Why did He create Satan, demons, unbelievers, pharaohs, felons, profligates, the wicked?' Why does He breed and sustain them, give them power — or respite? Why won't He destroy them?' Why does He this, why won't He do that? Such bitter complaints fill their hearts with mistrust and their souls with doubt and confusion.[494] To God these people are evil, and if they're good in your eyes, your boasting of them redounds only to your shame.

---

concepts of ego, sincerity to oneself and before God, and the curbing of such passions as braggadicio (*tafākhur*) and lust for domination (*ri'āsa*). See Michael Sells, ed. and tr., *Early Islamic Mysticism* (New York: Paulist Press, 1996), pp. 189–195. The conservative Iraqi preacher Abū'l-Faraj Ibn al-Jawzī devoted one of his works to Sufi excesses and the gullible masses taken in by them in *Talbīs Iblīs* (Beirut: Dār Kutub al-'Ilmiyya, 1975), tr. D. S. Margoliouth as 'The Devil's Delusion', *Islamic Culture*, 9–12 (1935–1938).

492 The devout sometimes vied in the numbers of their daily prostrations, emulating the extremes that pious traditions ascribed to the early caliphs. See William Muir, *The Caliphate: Rise, Decline, and Fall* (Beirut: Khayats, 1963). The practice continues today. The *zebība*, or forehead callus, is a fashionable mark of piety among Egyptian Muslims. The *New York Times* (December 18, 2007, p. A-4) quotes a hairdresser as saying, 'The *zebibah* is a way to show how important religion is for us', and a newspaper editor as saying that the mark makes 'a kind of statement', allowing the claimant to piety 'a way of outbidding others by showing them that he is more religious or to say that they should be like him.' A school security guard speaks of the *zebība* as giving an important first impression, and a female art student remarks that the *zebība* says '"I am a good person". . . . On Judgement Day, this sign, the *zebibah* on their forehead, will shine. It will say, "God is great"'.

493 Saadiah similarly finds that persons who make ascetic practice their overriding goal in life renounce many legitimate goods and grow bitter and misanthropic; see *Kitāb al-Mukhtār fī 'l-āmānāt wa'l-i'tiqādāt*, ed. Kafih, Book X.4. Dostoevsky's portrait of Father Ferapont in *The Brothers Karamazov* astutely observes the same weakness in modern ascetic extremists.

494 Just as ascetic excesses prompt misanthropy, mechanically repeated acts of penitence and piety may exacerbate doubts. The animals are proud of their unquestioning faith. But, as Saadiah argues, doubt is inherent in human finitude, and struggle with doubt gives authenticity to faith — which would be trivial, as the animals themselves suggest, were it mindless.

'As for your jurists and clerics, they're the ones who use and abuse their learning in the Law to win the world, lusting for rule, authority, and sway for their dicta and opinions — now allowing what God and His Prophet forbade, now banning what God and His Prophet permitted. With their mendacious glosses *they pursue what is unclear in it*,[495] and what's undisputable in God's revealed verses they reject and spurn *behind their backs, as though they never knew it, and follow the fancies demonically instilled* in their hearts,[496] ever worldly, avid for power not piety, not devout or God-fearing. *These are mere fuel for the fire*[497] hereafter, unless they turn to God and seek forgiveness.[498] What have you to boast of in them?

'Your judges and jurists are the basest, wickedest pharaohs and tyrants! Before his appointment to the bench you'll see such a man early at the mosque, rapt in prayer, or minding his own business, walking casually with his neighbours. No sooner is he given the post and power of a judge than you see him trotting along on a prancing mule or an ass out of Egypt with a saddle and a parasol trailing to the ground, borne by blacks, the gift of the despot, out of what he could wring from the due of orphans and divert from the charitable trusts. Such judges rule between parties by simply imposing a settlement. Where there's no satisfaction, they find for one side and impose their sentence on the other. They take graft and bribes, sops of ill-gotten goods, won by cabals and perjury, breach of trust and bond. They're condemned by God in the Torah, the Gospels, and the Qur'an. Will they fool God and get off scot-free?

'As for your caliphs, the self-styled heirs of the prophets, peace be upon them, suffice it to depict them as God's Messenger did: "No prophecy is without a tyranny to void it."[499] They're called successors to prophecy, but they live like tyrants. They're supposed to forbid wrong-doing, yet they breach every ban, slay God's saints and the scions of

495 Qur'an 3:7; see Chapter 3, note 50 above.

496 Qur'an 2:101–102. The charges echo the polemics of Islamic traditionalists against the seeming arbitrariness of independent reasoning.

497 Qur'an 3:10.

498 The Ikhwān rein in the condemnation, lest they replicate the censoriousness of the *takfīrī*, who leaps to prejudge God's sentence or close the door on a wrong-doer's repentance.

499 This report is not found among the canonical hadiths. But cf. Qur'an 25:31.

prophets, crucify and strip them of their rights. Wine drinkers and debauchers, they make God's creatures their chattels, take the days of His servants as their due and their wealth as their prize, repaying God's favour with unbelief, lording it over mankind. Forgetting the fact of resurrection, they sell the faith for the world, the hereafter for the here and now. Woe betide what their hands have wrought, and woe betide them, from what they've brought on themselves!

'As soon as one of them comes to power he arrests those who served his fathers and forebears and ends their preferments. He may slay his uncles, brothers, nephews, and kin, blind or imprison them, or renounce and exile them — all out of insecurity and mistrust, fear of losing what is destined, or eager to grasp what is never to be. Rapacious and greedy, they snatch at the world but forget the hereafter, unconvinced of requital, uncertain that resurrection will even occur. These are not the marks of free spirits or the traits of the great-souled.[500] So your boasting against us, O human, about your kings, sultans, and caliphs counts not for but against you. And your claims that we are your servants and you our lords are empty aspersions and canards. That is all I have to say. God grant pardon to me and to you.'

Chapter 38

When the parrot, spokesman of the birds of prey, had finished speaking, the King said to the sages of the jinn and humans gathered before him, 'Tell me, who brings the termite the clay she uses to build her vaulted cloisters, galleries, porticoes, and halls? For she crawls along without legs to run on or wings to fly with.'

'I can answer that, your majesty', said one of the Hebrews. 'We have heard that the jinn carry this clay to repay a favour that goes back to the days when the termite ate Solomon's staff, causing it to fall and allowing the jinn to realize he was dead and escape *the degrading chastisement* he had inflicted upon them.'[501]

500 The catalogue of caliphal excesses is not exaggerated but well attested by history.

501 Qur'an 34:12–14; see Chapter 8, note 122 above.

Said the King to the jinni scholars who stood about him, 'What do you say of this?'

They answered, 'We know of no such work by the jinn. If we jinn carried clay, water, and earth for the termite, that would just prolong the degradation. For the tasks that Solomon imposed on us were none other than bearing clay, water, and earth for his building projects.'

Said the Greek philosopher, 'Your Majesty, we have a scientific account of this business quite different from the lore this Hebrew has reported.'[502]

'Tell us what that is', the King directed.

'I shall, your Majesty. This tiny worm has an elegant structure, a marvellous nature. Her temperament is very cold, and her body laced with pores by which the air enters. Her intensely cold make-up chills the air into water that exudes on her body's surface. The dust in the air that falls steadily on her body is moistened by this liquid and collects like grime. She gathers it and with it builds her galleries to shelter her from

502 Contrasting Greek science with Hebraic lore, the Greek echoes Aristotle's suasion that philosophy must move beyond narrative and seek explanations not in the origins but in the essences of things. The notion of jinni subjection to the termites is meant to typify the fantastic tales that Islamic tradition calls *Isrā'īliyāt*, the Midrashic type of lore often discredited or disavowed in Islamic histories and Qur'an commentaries that seek a plane of seriousness, whether in the interest of critical handling of evidence or in a kind of chauvinistic winnowing of old traditions; see Goodman, *Islamic Humanism*, pp. 166–167. The daring, if oblique, suggestion is that a similar scepticism might spill over to undermine literalism about the Qur'an — exemplified in the Ikhwān's glossing of the jinn as natural forms and forces, God's Neoplatonic emissaries. The Ikhwān take a dynamic, Neoplatonizing view of the activity of the Forms. So in their essay on music (Epistle 5; *Rasā'il*, vol. 1, p. 238) they bracket as the view of particular philosophers the familiar, more static, Platonic model of the relation of the Forms to the world: 'Another said, "The fact is that the various animals in this world are mere spectres, images of those Forms and creatures in the realm of the spheres and the broad expanse of the heavens, just as the pictures and images painted on the surface of walls or ceilings are simulacra, likenesses that imitate or represent the flesh and blood forms of these animals. The creatures of flesh and blood are to these pure Forms as such painted decorations are to animals of flesh and blood."' Cf. Ian Netton, 'The *Rasā'il Ikhwān al-Ṣafā'* in the History of Ideas in Islam', in Nader El-Bizri, ed. *The Ikhwān al-Ṣafā' and their 'Rasā'il'*, pp. 126–127; Netton, *Muslim Neoplatonists*, pp. 16–19.

all harm.[503] She has two lips as sharp as knives that can chew through wood, grain, fruit, or plants, or tunnel through brick or stone.'

'This animal is one of the crawling creatures', said the King to the cricket. 'You are their spokesman. What do you think of what the Greek says?'

'What he says is true,' the cricket replied, 'but his account is incomplete.'

'Finish it, then', said the King.

'Certainly. When the Creator decreed the various types of creatures and parcelled out his gifts He dealt justly with them, as His wisdom determined, allotting his gifts with scrupulous fairness, justice, and equity.[504] Some creatures were given a great and powerful body but low and servile souls; such were the camel and the elephant. Others received a mighty and awesome soul, filled with wisdom and understanding, but a weak constitution and a tiny body. That is how the Creator balanced their gifts and talents, in keeping with His justice and wisdom.'

'Explain somewhat further', said the King to the cricket.

'Certainly. You see, your Majesty, the elephant, with all his bulk and his immense frame, is servile to be led by a youth riding on his shoulders, who treats him just as he pleases. How, if not out of servility, would a camel, with his great size and long neck, let himself be led by any tug at his nose, even by a mouse or a dung-beetle!

'Don't you see how a *jarāra* scorpion, one of the least of the crawling creatures — or even the *karura*, which is yet smaller — can strike an elephant with her stinger and kill it?[505] Termites, likewise, may have small bodies and a delicate build. But their soul is mighty. The same is true of all small bodied animals — the silkworm, pearl oyster, and wasp. Their souls are sagacious and sage, even though their bodies are small and their frames weak.'

503 The Ikhwān parody Greek science for purporting to explain the elegant and complex natural history of the termite using only simple notions of hot, cold, moist, and dry.

504 Cf. Aristotle, *De Partibus Animalium* IV.10.687a11–13: 'Nature's invariable plan in allotting organs is to give each to such animal as can make use of it; Nature acting in this matter as any prudent man would do.'

505 The *jarāra* would be a large scorpion, perhaps *Pandinus imperator*, whose females can reach upwards of 50 g; the *karura*, here as a tiny scorpion, may belong to the genus *Microtityus*, whose members reach only 12 mm.

'What is the wisdom in that?' asked the King.'

'The Creator understood', the cricket replied, 'that a powerful frame and mighty body are fit only for toil, brute labour, and bearing heavy loads. Had He linked great souls with such bodies they would not so readily be led to drudgery and menial labour. They'd be fractious and unruly and would refuse to bear a rider.[506] But praise be to God for the bounties of His creation. Small bodies and great souls full of learning befit the artistry of the bees, silkworms, pearl oysters, and their ilk.'[507]

'Go on', said the King.

'Certainly. With a real virtuoso one can't tell how he makes his goods, or from what. Such is the work of the bees. We have no idea how they build their dwellings and their six-sided cells without straight-edge or compass. Nor can we say where they get their honey and wax, how they work it, or set it apart. If bees had larger bodies all this would be patent and plain, observed and understood.

'Likewise the silkworm. If his body were large we could see how he extrudes his gossamer thread, spins, and plaits it. And the termites — if their bodies were large, we could see how they moisten their clay and how they build.[508]

'I'll tell you, your Majesty, the Creator signals His power in this way, to all the would-be Adamite philosophers who deny that the world came to be from no prior matter. For bees, by their art, make homes of wax, which they gather, and make honey for their food, from no prior matter. For if humans claim that bees collect it from flowers and tree leaves, why don't they collect any, with all their knowledge and supposed skill and philosophy? Or if bees gather it from the surface of the water or from thin air, why don't the humans see it or have any

506 Pliny has it that camels refuse to carry more than a regulation burden, *Natural History* VIII.26.67–68.

507 What the Greek left out in his naturalistic account was the spiritual side of animal nature.

508 Would a microscope void the wonderment? Probably not: God worked on a scale that strikes awe in the minds of nature's grosser observers. But ignorance is not the same as awe, and understanding does not obviate the marvel. Grasping the workings of a living design or recognizing how it evolved does not dissolve its brilliance. Marvel is not the same as mystery; see Goodman, *Creation and Evolution* (New York and London: Routledge, 2010).

idea how it's collected, carried, or saved, let alone how they build, or how they store their goods?[509]

'Through small creatures, too, the Creator has shown His power over human tyrants who insolently overstepped, when He had been gracious to them. Nimrod, for one, was killed by a gnat, the tiniest of swarming creatures. Pharaoh too, so brazen and wicked to Moses, was faced by God with hosts of locusts; and smaller still, lice, that vanquished him, since he did not take warning and repent.[510]

'Consider Solomon too. God gave him both prophecy and the crown, and he built up his kingdom and subjugated humans and jinn. He conquered and subdued the kings of the earth. But men and jinn alike doubted his dominion, imputing all to some trick or ruse, or to his own power and agency — although he denied it, saying *This was by the grace of my Lord — that He may try me, whether I am grateful or thankless.*[511]

'His words helped them not at all. They still did not believe him in their hearts, until God sent this termite, who gnawed Solomon's staff, and he fell on his face in his prayer niche. In dread and awe of him, not one human or jinni had dared approach, until God showed His power, as a caution to tyrants and monarchs who vaunt their great bodies, their bulk, and fierce onslaughts. Yet still men miss the warning. They don't repent or relent but mutter and mutiny, bragging against us of kings who are driven frantic by the weakest and frailest sons of our kind.[512]

---

509 The claim is not that bees make honey from nothing or out of thin air, but that the wondrous transformations used in honey making are no more incredible than creation. If *ex nihilo nihil fit* means that creation is impossible, the Ikhwān ask of such everyday miracles as the making of honey: whence comes the sweetness in what was not sweet?

510 See Qur'an 7:133; Exodus 8:16, 10:14. 'Lice are enough to vacate Sulla's dictatorship; and the heart of a great and triumphant emperor is the breakfast of a little worm.' Montaigne, *Apology for Raymond Sebond*, in *Complete Essays*, II, 12, p. 339.

511 Qur'an 27:40.

512 Human monarchs are great and powerful compared to an insect, but God showed those who stood in awe of Solomon that even a great king was mortal. The powers that led others to hold him in awe were God's gifts. Once those gifts were used up and the great king's life was ended, only his staff supported his body, and the gnawing of a termite brought his fall.

'The pearl oyster is the smallest sea-animal in bulk, the weakest, the most delicate, yet the greatest in soul, the most skilful and cunning. She lives in the depths of the sea-bed, minding her own affairs, seeking her food, until, at a certain season, she rises from the sea-floor to the surface on a rainy day and opens paired hatches like lips to catch the raindrops. Once she knows this is done, she snaps her hatches tight, careful admit no salty sea-water, and gently returns to the sea floor. There she patiently waits with closed shell until those water drops ripen and fuse within her to a pearl.[513] What human scholar could do such a thing, tell me if you know?

'God imbued human nature with a love of wearing silk, brocade, satin — clothing made from these fabrics, soft and fine, all from the spittle of this worm of tiny body and delicate build, but splendid soul. God made the food that humans find most delicious, the honey spat out by this animal of tiny body and delicate frame but noble soul and consummate art. The finest that humans can light in their assembly halls is the wax taken from the structures this animal builds.[514] And God made the choicest adornment humans use to bedeck themselves the pearl, extracted from the belly of this lowly worm, whose body is small but whose soul is lofty, as a sign of the wise Creator's wisdom, to heighten men's awareness of His bounties and increase their gratitude when they contemplate His works.[515]

'But even so, some are so blind, heedless, distracted, frivolous, grasping, and overweening, so insistently vicious, so ungrateful for God's blessings and gifts and so ready to disclaim His favours and

513 Of the pearl oyster, Isidore writes, 'the precious stone coalesces in its flesh. People who have written on the nature of animals say of these creatures that they seek the shore at night and conceive the pearls out of a celestial dew'; *Etymologies* 12.6.49. Pliny (*Natural History* IX.54.107) calls pearls 'the product of a dewy pregnancy', and explains that pearls correspond in quality to that of the dew received.

514 Paul of Aegina also describes bee's wax medically as 'attenuant and deobstruant'; *The Seven Books*, vol. 3, p. 311.

515 'Indeed, when I imagine man quite naked, yes, even in that sex which seems to have the greater share of beauty, his blemishes, his natural subjection, and his imperfections, I think we had more reason than any other animal to cover ourselves. We can be excused for having borrowed from those whom nature had favored more than ourselves in this, to adorn ourselves with their beauty and hide ourselves beneath their spoils — wool, feathers, fur, silk.' Montaigne, *Apology for Raymond Sebond*, in *Complete Essays*, II, 12, p. 356.

deny His art that they lord it over God's weakly creatures, and unjustly, despotically oppress them.'

When the cricket, delegate of the swarming creatures, had finished his speech, the King responded, 'God bless you! How understanding has He made you! What a wise philosopher and eloquent orator! How aware in your monotheism! How ready to acknowledge the gifts you've received!'

Chapter 39

Then said the King to the humans, 'You have heard what he said and understood his response. Have you anything to add?'

'We have. We have other qualities and distinctions to show that we are their masters and they are our slaves.'

'What are they? Cite them.'

'Our unity of form and their varied forms and contrarious shapes. For mastery and rule belong to unity, and servitude to diversity.'[516]

'What do you think of what he says?' the King asked the assembly.

All remained silent for a time, thinking over that argument.[517] Then the delegate of the birds, the nightingale, addressed them: 'He is right, your Majesty, in what he says. But though our forms are many and diverse, our souls are one, whereas these humans, while one in form, have many and conflicting souls.'

Said the King, 'How is that? Explain!'

'Their diverse notions, rival sects, competing schools, and varied religions.[518] Among them you find Jews, Christians, Sabians, Magians,[519]

516 The human spokesman adapts an axiom of Neoplatonic ontology to serve his cause.

517 The point gives the animals pause, since multiplicity means departure from God's ultimate unity. Cf. Plato, *Symposium* 211; *Republic* I.351d; *Sophist* 244b; and Proclus, *Elements of Theology*, Props. 1–13, ed. E. R. Dodds, pp. 1–17; e.g., Prop. 4, 'All that is unified is other than the One itself', and Prop. 5, 'Every manifold is posterior to the One'; Prop. 8, 'All that in any way participates in the Good is subordinate to the primal God which is nothing else but good.'

518 Like Rāzī, the Ikhwān associate religious differences with conflict. Kalonymos ascribes their deliberate anonymity to the religious and philosophical factionalism of their day, which, he remarks, did not vanish thereafter.

519 Iranian dualistic faiths remained prominent enough in Muslim eyes for al-Ghazālī to cite a hadith as to the impact of tradition: 'Everyone is born in a state of nature

pagans, idolaters, and worshippers of the sun and moon, stars and constellations, among other things. And you'll find that the followers of a single faith also split into many sects and schools. There are Samaritans, Ananites, and Exilarchs,[520] Nestorians, Jacobites, and Melkites,[521] Dualists, Khurramites, Mazdakites, and Manichaeans,[522] Brahmins, Buddhists, and Dīṣānites, Khārijites, Nāṣibites, Rāfiḍites, Murji'ites, Qadarites, Jahmites, Muʿtazilites, Sunnis,[523] Jabrites — among many other opinions and schools,[524] all calling each other unbelievers, cursing and killing each other.[525]

'But we are free of all such dissension. We have one outlook, one credo. We are all monotheists, faithful *muslims*, who assign God's divinity to no other and do not fall into hypocrisy and lawlessness. We have no doubts, confusions, or perplexities, no straying or misleading. We acknowledge our Lord, the Creator and Provider who gives us life and death and whom we praise, sanctify, celebrate, and exalt, morning

---

[*fiṭra*]. It is his parents who make him a Jew, a Christian, or a Magian'; *Munqidh*, tr. Watt, p. 21. For the sense of *fiṭra* here, see Qur'an 30:29, etc.; see also D. B. MacDonald, 'Fiṭra', *EI2*, vol. 2, pp. 931–932, where MacDonald explains that theological considerations drove the sense of the word in a direction that suggests that everyone is born a natural Muslim, and theological contention pushed the sense of the hadith, to make parents only a secondary or figurative cause — lest it give colour to Muʿtazilite notions of the efficacy of human efforts in reaching safe harbour in the true faith.

520 These three sects are Jewish.

521 These three are Christian sects.

522 These are Persian sects, following the religious traditions initiated by Zoroaster in the Avesta. See R. C. Zaehner, *The Dawn and Twilight of Zoroastrianism* (New York: Putnam, 1961).

523 The Ikhwān treat Sunnis as just another schism in the faith.

524 On these factions, see Appendix D: Religious Traditions. It is striking to note that the Ikhwān do not name the Shiʿa here.

525 A well-known body of hadiths ascribes to Muhammad the prediction that Islam will split into 'seventy-odd' sects. The Ikhwān underscore their point by their listing of sects, since most of the names cited were terms of vituperation in the mouths of rival sectaries. For a fine introduction to the history of Islamic sectarianism, see William Montgomery Watt, *The Formative Period of Islamic Thought* (Edinburgh: Edinburgh University Press, 1973). As Godefroid de Callataÿ points out, the Ikhwān themselves, in their seventh *risāla*, tellingly group religious and conventional studies together; see de Callataÿ, 'The Classification of Knowledge in the *Rasā'il*', in Nader El-Bizri, ed., *The Ikhwān al-Ṣafā' and their 'Rasā'il'*, pp. 66–67.

and evening — although these humans do not comprehend our songs of praise.'

The Persian responded, 'We do the same. We say our Lord is one, our Creator is one, our Provider is one, He who gives us life and death is one without peer.'

'Why, then,' asked the King, 'do you have different doctrines, sects, and creeds, if your Lord is one?'

'Because religions, schools, and sects are just different paths,[526] different avenues of approach. Our goal is one. Whichever path we take, *God's face is there.*'[527]

'So why do you slay one another, if the folk of all your religions have the same goal, of encounter with God?'

'You're right, your Majesty', said the thoughtful Persian. 'This does not come from faith, for there is *no compulsion in faith.*[528] It comes from faith's specious counterpart, the state.'

'How so? Explain that to me', demanded the King.

'Religion and the state are inseparable twin brothers. Neither can survive without the other. But religion is the elder. The state is the younger brother, the follower. A state cannot do without a religion for its people to live by; and religion needs a king to command the people to uphold his institutions, freely or by force. That is why the votaries of different religions slay one another — seeking political primacy and

526 The Ikhwān have tried to represent human diversity by varying the language each human speaker uses in narrating his own version of the creation story. Clearly, they do not intend (and are probably not able) to reflect the full extent of doctrinal differences among the cultures they represent. But they want to credit all of those cultures with the same foundational vision, of God as the Source, Ruler, and Judge of all.

527 Qur'an 2:115. The context (2:111–115) is revealing: *They say none shall enter paradise unless he be a Jew or a Christian . . . No! One who resigns his face to God and does what is good has his reward from God. They will have no fear or grief. . . . God's are the East and the West. Wherever you turn, there is God's face. God is all-encompassing and all-knowing.* The Ikhwān echo this thought in their own words: 'faith is found in every religion and current in every tongue. You must take the best and adapt to it. Do not make yourself busy finding faults in the religions others. Just see to it that your own is free of them' (*Rasā'il*, Epistle 42, vol. 3, p. 501, translated here after Bernard Lewis, *The Origins of Ismailism* (Cambridge: Heffer, 1940; repr., New York: AMS, 1975).

528 Cf. Qur'an 2:256.

sway. Each wants everyone to follow the ways of his own faith and the rules and practices of his own religion.[529]

'I'll tell you something, your Majesty — and may God help you understand the truth — what I'm saying is true, beyond doubt . . . '

'What is that?' said the King.

'The slaying of selves is practised in all faiths, creeds, and confessions, and all earthly dominions. But in religion, the mandate is for self-sacrifice.[530] In politics it usually means slaying others to gain power.'

Said the King, 'That kings kill to win power is plain enough. But how is it that seekers in the different religions slay themselves?'

'I'll explain. You know, your Majesty, that in Islam, this is clearly and plainly one's duty. For God says, *Lo, God hath bought of the faithful their substance and selves, since they shall have Paradise. Let them battle for God, slay and be slain. This is His promise, confirmed in the Torah, Gospels, and Qur'an. And who is truer to his pact than God?*[531] After which He says: *Rejoice in the sale of yourselves ye have made,*

529 Given the Qur'anic dictum (2:256; cf. 10:99) that there is no compulsion in faith, religious wars are clearly perversions of the aims of religion. It remains, then, for the Ikhwān to deal with Islamic militancy, which, by their standard, would register as a contradiction, and to address the Qur'anic tradition of *jihād*.

530 The 'self' in the pietist mode that the Ikhwān espouse is seen as its own worst enemy, a complex of passions, appetites, and drives that must be overcome before the soul's liberation can be attained. Al-Ḥakīm al-Tirmidhī reflects on the classical disparagement of this lower self (*nafs*), the ego, which the aspirant must root out like an old stump, 'a tree whose branches have been cut off but nonetheless continues to live. He may feel safe for a time, but then the tree sprouts new branches all over again. Whenever he cuts them off, new ones appear in their place . . . So he finally realizes that he will not be free of this evil until he has torn out that tree by its roots'; al-Tirmidhī, *Kitāb Khatm al-awliyā'* ed. 'Uthmān Yaḥya (Beirut: Catholic University Press, 1965), pp. 118–119. Many Muslim seekers of a pious life sought strategies to control the *nafs*, humble it, and curb its harmful effects. Early thinkers like al-Muḥāsibī developed a discipline of self-scrutiny to aid in the struggle (*mujāhada*). Ḥujwīrī sees the *jihād* against the self as a universal spiritual concern: 'The Apostle adjudged the mortification of the lower soul to be superior to the Holy War against unbelievers, because the former is more painful. You must know, then, that the way of mortification [*mujāhadat*] is plain and manifest, for it is approved of men of all religions and sects, and is observed and practised by the Sufis in particular.' Ḥujwīrī, *Kashf al-maḥjūb*, tr. Nicholson, pp. 200–201. Cf. Ben Zoma at Mishnah Avot 4.1.

531 Qur'an 9:111. The verse is commonly taken as an exhortation to warfare in behalf of the faith.

a splendid triumph![532] And, *God loveth those who do battle for Him, in ranks like a close-knit structure.*[533] In the Torah tradition, He says, 'Turn to your Creator and slay your selves. Your humbling is good in the eyes of your Creator.'[534] And Christ says in the Gospels, "*Who are my aides in the service of God?" The Disciples answered "We are God's helpers."*[535] He replied, "Prepare for death and the cross if you wish to aid me. Then shall you be with me in the Kingdom of Heaven, with my Father and yours. Else you are none of mine."[536] And they were slain but did not forsake Christ's faith.

'The Brahmins of India slay themselves and burn their bodies in their spiritual quest, convinced that the penitent comes closest to the Lord, exalted be He, by slaying his body and burning it to atone for his sins, certain of resurrection. And the godliest Manichaeans and dualists deny the self all gratifications and carry heavy loads of religious obligations, to slay the ego and free it from this realm of trial and degradation.

'The same pattern of self-sacrifice is found in the varied practices of people in all religions. All religious laws were laid down to deliver the soul, to save it from hell-fire and win blessedness in the hereafter, the realm to which we return and where we shall abide.[537]

---

532 Ibid.

533 Qur'an 61:4.

534 The reference may be to Leviticus 16:30–31, ordaining the Day of Atonement: *It shall be a sabbath of sabbaths for you, and ye shall afflict your souls — an everlasting statute.* The passage is perhaps conflated with verses like Hosea 14:2–3. The citations call for self-trial, not self-immolation, but certainly not for battle.

535 Qur'an 61:14.

536 See Matthew 16:24: 'Then said Jesus unto his disciples, "If any man will come after me, let him deny himself and take up his cross, and follow me."' Matthew 10:34–39: '"Think not that I am come to send peace on earth; I came not to send peace but a sword. For I am come to set a man at odds with his father, and daughter with mother, and daughter-in-law with mother-in-law. A man's foes shall be they of his own household. He that loveth father or mother more than me is not worthy of me. He that loveth a son or daughter more than me is not worthy of me. He that taketh not his cross and followeth not after me is not worthy of me. He that findeth his life shall lose it; and he that loseth his life for my sake shall find it."' Cf. Luke 9:23–26.

537 The Ikhwān adopt a quasi-gnostic, quasi-Neoplatonic Sufi conceit: the soul is liberated by severing its attachment to everything in this world. Gnostics called

'Frankly, your Majesty, there are good people and bad in all creeds and sects. But the worst of the wicked are those with no faith in the Day of Reckoning — no hope of reward for good deeds or fear of requital for evil — who find no solace in the unity of the Creator, the All-Wise, All-Providing Author of life, and death, and resurrection — to whom we all return and in whom is our destiny.'

Chapter 40

Said the Indian spokesman: 'We children of Adam are the most multifarious of animals in number, in nations and kinds, types, varieties, and individuals.[538] Our distinction is our experience of the changing ages and diverse conditions of man, the varied regimes and aspirations, the wonders we have seen.'

'How so?' asked the King. 'Explain this.'

'Why, the inhabited quarter of the earth comprises some seventeen thousand cities, of numberless different nations.[539] Among these countless peoples are those of China, India, Sind, Zanj, the Ḥijāz and the Yemen, Abyssinia, the Nejd, Nubia, Egypt, Ṣaʿīd, Alexandria, Cyrenaica, Qayrawān, the Berber and Bedouin lands, Tangier, Britain, the Canary Islands, Andalusia, Rome, Constantinople, Killa, and Miyyāfārqīn. There are Bulgarians, Slavs, Russians, the people of Malaga and those of Bāb al-Abwāb, Azerbaijanis, Armenians, Damascenes, Greeks, the folk of the Diyārs, Iraq, Khūzistān, Jibāl, Jilān, Daylam, Ṭabaristān, Jurjān, Nishapur, Kirmān, the people of Iran, Makrān, Kābulistān, Multān, and Sijistān. There are the lands of Māh, Jordan, Tukhāristān,

---

the body the crypt of the soul, from which it can be freed only by renunciation. Plotinus summed up his ethical teaching in the words 'cut away everything'; Plotinus, *Enneads* V.3.17. In Neoplatonism, matter (the principle of otherness and privation) is the sole opposing polarity to God's oneness. So, freedom from matter assures entry to the divine Intellectual world. The Ikhwān allegorize *jihād* and paradise here, by reference to the soul's struggle for liberation through self-renunciation.

538 Here the claim to human unity is abandoned — not a sharp inconsistency. For, from a Neoplatonic standpoint, this world is riven by diversity, yet given stability by the unity imparted to its denizens from above. Human uniqueness, too, figures in the new argument, as the Indian spokesman mentions diversity not only of types but of individuals.

539 For further information on these cities and nations, see Appendix B.

Bāmiyān, Khatlān, Khurāsān, Transoxiana, and Khwārizm. There are the peoples of Chāch and Farghāna, Khāqān and Sīstān, and the lands of the Kirgiz, the Tibetans, and the dwellers in the Land of Gog and Magog[540] — not to mention the island and desert peoples, and those of coastal and mountain regions, nor the folk of villages and hamlets, nor the Arabs,[541] or Kurds,[542] the nomads of the deserts and wastes, and the people of the forests and jungles — all of whom are nations of humans, all of the race of Adam, of diverse colours and tongues, characters and natures, opinions and doctrines, crafts, ways of life and religions, of number known but to God, exalted be He, who created and raised them up, and provided their sustenance. *He knows their inmost being*, their *every lair and refuge — all in a book writ plain.*[543]

'Our vast numbers and divers conditions, our varied ways of life, and our marvellous projects show that we are superior, the noblest creatures on earth, better than all animals put together. These facts show that we are the masters and that all animals are our property — our slaves and chattels. We have a host of other virtues, varied distinctions too many to list. I've said what I had to say. God grant pardon to me and to you.'

Chapter 41

When the human had finished, the frog spoke up: 'Praised be God, great, sublime and supernal, exalted, revered, almighty, and forgiving, Creator of rivers flowing with sweet water and the rolling salt seas, vast and deep, with their tumultuous waves, a mine of pearls and

540 See Chapter 33, note 336 above.

541 Arabs in mediaeval texts are typically Bedouins, an impression confirmed here by their linkage with the nomadic Kurds. Cf. the figure of the Bedouin in Chapter 28.

542 The Kurds were known from antiquity and are thought of as tribal nomads in mediaeval sources. Mas'ūdī, ca. 943, just a few years before the Ikhwān put pen to paper, and the *Shahnameh,* somewhat later, make them out to be Iranians who escaped the tyranny of the legendary dragon king Ḍaḥḥāk (see Appendix C). There were several Kurdish dynasties in the first half millennium of Islam; and Saladin, the Sunni ruler of Egypt in the twelfth century, was perhaps history's most famous Kurd. But the Buwayhid rulers of the late tenth century were often engaged in battle with Kurdish insurgents.

543 Qur'an 47:26, 11:6.

coral. He it was who created in the dark depths of the sea-bed and the clashing waves of the sea all manner of creatures in all their diverse kinds — some with gigantic bodies and huge hulking frames, some clothed by their Maker in tough skins, or stiff, layered scales, or fine spiral shells.

'Some have many legs for creeping, others have wings for flying. Some have cavernous bellies, great heads, gaping maws, gleaming eyes, flaring jaws, shearing teeth, razor claws, vast gullets, muscled flanks, and long tails to swim fast and light. Others have small bodies, smooth skins, no tool or device, and little perception or movement — all for reasons and causes known ultimately only to Him who created and formed them, who reared them and cared for them, brought them to maturation, to their peak of development and final fulfilment. *He knows their every lair and refuge — all in a book writ plain*[544] — not for fear of error or lest He forget but for sheer clarity and lucidity.[545]

'Happy Majesty,' the frog continued, 'this human has mentioned the numbers, classes, and ranks of his fellows and bragged that these make them better than the animals. But if he saw the water animals and beheld their diverse forms and wondrous shapes, their exquisitely varied structures, he would be amazed, and all the diversity of human types that he cited, the many nations of Adamites that he says fill cities and towns on dry land, would seem paltry to him. For, the inhabited quarter of the earth has some fourteen great seas — the Mediterranean, the Caspian, the Red Sea, Persian Sea, Indian Ocean, Sindian Sea, the China Sea, the Sea of Gog and Magog, the Arabian Sea, the Western Sea, the Northern Sea, the Abyssinian, Southern, and Eastern Seas.

'In the inhabited quarter of the earth there are also some five hundred small rivers and some two hundred long rivers like the Oxus, the Tigris, the Euphrates, the Nile of Egypt, the rivers Kura and Aras in Azerbaijan, the Helmand in Sijistān, and other such great rivers, each 100–1,000 *farasangs* long.[546] And the lakes, ponds, streams, rivulets, and creeks, are without number! In every one of them live all sorts of

544 Qur'an 11:6.

545 The Book, as we've had occasion to note, is a symbol of the clarity of God's design, not a literal codex in the Kingdom of Heaven. See Chapter 19, note 248 above.

546 A *farasang* is roughly 3.5–4 miles (approximately 6 km). For example, the Nile is 4,180 miles (6,727 km) in length; the Helmand, about 715 miles (1,150 km).

fish, crabs, turtles, sea-serpents, swordfish, dolphins, crocodiles, and other species beyond tally or count, known but to the Creator of all. There are said to be seven hundred genera, to say nothing of species and individuals. And on land there are five hundred genera — not to mention species or individuals — of wild creatures, predators, beasts, cattle, creeping and swarming creatures, birds of prey, and wild and domestic fowl. All these are God's worshippers, His property, created by His power, formed by His wisdom, raised, sustained, and protected by Him. Nought of theirs is concealed from Him,[547] who *knows their every lair and refuge — all in a book writ plain.*[548]

'If you took thought and considered all I have told you, O human,' the frog concluded, 'you would realize and understand that your boasts of the multiplicity and diversity of the sons of Adam and their many kinds and classes are no proof at all that men are masters and others are their slaves.'

When the frog had finished speaking, a jinni sage said, 'One thing escapes you, O humans, ye children of Adam, and your earthly race too, O animals, with your gross, coarse, heavy bodies, your frames spread in three dimensions, whether you dwell on land or sea, or in the air. You overlook the many spiritual creatures, luminous wraiths, lithe spirits, subtle spectres, uncompounded souls and disembodied forms that dwell in the wide expanses between the storeys of the heavens and traverse the vast spirit world amidst the spheres — all sorts of angels, cherubs, and throne-bearers — all the fiery spirits in the globe of the aether, and all the nations of jinn and troops of demons, the ranks of Satan all together, who dwell in the sphere of the Zamharīr.

'If you of the human and animal kinds knew how many kinds of these creatures there are that are not bodies compounded of the elements or objects extended in the dimensions, if you knew how many species and diverse forms they have, and how widely even our individuals vary, why then the many genera and species and individuals of corporeal beings would seem small to you. For the sphere of the Zamharīr is more than ten times the measure of earth and sea. The sphere of the aether is more than ten times wider that of the Zamharīr.

547 Cf. Qur'an 69:18.
548 Qur'an 11:6.

The sphere of the moon is more than ten times the size of that entire globe. And in the same proportion is the sphere of Mercury to that of the moon. All seven concentric spheres are in the same ratio, up to the highest encompassing sphere. All this vast expanse[549] is filled through and through with spiritual creatures. Not a span is devoid of some kind of unearthly being, as the Prophet related, peace be upon him, when asked of God's words *None but He knows His hosts*:[550] "In all the seven heavens there is not a hand's breadth without some ministering angel, standing, bowing, or kneeling to God."[551]

'If you gave thought to what I have said, O human and animal kinds,' the jinni sage continued, 'you would realize that you are the least of all creatures in number and the lowest in standing and rank. Your vaunted numbers do not show that you are masters of others or that they are slaves to you. For all of us are slaves to God, exalted be He. We are His hosts and subjects, subject to one another by His

---

549 As the Harvard astronomer Owen Gingerich remarks, the scriptural cosmos seems small by comparison with that of late antiquity. The psalmist, at home in his world, compares the heavens to a tent. Genesis (1:6–8) speaks of a kind of pounded metallic roof. But 'In the five centuries between Aristotle and Ptolemy, other Greek philosophers had conceived ingenious methods to deduce not only the size of the Earth but even the distance to the moon, approximately 60 earth-radii away. . . . A clever but highly faulty scheme for getting a distance to the sun yielded a result of nineteen times farther than the moon, or (19 x 60 =) 1,140 earth radii. This number held sway until the end of the sixteenth century, well past the time of Copernicus. Working with this spurious dimension, approximately twenty times too small, Ptolemy and his successors carefully nested the mechanisms for the planets next to one another, finally placing the spherical shell of the fixed stars just beyond Saturn, to give a total distance of 20,000 earth radii from earth to sky.' Owen Gingerich, 'An Astronomical Perspective', in *How Large is God?*, ed. John Marks Templeton (Philadelphia: Templeton Foundation Press, 1997), p. 24. Robert Jastrow and Malcolm M. Thompson, in *Astronomy: Fundamentals and Frontiers* (New York: Wiley, 1972), explain that in the modern cosmos, if the sun is the size of an orange, the earth would be a grain of sand circling it at a distance of thirty feet, Jupiter would be a cherry-stone at two hundred feet; our galaxy would be a hundred billion oranges, averaging one thousand miles apart. And, as we now know, there are hundreds of billions of galaxies.

550 Qur'an 74:31.

551 This hadith, not included in the major collections, is meant to signify the plenitude of the Great Chain of Being, which dwarfs all sublunary creation. For the prostration of the celestial bodies, see Chapter 35, note 443 above.

wisdom's decree and the demands of His rule. His is the praise for that; and for all the rest of His blessings, praises abounding.'

When the jinni sage had finished speaking, the King said, 'We have heard your claims, O race of humans, and what you have gloried in, and you have heard the response. Have you anything to add beyond what you have mentioned? If so, present your proofs, adduce your arguments, elucidate your claims, and we shall heed them, if you speak truly.'

Chapter 42

At that, the orator from the Ḥijāz, from Mecca and Medina, rose and said, 'Yes, your Majesty. We have other virtues and distinctions which show that we are lords and that these animals are slaves to us and we are their masters and owners.'

'What are they?' asked the King.

'The promises our Lord gave us, that we of all living beings will be resurrected and raised up, brought forth from our graves and dealt our reckoning on the Day of Judgement, admitted by the Straight Path and entered into Paradise, the Lovely Garden, the Eternal Garden, the Garden of Eden, Garden of Sanctuary, the Realm of Peace and Abiding, Abode of the Faithful, the Tree of Beatitude, the Spring of Salsabīl, rivers of wine, of honey, of milk, and pure, sweet water, with tiered palaces and dark-eyed maidens to wife, and God close by, all-merciful, all-glorious, all-bountiful, and the scent of the breeze and the verdure, all described in the Qur'an in some seven hundred verses.[552] All this these animals lack, and it shows that we are the masters and they are our slaves. We have further distinctions too that would take too long to list. I have said my say. God grant pardon to me and to you.'

At this point the delegate of the birds, the nightingale, rose and said, 'Yes, as you say, O human. But bear in mind the rest of the promise, O humans — chastisement in the grave, the interrogation of Nakīr and Munkar,[553] the terrors of Judgement Day, the strict reckoning,

552 E.g., Qur'an 15:45–48, 37:40–49, 38:50–52.

553 Nakīr and Munkar are the angels that interrogate the dead in the grave and torment those who deserve chastisement. Qur'an 6:93, 8:52, 47:29, etc., allude to

the threat of the flames and torments of hell, the blazing hell-fire, the inferno, the furnace, the abyss, the Crush,[554] and the Pit,[555] shirts of pitch,[556] pus to drink, eating of the Tree of Zaqqūm,[557] the Master of Wrath standing by, Gatekeeper of the Fire, the demons at hand, Satan's massed hordes — all described in the Qur'an — for every verse of promise, another of warning and threat.[558] All this is for you, not for us. We are exempt. We have no promised reward, but we face no threat of retribution. We accept our Lord's judgement, neither for nor against us. He withheld the blessing of His promise but spared us the dread of His threat. So the evidence is balanced. You stand on equal footing with us and have no advantage to boast of.'

'How are we equal?' demanded the Ḥijāzī. 'How do we stand on a par, when we have among us prophets and their devisees,[559] imams, sages, poets[560] and paragons of goodness and virtue, saints and their seconds,[561] ascetics, pure and righteous figures, persons of piety,

---

these trials, but the angels are named in only one canonical hadith, in Tirmidhī, *Janā'iz*, Bāb 70. Muslim creeds stress the reality of the ordeal, reacting against the Muʿtazilites, who were castigated for not regarding such terrors concretely enough. See *Waṣiyat Abī Ḥanīfa* §§ 18–19, and *al-Fiqh al-akbar*, I, § 10 and II, § 23, in Wensinck, *Muslim Creed*, pp. 104, 129, 195–196; see also Wensinck's discussion, ibid., pp. 117–121, 163–178, 235–236; G. H. A. Juynboll, 'Munkar', *EI2*, vol. 7, pp. 576–577. The doctrine in brief: both believers and non-believers will be sat up in their tombs and asked what they think of Muhammad. The faithful will declare him God's Messenger and will be left in peace until the Resurrection. But sinners and infidels, unable to answer properly, will be beaten by the angels as long as God pleases — perhaps until Judgement Day. Al-Ghazālī includes a famous discussion of the interrogation in the *Iḥyā' ʿulūm al-dīn*; tr. T. J. Winter as *The Remembrance of Death and the Afterlife* (Cambridge: Islamic Texts Society, 1995), Book 40, pp. 135–147.

554 Qur'an 104:4–5.

555 Qur'an 101:9.

556 Qur'an 14:50.

557 Qur'an 37:60–64, 44:43–44, 56:52–53.

558 E.g., Qur'an 11:106–108, 22:20–24, 38:49–64.

559 The devisees (*awsiyā'*) of prophets are those whom God's messengers have appointed to carry forward their message. Both the term and the concept are redolent of Shiʿi theology. In Sunni theory, the saints (*awliyā*) are inheritors (*wārithūn*) of a given prophet's mission. But in Shiʿi thinking, the prophetic role is passed by inheritance, as it were, to a designated successor.

560 Note the inclusion of poets here, along with others who exercise holy responsibility.

561 The 'seconds' here, (*abdāl*) are a rank of saintly persons capable of rising to the

insight, understanding, awareness and vision, who are like the angels on high! They quest after the highest goods, yearn after their Lord, turn to Him in all things and ever hearken to Him. They look to Him, contemplate His greatness and splendour, trust Him in all things, beseech Him alone, seek Him alone, and hope in Him alone, since their care is His dread.'[562]

Then the animal delegates and jinni sages all said together, 'Ah humans, now at last you've come to the truth. You've spoken well and answered aright. For what you claim now is something indeed to take pride in. The deeds you cite are indeed worth performing. The lives and characters of these saintly persons, their manners and thoughts, the studies in which they are versed, are indeed worth vying for. But tell us, O humans, of the qualities and lives of these persons, inform us of their insights and ways, their virtues and godly doings, if you know aught of these. Enlighten us about these, if you can.'

The whole body fell silent, pondering the question. But no one had an answer.

Finally arose a learned, accomplished, worthy, keen, pious, and insightful man.[563] He was Persian by breeding, Arabian by faith, a *ḥanīf*

---

highest rung in the celestial hierarchy.

562 Montaigne qualifies his strictures on illusory physical beauty in a similar vein: 'This dissertation concerns only the common run of us, and is not so sacrilegious as to mean to include those divine, supernatural, and extraordinary beauties that we sometimes see shine among us like stars under a corporeal and terrestrial veil.' *Apology for Raymond Sebond*, in *Complete Essays*, II, 12, p. 357. The argument offered by the Ḥijāzī might not be clear at first blush. It belongs to an ancient topos, aimed at cynics and satirists: a group (or humankind at large) should not be judged by the worst but by the best among them. Compare Abraham's plea for the Cities of the Plain (Genesis 18), asking God to spare Sodom and Gomorrah for the sake of even a handful of righteous individuals who might be found among them: far be it from the Judge of all the earth to sweep away the righteous with the wicked. God agrees that the whole place should be spared for the sake of the righteous who live there. Their goodness does not exonerate the rest, but it does exclude a global condemnation. Even if one cannot say that all are corrupt, the rest might be worth preserving for the sake of those few.

563 The final speaker, a composite of the highest human attributes, carries the day, establishing human merit and superiority over the animals by appeal to the special status of saints in the order of creation. Animals and jinn alike recognize the wisdom and exemplary lives of these rare figures. Building on that acknowledgment, the final speaker points to the limitless and ineffable virtues of the saintly in language that would resonate with any audience, Jewish, Christian,

by confession,[564] Iraqi in culture, Hebrew in lore, Christian in manner, Damascene in devotion, Greek in science, Indian in discernment, Sufi in intimations,[565] regal in character, masterful in thought, and divine in awareness. 'Praised be God, Lord of all worlds,' he said, 'Destiny of the faithful, and foe to none but the unjust. God bless the Seal of Prophets, foremost of God's messengers, Muhammad, God's elect, and all his worthy house and good nation.

'Yes, just Majesty and assembled hosts', he began. 'These saints of God are the flower of creation, the best, the purest, persons of fair and praiseworthy parts, pious deeds, myriad sciences, godly awareness,

---

Shi'i, or Sunni, or, as the Ikhwān reckon, with any sound and upright human creed or culture. Early in the Shi'i tradition the perfect man was identified with the imams whose very existence justified and sustained creation; see M. Amir-Moezzi, *The Divine Guide in Early Shi'ism*, tr. D. Streight (Albany, NY: SUNY Press, 1994), pp. 99, 125. Among the Sunnis, a similar role was given to the loftiest saints of each era; see R. McGregor, *Sanctity and Mysticism in Medieval Egypt* (Albany, NY: SUNY Press, 2004), pp. 24–26, 107–117, 147–155. Here, however, the ideal man here is more than a figure of eschatology or fixture in the pleroma but a real person. Consummating the history of creation, 'the perfect man who has realized his Divine Origin', as Nasr writes (*Islamic Cosmological Doctrines*, p. 73), and all those who fulfil mankind's angel-like potential, justify, by the lives they lead, man's dominion over nature. Lofty as these characters may be, and critical as their lives are to human claims of excellence, it is the final irony in the case of the animals versus man that none of the many eloquent and thoughtful speakers present can adequately describe them. Yet the clear moral message is that human life itself is given its true purpose by taking up their path in pursuit of perfection.

564 A pure, generic monotheism in the spirit and tradition of Abraham; see Qur'an 3:95, 2:135. The Ikhwān preserve the cosmopolitan outlook they have cultivated throughout the essay, careful, here at least, to avoid giving colour to Islamic exclusivism or triumphalism.

565 'Intimations' (*ishārāt*) are the esoteric hints characteristic of Sufi thought, which fights shy of overt reference to its monistic thrust but (like other mystical traditions) often finds little resonance for its interests in the plain sense of a scriptural passage. Following a distinction ascribed to Ja'far al-Ṣādiq, Sahl al-Tustarī distinguishes the *'ibāra* ('lesson') of a verse taken at face value and open to the common man, from the *ishāra* (its allegorical allusion), the special province of the mystic elite (*khawāṣṣ*). See Gerhardt Böwering, *The Mystical Vision of Existence in Classical Islam: The Qur'anic Hermeneutics of the Sufi Sahl al-Tustari* (New York: de Gruyter, 1980), p. 141. By the time of the Ikhwān, this idea of *ishārāt* was well established in mainstream Sufism, represented, for example in the manual of al-Kalābādhī, *Kitāb al-Ta'arruf li-madhhab ahl 'l-taṣawwuf*, tr. Arberry, p. 76. Not long after the Ikhwān wrote, Avicenna fused the Sufi hermeneutical approach with his own Neoplatonic philosophy in his *Kitāb al-Ishārāt wa'l-tanbīhāt*.

regal character, just and holy lives, and awesome ways. Fluent tongues weary to name their qualities, and no one has adequately described their inmost core. Many have cited their virtues, and preachers in public assemblies have devoted their lives down through the ages to sermons dilating on their merits and their godly ways, without ever reaching the pith of the matter.'[566]

****

We have now laid out our story in fifty-one epistles[567] as clearly and concisely as possible, and this essay is one of them. God grant you success, dear brothers, in reading and grasping it fully. May He open your hearts, lay wide your breasts, and enlighten your eyes with the inner meaning of these words, and smooth the way for you to put these thoughts into practice, as He has done with His pure, holy, and devoted saints. For He has the power to effect what He will.

566 The modern printed editions of the Arabic text fill out the story here, as if to compensate for the seeming abruptness and surprising turn of the last few pages. The Ziriklī, Tāmir, and Bustānī editions add the following:

> And how did the just King rule on the claims of these human strangers, and their responses to the counter-claims of the animals? His order was that all of the animals were to be subject to the commands and prohibitions of the humans and remain subject to them until a new age had dawned. But then they would have a new fate. At this, one of the King's attendants rose and announced, 'You have heard, O animals, the explanations of these humans and you have conceded the that their arguments are sound. You have acknowledged that you are satisfied. So retire and return under God's protection and safe conduct.'
>
> ***************
>
> Know, dear brother, that we have now attained our object in this essay. Don't think the less of us, as if this were just a fairytale, some childish story that we brethren have told to entertain ourselves. Our choice of language and our indirect modes of expression may have veiled the truths we wished to convey. But this was only to prevent our losing sight of our true target.

567 The numbering of the epistles differs from one manuscript to another, based on discrepancies regarding the classification of the sciences; in some manuscripts, the total number of epistles is fifty-two, which corresponds with the enumeration in this present series.

He hears every prayer. He is our bounteous lot and most generous counsel. Blessings upon God's chosen Prophet, Muhammad, and all his House together.

Appendix A: Authorities Cited

ʿAbbās ibn al-Muṭṭālib (d. ca. 653)
Abū Tammām (804 or 806–845 or 846)
Aesop (6th century BCE)
Alfonso X of Castile (1221–1284)
Apion (fl. ca. 40)
Ardashir (ca. 226)
Aristotle (384–322 BCE)
al-Ashʿarī (d. 935)
ʿAṭṭār (d. 1229)
Baradaeus, Jacob (fl. 541)
al-Baqlī, Rūzbihān (d. 1209)
al-Bīrūnī (d. post 1050)
al-Bisṭāmī (d. 875)
Damascius (d. 553)
al-Fārābī (d. 950)
al-Farghānī (Alfraganus, 9th century)
Ḥunayn ibn Isḥāq (ca. 809–877)
Ibn ʿArabī (1165–1240)
ibn Ḥanbal, Aḥmad (d. 855)
ibn al-Jawzī, Abū al-Faraj (d. 1201)
Ibn Karrām (d. 869)
Ibn al-Munayyir (1223–1284)
Ibn al-Muqaffaʿ (ca. 720–ca.756)
ibn Naqīb al-Miṣrī, Aḥmad (d. 1368)
Ibn Ṭufayl (ca. 1100–1185)

al-Jāḥiẓ (ca. 776–868)

al-Junayd (d. 910)

al-Kalābādhī, Abū Bakr (d. ca. 990)

al-Khwārizmī (ca. 780–ca. 850)

al-Māwardī (974–1058)

al-Muḥāsibī (d. 857)

Mullā Ṣadrā (1571/2–1640)

Nābigha al-Dhubyānī (fl. ca. 570–600)

Nestorius (ca. 386–ca. 451)

Niẓām al-Mulk (1018–1092)

Paul of Aegina (ca. 625–ca. 690)

Plato (429–347 BCE)

Plotinus (205–270)

Proclus (410–485)

Sergius of Resh ʿAyn (d. 536)

Simplicius (ca. 490–ca. 560)

Suhrawardī (1145–1234)

al-Ṭabarsī (d. 1153)

Thābit ibn Qurra (ca. 826–901)

Themistius (ca. 317–ca. 387)

al-Tirmidhī, al-Ḥākim (d. ca. 937)

al-Tustarī, Sahl (ca. 818–896)

Yaḥyā ibn ʿAdī (ca. 893–974)

al-Zamakhsharī (1075–1144)

Appendix B: Geographical Regions

The Ikhwān look out upon a vast geography. Their world to the east is bordered by China and the Indian Ocean. To the north, their horizon extends to Russia and even Britain, its western extreme marked by the Canary Islands. In Chapter 40 of our story, the Indian spokesman offers a wide-ranging overview of the lands and peoples of the world known to the Ikhwān. Clearly, they take pride in its scope. The following comments, roughly following northern and southern trade routes from east to west, situate the places and peoples mentioned in the Indian's speech.

Sind, a large region of the northern Indian subcontinent centred in the Indus delta, is today a province of Pakistan bounded in the north by Baluchistan and Punjab, to the east and south by India, and in the southwest by the Arabian Sea. **Zanj** is the East African coastal region now known as Tanzania and including the archipelago of Zanzibar. The presence of Arabian and Iranian Muslim trading communities on Zanzibar dates from the turn of the twelfth century.

The **Ḥijāz** is the arid western steppe of Arabia. Its principal cities are Mecca and Medina and the Red Sea port of Jidda. The **Nejd** is the central Arabian highland. **Yemen**, further south in the Arabian peninsula, was home to the ancient Sabaeans, the people of the legendary Queen of Sheba. Their language, Old South Arabic, gave rise to the Ethiopian tongue known as Ge'ez, and to classical Arabic. **Abyssinia**, Ethiopia, faces Arabia across the Red Sea. Ruled by Christian kings from early times, it was celebrated in Islamic tradition for providing asylum to some of Muhammad's earliest followers.

Nubia, today known as Sudan, lies to the south of Egypt and north of Abyssinia. A Christian kingdom in the early Muslim era, it was increasingly Islamized in the Middle Ages. **Ṣaʿīd** in Upper Egypt is the region of the city of Aswan, the ancient Syene, named after an ancient Egyptian goddess. Located opposite the Byzantine settlement of Elephantine, at the first cataract of the Nile (site of the modern High Dam), the city is not far from the Tropic of Cancer, at about the twenty-fourth parallel of latitude, and was thought to be the place at which the sun would cast no shadow at the summer solstice. In the third century, the Greek scientist Eratosthenes used measurements taken there to refute the notion of a flat earth and to estimate the circumference of the globe. **Alexandria**, the Egyptian entrepôt on the western Nile delta, was the world's second greatest city in the Ptolemaic age and long a centre of inter-cultural exchange. It was founded by Alexander the Great in 332 BCE, and conquered by the Arabs almost a thousand years later, in 642. Still a centre of scientific and philosophical learning, it was an important source of the varieties of knowledge that the Ikhwān most prized. The story told by a thirteenth-century Arab author that the caliph ʿUmar ordered the burning of its famous library is now thought to be apocryphal. Indeed, the lighthouse on the island of Pharos, marking the entry to Alexandria's harbour and celebrated as one of the Seven Wonders of the Ancient World, survived the Islamic conquest, and was carefully described two centuries after the time of the Ikhwān. It later crumbled in earthquakes.

Cyrenaica was an ancient North African province in what is now eastern Libya. Socrates' friend Aristippus came from the capital city of Cyrene, and the notoriously sybaritic school of philosophy founded by him and continued by a grandson of the same name preserves the designation 'Cyrenaic'. **Qayrawān**, a major city and religious centre in the time of the Ikhwān, lies about 160 km south of Tunis. It was the home of the Jewish philosopher, physician, and centenarian Isaac Israeli (855–955). The **Berbers** are the indigenous people of North Africa, converted to Islam after the Muslim conquest of the seventh century. Although they adopted Arabic, they preserve their own language, culture, and ethnic identity. **Tangier** ('Ṭanja' in Arabic, a name probably of Berber origin) is a port city facing the Strait of Gibraltar at the western extreme of the Mediterranean. Founded in the seventh century BCE, it has seen Phoenicians, Carthaginians, Romans, Vandals, Portuguese, Spanish, and English denizens. Governed after the Muslim conquest by a Berber Muslim officer, Ṭāriq ibn Ziyād, after whom the Strait of Gibraltar (Jabal Ṭāriq) is named, it became a key North African city in the conquest of Spain. The **Canary Islands** (al-Khālidāt), now belonging to Spain, are situated near northwest Africa and were once thought of as the western limit of the habitable world.

Andalusia, Muslim Spain, under Islamic rule from the conquest of 711 to the completion of the Reconquista in 1492, was a region synonymous with high literary culture and scientific achievement among Muslims. Hebrew and Judaeo-Arabic culture blossomed there as well in the time of the Ikhwān, under the aegis of Hasdai ben Shaprut (ca. 915–970 or 990). Within Andalusia, **Malaga**, on the southern coast of the Iberian peninsula, west of Granada, south of Cordoba, and east of Gibraltar, was known for its trade, its fine produce, and handsome mosques.

Killa (or Kalla) was perhaps a Southeast Asian port on the Malay Peninsula at the Strait of Malacca; or the name may refer to a port in Ceylon. **Multān,** in the Punjab, the region defined by the five great tributaries of the Indus, was invaded by the Arabs in 711–714. A centre of Islamic hegemony and commerce in western India, it was called the 'Gateway to the House of Gold' by the conquerors. It was the first and most prominent city in which Hindus were treated as *dhimmīs*, and its temple, long a Hindu pilgrimage site, paid much of its income to the new rulers to secure its toleration, until it was finally destroyed by an Ismaili *dāʿī* in the time of the Ikhwān. Multān's days as an independent Shiʿi enclave in the long shadow of the Fāṭimid regime in Cairo came to an end when Maḥmūd of Ghaznā reduced the province. His son's unsuccessful rebellion against a brother in 1031 led to the extinguishing of Ismaili allegiance in Multān.

Rūs, or Rūsiyya, refers to the people of Russia, Ukraine, and Belarus. The Ikhwān's citation is a very early mention of them in an Arabic source. Jilān, although protected from land invasions by the mountains behind it, was raided by Rūs from the Caspian in 913–914. The marauders were pretty clearly Slavs, although the name was also applied to Vikings in the Islamic West. Rūs attacked Byzantine Constantinople, probably from Kiev, in 860. A century later, in the time of the Ikhwān, it was the Rūs, incited by the Byzantines, who defeated and dispersed the Khazars (a Turkic people, and their former allies), many of whom had converted to Judaism in the eighth and ninth centuries and who, at the height of their power, controlled the lower Volga, the Caspian coast, and the Crimea.

Bāb al-Abwāb (literally 'Gate of Gates') was a fortified city and harbour on the western shore of the Caspian, at the eastern margin of the Caucasus, in the Persian province of Derband. Masʿūdī notes the fine black fox pelts from the Volga that were traded there. The city remained Persian rather than Arab in character, and there was fighting with Russian raiders in the area not long after the time of the Ikhwān.

Azerbaijan, west and southwest of the Caspian and northeast of Iraq, was named for the general Atropates, who declared his independence from Alexander the Great in 328 BCE. It was ruled by a Sāsānian frontier commander until the Islamic conquest some twenty years after the Hijra. The treaty of surrender specified that the polyglot, largely Iranian populace would not be enslaved, that the fire temples would be respected, and Kurdish marauders held at bay. After various revolts, the region came under the sway of Daylamites of Ismaili persuasion; it was taken over by Kurdish dynasts not long after the Ikhwān composed their *Rasāʾil*.

Armenia, northwest of Azerbaijan, between the Caspian and the Black Sea, is hemmed in by the Pontic mountains to the north and the Taurus range to the south. Its highlands hold the headwaters of the Tigris and Euphrates. Mount Ararat, the volcanic peak that is the traditional landing place of Noah's ark, rises to nearly 17,000 feet in today's Turkey, but it is in sight of Yerevan, and its stately presence has long inspired Armenians. Severe in climate and cut up by its mountain ranges into well-watered basins whose denizens were not readily united, Armenia was a vassal to the Medes and then the Persians and Parthians, Romans, Sāsānians, and Byzantines. Christianity came in the late third century, and some of the works of Philo, the Alexandrian Jewish philosopher admired by early Christian thinkers, survive only in Armenian translation. Inured to long resistance against Persian Zoroastrian overlords, the Armenians never accepted Islam, despite the Arab raids, incursions, and occupations of the mid-seventh century, and the long periods of Arab domination and battles for control with the Byzantines and with one another down to the time of the Ikhwān.

The **Diyārs**, or tribal realms, were parts of upper Mesopotamia: Diyār Rabīʿa, the territory of the Rabīʿa tribe along the Tigris; Diyār Muḍar, that of the Muḍar tribe along the Euphrates; and Diyār Bakr in the upper basin of the Tigris near Armenia, home of the Bakr branch of Rabīʿa. Arab tribal elements had moved into Mesopotamia even before the coming of Islam, but the regions known as the Diyārs were established more formally and settled more systematically by Muʿāwiya (who later became caliph), when he was serving as governor of the region soon after the Muslim conquest in the caliphate of ʿUthmān. **Miyyāfārqīn**, also known as Silvan, is a chief town of Diyār Bakr.

Khūzistān, a province of southwest Iran at the northern end of the Persian Gulf, is the ancient Elam; it was later ruled from the biblical city of Susa. Its present capital is Ahwāz, and its people are Arab and/or Persian. Low-lying, hot, and humid, exposed to desert winds from Syria and Arabia, Khūzistān was known as an unhealthful land, although the perfume made there from local violet blossoms was highly prized. Despite its drawbacks, Khūzistān was always well watered and thought of as prosperous. It was the bread-basket of the Achaemenid empire, and its grain and barley harvest gave yields along the lines reflected in the lark's sermon, as promised in the Qur'an.

Jibāl, or ʿIrāq ʿAjamī ('Persian Iraq'), is, as its Arabic name implies, a mountainous region. Bounded in the east by the Great Desert of Khurāsān, it lies north of Fārs (Persia proper) and Khūzistān. To the west is 'Arabian Iraq', and to the north, the Elburz Mountains that ring the southern Caspian. The area can be cold and snowy, especially in the rugged mountains of the northeast. Isfahan is its best known city.

Māh, Arabic for 'Media', was a term applied to an area whose revenues supported a city after the Arab conquest. Both Basra and Kūfa had a Māh sustaining the garrison city of the Muslim conquerors. Māh al-Kūfa was Dīnawar in Jibāl. The Māh of Basra, which the Ikhwān probably intend here, was the district of Nihāwand, which fell to the

Muslims in 642. The name is inscribed on its coinage as early as the late seventh century.

Jilān (or Gilān), the warm, humid region southwest of the Caspian and west of Ṭabaristān, lies in the delta of the Safīd-rud. The name Jilān derives from that of its early inhabitants, the Gel people. In Islamic times, Jilānīs raised rice and silkworms and were known for their short trousers and their wooden homes with verandas built from the lumber of the rich forests of the province. **Daylam** lies in the Elburz highlands above Jilān on the Caspian, which Arab sources call the Sea of Daylam. Warlike Daylamite tribes from the valley of the Shāh-rud, a tributary of the Jilān River, were drawn to the fertile plains from antiquity, and in 945 Daylamite troops captured Baghdad and established the Būyid (Buwayhid) dynasty, which largely controlled the caliphate in the time of the Ikhwān. **Ṭabaristān**, the narrow littoral plain between the south coast of the Caspian and the Elburz mountains, was called Māzandarān after the Mongol conquests. Its old name derives from the axe (*tabar*) wielded by its woodsmen. A large Zoroastrian population still lived there in the twelfth century.

The city of **Jurjān**, now more commonly known as Astarābādh, lies about 50 km east of the southern tip of the Caspian. Watered by the Atrak and Gurgān rivers, its province is fertile but feverish. A marchland of the Sāsānids against incursions by nomads from the northern steppes, by the time of the Ikhwān it was a prosperous silk centre and a way station on the caravan route to Russia. Long receptive to ʿAlid emissaries, Gurgān, as it was also called, was ruled with Daylamite support by nominal vassals of the Sāmānids. The city lay in ruins after the thirteenth-century massacres perpetrated by the Mongols, and the province never recovered. **Nishapur** (meaning 'Fair Shāpūr' in Fārsī, after its presumed founder, Shāpūr I), a key city of Khurāsān, is sometimes honorifically called Iranshahr. It was wrested from the Persians in 652 by the Muslim governor of Basra, and succeeded Marw as the Muslim capital of Khurāsān in the mid-ninth century. Its fine climate, prized textiles, and active industries made it a cultural and commercial centre under the rule of the Sāmānids in the time of the Ikhwān.

Kirmān is the Iranian city in the highlands southwest of the Persian desert (Dasht-i-Lūt), and the province extending down to the coastal plain at the Strait of Hormuz. To the north lie Yazd and Khurāsān; to the east, Makrān and Sīstān. The fertile uplands include orchards, fields, and streams; and the region was known for its grains and fruits, sugar and dates, as well as its sheep, goats, and beasts of burden. Before the Muslim conquests of 638–649, Zoroastrians mingled with Nestorian Christians in the region, and conversion to Islam proceeded very slowly thereafter. Protected by the desert, dissidents, including Azraqite Khārijites, thrived in the region, and both the Sāmānids in the tenth century and the Ghaznavids in the eleventh sought to wrest it from Būyid suzerainty, before it fell under the control of the Seljuqs. **Makrān** is the rather arid region southeast of Kirmān, running through Iran toward Sind, along the Arabian Sea. Today, it lies half in Iran and half in Pakistan. Alexander the Great passed this way on returning from the Indus valley in 325 BCE, and the area was raided by Arabs during the caliphate of ʿUmar and Islamized thereafter; but it was considered a poor and lightly populated area, best known for its cane syrup and coastal fishing, so its history tended to be something of a footnote to that of Kirmān.

Kābulistān, the province of Kabul, capital of modern day Afghanistan, centres on the Kabul River, between Bāmiyān in the west and Lamghān in the east. Generally viewed as lying north of Multān, Ghaznā, and Zābulistān, its well-watered highland plains were of commercial and strategic importance, since it was nestled between the Hindu Kush in the southwest and the Pamir mountains to the northeast. Part of the Hellenized Bactrian states system of the post-Alexander era, the region was dominated by tribal peoples from the steppes in early Christian times. Its people were Buddhist or Hindu before the Muslim conquest. They resisted Arab domination until the ninth century and were not Islamized to any great extent until the time of the Ikhwān.

Sijistān (or Sīstān) in eastern Persia, south of Khurāsān and north of Balūchistān and Makran, draws its name from an ancient Scythian people. In his epic, the *Shahnameh*, Firdawsī calls it Nīmrūz, or 'midday'. Its basin-like topography, severe winds from May to October, shifting river courses, and alluvial soil allowed cultivation of winter wheat, barley, and legumes; but windstorms, erosion, insect pests, and vipers made the land a kind of object lesson as to the fragility of human hopes. Many of the Tajiks and Balūchīs of Sīstān even today hunt and fish from reed rafts on its lakes and marshes. Although the area was conquered by Arabs in the seventh century, Zoroastrian fire temples seem to have remained active even in the time of the Ikhwān.

Jordan has been known since biblical times for its river, which is the world's lowest, and whose shallow, unnavigable, readily forded waters spring (with much seasonal fluctuation) from the foothills of Mount Hermon into the long, malarial papyrus swamp of the Huleh depression, and then (with many a meander and treacherous current) into the Sea of Galilee, and finally to the Dead Sea. **Petra** (originally 'Rekem') in today's Kingdom of Jordan, is named in the Dead Sea Scrolls, and by Josephus, Eusebius, and Jerome. Associated with the biblical Mount Seir, home of the Edomites, it was the ancient Nabataean capital, thriving with the aid of a man-made oasis that used cisterns and conduits to control the flash floods. The trinity of Nabataean goddesses, Allāt, Manāt, and al-ʿUzza are acknowledged in the famous cancelled verses of the Qur'an (53:19–22; cf. 17:73–75, 22:52–53, and 2:100). The most prominent of Petra's brilliant ruins described by Johann Burckhardt in 1812, 'a rose-red city half as old as time', as one sonneteer called it, date from a Hellenizing era in the first century BCE. **Palmyra**, a commercial rival to Petra, is the ancient Tadmor. Located some 215 km northeast of Damascus, it was a significant caravan city from earliest times until the sixteenth century. It rebelled against Rome in the reign of Zenobia (Zaynab, fl. 240–274), whose forces conquered Egypt and expelled its Roman prefect. On the defeat of her armies, the audacious queen was brought to Rome in golden chains, granted a luxurious villa in Tibur (Tivoli), and became a prominent philosopher and socialite. The land to the east of the Jordan prospered as a Byzantine province under their Ghassānid vassals in the sixth century. Held by the Sāsānids for a time, it was conquered decisively by Muslim forces at the Yarmūk in 636. The Umayyad rulers built prominent desert castles in the region, and the ʿAbbāsid revolt of 750 was planned in the area, but it fell into neglect as the interests of the new dynasts shifted eastward. By the time of the Ikhwān, Jordan lay in the sphere of Egyptian rulers, including, at times, the Fāṭimids.

Tukhāristān, the former Bactria, follows the Oxus through today's Afghanistan, Turkmenistan, Uzbekistan, and Kyrgyzstan. Balkh was its capital. The Arab conquest here was long and difficult, beginning with raids seeking a bulwark against the formidable Hephthalite and Chinese allies called upon by the son of the defeated Sāsānid emperor Yazdijird. The region was more or less secured only after the Muslim governor of Khurāsān treacherously slew a key local ruler. But other local leaders continued to seek aid against Muslim hegemony even after their Chinese allies suffered a decisive defeat at Talas in 751. **Khatlān** is a south-western province in what is today Kyrgyzstan. **Bāmiyān** is a city and province of Afghanistan, in the Hindu Kush, some 8,500 feet above sea level, between the watersheds of the Oxus and the Indus. Long a major Buddhist centre and pilgrimage site, Bāmiyān is well known today after the destruction of its two monumental Buddhas by the Taliban regime in March of 2001. In the ʿAbbāsid era, Bāmiyān dynasts held prominent positions at the caliphal court in Baghdad, but the standing of their house was sapped by the rise of the Ghaznavids. Under the Ghūrids in the twelfth century, Bāmiyān became the capital of Tukhāristān. The Mongols razed the town in 1221, but a modern settlement survived at the foot of the cliff into which the two great Buddhas were carved.

Khurāsān, one of the four great provincial satrapies of the Sāsānian empire, was ruled from Marw, where Yazdijird III made his last stand. Betrayed to the Muslim invaders by his *marzban*, that is, his march warden or military governor, he was murdered in 651. Even after the Arab conquests, many local rulers were kept in office on payment of tribute to the conquerors. But there were frequent rebellions, first of non-Muslim potentates and pretenders who sought Hephthalite, Turkic, or Chinese aid against Arab domination, and later by tribal factions among the Islamized population of mingled Arab and Persian origins. Khurāsān was the power base of the ʿAbbāsid revolution, and it prospered under their Tāhirid vassals, exporting luxury goods, Turkic slaves, and talented personnel to Iraq. Among the migrants were the famous Barmecid family of viziers. The Saffārid rulers, who ousted the

Tāhirids, were themselves overthrown by the Sāmānids, whose orderly and effective rule was widely appreciated in the time of the Ikhwān; see also Chapter 20, p. 219 and note 265 above. **Transoxiana** is called Mā Warā'a al-Nahr in Arabic, meaning 'What Lies Beyond the River' (beyond the Oxus, or Āmū Daryā, and extending to the Syr Daryā, or Jaxartes, both of which flow into the Aral Sea). Bukhara and Samarqand were its great cities. Hellenized after the conquests of Alexander, the land was called Soghdiana by the Achaemenids, a name kept alive by the Sāsānians, under whom the traffic of the Silk Road gave it prosperity. For Firdawsī the Oxus marked the boundary between Iran and Tūrān. The region became a fountainhead of the revival of Persian culture under the Sāmānids.

Khwārizm, called Khīva after the Mongol invasions, is the lowland watershed of the Āmū Daryā and its intricate and fertile delta south of the Aral Sea. Located on the ancient Silk Road in today's Uzbekistan, Khwārizm may have been the land of origin of the Gāthās, the oldest part of the Avesta; its blue stones decorated the palace of Darius at Susa. In 328 BCE, Alexander the Great declined an alliance with the Chorasmian king, as he is called in the Greek sources, who claimed power extending to Colchis and the Black Sea. The land seems to have remained independent during the Arsacid and Seleucid eras but was absorbed into the Persian empire by the Sāsānids. The polymath genius al-Bīrūnī (d. post 1050) took special pride in Khwārizm, since it was his homeland. It fell to the Arabs in 712, who slew its king and, Bīrūnī writes, massacred all who knew its ancient script and traditions. Still resistance continued for decades, and the Khwārizmian language continued to find uses for several centuries, particularly in Buddhist and Manichaean texts, written in an alphabet of Aramaic origin. Among notable Khwārizmian thinkers were the great Muʿtazilite exegete and philologist al-Zamakhsharī (1075–1144), whose love of Arabic made him a vehement adversary of the Shuʿūbiyya, despite his Iranian descent; and al-Khwārizmī (ca. 780–ca. 850), whose surname, reflecting his origins, was bequeathed to the world in the word 'algorithm', crediting his work in founding algebra, the branch of mathematics whose name derives from one portion of his work.

Chāch is today's Tashkent, the capital of Uzbekistan, its current name first attested by Bīrūnī. Controlled by Turkic tribal leaders in antiquity and known to Chinese sources as early as the third century, Chāch was conquered by Muslim forces after they severely defeated its Chinese overlords in 751. ʿAbbāsid rulers built a wall there against Turkic raiders, but the city fell under Turkic control for a time in the early ninth century. It then came under the rule of Sāmānids. The Syr Daryā in the heart of the region was often called the River of Chāch. Muslim geographers describe the district as wide, rich, well irrigated, and filled with eager fighters for the faith, many of them archers.

Farghāna, a city and the surrounding valley of the Syr Daryā nestled beneath spurs of the Tien Shan Mountains, is populous and well supplied with water from the surrounding highlands. The district was mentioned in Chinese sources as early as 128 BCE. Chinese and Turkic powers fought with local Iranian and Soghdian rulers for control, and both Umayyad and ʿAbbāsid rulers sought to conquer the rich valley, despite continued Chinese pressure and much resistance to Islam. Many Soghdians moved east, and in the end it was under Sāmānid rule that a firm Islamic government was established in the time of the Ikhwān, when the region's prosperity only grew. In the surrounding mountains there were gold, silver, coal, iron, copper, lead, turquoises, and sal-ammoniac for medicinal use, and the area was a prolific exporter of swords and armour, textiles, and Turkic slaves. An inscription from 1041 shows dates in Sāsānian, Christian, and Muslim style, indicating the still polyglot and commercial character of the area in the time of the Ikhwān.

Khāqān is not a region but a title, Khagan, used by Turkic leaders and applied by Muslim writers to the leaders of Turkic confederations. The **Kyrgyz** (or Kirgiz), a Turkic people mentioned in Chinese narratives as early as the second century, came from the upper Yenisei valley in Siberia and conquered the Uigurs in Mongolia to the south in 840. The red hair, fair skin, and blue eyes, described in early sources, were thought by mediaeval Muslim writers to indicate a connection with Slavic populations. These features have now disappeared, but the connection is confirmed by DNA comparisons with Poles, Ukrainians, and Icelanders, as well as Tajiks. After the Mongol conquests the Kyrgyz moved further south. Today's Kyrgyzstan lies in the Tien Shan Mountains, south of Kazakhstan, east of Uzbekistan, northeast of Tajikistan, and northwest of the Chinese border, but there are Kyrgyz minorities in Afghanistan, western China, and eastern Turkey.

Muslims first encountered **Tibetans** during the conquest of Transoxiana, when Tibetans fought alongside Hephthalite and Turkic forces. The caliph ʿUmar II (r. 717–720) was said to have received a Tibetan embassy requesting the dispatch of teachers of Islam; and an idol on a golden throne was reportedly sent to Khurāsān by a Tibetan king, in token of his renunciation of paganism in the time of Maʾmūn (r. 813–833). 'Tibet' here would be 'Little Tibet', south of the Karakorum Mountains. Tibetans living between Badakhshān and the upper Oxus levied a steep duty on goods moving through the high pass that bore the risk of mountain sickness but also gave access to Tibet proper and the precious musk of its mountain gazelles.

Appendix C: Iranian Kings and Heroes of History and Legend

Afrāsiyāb
The king of Tūrān and enemy of Iran, killed in Azerbaijan by his grandson Kay Khusraw.

Afrīdūn (Farīdūn)
Son of Ābtīn, a descendant of Jamshīd, he had three sons, Salm, Tūr, and Īraj, among whom he divided his kingdom. The jealous Tūr and Salm killed their brother Īraj, but before his death Afrīdūn enthroned Īraj's son Manūjahr as king over them all. Afrīdūn is known in Persian as Feraydun, modelled on the Thraetaona of the Avesta, or Thraitana in Sanskrit (see 'Farīdūn', *EI2*, vol. 2, p. 798; E. G. Browne, *A Literary History of Persia*, vol. 1, pp. 114–115). As a hero in the *Shahnameh,* he is nursed by a magical cow and reared by a holy man atop Mount Alburz. Supported by the oppressed folk of Iran, inspired by his mother, and instructed by an angel, he grows to a godly youth who defeats the demon armies of the Arab tyrant Ḍaḥḥāk, who slew his father and seized the throne of Iran when its great king Jamshīd lost his power through a tragic moment of hubris. Having subdued the monstrous Ḍaḥḥāk and chained him to mount Damavand, the mighty peak seen to the northeast of today's Tehran, Afrīdūn reigned wisely and well for five hundred years.

Anūshirwān (Khusraw I, or Chosroes I)
The twentieth Sāsānid king (r. 531–579), he presided over the dynasty's golden age, trading across the Indian Ocean with lands as far as Vietnam and China, promoting scholarship, the arts, commerce, agriculture, and industry. Anūshirwān sponsored the codification of the Avesta, the Zoroastrian scriptures, but was tolerant of a variety of faiths and hosted philosophers from the East and the West, including Simplicius and Damascius, whom Justinian had banned from teaching philosophy at Athens when he closed Plato's Academy in 529. Kisra, as he was called in Arabic, personified the Iranian monarchy in the eyes of Muslim writers, who looked back on his capital at Ctesiphon (Madā'in) as the epitome of luxury, fine food, polished manners — and despotism. Muslim traditions fondly contrasted the emperor's pomp with Muhammad's modesty and pictured him tearing up the Prophet's invitation to embrace Islam. Militant traditions promised to bring down both Kisra and Qaysar, that is, both shah and Caesar, the rulers of Byzantine Rome and Sāsānid Persia.

Ardashīr son of Bābakān (Artaxerxes)
Founder of the Sāsānid dynasty (r. 224–241), he defeated his brother to gain control of a vassal kingdom in Parthia, conquered both Persia and Parthia, and declared himself Shāhanshāh ('King of Kings'), even claiming divine descent. Expanding his empire into Sistān, Khurāsān, Balkh, Khwārizm, Bahrain, Mosul, and what is today Turkmenistan, he centralized state authority and established a state-sponsored version of Zoroastrianism, centred in fire temples, and canonized in a new text of the Avesta for his time. Maintaining his power base in Fārs, Ardashīr built a capital at Ctesiphon, on the Tigris, and rebuilt Seleucia on the opposite bank, a city the Romans had destroyed. He ended his reign in years of battle for Mesopotamia against Rome and her Armenian allies. Pāpak (the name Bābakān is given in Pahlavi) was a warrior king; and Ardashīr, although called his son in later sources, was actually the son of his son-in-law, Sāsān, whom Pāpak had recognized as a descendant of the last Achaemenid king.

Bahmān
Persian hero, the son of Isfandiyār and founder of the vagabond legion of the Banū Sāsān; see Chapter 2, note 43 above.

Bahrām
The Zoroastrian god of victory and the planets, who presides over the twentieth day of the solar calendar. In the Avesta he takes both human and animal form. Five Sāsānid rulers bore his name.

Bahrām Gur (Bahrām V)
Sāsānid king of Persia (r. 421–438) and son of Yazdijird I and of the daughter of the Jewish Exilarch. He was raised at Ḥīrā' after the sudden death or assassination of his father, and was aided to the throne by Mundhīr, the Lakhmid Arab vassal of the Sāsānians. He did battle against the Byzantines in Armenia, which he annexed, and against the Huns, whom he defeated in the far north of Iranian lands. That victory was commemorated for centuries in the Bukharan coinage. He built many fire temples and vigorously persecuted the Christians in his domains, many of whom fled to Byzantine controlled lands. Bahrām's exploits in war, in love, and in the hunt are celebrated in the *Shahnameh*, in Persian miniatures, and in popular legend in Iran and the Punjab.

Bīwarāsp
Meaning 'Ten Thousand Horses' in Pahlavi, 'Bīwarāsp' was an epithet of Ḍaḥḥāk, the dragon king of Firdawsī's *Shahnameh*; see *The Sháhnáma of Firdausí done into English*, tr. A. G. Warner and E. Warner (London: Kegan Paul, 1905–1925), vol. 1, p. 135. The Ḍaḥḥāk of legend was descended from ancient Iranian world-kings. But Iranian sources make him the son of an Arab king, Mardas. Although blessed by the day and the night and 'meant for greatness, not for hate,' Ḍaḥḥāk was without love. Brutal, impious, and tempted by Iblīs (who is substituted for the Ahriman of the Zoroastrian sources), he slew his father and

took the throne. Defeating Jamshīd in battle, he sawed the great king in half, seized Iran, and took Jamshīd's sisters to his bed, turning the two princesses to witchcraft. He oppressed the Zoroastrian sages, and Ahriman led him to introduce meat eating, hitherto unknown. The Arab tyrant's reign of bloodshed, rapine, fire, famine, and drought lasted a thousand years. Tormented by two black snakes that grew from his shoulders where Iblīs had kissed him, he fed each on the brain of a youth every day, until finally subdued with a bull-headed mace by Afrīdūn, who confined him on a mountain until the world's restoration. Our fable suppresses all this, relying, perhaps, only on the ominous repute of Bīwarāsp the Wise under another name, so as to suggest a judge whose outlook will not necessarily favour the human cause. Ḍaḥḥāk's eerie side comes to life in manuscript illustrations, where the jinni king repeatedly shifts guises.

Buzurgmihr (Burzoe)
The legendary multi-talented minister of Khusraw I (Anūshirwān). Unknown in our earliest Persian sources but celebrated as the ideal vizier by later writers like Thaʿlabī, Firdawsī, and Masʿūdī, he was made the author of many wise sayings and cunning discoveries, a master of chess and inventor of backgammon, and translator of the *Pañcatantra* into Pahlavi, the source of Ibn al-Muqaffaʿ's *Kalīla wa-Dimna*.

Ḍaḥḥāk (Zaḥḥāq)
A legendary shah, fancifully identified with Bīwarāsp, q.v.

Darius I
The Achaemenid ruler of Iran (r. 522–486 BCE), whose struggles to reach the throne are engraved in old Persian, Elamite, and Babylonian scripts, along with a relief of the monarch seated on his throne, on a mountain-side not far from today's Kirmanshāh. Tolerant of diverse religions and supportive of the arts and learning, Darius built Susa and Persepolis, established highways and forests, and expanded his empire

in northern India. Defeated by the Greeks at Marathon, he died facing a revolt in his Egyptian province.

Isfandiyār

Son of the legendary King Goshtasb, in the *Shahnameh* he fought the hero Rustam after a sequence of trials like that of his adversary. Rustam slew him with an arrow to the eye — his only point of vulnerability after having bathed himself in a pool of invincibility.

Jamshīd

Counted in Firdawsī's *Shahnameh* as fourth and greatest of the world's early monarchs, he is a legendary figure associated with the equally legendary Kayanid dynasty. His story is based in part on those of the Zoroastrian heroes of the Avesta, and on the Vedas. In Persian myth, Jamshīd commanded all angels and demons; and early Arab historians, as E. G. Browne notes (in A *Literary History of Persia*, vol. 1, pp. 112–113), often identify him with King Solomon. Both king and high priest, Jamshīd was credited with the invention of many weapons and elements of armour and with the crafts of weaving, masonry, mining of metals and gems, wine-making, perfumery, and navigation. He was slain by his rebellious vassal Ḍaḥḥāk, the ruler of Arabia.

Manūjahr (Manūchihrī)

The son of Īraj and grandson of Afrīdūn, he slew his wicked uncles and sent their heads to his grandfather, who named him his successor.

Rustam

The son of Zāl, dragon slayer, and heroic opponent to Isfandiyār.

Siyāwush

A legendary Persian prince, slain by Afrāsiyāb, King of Tūrān, and later avenged by his son Kay Khusraw.

Yazdijird I

The thirteenth Sāsānid king of Persia (r. 399–421), son of Bahrām IV.

Yazdijird III

The twenty-ninth and last Sāsānid shah (r. 632–651), he was defeated by the Muslim Arab armies at Qādisiyya (636) and murdered at Marw in 651 after the fall of his capital at Ctesiphon (Madā'in).

Zāl

Mythical warrior of the *Shahnameh* and father of Rustam, he was born with white hair, rejected by his father Sām, but nurtured by the great Simurgh on Mount Damavand.

Appendix D: Religious Traditions

Ananites are Karaites, so called after their founder, Anan ben David (eighth century), a sect who reject the Talmud and the authority of rabbis.

Sumanites, as **Buddhists** were called in the Islamic context, were often encountered in eastern Iraq and Persia. Relations were not irenic in the wake of the Islamic conquests, and Buddhism (like Zoroastrianism) was all but eradicated where Islam held sway. The great figures celebrated in Islamic scripture were demonized among Buddhists whose traditions preserved the scars of that traumatic epoch.

Dīṣānites or Dayṣānites, were followers of Ibn Dayṣān of Edessa (ca. 154–222), called Bardesan in Europe (after the Syriac version of his name — Bar Dīṣān). The founding figure was a Christian influenced by Platonic and Stoic ideas as well as astrological notions. He fled to Armenia when the Romans took prisoner his king, Abgar IX in 216. A dialogue of his on fate and freedom mingles Greek, Hebraic, and Christian ideas. Ephraem the Syrian (306–373), who wrote ecstatic and vivid descriptions of paradise that are thought to have influenced Muhammad, reflecting on his predecessor's pessimism about this world, at least in its present dark era, condemned him as a Manichaean heretic. Muslim writers, following that Christian appraisal, tend to represent the Dayṣānite tradition in broadly dualistic terms. See 'Bardaisan' in the *Encyclopedia of Religion* and A. Abel, 'Dayṣāniyya', *EI2*, vol. 2, p. 199.

Exilarchs were followers of the (Rabbanite) Exilarchs of Babylonia, whose leadership of Diaspora Jewry was established in the centuries following the Roman exile (in 135) of Jews from the land of Israel and especially after the completion of the Talmud, down to the time of the time of Saadiah and the Ikhwān. The Exilarchs in the time of the Ikhwān had their head-quarters in Baghdad, as did the two great talmudic academies of Babylonia, formerly located at Sura and Pumpedita.

Jabrites were determinists, or fatalists, the term applied to Ashʿarites and others by defenders of human free will such as the Muʿtazilites; see W. Montgomery Watt, 'D̲j̲abriyya' *EI2*, vol. 2, p. 365.

Jacobites, or Monophysites, followers of the teachings of Jacob Baradaeus (sixth century), hold that Christ had one, divine nature: God was not actually crucified.

Jahmites, a little known sect named after Jahm ibn Safwān (executed in 746), a Muslim official, war-lord, and religious thinker allied with a rebel against the Umayyads in Khurāsān. Jahm is said to have debated with Buddhists, but his own views are obscure. The eponymous sect is first mentioned some seventy years after his death, mainly in polemics like the book Aḥmad ibn Ḥanbal wrote against them. Jahmites are said to have deemed the Qurʾan created (whereas more traditionalist Muslims made it a key tenet of their faith that it was eternal) and to have denied that God had an eternal attribute of knowledge, or, for that matter, any separate attributes at all. Jahmite theology may have anticipated that of the Muʿtazilites, and their views regarding sin, like those of the Murjiʾites. But Muʿtazilites refused to call their views Jahmite, understandably, given the opprobrium the name took on, not to mention the reports that Jahmites held that human beings can be said to act only in a metaphorical sense, as the sun is said to set.

Khārijites (or Khawārij, literally, 'seceders'), an extremist Islamic sect, are traced back to a critical juncture during the battle of Ṣiffīn, which had been provoked by the assassination of the caliph ʿUthmān. Muʿāwiya, championing the cause of the dead caliph, offered his ʿAlid adversaries negotiations and settlement 'according to the Qur'an'. Most of 'Alī's forces agreed, but dissidents protested, insisting that judgement belongs to God alone. They withdrew to a nearby village, where they elected a leader and drew successive waves of rebels to their cause. The Khārijites were *takfīrīs*, that is, they damned as unbelievers the perpetrators of grave sins. Allegiance to rival authorities was such a sin, so those who rejected Khārijite claims were, in their estimation tantamount to apostates, who had forfeited the civil protection owed to believers. The Khārijite movement fomented rebellions for centuries; see G. Levi Della Vida, 'Khāridjites', *EI2*, vol. 4, pp. 1074–1077; C. Pellat, 'Isti'rāḍ', *EI2*, vol. 4, p. 269; A. J. Wensinck, 'Nāfi' ibn al-Azra', *EI2*, vol. 7, pp. 877–878. Isti'rāḍ was the Khārijite inquisition and mandated slaying of those who rejected their doctrine: all such adversaries were damned, and it was licit to slay them and their women and children. Ibn al-Azraq was the seventh-century Khārijite leader who used such 'testing' egregiously.

The **Khurramites** were a quasi-Mazdakite syncretistic sect, whose name has been thought to suggest a cheerful attitude towards life (cf. Nietzsche's *Fröhliche Wissenschaft*); see Hastings, *Encyclopedia of Religion and Ethics* (New York: Scribner's, 1951), vol. 8, p. 508. See Wilferd Madelung, 'Mazdakism and the Khurramiyya', in his *Religious Trends in Early Islamic Iran* (Albany, NY: Bibliotheca Persica, 1988), pp. 1–12.

Manichaeans were followers of the Persian prophet Manes, or Mani, whose religion arose in mid-third-century Babylonia. Its quasi-gnostic dualism rivalled both the monotheistic and the dualistic faiths of the late ancient world. The young Augustine was a celebrated adherent. See Shahrastānī, *Kitāb al-Milal wa'l-niḥal*, ed. W. Cureton (Piscataway, NJ: Gorgias, 2002), pp. 173, 188, 192–193.

The **Mazdakites** were a prominent heresy of Zoroastrianism, allegedly communistic in practice. Mazdak, the founder, had won favour in the reign of the monarch Kavāt but was deceived into a ghastly death. His followers were massacred by Khusraw in the sixth century, the same monarch who sought the aid of the last members of Plato's Athenian Academy, reportedly in his efforts to establish a Zoroastrian dualistic orthodoxy as a foundation of his state.

Melkites, Eastern in rite but Catholic in doctrine and communion, like other Catholics and the Orthodox, accept the Christology of the creed of Chalcedon.

The **Murji'ites** were classically identified as opponents of the Khārijites, holding that grave sins did not exclude Muslims from the ranks of the faithful. Their view was that grave sinners will be judged by God alone. Their name is based on the Qur'anic (9:106) term '*irjā*'' ('deferred judgement'): the standing of grave sinners *vis à vis* the faith need not be settled in this world. Murji'ism came to be regarded as heretical, and its history may have been rewritten to remove key early figures later deemed orthodox from the ranks of its supporters. The movement seems to have represented a middle ground between the Khārijite and ʿAlid extremes. 'Politically,' as Wilferd Madelung writes, 'the early Murdji'a were primarily concerned to restore the concord of the Muslim community by opposing radical religious groups'; see W. Madelung, 'Murdji'a', *EI2*, vol. 7, pp. 605–607. As he adds, the movement took on a new role, in support of non-Arab converts to Islam, around the turn of the seventh century. A strong advocate was Abū Ḥanīfa. But, given the heretical connotations the name acquired, he is said to have rejected that label. Murji'ism developed a powerful following in Balkh, and there was strong opposition in Kūfa and Basra. Aḥmad ibn Ḥanbal (780–855) went so far as to class Murji'ites as non-Muslims, but other theologians were more tolerant, partly because Murji'ite views were formative in the Ashʿarite doctrine that Islam is a matter of faith, and that actions are secondary.

The **Muʿtazilites** called themselves the exponents of monotheism and theodicy. They upheld God's unity by denying God attributes distinct from His identity (an approach perhaps first devised as a defence against Christian attempts to promote the idea of the Trinity by way of appeal to the reality of God's attributes). Muʿtazilites upheld

God's justice by defending human free will and moral responsibility: God rewards the obedient and punishes the disobedient. The fate of sinners was left in God's hands, but His judgement, perforce, was fair. Muʿtazilite theology remained strong in Shiʿi circles, and its flavours are evident in the thinking of the Ikhwān. But the school came into disrepute with other Muslims for seeming to bind God to human moral standards, for deeming the Qur'an created (perhaps an outcome of the Muʿtazilite view that a just God must reveal His will), and for the *miḥna*, or inquisition into the faith of Muslims, that Muʿtazilites instituted during their ascendancy in the ninth century — a policy that bore ugly Khārijite overtones. For the moral objectivism of the Muʿtazilites, see George Hourani, *Islamic Rationalism: The Ethics of ʿAbd al-Jabbār* (Oxford: OUP, 1971).

Nāṣibites, likely one of the late seventh-century Shiʿi groups among the Kaysāniyya, who were supporters of al-Mukhtār al-Thaqafī, a rebel leader in Iraq.

Nestorians, followers of the teaching of Nestorius, Patriarch of Constantinople, held that Christ had separate divine and human natures, avoiding the ignominy of a crucified God.

Qadarites, Islamic voluntarists, held that not all human actions are predetermined by God, a view crucial for the Muʿtazilites. The term 'Qadarite' actually denotes a determinist, and its valence was consistently pejorative, applied by rival sects to one another: the upholders of predestination were voluntarists with respect to God. They called the advocates of human agency and moral freedom the real determinists, since these adversaries believed that man 'creates' his own actions. That seemed to tie God's hands, leaving Him bound, if not by human choices, then by His own goodness. The heresiographers ensured that this was the account that stuck: it was those who upheld human freedom who were called determinists.

Rāfiḍites rejected the leadership of the three caliphs before ʿAlī. By the time of the Ikhwān the name is mainly a term of abuse hurled at early Shiʿa groups, the largest of which was to become the Imāmīs or Twelvers. Each major Shiʿa group had its own favoured line of succession, typically stressing *naṣṣ* (designation by the prior imam), in contrast to the Sunni consultative ideal.

The **Sabians** were deemed scriptural monotheists (*ahlu'l-kitāb*), grouped with Jews and Christians in the Qurʾan (2:62, 5:69, 22:17). By a genial fiction, the pagan star-worshippers of Ḥarrān in Syria were also identified as Sabians, and thus were tolerated as *dhimmīs* after the Muslim conquests; a number of important mathematicians, astronomers, physicians, and translators of Greek scientific works stemmed from this community, including Thābit ibn Qurra (d. 901), his son Sinān, two grandsons, and generations of later descendants. See F. C. de Blois, 'Ṣābi'', *EI2*, vol. 8, pp. 672–675; T. Fahd, 'Ṣābiʾa', *EI2*, vol. 8, pp. 675–692.

Samaritans, whose claims to be true Israelites caused friction in the fifth century BC (see Nehemiah 6), are called 'Kuthites' in the Talmud but 'B'nei Yisrael' in their own usage.

Bibliography

Ikhwān al-Ṣafāʾ

Rasāʾil Ikhwān al-Ṣafāʾ wa-Khullān al-Wafāʾ, ed. Aḥmad ibn ʿAbd Allāh. Bombay: Maṭbaʿat Nukhbat al-Akhbār, 1888.

Rasāʾil Ikhwān al-Ṣafāʾ wa-Khullān al-Wafāʾ, ed. Khayr al-Dīn al-Ziriklī. Cairo: al-Maṭbaʿat al-ʿArabiyya, 1928.

Rasāʾil Ikhwān al-Ṣafāʾ wa-Khullān al-Wafāʾ, ed. Buṭrus al-Bustānī. Beirut: Dār Ṣādir, 1957.

Mensch und Tier vor dem König der Dschinnen, tr. Alma Giese. Hamburg: F. Meiner, 1990.

Thier und Mensch vor dem König der Genien, ed. F. Dieterici. Leipzig, 1879, 1881. Reprint, Hildesheim: Olms, 1969. Tr. F. Dieterici as *Der Streit zwischen Mensch und Thier*. Berlin, 1858. Reprint, Hildesheim: Olms, 1969.

Iggeret Baʿalei Ḥayyim, tr. Kalonymos ibn Meir. Wilno, 1802, 1874. Reprint, Warsaw, 1879; Jerusalem: Mossad ha-Rav Kook, 1949.

'A Treatise on Number Theory from a Tenth Century Arabic Source', tr. B. R. Goldstein. *Centaurus*, 10 (1964), pp. 129–160.

Classic Texts

The Holy Qurʾān: English Translation of the Meanings and Commentary [bilingual edition], ed. The Presidency of Islamic Researches IFTA. Medina: King Fahd Complex for the Printing of the Holy Qurʾān, n.d.

An Interpretation of the Qurʾan: English Translation of the Meanings, ed. and tr. M. Fakhry. New York: New York University Press, 1975.

Mishkāt al-maṣābiḥ, tr. James Robson. Lahore: M. Ashraf, 1975.

Actuarius, John. *De Spiritu Animali*. Venice: apud Petrum de Nicolinis de Sabio, 1547.

Aesop. *The Complete Fables*, tr. Olivia and Robert Temple. London: Penguin, 1998.

Aristotle. *The Complete Works of Aristotle: The Revised Oxford Translation*, ed. Jonathan Barnes. 2 volumes. Princeton: Princeton University Press, 1984.

—— *Politics*, ed. and tr. R. F. Stalley (rev. after Ernest Barker). Oxford: Oxford University Press, 1995.

Arnim, Hans Friedrich von, ed. *Stoicorum Veterum Fragmenta*. 4 volumes. Stuttgart: Teubner, 1903–1905.

ʿAṭṭār, Farīd al-Dīn. *Tadhkirāt al-awliyā'*, ed. M. Istilami. Tehran: Intisharāt-i Zuwwār, 1968.

—— *Manṭiq al-ṭayr*, tr. A. Darbandi and D. Davis as *The Conference of the Birds*. New York: Penguin, 1984.

Augustine. *Confessions*, tr. E. B. Pusey. Oxford: J. H. Parker, 1838, 1853.

Avicenna. *Avicenna Latinus*, ed. S. van Riet. Leiden: Brill, 1968–1972.

—— *Kitāb al-Najāt*, tr. Fazlur Rahman as *Avicenna's Psychology*. London: Oxford University Press, 1959.

al-Baghdādī, Khāzin. *Lubab al-ta'wīl fī ma'ānī al-tanzīl*. Beirut: Dār al-Maʿrifa li'l-Ṭibāʿa wa'l-Nashr, 1970–1979.

Baiḍāwī. *Commentary on Sura 12 of the Qur'an*, ed. and tr. A. F. L. Beeston. Oxford: Oxford University Press, 1963, 1978.

Cicero. *De Natura Deorum*, tr. Horace Rackham. Cambridge, MA: Harvard University Press, 1957.

Diogenes Laertius. *Lives of the Eminent Philosophers*, ed. and tr. R. D. Hicks. 2 volumes. Cambridge: Harvard University Press, 1965. First published 1925.

Epicurus. *Letters, Principal Doctrines, and Vatican Sayings*, tr. Russel Geer. Indianapolis: Bobbs-Merrill, 1964.

al-Fārābī, Abū Naṣr. *Commentary on Aristotle's 'De Interpretatione'*, ed. Wilhelm Kutsch and Stanley Marrow. Beirut: Catholic University Press, 1960. Tr. F. Zimmermann as *Al-Farabi's Commentary and Short Treatise on Aristotle's 'De Interpretatione'*. London: Oxford University Press, 1981.

—— *Kitāb Iḥṣā' al-ʿulūm*, ed. C. Baeumker as 'Alfarabi, Über den Ursprung den Wissenschaften', *Beiträge zur Geschichte der Theologie und Philosophie des Mittelalters*, 19 (1916), pp. 17–24. Tr. John L. Longeway as *The Book of Al Farabi on the Origin of the Sciences*, http://uwp.edu/~longeway/Al%20Farabi.htm

—— *Fuṣūl al-madanī*, ed. and tr. D. M. Dunlop as *Aphorisms of the Statesman*. Cambridge: Cambridge University Press, 1961.

—— *Kitāb Mabādi' ārā' ahli'l madīnati'l-fāḍila*, ed. and tr. Richard Walzer as *Al-Farabi on the Perfect State*. Oxford: Oxford University Press, 1985.

——. *Fī Taḥṣīl al-ṣa'ādah*. Hyderabad: Maṭba'at Majlis Dā'irat al-Ma'ārif al-'Uthmāniyya, AH 1345 (1926). Tr. Muhsin Mahdi as *Alfarabi's Philosophy of Plato and Aristotle*. Ithaca, NY: Cornell University Press, 1969.

Firdawsī. *The Sháhnáma of Firdausí done into English*, tr. Arthur George Warner and Edmond Warner. 9 volumes. London: Kegan Paul, 1905–1925. Tr. Dick Davis as *Shahnameh: The Persian Book of Kings*. 3 volumes. Washington, DC: Mage, 2009.

Galen. *De Usu Partium*, tr. Margaret Tallmadge May as *On the Usefulness of the Parts of the Body*. 2 volumes. Ithaca, NY: Cornell University Press, 1968.

—— *Galen on Food and Diet*, ed. and tr. Mark Grant. London: Routledge, 2000.

—— *Opera Omnia*, ed. C. G. Kühn. Leipzig: Knobloch, 1821–1833.

—— *Precis of the 'Timaeus'*, tr. Ḥunayn ibn Isḥāq, in *Plato Arabus*, Volume 1: *Galeni Compendium Timaei Platonis*, ed. with Latin tr. Paul Kraus and Richard Walzer. London: Warburg Institute, 1951.

al-Ghazālī, Abū Ḥāmid. *Faḍā'iḥ al-bāṭiniyya*, ed. A.-R. Badawi. Cairo: Dār al-Qawmiyya, 1964.

—— *Iḥyā 'ulūm al-dīn*. Cairo: Dār al-Ḥadīth, 1992. Book 40, tr. T. J. Winter as *The Remembrance of Death and the Afterlife*. Cambridge: Islamic Texts Society, 1995.

—— *Mishkāt al-anwār*, ed. and tr. David Buchman as *The Niche of Lights*. Provo: Brigham Young University, 1998. Tr. W. H. T. Gairdner as *Al-Ghazzali's 'Mishkat al-Anwar' ('The Niche for Lights')*. London: The Royal Asiatic Society, 1924. Reprint, Lahore: Ashraf, 1952.

—— *Al-Munqidh min al-ḍalāl*, in *The Faith and Practice of al-Ghazālī*, tr. William Montgomery Watt. London: Allen Unwin, 1953.

Halevi, Judah. *Kitāb al-Radd wa'l-dalīl fī'l-dīn al-dhalīl* (The Book of Rebuttal and Evidence in behalf of the Abased Religion, known as the *Kuzari*), ed. David H. Baneth. Jerusalem: Magnes Press, 1977. Tr. Hartwig Hirschfeld as *Kuzari*. New York: Schocken, 1964; first English edition, 1905.

Hippocrates. *Opera Omnia*, ed. C. G. Kühn. Leipzig: Knobloch, 1825–1827.

Hobbes, Thomas. *The Elements of Law, Natural and Politic* (1640), ed. J. C. A. Gaskin. Oxford: Oxford University Press, 1994.

Ḥujwīrī. *The Kashf al-maḥjūb: the Oldest Persian Text on Sufism* (Revealing What Was Veiled), tr. R. A. Nicholson. London: Luzac, 1967. First published 1911.

ibn 'Arabī, Muhyiddin. *Fuṣūṣ al-ḥikam*, ed. Abū'l-'Alā' 'Afīfī. Cairo: Dār al-Kitāb al-Arabī, 1946. Reprint, Beirut: Dār al-Kitāb al-Arabī, 1966.

ibn Ḥanbal, Aḥmad. *Al-Zuhd*. Cairo: al-Sadr li-Khidmati'l-Ṭibā'a, 1992.

ibn al-Jawzī, Abū'l-Faraj. *Talbīs Iblīs*. Beirut: Dār Kutub al-'Ilmiyya, 1975. Tr. D. S. Margoliouth as 'The Devil's Delusion by Ibn-al-Jauzi'. *Islamic*

Culture, 9–12 (1935–1938), pp. 1–21, 187–208, 377–399, 551–553 of the volumes respectively.
Ibn Khaldūn. *Muqaddimah*, tr. Franz Rosenthal. New York: Pantheon, 1958.
Ibn al-Muqaffaʿ. *La version arabe de Kalīlah et Dimnah*, ed. Louis Cheikho. Beirut: Catholic University Press, 1905. Selected and tr. Saleh S. Jallad as *The Fables of Kalilah and Dimnah*. London: Melisende, 2002.
—— *Kalilah and Dimnah: An English Version based upon Ancient Arabic and Spanish Manuscripts*, tr. Thomas B. Irving. Newark, DE: Juan de la Cuesta, 1980.
ibn Paqūda, Baḥyā. *Kitāb al-Hidāya ilā farāʾiḍ al-qulūb*, ed. A. S. Yahuda. Leiden: Brill, 1912, 1942. Tr. Menahem Mansoor as *The Book of Direction to the Duties of the Heart*. London: Routledge and Kegan Paul, 1973.
Ibn Rushd. *Commentary on Plato's Republic*, ed. E. I. J. Rosenthal. Cambridge: Cambridge University Press, 1966.
Ibn Ṭufayl. *Ḥayy ibn Yaqẓān*, tr. L. E. Goodman. Chicago: University of Chicago Press, 2009.
Isidore of Seville. *Etymologiae*, tr. Stephen A. Barney et al. as *The 'Etymologies' of Isidore of Seville*. Cambridge: Cambridge University Press, 2006.
Al-Jāḥiẓ. *On Singing-Girls*, ed. and tr. A. F. L. Beeston. Warminster: Aris and Phillips, 1980.
al-Jayyānī, Abū Ḥayyān. *Al-Baḥr al-muḥīṭ*. Riyadh: Maktabat al-Nashr al-Ḥadītha, 1960.
al-Kalābādhī, Abū Bakr. *Kitāb al-Taʿarruf li-madhhab ahl al-taṣawwuf*, tr. A. J. Arberry as *The Doctrine of the Sufis*. Reprint, New York: Cambridge University Press, 1989.
Kant, Immanuel. *Critique of Practical Reason* (1788), tr. Lewis White Beck. Indianapolis: Bobbs-Merrill, 1956.
—— *Groundwork of the Metaphysic of Morals* (1785), tr. H. J. Paton. 2nd ed. New York: Harper and Row, 1956.
Al-Kindī. *Metaphysics*, tr. Alfred Ivry. Albany, NY: State University of New York Press, 1974.
—— *Rasāʾil falsafiyya*, ed. Muḥammad Abū Riḍā. Cairo: Dār al-ʿArabī, 1950–1953.
—— *Uno Scritto Morale*, ed. Helmut Ritter and Richard Walzer. Rome: Accademia dei Lincei, 1938.
Kirk, G. S., J. E. Raven, and M. Schofield, ed. *The Presocratic Philosophers*. 2nd ed. Cambridge: Cambridge University Press, 1984.
Al-Kisāʾī. *Qiṣaṣ al-anbiyāʾ*, tr. Wheeler M. Thackston as *The Tales of the Prophets of al-Kisaʾi*. Boston: Twayne, 1978.
Lactantius. *The Divine Institutes*, ed. Mary Francis MacDonald. Washington, DC: Catholic University Press, 1964.

Long, A. A., and D. N. Sedley, ed. and tr. *The Hellenistic Philosophers*. 2 volumes. Cambridge: Cambridge University Press, 1987.

Lucan. *Pharsalia*, tr. Robert Graves. Baltimore, MD: Penguin, 1957.

Lucretius. *De Rerum Natura*, ed. and tr. Cyril Bailey. Oxford: Oxford University Press, 1947.

Macrobius. *Saturnalia*, tr. P. V. Davies. New York: Columbia University Press, 1969.

Maimonides (Moses ben Maimon). *Dalālat al-Ḥā'irīn* (*Guide to the Perplexed*), ed. and tr. [into French] Salomon Munk. 3 volumes. Paris: A. Franck, 1856–1866. Reprint, Osnabrück: Zeller, 1964.

—— *Maimonides' Treatise on Resurrection (Maqāla fī Teḥiyyat ha-Metim): The Original Arabic and Samuel ibn Tibbon's Hebrew Translation and Glossary*, ed. Joshua Finkel. New York: American Academy for Jewish Research, 1939.

—— *Crisis and Leadership: Epistles of Maimonides*, tr. Abraham Halkin. Philadelphia: Jewish Publication Society of America, 1985.

al-Maqrīzī, Taqī al-Dīn. *The Book of Contention and Strife Concerning the Relations between the Banū Umayya and the Banū Hāshim*, tr. C. E. Bosworth. Manchester: University of Manchester Press, 1980.

al-Māwardī, Abū'l-Ḥasan. *Aḥkām al-sultāniyya wa'l-wilāyāt al-dīniyya*, tr. Wafaa H. Wahba as *The Ordinances of Government*. Reading: Garnet, 1996.

al-Miṣrī, Aḥmad ibn Naqīb. *'Umdat al-sālik*, ed. N. Keller. Beltsville, MD: Amana, 1994.

Monawwar, M. *Asrār al-tawḥīd fī manāqib Abī Sa'īd*, tr. John O'Kane as *The Secrets of God's Mystical Oneness*. Costa Mesa, CA: Mazda, 1992.

Montaigne, Michel Eyquem. *Complete Essays*, tr. Donald Frame. Stanford, CA: Stanford University Press, 1958.

Nābigha al-Dhubyānī. *Dīwān*, ed. G. Shaykh. Beirut: Mu'assasat al-A'lamī li'l-Maṭbū'āt, 2000.

Nicomachus of Gerasa. 'Introduction to Arithmetic', in *Thābit ibn Qurra's arabische Übersetzung der Arithmêtikê Eisagôgê des Nikomachos von Gerasa*, ed. Wilhelm Kutsch. Beirut: Catholic University Press, 1959.

Nizām al-Mulk. *Siyāsat-nāma*, tr. Hubert Darke. London: Routledge and Kegan Paul, 1960.

Origen. *De Principiis*, tr. G. W. Butterworth. New York: Harper and Row, 1966.

Paul of Aegina. *The Seven Books of Paulus Aegineta*, tr. Francis Adams. London: Sydenham Society, 1844–1847.

Philo. *De Opificio Mundi*, tr. F. H. Colson and G. H. Whitaker. Cambridge, MA: Harvard University Press, 1929.

Philoponus, John. *De Caelo*, apud Simplicius *De Caelo*, ed. J. L. Heiberg. Berlin: Reimer, 1894.

—— *De Opificio Mundi,* ed. W. Reichardt. Leipzig: Teubner, 1897.
Plato. *Complete Works*, ed. and tr. John M. Cooper. Indianapolis: Hackett, 1997.
Pliny. *Natural History*, ed. and tr. Horace Rackham. Cambridge, MA: Harvard University Press, 1940.
—— *The Elder Pliny on the Human Animal: 'Natural History Book VII'*, ed and tr. Mary Beagon. Oxford: Oxford University Press, 2005.
Plutarch. *Moralia*, ed. and tr. F. C. Babbitt. 12 volumes. Cambridge, MA: Harvard University Press, 1927–1969.
Porphyry. *De Abstinentia*, tr. T. Taylor as *On Abstinence from Animal Food.* London: Centaur Press, 1965.
Proclus. *Commentary on 'Alcibiades I'*, tr. William O'Neill. The Hague: M. Nijhoff, 1965.
—— *A Commentary on the First Book of Euclid's 'Elements'*, tr. Glenn Morrow. Princeton: Princeton University Press, 1970.
—— *The Elements of Theology*, ed. and tr. E. R. Dodds. Oxford: Oxford University Press, 1963.
Rūzbihān al-Baqlī. *'Arā'is al-bayān fī ḥaqā'iq al-Qur'ān.* www.altafsir.com (accessed 2 April, 2009).
—— *Le livre Bilawhar et Budasf selon la version arabe ismaelienne*, ed. and tr. D. Gimaret. Paris: Droz, 1971.
Saadiah ben Joseph al-Fayyūmī. *Kitāb al-Mukhtār fī'l-āmānāt wa'l-i'tiqādāt* (= *Sefer ha-Nivḥar ba Emunot ve-De'ot*), ed. and tr. J. Kafih. Jerusalem: Sura, 1970. Tr. Samuel Rosenblatt as *The Book of Beliefs and Opinions.* New Haven: Yale University Press, 1948.
—— *The Book of Theodicy: Translation and Commentary on the Book of Job*, tr. Lenn E. Goodman. New Haven: Yale University Press, 1988.
Sells, Michael, ed. and tr. *Early Islamic Mysticism.* New York: Paulist Press, 1996.
Sextus Empiricus. *Outlines of Pyrrhonism*, tr. R. G. Bury. Cambridge, MA: Harvard University Press, 1933.
Shahrastānī. *Kitāb al-Milal wa'l-niḥal*, ed. William Cureton. Leipzig: Harassowitz, 1846, 1923. Reprint, Piscataway, NJ: Gorgias, 2002.
Spinoza, Baruch. *The Collected Works*, tr. E. Curley. Princeton: Princeton University Press, 1985. *Complete Works*, tr. Samuel Shirley. Indianapolis, Hackett, 2002.
Suhrawardī. *The Philosophical Allegories and Mystical Treatises*, ed. and tr. Wheeler M. Thackston. Costa Mesa, CA: Mazda, 1999.
al-Sulamī, Abū 'Abd al-Raḥmān. *Dhikr al-niswa al-muta'abbidāt al-sūfiyyāt*, ed. and tr. R. Cornell as *Early Sufi Women.* Louisville, KY: Fons Vitae, 1999.
al-Ṭabarsī (Ṭabrizī), Amīn al-Dīn. *Majmū' al-bayān fī tafsīr al-Qur'ān.* www.altafsir.com (accessed 2 April, 2009).

al-Tawḥīdī, Abū Ḥayyān. 'The Zoological Chapter of the *Kitāb al-Imtā' wal-Mu'ānasa* of Abū Ḥayyān al-Tauḥīdī (10th century)', tr. L. Kopf. Osiris, 12 (1956), pp. 390–466.

Al-Thaʿlabī. *'Arā'is al-majālis fī qiṣaṣ al-anbiyā'*, tr. William Brinner as *Lives of the Prophets*. Leiden: Brill, 2002.

—— *Kitāb Laṭā'if al-maʿārif*, tr. C. E. Bosworth as *The Book of Curious and Entertaining Information*. Edinburgh: Edinburgh University Press, 1968.

al-Tirmidhī, al-Ḥakīm. *Kitāb Khatm al-awliyā'*, ed. 'Uthmān Yaḥyā. Beirut: Catholic University Press, 1965. Tr. B. Radtke and J. O'Kane as *The Concept of Sainthood in Early Islamic Mysticism*. Surrey: Curzon, 1996.

Vishnu Sharman. *Pañcatantra*, ed, and tr. Patrick Olivelle as *Five Discourses on Worldly Wisdom*. New York: New York University Press, 2006.

Yaḥyā ibn 'Adī. *Tahdhīb al-akhlāq*, ed. and tr. Sidney Griffith as *The Reformation of Morals*. Provo: Brigham Young University Press, 2002.

Modern Studies

Altmann, Alexander. 'The Delphic Maxim in Medieval Islam and Judaism', in *Studies in Religious Philosophy and Mysticism*. Ithaca, NY: Cornell University Press, 1969, pp. 1–40.

Altum, Bernard. *Der Vogel und sein Leben*. Münster: Niemann, 1868.

Amir-Moezzi, M. *The Divine Guide in Early Shi'ism*, tr. D. Streight. Albany, NY: State University of New York Press, 1994.

Arnold, T. W. *The Caliphate*. London: Clarendon, 1924.

Asín Palacios, Miguel. *Islam and the Divine Comedy*, tr. Harold Sutherland. London: John Murray, 1926. Reprint, London: Frank Cass and Co., 1968. First Spanish edition, 1919.

Ayoub, Mahmoud. *Redemptive Suffering in Islam: A Study of the Devotional Aspects of Ashura in Twelver Shiʿism*. The Hague: Mouton, 1978.

Becker, C. H. 'Ubi sunt qui ante nos in mundo fuere', in *Islamstudien*. 2 volumes. Leipzig: Quelle and Mayer, 1924, vol. 1, pp. 501–519.

Blumenthal, David. 'A Comparative Table of the Bombay, Cairo, and Beirut Editions of the *Rasā'il Iḫwān al-Ṣafā*", *Arabica*, 21 (1974), pp. 186–203.

Bosworth, C. E. *The Medieval Islamic Underworld: The Banū Sāsān in Arabic Society and Literature*. 2 volumes. Leiden: Brill, 1976.

Böwering, Gerhardt. *The Mystical Vision of Existence in Classical Islam: The Qur'anic Hermeneutics of the Sufi Sahl al-Tustari*. New York: de Gruyter, 1980.

Browne, E. G. *A Literary History of Persia*. 4 volumes. Cambridge: Cambridge University Press, 1902–1924. Reprint, 1964.

Chittick, William. *The Sufi Path of Knowledge*. Albany, NY: State University of New York Press, 1989.

Cook, Michael. *Commanding Right and Forbidding Wrong in Islamic Thought.* Cambridge: Cambridge University Press, 2000.

Corbin, Henry. *Avicenna and the Visionary Recital*, tr. Willard R. Trask. London: Routledge and Kegan Paul, 1960.

—— *En Islam iranien: Aspects spirituels et philosophiques.* 4 volumes. Paris: Gallimard, 1971.

Daniel, Elton L. *The Political and Social History of Khurasan under Abbasid Rule* 747–820. Minneapolis: Bibliotheca Islamica, 1979.

Darwin, Charles. *The Descent of Man, and Selection in Relation to Sex* (1871). Princeton: Princeton University Press, 1981. Also in *The Works of Charles Darwin*, ed. Paul H. Barrett and R. B. Freeman. 29 volumes. London: Pickering, 1986–1990.

—— *The Origin of Species* (1859), in *The Works of Charles Darwin*, ed. Paul H. Barrett and R. B. Freeman. 29 volumes. London: Pickering, 1986–1990.

Davidson, Olga M. *Poet and Hero in the Persian Book of Kings.* Ithaca, NY: Cornell University Press, 1994.

De Boer, T. J. *History of Philosophy in Islam*, tr. Edward R. Jones. London: Luzac, 1903. Reprint, London, 1961.

Dieterici, Friedrich. *Die Anthropologie der Araber im zehnten Jahrhundert n. Chr.* Leipzig: J. C. Hinrichs, 1871.

—— *Der Darwinismus im X. und XI. Jahrhundert.* Leipzig: J. C. Hinrichs, 1878.

Douglas, Mary. *Purity and Danger: An Analysis of the Concepts of Pollution and Taboo.* London: Routledge and Kegan Paul, 1966.

El-Bizri, Nader, ed. *The Ikhwān al-Ṣafāʾ and their ʻRasāʾilʼ: An Introduction.* Oxford: Oxford University Press in association with the Institute of Ismaili Studies, 2008.

Encyclopaedia of Islam, ed. H. A. R. Gibb et al. 2nd ed. 12 volumes. Leiden: Brill, 1960–2004.

Fakhry, Majid. *Islamic Occasionalism and its Critique by Averroes and Aquinas.* London: Allen Unwin, 1958.

van Gelder, Geert Jan. 'The Conceit of the Pen and Sword: On an Arabic Literary Debate'. *Journal of Semitic Studies,* 32 (1987), pp. 329–360.

Gibb, Hamilton Alexander Rosskeen. 'Al-Mawardi's Theory of the Caliphate', in *Studies in the Civilization of Islam*, ed. Stanford J. Shaw and William R. Polk. Boston: Beacon, 1962, pp. 151–165.

—— 'The Social Significance of the Shuʿūbiyya', in *Studies in the Civilization of Islam*, ed. Stanford J. Shaw and William R. Polk. Boston: Beacon, 1962, pp. 65–73.

Gingerich, Owen. 'An Astronomical Perspective', in *How Large is God?*, ed. John Marks Templeton. Philadelphia: Templeton Foundation Press, 1997, pp. 23–46.

Ginzberg, Louis. *Legends of the Jews*, tr. Henrietta Szold, vol. 3 tr. Paul Radin, vol. 7 tr. Boaz Cohen. 7 volumes. Philadelphia: Jewish Publication Society, 1908–1938. Reprint, 2003.

Goldziher, Ignaz. *Muslim Studies*, tr. Samuel Stern. London: Allen and Unwin, 1971. First German edition, 1890.

Goodenough, H. Ward. 'Comments on the Question of Incestuous Marriages in Old Iran'. *American Anthropologist*, 51 (1949), pp. 326–328.

Goodman, Lenn E. 'Al-Fārābī's Modalities'. *Iyyun*, 23 (1972), pp. 100–112.

—— 'Razi's Myth of the Fall of the Fall of the Soul', in *Essays on Islamic Philosophy and Science*, ed. G. Hourani. Albany, NY: State University of New York Press, 1975, pp. 25–40.

—— 'Maimonidean Naturalism', in *Neoplatonism and Jewish Thought*, ed. L. Goodman. Albany, NY: State University of New York Press, 1992, pp. 139–172. Reprinted in *Maimonides and the Sciences*, ed. Robert Cohen and Hillel Levine. Boston: Kluwer Academic, 2000, pp. 57–85.

—— *God of Abraham*. New York: Oxford University Press, 1996.

—— *Jewish and Islamic Philosophy: Crosspollinations in the Classic Age*. Edinburgh: Edinburgh University Press, 1999.

—— 'Rāzī vs Rāzī: Philosophy in the Majlis', in *The Majlis: Interreligious Encounters in Medieval Islam*, ed. Hava Lazarus-Yafeh et al. Wiesbaden: Harrassowitz, 1999, pp. 84–107.

—— *Islamic Humanism*. New York: Oxford University Press, 2003.

—— *Love Thy Neighbor as Thyself*. New York: Oxford University Press, 2008.

—— 'Baḥyā and Maimonides on the Worth of Medicine', in *Maimonides and His Heritage*, ed. I. Dobbs-Weinstein, L. Goodman, and J. Grady. Albany, NY: State University of New York Press, 2009.

—— *Creation and Evolution*. New York and London: Routledge, 2010.

Hadas, Moses. *Hellenistic Culture, Fusion and Diffusion*. New York: Columbia University Press, 1959.

Hallie, Philip P. 'The Ethics of Montaigne's "De la cruauté"', in *O Un Amy! Essays in Honor of Donald M. Frame*, ed. Raymond C. La Charité. Lexington, KY: French Forum, 1977, pp. 156–171.

Hamdani, Abbas. 'The Arrangement of the *Rasā'il Ikhwān al-Ṣafā'* and the Problem of Interpolations', updated version in *The Ikhwān al-Ṣafā' and their 'Rasā'il'*, ed. Nader El-Bizri. London: OUP–IIS, 2008, pp. 83–100.

—— 'Brethren of Purity, a Secret Society for the Establishment of the Fāṭimid Caliphate: New Evidence for the Early Dating of their Encyclopaedia', in *L'Egypte Fatimide: son art et son histoire*, ed. Marianne Barrucand. Paris: Presses Universitaires de Paris–Sorbonne, 1999, pp. 73–82.

—— 'Religious Tolerance in the Rasā'il Ikhwān al-Ṣafā'', in *Adaptations and Innovations*, ed. Tzvi Langermann and Josef Stern. Peeters, Leuven: 2008, pp. 137–142.

Hamori, Andras. 'Ascetic Poetry (*zuhdiyyāt*)', in *The Cambridge History of Arabic Literature: 'Abbasid Belles-Lettres*, ed. J. Ashtiany et al. New York: Cambridge University Press, 1990, pp. 265–274.

Hartshorne, Charles. *Born to Sing: An Interpretation and World Survey of Bird Song*. Bloomington, IN: Indiana University Press, 1973.

Hastings, James, ed. *Encyclopedia of Religion and Ethics*. New York: Scribner's, 1951.

Horovitz, Josef. *Koranische Untersuchungen*. Berlin: de Gruyter, 1926.

—— 'Muhammeds Himmelfahrt'. *Der Islam*, 9 (1919), pp. 159–183.

Hourani, George. *Islamic Rationalism: The Ethics of 'Abd al-Jabbār*. Oxford: Oxford University Press, 1971.

Howard, Henry E. *Territory in Bird Life*. London: J. Murray, 1920.

Howard, Walter E. *Animal Rights vs. Nature*. Davis, CA: privately published, 1991.

Hughes, Thomas. *A Dictionary of Islam*. London: W. H. Allen, 1885. Reprint, Lahore: Premier Book House, 1965.

Irwin, Robert. *Islamic Art in Context: Art, Architecture, and the Literary World*. New York: Prentice Hall, 1997.

Jastrow, Robert, and Malcolm M. Thompson. *Astronomy: Fundamentals and Frontiers*. New York: Wiley, 1972.

Johns, Catherine. *Horses: History, Myth, Art*. Cambridge, MA: Harvard University Press, 2006.

Karamustafa, Ahmet. *God's Unruly Friends: Dervish Groups in the Later Middle Period, 1200–1550*. Salt Lake City: University of Utah Press, 1994.

Khalidi, Tarif. *Arabic Historical Thought in the Classical Period*. Cambridge: Cambridge University Press, 1994.

Kister, M. J. 'Adam: A Study of Some Legends in Tafsīr and Ḥadīth Literature'. *Israel Oriental Studies*, 13 (1993), pp. 113–176.

Lane, Edward. *The Manners and Customs of the Modern Egyptians*. London: J. Murray, 1860. Reprint, London: Everyman, 1963.

Langermann, Y. Tzvi and Josef Stern, eds., *Adaptations and Innovations: Studies on the Interaction between Jewish and Islamic Thought and Literature from the Early Middle Ages to the Late Twentieth Century, Dedicated to Professor Joel L. Kraemer*. Paris, Louvain, and Dudley, MA: Peeters, 2007.

Leaman, Oliver. *Islamic Aesthetics: An Introduction*. Notre Dame: University of Notre Dame Press, 2004.

——, ed. *The Qur'an: An Encyclopedia*. London: Routledge, 2006.

Lethaby, William. *Architecture, Mysticism and Myth*. New York: Macmillan, 1892. Reprint, New York: Braziller, 1975.

Lévi-Strauss, Claude. *The Raw and the Cooked*, tr. John and Doreen Weightman. New York: Harper and Row, 1970. First French edition, 1964.

—— *The Savage Mind*, tr. John and Doreen Weightman. Chicago: University of Chicago Press, 1966. First French edition, 1962.

Lewis, Bernard. *Race and Color in Islam*. New York: Harper and Row, 1971.

Lichtenstadter, Ilse. 'Das Nasīb der altarabischen Qasīde'. *Islamica*, 5 (1931), pp. 17–96.

Lovejoy, Arthur. *The Great Chain of Being*. Cambridge, MA: Harvard University Press, 1936, 1960. 2nd ed., 1976.

Madelung, Wilferd. *Religious Trends in Early Islamic Iran*. Albany, NY: Bibliotheca Persica, 1988.

Mahdi, Muhsin. *Alfarabi and the Foundation of Islamic Political Philosophy*. Chicago: University of Chicago Press, 2001.

Marquet, Yves. *La philosophie des Iḫwān al-Ṣafā'*. Algiers: Société Nationale d'Édition et de Diffusion, [1975]. Reprint, Paris: Société d'Études de l'Histoire de l'Alchimie, 1999.

Mayhew, Robert. *The Female in Aristotle's Biology: Reason or Rationalization*. Chicago: University of Chicago Press, 2004.

McGregor, Richard. *Sanctity and Mysticism in Medieval Egypt*. Albany, NY: State University of New York Press, 2004.

Melamed, Abraham. *The Philosopher King in Medieval and Renaissance Jewish Political Thought*. Albany, NY: State University of New York Press, 2003.

Melehy, Hassan. 'Montaigne and Ethics: The Case of Animals'. *L'Esprit Créateur*, 46 (2006), pp. 96–107.

Meyerhof, Max. 'New Light on Ḥunayn Ibn Ishāq and his Period'. *Isis*, 8 (1926), pp. 685–724.

Midgley, Mary. 'The Concept of Beastliness'. *Philosophy*, 48 (1973), pp. 111–135.

Muir, William. *The Caliphate: Rise, Decline, and Fall*. Beirut: Khayats, 1963. First published 1898.

Nasr, Seyyed Hossein. *Islamic Cosmological Doctrines*. Cambridge, MA: Harvard University Press, 1964.

Oakeshott, Michael. *Rationalism in Politics and Other Essays*. 2nd ed. Indianapolis: Liberty Press, 1991. First published, London: Methuen, 1962.

Onians, Richard Broxton. *The Origins of European Thought about the Body, the Mind, the Soul, the World, Time, and Fate: New Interpretations of Greek, Roman, and Kindred Evidence*. Cambridge: Cambridge University Press, 1951.

Ormsby, Eric. *Theodicy in Islamic Thought: The Dispute over al-Ghazālī's 'Best of all Possible Worlds'*. Princeton: Princeton University Press, 1984.

Ramsey, Paul. *Fabricated Man*. New Haven, CT: Yale University Press, 1970.

Richards, Robert J. *Darwin and the Emergence of Evolutionary Theories of Mind and Behavior*. Chicago: University of Chicago Press, 1987.
Ryle, Gilbert. *Dilemmas*. Cambridge: Cambridge University Press, 1954.
Sambursky, S. *The Physical World of Late Antiquity*. London: Routledge, 1962.
Sasson, Jack, ed. *Civilizations of the Ancient Near East*. Peabody, MA: Hendrickson, 1995.
Sasson, Jack. *Hebrew Origins: Historiography, History, Faith of Ancient Israel*. Hong Kong: Chung Chi College, 2002.
Serjeant, R. B. *South Arabian Hunt*. London: Luzac, 1974.
Singer, Peter. 'Down on the Factory Farm', in *Animal Liberation*. New York: Harper Collins, 1991; 1st ed., 1975.
Slotkin, J. S. 'On a Possible Lack of Incest Regulations in Old Iran', *American Anthropologist*, 49 (1947), pp. 612–617.
Sourdel, Dominique. Le Vizirat *'Abbāside de 749 à 936*. Damascus: Institut français de Damas, 1959–1960.
Stern, S. M. 'Some Fragments of Galen's *On Dispositions* in Arabic'. *The Classical Quarterly*, 6 (1956), pp. 91–101.
Storer, Tracy I., and Robert L. Usinger. *General Zoology*. New York: McGraw Hill, 1957.
Sviri, S. 'Hakim Tirmidhi and the *Malamati* Movement in Early Sufism', in *The Heritage of Sufism*, ed. L. Lewisohn. Oxford: Oneworld, 1999.
Taylor, A. E. *Commentary on Plato's 'Timaeus'*. Oxford: Clarendon, 1928. Reprint, 1962.
Temkin, Oswei. *Galenism: Rise and Decline of a Medical Philosophy*. Ithaca, NY: Cornell University Press, 1973.
van Ess, Joseph. 'Ibn ar-Rewandi, or the Making of an Image'. *Al-Abhath*, 27 (1978/1979), pp. 5–26.
Walsh, Joseph. 'Galen's Discovery and Promulgation of the Function of the Recurrent Laryngeal Nerve'. *Annals of Medical History*, 8 (1926), pp. 176–184.
Walzer, Richard. *Galen on Jews and Christians*. London: Oxford University Press, 1949.
—— *Greek into Arabic*. Oxford: B. Cassirer, 1962.
Watt, William Montgomery. *Free Will and Predestination in Early Islam*. London: Luzac, 1948.
—— *Companion to the Qur'ān*. London: Allen Unwin, 1967.
—— *The Formative Period of Islamic Thought*. Edinburgh: Edinburgh University Press, 1973.
Wensinck, A. J. *The Muslim Creed: Its Genesis and Historical Development*. London: Frank Cass, 1965. First published 1932.
—— *Concordance et Indices de la Tradition Musulmane*. Leiden: Brill, 1992.

Wheeler, Brannon M. *Moses in the Quran and Islamic Exegesis*. London: Routledge Curzon, 2002.
Yarshater, E., ed. *Encyclopaedia Iranica*. Boston: Routledge and Kegan Paul, 1985– .
Zaehner, R. C. *Zurvan: A Zoroastrian Dilemma*. Oxford: Oxford University Press, 1955.
—— *The Dawn and Twilight of Zoroastrianism*. New York: Putnam, 1961.

Index Nominum

ʿAbbās ibn al-Muṭṭalib, 103
Abel, 136, 160, 258, 264
Abraha, 168
Abraham, xi, 10, 121, 132, 137, 173, 174, 186, 204–205, 208, 211, 224, 255, 281, 283–285, 313–314
Abū Bakr, 213
Abū Bishr Mattā, 11
Abū Dharr, 105
Abū Sufyān, 265
Abū Tammām, 117
Abyssinia, 168, 306, 319, 320
Achaemenids, 93, 323, 328, 332, 334
ʿĀd, 178, 280, 284
Adam, 7, 43–44, 64, 68, 99, 103, 106–107, 109, 111, 116, 118, 121, 128, 130, 131, 132, 133–135, 136, 168, 174, 176, 179, 183, 201, 203, 206, 208, 210, 212, 219, 255, 260, 261, 263, 264, 274, 279, 285, 288, 306, 307, 309
Aesop, 4–5, 11, 79, 129
Aetius, 80, 250
Afghanistan, Afghans, 13, 325, 327, 330
Afrīdūn, 204, 264, 331, 334, 335
Agade, 116
Ahasuerus, 142
Ahriman, 194, 334, 335
Alexander of Aphrodisias, 190, 198
Alexander the Great, 29, 136, 143, 204, 227, 264, 320, 322, 324, 325, 328
Alexandria, 82, 217, 306, 320, 322
Alfonso X, 157
ʿAlī, (Imam), 213, 220, 339, 341, 343
Alpha Draconis. *See* Thuban
Amram, 186, 208, 255, 281, 284
Ananites, 302
Anaxagoras, 69, 142, 152
Andalusia, 306, 321
Androcles, 267
Antar romance, 173
Antiochus Epiphanes, 120
Anūshirwān, 168, 204, 332
Apion, 267
Arabia, 29, 122, 137, 140, 143, 210, 212–213, 264, 280, 319, 323, 335
Arabian Sea, 308, 319, 325
Arafat, Mount, 212
Ararat, 203, 322
Aras, 308
Arcturus, 273
Ardashīr, 143, 204, 332
Aristotle, xviii, 3, 24, 28–29, 35–36, 45, 63, 64–69, 74, 75, 76, 81, 82, 86, 88, 90, 93, 94, 109, 115, 124–125, 142, 144, 152, 172, 173, 175, 178, 185, 189, 200, 204, 211, 215, 217, 228, 234, 238–239, 253, 274, 283, 296, 297, 310
Armenians, 120, 306, 322–323, 332
Artaxerxes, 143, 332
Āṣaf son of Barkhiyya, 140
Asclepiades, 82
Ashʿarites, 29, 64, 338, 340
ʿĀshūrāʾ, 221
al-Aswad ibn Yaʿfūr, 179
Augustine, 279, 339
Averroes, 3, 90, 154, 250

Avesta, 162, 302, 328, 331, 332, 333, 335
Avicenna, xi, 162, 195, 204, 233, 250, 314
Azerbaijan, 308, 322, 331

Bāb al-Abwāb, 306, 322
Bābakān, 204, 332
Babel, 174, 281
Babylonians, 93, 220, 284, 334, 338–339
Bacon, Francis, 8, 85
Badr, 103
Baghdad, xvii, 35, 143, 265, 291, 324, 327, 338
Bahrām, 127–128, 204, 264, 333, 336
Baḥtikān, 204
Baḥyā ibn Paqūda, 166, 196, 286, 289
Bahmān ibn Isfandiyār, 108, 162, 264, 333, 335
al-Baladī, 80
Balāsaghūn, 101
Bāmiyān, 307, 325, 327
Bāriq, 178
Basra, xvii, 266, 323, 324, 340
Bedouins, 247, 306–307
Beirut, xxi, xxiii, xxiv, 59, 120, 157
Berbers, 306, 322–323
Bidpai, 10, 157, 174, 336
Bilawhar, 206, 207
Bilqīs, 10, 108, 140
Birjīs, 127
al-Bīrūnī, 134, 142–143, 328–329
al-Bisṭāmī, 72, 266
Bīwarāsp, 2, 101, 102, 137, 333–334
Bosworth, C. E., 108, 213
Brahmasphuta Siddhanta, 143
Brahmins, 50, 206, 302, 305
Britain, 306, 319
Budasf, 206–207
Buddha, 206, 327
Buddhists, 13, 203, 302, 325, 327–328, 337–338
Bukhara, 204, 218, 328, 333
al-Bustānī, Buṭrus, xxi, 4, 63, 133, 315
Būyids (Buwayhids), 307, 324
Buzurgmihr, 204, 334
Byzantines, 13, 83, 120, 214, 242, 252, 320, 322–323, 326, 332–333

Caesar, 282, 332
Cain, 32, 136, 160, 258, 264
Canary Islands, 306, 319, 321
Caspian Sea, 162, 218, 308, 321–324
Castile, 157
Ceylon, 206, 321
Chāch, 307, 329
Chaldeans, 144
China, 203, 306, 308, 319, 330, 332
China Sea, 308
Christ, 49, 141, 209, 220, 256, 305, 338, 341
Christians/Christianity, 13, 51–53, 63, 103, 120, 132, 209–210, 217, 265, 267, 301–303, 313–314, 319–320, 322, 325, 329, 333, 337, 340, 342
Constantine, 264
Constantinople, 217, 306, 322, 341
Copernicus, 310
Corbin, Henry, 162, 163
Cordoba, 8–9, 143, 321
Cynics, 265
Cyrenaica, 306, 320
Cyrus, 142

Ḍaḥḥāk, 264, 307, 331, 333, 334, 335
Darius, 204, 264, 328, 334
Darwin, Charles, 19, 24, 75, 76, 85, 113, 233, 234
David, 139–140, 142, 164, 218, 264
Daylam, 306, 324
Delphi, 203
Demetrius of Phalerum, 217
Desert Fathers, 267
Dhū'l-Qarnayn, 227
Dieterici, F., xxi, 4, 24, 67, 78, 248, 255, 264
Dimna, 3, 10, 117, 155, 156–157, 259, 334
Dīṣānites, 302, 337
Diyārs, 306, 323
Dualists, 50, 211, 301–302, 305, 337, 339–340

Eden, 36, 99, 110, 172, 311

Egypt, xi, xvii, xxiii, 9, 80, 217, 228, 281, 284, 294, 306–308, 314, 320, 322, 326
Elburz, 162, 325–326
Elijah, 136, 267
Empedocles, 25, 66, 69, 275
Enoch, 108, 136
Epicureans, 25, 34, 182, 251, 265
Erasmus, 85
Erisistratus, 82, 83
Ethiopians, 129, 319
Euphrates, 205, 308, 322, 323
Eve, 99, 109, 133–135, 203, 212
Exilarchs, 302, 333, 338
Ezra, 136, 143, 256

al-Fārābī, 7, 28, 63, 81, 115, 138, 217, 218, 230, 241, 275, 283
Farghāna, 204, 307, 329
al-Farghānī, 71
Fārs, 218, 323, 332
Fāṭimids, xvii, 80, 228, 321, 327
al-Fazārī, 143
Firdawsī, 162, 204, 325, 328, 333, 334, 335

Gabriel, 162, 174, 216
Galen, xviii, 3, 22, 24, 70, 80–84, 93, 112, 113, 151–152, 154, 191–192, 194–195, 233, 250–252, 273
Garuda, 162
Gelder, Geert Jan van, 117, 122, 157, 158
Gerard of Cremona, 71
Ghassan, 273
al-Ghazālī, 28, 102, 110, 111, 156, 162, 200, 219, 288, 301, 312
Gog, 18, 227, 307–308
Gomorrah, 313
Greeks, 1, 33, 52–53, 70–71, 78, 82, 112, 115, 120–121, 126, 134, 137, 143, 153, 156, 204, 206, 214–217, 222, 273, 290, 296–298, 306, 310, 314, 320, 328, 335–337, 342

Ḥaḍramawt, 264
Halevi, Judah, 11, 101, 179, 191
Hamadhānī, 9, 108
Hamori, Andras 179, 265
al-Ḥarīrī, 9
al-Ḥarīzī, 101
Harris, Joel Chandler, 4, 157
Hartshorne, Charles, 97, 163, 181
al-Ḥasan, 213
Hasmoneans, 120
Hebrew (language), Hebrews, 3, 5–6, 51–52, 71, 108, 136, 141, 143, 157, 179, 190, 206, 207, 217–218, 228, 254–255, 282, 295–296
Helmand, 308
Hermes Trismegistus, xviii, 136
Hezekiah, 140
Ḥijāz, 51, 205, 306, 311, 319
Hindus, 13, 51, 143, 162, 265, 321
Hipparchus, 144
Hippocrates, 81–82, 85, 152, 250, 252
Hobbes, Thomas, 235–236
Horace, 8, 251
al-Ḥujwīrī, 266, 292, 304
Ḥunayn ibn Isḥāq, 70, 82, 273
al-Ḥusayn, 213, 220–221, 267

Iblīs. *See* Satan
Ibn ʿArabī, 70, 72, 136, 272, 289
Ibn Gabirol, 11
Ibn Ḥazm, 256
Ibn al-Jawzī, 293
Ibn al-Kalbī, 143
Ibn Karrām, 194
Ibn Khaldūn, 99, 178
Ibn al-Muqaffaʿ, 156–157, 162, 267, 334
Ibn Rushd. *See* Averroes
Ibn Sīnā. *See* Avicenna
Ibn Ṭufayl, xi, 68, 80, 82, 111, 206
Idrīs, 108, 136–137, 204
Imruʾ al-Qays, 97, 273
India, 3, 50, 203, 206, 218, 305–306, 319, 321, 335
Indian Ocean, 101, 308, 319, 332
ʿIrām, 178
Iran, xxiii, 127, 143, 202, 204, 221, 222, 306, 323, 325, 328, 331, 333, 334, 339
Iraq, 202, 204–205, 220, 291, 306, 322, 323, 327, 337, 341
Irāq Ajamī, 202, 323
Isfahan, 127, 323

Ishmael, 136–137, 143, 208
Isidore of Seville, 77, 79, 114, 118, 120, 121–122, 150, 154, 163, 168, 175, 176, 187, 193, 223, 226, 243, 244, 251, 257, 276, 277, 300
Islam, 1, 9, 12–13, 20, 40, 44, 49–51, 72, 100–107, 110, 113, 116–117, 120, 122, 125, 127, 132, 134, 136, 137–145, 147, 149, 153, 157, 175, 179–181, 201, 204, 209–213, 217–218, 223, 252, 255, 259, 265, 267, 280, 284, 288–289, 294, 296, 302, 304, 307, 314, 319–327, 329, 332, 337–340
Israel, 5, 116, 133, 138, 142, 205, 207–209, 218, 255, 338

Jabrites, 302, 338
Jacob Anatoli, 71
Jacob ben Elazar, 3, 101
Jacobites. *See* Monophysites
Jaʿfar al-Ṣādiq, 314
Jāhiliyya, 179
al-Jāḥiẓ, 157–158, 168
Jahmites, 302, 338
Jamshīd, 264, 331, 334, 335
Japan, 203
Jerome, 267, 326
Jesus. *See* Christ
Jethro, 285
Jews, Judaism, 52–53, 103, 120, 132, 137, 207, 221, 246, 256, 301–303, 313
Jibāl, 306, 323
Jilān, 306, 321, 324
Jinn, King of. *See* Bīwarāsp
Job, xi, 14, 34–35, 122, 199, 228, 232, 277, 289, 291
Joel (Rabbi), 3, 157
John Actuarius, 83
John of Capua, 157
John of Seville, 71
John Philoponus, 124–125
Jonah, 101, 284–285
Jordan, 306, 326, 327
Joseph, 137–138, 284
al-Junayd, 266
Jupiter, 93, 127, 197, 237–238, 310
Jurjān, 306, 324

Kaʿb al-Aḥbār, 105, 178
Kābulistān, 306, 325
al-Kalābādhī, 212, 314
Kalīla, 3, 10, 117, 155, 156–157, 162, 259, 262, 268, 334
Kalonymos ben Kalonymos, 3, 6–7, 10, 101–105, 110, 141, 176, 179, 190, 208, 212, 213, 301
Kant, Immanuel, 37, 114, 125
Kaskar, 163
Kaywān, 127, 130, 140
Kenya, 79
Khāqān, 108, 307, 329
Khārijites, 270, 302, 325, 338–341
Khatlān, 307, 327
Khawārij, 270, 338
Khawarnaq, 178
Khurāsān, 204, 218, 220, 307, 323, 324, 325, 327, 330, 332, 338
Khurramites, 302, 339
Khūzistān, 306, 323
Khwārizm, 307, 328, 332
al-Khwārizmī, 143, 328
Killa, 306, 321
al-Kindī, 3, 8, 12, 28, 73–74, 181, 217, 252, 273, 289, 291
Kirgiz (Kyrgyz), 307, 329
Kirmān, 127, 306, 325
al-Kisāʾī, 133, 137, 140, 164, 173, 178, 224, 284, 285
Kura, 308
Kurds, 108, 115, 148, 307

La Fontaine, Jean, 4, 157
Lévi-Strauss, Claude, 99, 187
Levites, 140
Lucan, 79, 263
Lucretius, 22, 100
Luqmān, 127, 129
Luther, Martin, 21

MacDonald, D. B., 302
Machiavelli, Nicolo, 128
Maghrib, 256
Magians, 301–302

Magog, 18, 227, 307–308
Māh (Media), 306, 323
Māhān, 127
Maimonides, 9, 28, 34–35, 71, 75, 76, 106, 138, 173, 198, 208, 286
Makrān, 306, 325
Malaga, 306, 321
Manichaeans 50, 206, 302, 305, 328, 337, 339
Manūjahr, 204, 264, 331, 335
al-Maqrīzī, 213
Marathon, 143, 335
Marcus Aurelius, 290
Mars, 93, 197, 237–238
Marw Shāhān, 218, 219, 324, 327, 336
Marwānids, 220, 265
Mazdakites, 302, 339
Mecca, 52, 137, 168, 203, 212–213, 311, 319
Medina, 52, 137, 221, 311, 319
Mediterranean, 308, 321
Melkites, 302, 340
Mercury, 93, 237–238, 310
Mesopotamia, 202, 217, 323, 332. *See also* Iraq
al-Miṣrī, 263
Mithridates, 195, 290
Miyyāfārqīn, 306, 323
Mongols, 265, 324, 327, 328, 329
Monophysites, 63, 302, 338
Montaigne, Michel, 8, 21–23, 44, 70, 113, 117, 123, 174, 223, 227, 229, 244, 267, 299, 300, 313
Moriah, 203
Moses, 112–113, 134, 138, 186, 208, 220, 245, 281, 284–285, 299
Muhammad, xvii, 10, 29, 52, 72, 100, 101, 103, 105–106, 110, 116, 120, 136, 137, 140, 141, 146, 147, 149, 168, 202, 208–210, 212, 213, 216, 220–221, 240–241, 246, 268, 280, 285, 302, 312, 314, 316, 319, 332, 337
Muḥarram, 221
Muḥarriq, 178
al-Muḥāsibī, 266, 292, 304
Mullā Ṣadrā, 289
Multān, 306, 321, 325
Munkar, 311, 312
Murghab River, 218
Murji'ites, 302, 338, 340
Mu'tazilites, 12, 29, 36, 72, 119, 165, 211, 268, 273, 286, 302, 312, 328, 338, 340–341

Nābigha al-Dhubyānī, 125, 273
Nāhīd, 127–128
Nahum of Gimzo, 191
Nakīr, 311
Nanna, 116
Nāṣibites, 302, 341
Nasr, S. H., 24, 40, 67, 71, 72, 74, 91–92, 105, 132, 133–134, 143, 144, 225, 274, 281, 314
Nebuchadnezzar, 142, 205, 220, 264
Nejd, 306, 319
Nestorians, 10, 302, 325, 341
Nicomachus of Gerasa, xviii, 64, 91–92
Nile, 308, 320
Nimrod, 10, 27, 31, 132, 137, 173–174, 186, 205, 224, 269, 280–281, 283–284, 299
Nishapur, 267, 306, 324
Noah, 99, 136, 204, 208, 255, 287, 322
Northern Sea, 308
Nubia, Nubians, 115, 306, 320

Oribasius, 80, 250, 252
Oxus, 218, 308, 327, 328, 330, 337, 328

Palestine, 218, 254
Palladius, 250
Parsees, 222
Paul of Aegina, 80, 84, 121, 194, 195, 206, 250, 251, 252, 300
Paul of Thebes, 267
Peripatetics (Aristotelian), 2, 28, 36, 63, 66, 74, 81–82, 92, 124, 190, 198, 202, 217, 275, 287
Persia, 127, 203, 218, 220, 221, 273, 323, 325, 331, 332, 333, 335, 336, 337
Persians, 1, 3, 12–13, 48–50, 52, 108, 115, 127, 134, 143, 147, 156–157, 162–163, 202, 204, 213, 218, 221–222, 268, 292, 302–303, 308, 313, 322–324, 327–328, 331, 333–339

Persian Sea, 308
Petra, 287, 326
Pharaoh, 31, 142, 186, 208, 280–281, 284, 299
Philo, 124, 138, 217, 322
Philotimus, 82
Pingree, David, 143
Plato, xviii, 11, 65, 70, 107, 112, 115, 123, 125, 138, 152, 156, 188, 201, 215, 217, 228, 242, 250, 253, 274–275, 301
Pliny the Elder, 78, 79, 114, 120, 122, 154, 173, 185, 223, 243, 257, 261, 298, 300
Plotinus, xviii, 35, 125, 171, 215, 217, 306
Plutarch, 41, 277
Pontus, 290
Porphyry, xviii, 34, 35, 125
Praxagoras, 82
Proclus, xviii, 126, 214, 301
Ptolemy, Claudius, xviii, 71, 143, 310
Ptolemy Soter, 217
Pythagoras, xviii, 91

Qadarites, 302, 341
Qādisiyya, 143, 336
Qalandar, 292
Qara-Khans, 101
Qayrawān, 306, 320
Quraysh, 210, 213

Rāfiḍites, 302, 341
Rajastan, 143
Ramadan, 211–212
Rami ben Ḥama, 266
al-Rāzī, Abū Ḥātim, 10
al-Rāzī, Muḥammad ibn Zakariyā', 11, 12, 25, 28, 65, 194, 195, 250, 265, 287, 301
Red Sea, 308, 319
Romans, 33, 120, 143, 221, 250, 279, 290, 322, 326, 332, 337–338
Rome, 3, 81, 306, 326, 332
Russia, Russians, 306, 319, 321, 322, 324
Rustam, 162, 264, 335, 336
Rūzbih. *See* Ibn al-Muqaffaʿ

Saadiah, 14, 25, 35, 80, 132, 166, 288, 291, 293, 338
Sabaeans, 143, 264, 319
Sahl al-Tustarī, 266, 314
Saladin, 307
Ṣāliḥ, 285
Samānids, 204, 265, 324–325, 328–329
Samaritans, 302, 342
Sanskrit, 10, 157, 162, 331
Sargon, 116
Sāsān, Sāsānians, 108, 143, 202, 204, 322, 324, 326–329, 332–333, 336
Satan, 7, 28, 132, 133, 135, 136, 138, 164, 274, 293, 309, 312
Saturn, 93, 197, 237, 310
Seleucids, 143, 328
Sennacherib, 142
Septimus, Bernard, 207
Seth, 136
Sextus Empiricus, 79, 146, 221
Shaddād, 178
Shayṣabān, 108
Sheba, Queen of, 10, 108, 140, 164, 220, 319. *See also* Bilqīs
Shiʿis, 10, 12, 110, 163, 213, 220–221, 264–265, 267, 289, 302, 312, 314, 321, 341–342
Shuʿayb, 285
Shuʿūbiyya, 12, 147, 202, 221, 328
Ṣiffīn, 220, 338
Sijistān, 306, 308, 325
Simplicius, 142, 228, 332
Simurgh, 10, 16, 24, 27, 162–163, 172, 269, 336
Sinai, 212
Sind, 143, 306, 319, 325
Sindbad, 6, 176
Sindhind, 143
Sindian Sea, 308
Sindians, 115, 306, 308, 319, 325
Singer, Peter, 100
al-Sīrāfī, 10
Sīstān, 307, 325, 326, 332
Siyāwush, 264, 336
Slavs, 306, 321, 329
Socrates, xviii, 152, 289, 320
Sodom, 313

Solomon, 6, 10, 138–141, 163–164, 192, 205, 218–219, 239, 278, 295–296, 299, 335
Sophists, 17, 33, 149, 278
Spinoza, Baruch, 37, 40, 192, 211
Stoics, 8, 22–23, 31, 34–35, 69, 82, 114, 181, 192, 197–198, 200, 233, 254, 265, 273, 277, 282, 290, 337
Sufis, 52, 63, 64, 110, 162, 164, 200, 212, 266, 272, 289, 292–293, 304–305, 314
Sufyānids, 265
Suhrawardī, 162–163, 289
Sunnis, 12, 17, 110, 221, 302, 307, 312, 314, 342
Syria, 120, 207, 213, 218, 254, 323, 342
Syrians, 35, 209, 220, 337

Ṭabarī, 173, 256
Ṭabaristān, 306, 324
Tāmir, ʿĀrif, xxi, 315
Tangier, 306, 320
al-Tawḥīdī, xvii, 163, 170, 228
Terah, 224
Thābit ibn Qurra, 64, 91, 342
al-Thaʿlabī, 133, 162, 183, 186, 192, 204, 334
Thamūd, 284–285
Themistius, 217
Theophrastus, 217
Thrasymachus, 152
Thuban, 144
Tibetans, 307, 330
Tigris, 308, 322, 323, 332
Tihāma, 210
Tīrān, 127
al-Tirmidhī, 64, 212, 266, 304, 312
Toledo, 157
Torah, 49, 104, 117, 205, 208, 220, 240, 256, 285, 294, 304–305
Transoxiana, 204, 205, 307, 330, 328
Tubbaʿ, 143, 264
Tukhāristān, 306, 327
Tunis, xxiii, 322
Turkey, 322, 330
Turkmenistan, 218, 327, 332
Turks, xxiii, 13, 108, 115, 148, 204, 273, 292, 322, 327, 329–330, 332

ʿUmar, 213, 264, 320, 325, 330
Umayyads, 157, 213, 220, 265, 326, 329, 338
Ur, 116
ʿUthmān, 213, 264, 323, 338

Venus, 93, 127, 237–238
Vishnu, 162
Vishnu Sharman. *See* Bidpai
Watt, William Montgomery, 139
Western Sea, 308

Yaḥyā ibn ʿAdī, 63, 266
Yaʿsūb, 45, 232, 236–237, 239, 241
Yazdijird, 265, 327, 333, 336
Yazīd, 213, 220
Yemen, 164, 168, 306, 319

Zāl, 162, 335, 336
al-Zamakhsharī, 211, 273, 328
Zamharīr, 225–226, 309
Zanj, 306, 319
Zaqqūm, 312
al-Ziriklī, Khayr al-Dīn, xxi, 315
Zoroaster, 302
Zoroastrians, 13, 194, 222, 302, 323–326, 332–335, 337, 339–340

Index Rerum

Active Intellect, 162, 189–190, 199, 214–215, 216, 238
adab, 9, 131, 156, 157
adaptation, 22, 24, 25–26, 31, 67, 112–113, 228, 273. *See also* metamorphosis; natural selection
admonition, 30, 166, 279, 289
agency, 37, 40, 67, 299, 341. *See also* determinism
agriculture, 32–33, 99, 231, 253, 290, 332. *See also* husbandry
air, 34, 36, 39, 65, 83, 85, 86, 87, 90, 92, 95, 96, 97, 101, 110, 113, 152, 165, 169–170, 171, 179, 184, 187, 189, 192, 197–198, 201, 203, 216, 219, 224–225, 227, 229, 232, 234, 245, 254, 258, 276, 279, 296, 298, 309
alchemy, 137, 214
ambition, 15, 176
anatomy, 24, 81–82, 91, 191, 237
angel, xix, 2, 5, 7, 13, 25, 28, 43–44, 45–46, 53, 55, 63, 64–65, 71–72, 105, 108, 117, 125, 131, 132, 133, 135, 136, 155, 162, 174, 183, 189, 201, 207, 209, 212, 215–216, 218, 219, 226, 238, 239, 240, 253, 272, 273, 274, 275, 279, 309, 310, 311–312, 313, 314, 331, 335. *See also* demon; jinn
animal-baiting, 38
ant, 17, 18, 20, 22, 24, 30, 46, 76, 79, 140, 187, 192, 193, 223, 227, 232, 244, 270, 271, 277, 279
antennae, 76
anthropocentrism, 23, 34–35, 39, 41, 66, 216
anthropomorphism, 23, 39
antinomianism, 292
antivenin, 195
ape, 68, 82, 152, 154, 160, 207, 208
apostasy, 269–270, 339
appetite, 7, 15, 159, 250, 266, 289, 304
armour, 20, 122, 151, 174, 185, 192, 329, 335. *See also* weapon
arts and industries, 17, 18, 22, 25, 32, 54, 101, 114, 136, 151, 183, 204, 216, 217, 227, 231, 242, 253, 269, 276, 282, 324, 332, 334
asceticism, 30, 51, 52, 99, 176, 207, 265–266, 293, 304, 312. *See also* saint
ass, 5, 14, 26, 35, 40, 79, 88, 114, 116–117, 120–123, 125, 222, 294
astrology, 78, 92, 116, 137, 143, 197, 207, 214, 256–257, 269, 280–287, 289–290, 337
astronomy, xix, 3, 71, 91, 93, 143–144, 214, 216, 218, 237–238, 269, 310, 342
astrospectroscopy, 125
Atonement, Day of, 221, 305
autonomy, 10, 102. *See also* freedom
autumn, 94, 157, 230, 245

bamboo, 206, 224
basilisk, 223
beak, 27, 77, 87, 90–91, 95–96, 175, 188, 224
bear, 4, 35, 38, 47, 152, 158–161
beast of burden, 14, 102, 104, 129, 325

beast of prey, 16–17, 27, 77, 90, 99–100, 103, 120, 150–161, 259–268, 270
beauty, 6, 13, 35, 110–113, 134, 172, 197, 229, 238, 300, 313
bee, 14, 17, 22, 27, 30, 31, 45, 76, 172–173, 175, 232–236, 242, 243, 245–248, 252, 258, 270, 275, 279
beetle, 198, 297
belly, 17, 77, 81, 107, 157, 184, 227, 257, 267, 300. *See also* oesophagus, rumen
bile (yellow or black), 83–84, 92, 237, 251
biodiversity, 42, 63
bird. *See* fowl
bird of prey, 27, 77, 96, 121, 150, 165, 175–182, 187, 196, 224, 229, 233, 264, 282, 295
Black Stone, 211
bladder, 77, 86–87
blood 12, 38, 45, 49, 64, 82–84, 89, 92–93, 118, 133, 148, 160, 193, 200, 205, 210, 235, 237, 241, 262–263, 265, 296, 334; blood vessel, 67, 77–78, 82–86, 89, 93, 193, 313
boar, 192
bowel, 14, 21, 77, 79, 84, 88, 118, 123, 187, 193, 235, 288
brain, 11, 14, 70, 77, 81–82, 118, 174, 193, 238, 289, 293, 334
bribe, 147, 294
bridle, 99, 118, 122, 257
brigands, 230, 244, 250, 270
buffalo, 16, 78, 111, 176, 192, 223–225, 263
bulbul, 163, 167, 279
butcher, 14, 82, 118, 198, 249
butterfly, 138

calendar, 13, 93, 333
caliph, xviii, 12, 143, 146–147, 180, 213, 220, 228, 237–238, 264–265, 268, 274, 293–295, 320, 323–325, 327, 330, 338, 341. *See also* monarch
camel, 10, 14, 26, 78, 88–89, 95, 99, 106, 111–113, 117–121, 155, 161, 176, 178, 219, 263, 297–298
carnivore. *See* beast of prey
cat, 27, 32, 47, 152, 154, 159–162, 168, 198, 222, 251
caterpillar, 74
causality, 25, 29, 64, 67, 86, 89–90, 112, 144, 181, 197–198, 200, 203, 206, 214–215, 233, 242, 248, 251, 252, 282, 302,
celebration, 248, 253–254
centipede, 76
chameleon, 187
character, 25, 44, 47–48, 52–53, 64, 72, 103, 115, 119, 122, 131, 153, 155–156, 158–159, 192, 222, 224, 226, 241, 266, 268–71, 307, 313–315
charity, 167, 181–182, 255, 257–258, 282, 285, 287, 291. *See also* kindness
chauvinism, 12, 204, 205, 217, 296. *See also* pride
cheetah, 27, 152, 154, 160, 180, 222, 263
chick, 24, 46, 80, 94–96, 251, 271, 277–278
child, 27, 38, 46, 79, 108, 126, 134, 137, 153, 162, 181, 184, 190, 208, 223, 246, 251, 272, 274, 277, 280–281, 283, 339. *See also* parent
chrysolite, 206
chyme, 83, 193
city, city folk, 17, 32–33, 99, 106, 148, 204, 219, 231, 306, 308
claw, 16, 22, 27, 76–77, 90, 151–152, 160, 175, 185, 188, 191–192, 222–223, 259, 262–263, 308
clay, 31, 41, 66, 68, 74, 78–79, 94, 105, 111, 135, 193, 276–277, 295–296, 298
clothing, 32, 66, 95, 99, 109–110, 115, 126, 134, 136, 148, 151, 174, 192, 231, 249, 253, 259–262, 300, 308
cock, 38, 47, 79, 157–158, 163–165, 169, 251, 279
commerce, 18, 101, 148, 166, 227, 242, 249, 253, 319, 321, 324–326, 329, 332
compass, 17, 123, 275, 298
compassion, 15, 30, 33, 38, 46, 74, 102, 115–119, 146, 153, 187–188, 190, 202, 209–210, 232, 239, 246, 261, 270–274, 278. *See also* kindness; mercy

composite, 27–28, 65, 206, 215, 313
conquest, xviii, 12, 108, 143, 213, 265, 320–330, 337, 342
conscience, 132, 286
consciousness, 27, 37–38, 43–44, 54, 238
consultation, 44, 127, 145–146, 150, 152, 342
cookery, 88, 107, 136, 248–249, 263
copper, 79, 183, 329
cormorant, 163
corruption, moral, 29, 32, 44, 64, 119, 132–133, 160, 280–281, 313; physical 92, 197–198
cosmetics, 157
cosmopolitanism, 50, 52, 217, 265, 314
cosmos, 12–13, 19, 21, 25, 28, 91–92, 125, 143–144, 172, 203, 208, 310
country folk, 32–33, 41, 180
courtesy. *See adab*
court, 9, 11, 27, 44, 102, 108, 127–128, 137, 142, 146, 153, 155, 157, 164, 174, 178, 184, 268, 290, 327
cow, 41, 99, 107, 111, 114, 121, 123, 173, 227, 257, 260, 263 331
crab, 84, 183, 185, 192, 226, 309
crane, 46, 95–98, 163, 169–170, 271, 279
crawling creature, 26–27, 67, 75–77, 85, 90–91, 96, 112, 187–199
creatureliness, 20, 24, 30, 146, 153
cricket, 26, 84–85, 172, 187–197, 225, 279, 297–298, 301
cry, 21, 38, 41, 53, 85, 126, 177, 188, 240, 268
crocodile, 16, 183–186, 196–197, 223, 226, 229, 309
cross (hybrid), 26, 120, 277
cruelty, 14, 107, 229, 290
cube, 92–93, 234
cud, 88. *See also* rumen
culture, 8–9, 33, 52, 70, 99, 136, 138, 153, 156, 183, 269, 278, 280, 314, 321, 328
cycle, 29, 31, 36, 93, 142–144, 198, 202, 218, 229, 237, 290
cynicism, 10, 137, 152, 265, 267, 313
death, 33, 35–37, 49, 148, 165–167, 171, 177–179, 196, 201, 207, 237, 252, 260, 302–303, 305, 306
demon, 7, 74, 81, 100–101, 138–139, 141, 155, 201, 219, 238, 274, 293, 309, 312, 331, 335, 337. *See also* angel; jinn
desert (sand) 94, 97, 105, 107, 126, 163, 170, 182–183, 203, 205–209, 240, 242, 267, 287–288, 307, 323, 325–326
deserts (worth), 35–37, 39, 43
design, 1, 6, 24–25, 30, 73, 79, 113, 190, 200, 298, 308. *See also* adaptation
destiny, 29, 52, 71, 116, 133, 137, 199, 219, 228, 281–282, 285, 306, 314. *See also* fortune
determinism, 282, 338, 341. *See also* agency
dhimmī, 321, 342
dialogue, 10–12, 337
diet, 32, 66, 99, 175, 250, 252, 260, 289
digestion, 17, 83, 196, 227
dimensions, xix, 65, 201, 214–215, 309
disaster, 282–287
discernment, 52, 54, 65, 76, 80, 113–114, 135, 150–152, 155, 175, 183, 186, 216, 238, 242–247, 314
disease, 193, 218, 250–252, 285, 289–291
disgrace, 135, 142, 254, 256
diversity, 48–51, 70, 91, 124, 187, 199, 214–215, 231, 288, 301–303, 306, 308–309
divine right, 146
diviner, 269, 279–280. *See also* astrology
dogma, 28, 119, 288
dog, 20, 27, 32, 35, 38, 47–48, 88, 121, 154, 157–162, 222, 251, 257
dolphin, 183–184, 226, 309
dominion, 15, 29, 49, 53, 104, 146, 208, 218, 221, 235, 242, 299, 314
dove, 94, 96, 251, 278–279
dragon, 16, 26–27, 31, 85, 187–188, 193–194, 225–226, 229, 307, 333, 335
drum, 79, 154, 236
duck, 163
dung, 74, 164, 187, 193, 198, 235, 249

eagle, 18, 162, 174–175, 183, 190, 193, 196, 227
earwig, 187
eclogue, 33
ecology, 30–31, 41–42
effeminate, 270
egg, 27, 67, 75, 79–80, 86, 94–95, 243, 245–246, 277
elegy, 18, 21, 33, 166, 176, 179, 183
element, 65, 71, 86, 92, 204, 206, 215, 238, 242, 246, 250, 309. *See also* humours
elephant, 14–16, 20–21, 26, 42, 78–79, 111–112, 118, 120, 122, 168, 176, 191–192, 206, 223–225, 263, 297
emanation, 12, 46, 78, 125–126, 162–163, 172, 190, 214–215, 233, 240, 272
embodiment, 43, 71–72, 275, 309
embryology, xix, 68, 78, 89, 237. *See also* development; gestation; metamorphosis
emissary, 156, 163, 183, 232, 236, 241
empire, 50, 93, 120, 168, 218, 264, 323, 327–328, 332, 334
enlightenment, 132, 215, 315
environment, 24, 26–27, 30–32, 41, 100–101, 106, 134
equality, 26, 191
equator, 68, 78, 101, 206, 224, 262
equinox, 71, 144
erect stature, 69, 109
eremite, 30
eschatology, 72, 119, 165, 314
essay form, 1–3, 8–9, 21
essence, 28, 82, 92, 111, 171, 215, 219, 296
eternity, 13, 28–29, 53, 66, 74, 86, 116, 124–125, 135, 143–144, 189–190, 198, 200–201, 203, 206–207, 266, 275, 279, 281, 287–288, 311, 338. *See also* immortality
ethics, 30, 37–43, 64, 102, 125–126, 132, 136, 182, 266, 306
ethnicity, 12–13, 39, 50, 108, 113, 320
ethos. *See* character
evolution, 24, 26–27, 31, 67, 144, 198, 234
exile, 73, 99, 262, 295, 338
exploitation 13, 15, 20, 24, 30–32, 35, 41, 53, 69, 100, 107, 152, 204, 213, 264
extinction, 160, 196
eye, 15–17, 21, 26, 38, 48–49, 70, 73, 75, 79–80, 96, 111–112, 117, 122, 140, 148, 159, 162, 164, 176, 185–188, 199–200, 218, 223, 227, 233–235, 238, 276–280, 291, 301, 305, 308, 311, 315, 329, 335

fable, 1–7, 10–15, 19, 23, 26, 28, 29, 33–34, 40–41, 44, 50–52, 54, 63–64, 69, 101, 117, 145, 157, 164, 172, 176, 190, 334
factionalism, 12, 301
faith, 12, 43, 48–52, 131–132, 137–138, 141, 146–147, 201, 209, 211–213, 220, 231, 283–284, 287–293, 295, 302–306, 313, 329, 338, 340–341
falcon, falconry, 18, 175, 180–181, 187, 227
fast, 176, 181, 211–212, 221, 255–257, 282, 287. *See also* asceticism
fatalism, 282. *See also* determinism
fate, 20, 28–29, 33, 35, 116, 136, 148, 167, 178–179, 201, 207, 214, 228, 253–254, 263, 280–282, 285, 287, 315, 337, 341
fear, 8, 16–18, 20, 27, 31, 69, 79, 99, 101, 116, 123, 130–131, 156, 161, 176, 184–186, 192, 207, 223, 226–227, 232, 240, 247, 250, 252, 256, 283–287, 295, 303,
fellowship, xv, xix, 8, 12
festival, 212, 255, 258
fever, 250, 324
finch, 163
finitude, 25, 30, 288, 293
fire, 65, 69, 92, 100, 105, 107, 125, 135, 142, 202, 207, 216, 249, 263, 291, 334; Abraham cast into, 137, 173–174, 186; jinn, 100; worship, 221, 322, 326, 332–333. *See also* hell-fire
fish, 31, 84, 140, 152, 183–183, 191–193, 223, 263, 309, 326
flea, 77, 164, 187, 246
fleece, 14, 22, 107, 109, 116,123, 148, 173, 188, 203, 261, 264

flock, 44, 95, 114, 139, 152, 168, 175, 181–182, 209, 243, 270, 283–284
flower, 31, 52, 73, 75, 134, 233, 238, 242–243, 249, 262, 298, 314
flute, 69, 152, 236
fly, 18, 74, 76–77, 84, 112, 173–174, 191, 198, 227, 246, 276–277
folklore, 6, 108, 178
food chain, 30–31, 41, 198, 229
fool, 23, 70, 79, 145, 155, 181, 270, 280, 291, 294
foot, 14, 69–70, 77, 81, 95–96, 114, 117, 135, 253
forest, 19, 42, 100, 107, 121, 229, 259, 263, 266, 268, 291, 307, 324, 334
form, 7, 13, 24, 28, 31, 66–67, 71, 90, 140, 189, 198–202, 214–215, 238–239, 272, 274–275, 286, 296, 309
fortune, 22, 78, 115–116, 123, 143, 161, 171, 206, 232, 254, 280, 282, 285, 289. *See also* destiny
fowl, 16–18, 21, 24, 26–27, 29, 31, 42, 54, 70, 73, 77, 87–88, 90–91, 94–98, 134, 137, 139, 140, 150, 162,–172, 187, 190, 192, 227, 233, 245, 248–256, 269–270, 276–278, 309
fox, 4, 47, 152, 154, 158, 222, 322
francolin, 94–96
free will. *See* agency
freedom, 47, 49, 69, 99, 103, 119, 121, 126, 128–130, 137, 142–143, 145–149, 248–251, 271, 290, 295, 303. *See also* exploitation; slavery
frog, 27, 84, 183, 186, 226, 228–229, 279, 307–309
fruit, 47, 66–67, 73–74, 90, 95–96, 99, 101, 109–110, 134–136, 158–161, 166, 171–172, 181, 187, 216–217, 233–235, 247, 249, 252, 254, 262, 273, 291, 297, 325
fugitive, 107
fur, 75, 77, 86–87, 116, 259, 261, 300
furnishings, 14, 148, 203, 231
future, 168, 244, 250, 280

gall-bladder, 83–84, 86, 89, 193, 238
garden. *See* paradise
gazelle, 20, 96, 100, 121, 129, 192, 330
gecko, 91, 186–187
generosity, 2, 13, 16, 24, 44–46, 54, 67, 102–103, 125, 130, 137, 156, 158, 164–165, 190, 193, 223, 232, 246, 261, 270–271, 316
geography, xix, 50, 203, 319
geology, 234
geometry, xix, 3, 91, 214, 216
gestation, 78–79. *See also* embryology
giraffe, 26–27, 79, 120
gizzard, 77, 87, 193
glory, 35, 124, 136, 200, 219
gnat, 18, 20, 24, 26, 31, 76–77, 79, 84, 98, 112, 173–174, 191, 198, 223, 227, 246, 299
God, attribute of, 338, 340; constancy of, 260; infinitude of, 9, 171, 215; providence of, 2, 12, 22, 24, 34, 46, 67–70, 85, 89–90, 124, 144, 175, 198–202, 231, 233, 245, 247, 272, 273, 277–278; unity of, 256; wrath of, 53, 208, 266, 284, 312
gods, 19, 69–71, 116, 124, 152, 208, 215–219, 237, 256, 282, 326, 333
gold, 132, 183, 208, 257, 326, 329, 330
Gospels, 49, 104, 220, 240, 294, 304–305
government, 18, 22–23, 48–49, 76, 106, 128, 153, 204, 222, 227, 230–231, 234–235, 238, 250, 270, 291, 303, 329
grain, 17, 66–67, 74, 80, 88, 90, 95–96, 101, 166, 171, 187, 200, 244, 247, 249, 252, 254, 278, 297, 310, 323, 325
grass, 19, 35, 94, 110, 112, 120, 151, 171, 203, 206, 224, 242–243, 245, 249, 276
grasshopper, 17–18, 24, 30, 76–77, 84, 98, 187, 227
gratitude, 1, 15–16, 29, 46–47, 65, 106, 123, 139–140, 146, 182, 271, 299–300
grave, 80, 155, 167, 177, 227, 247, 254, 290, 311
Great Year, 144
grief, 9, 41, 73, 114, 122, 130, 136, 165, 178, 220, 252, 254, 291, 303
griffin, 10, 16, 175–176, 179–182, 224
grub, 26, 74, 193
guilt, 33, 54, 208

habit, 63, 90, 94, 138, 161, 199
habitat, 15, 27–32, 67, 99–101, 105, 129, 160, 187, 208, 229–230, 236, 253, 306
hadith, 10, 74, 100, 105, 111, 133, 149–150, 161, 200, 210, 219–220, 256, 289, 292, 294, 301–302, 310, 312
hair, 22, 32, 70, 77, 86–87, 107, 113, 121, 134–135, 148, 173, 188, 203, 205, 261–264, 292, 329, 336. *See also* fleece; fur
hand, 69, 77, 81, 109, 117, 151–152, 188, 193, 208, 234, 264
happiness, 40, 74, 97, 115, 254
harmony, 91, 93, 101, 188
hatred, 97, 120, 130–131, 134–136, 142, 154–155, 159, 179–181, 194, 235, 268
hawk, 18, 175, 180, 183, 193, 196–197, 227
health, 14, 66, 85, 195, 197, 249, 285, 289
hearing, 75–76, 96, 193, 268
heart, 1, 7, 16, 38, 63, 77, 81–83, 85–86, 110, 136–138, 157, 178, 181–182, 187–188, 192, 197, 199, 204–205, 209, 219, 223, 233, 236–237, 241, 250, 254, 261–262, 266, 273, 282, 285, 289–291, 293–295, 315
heaven, 22, 49, 74, 80–81, 97, 101, 105, 133, 136, 141, 143, 150, 164, 174, 179, 207, 211–212, 218, 239, 258, 305, 308
heavenly (celestial) body, 19, 31, 45, 70, 93, 106, 124, 144, 198, 206, 215–216, 237–239, 273, 281. *See also* star, planet, moon
hegemony, 15, 29, 99, 116, 143, 203, 205, 321, 327; Arab, 12–13, 147, 265, 323
hell-fire, 50, 80, 149, 167, 294, 305, 312,
Hellenism, 80, 120, 144, 217, 265
helplessness, 26, 188–192, 229, 282, 308
herb, 88, 95–96, 99, 101, 134, 245, 249, 253, 263, 273
heron, 96, 98, 163
homosexuality, 113, 221, 257. *See also*, sex
honey, 14, 47, 89, 158, 224, 235, 243, 252, 298–300, 311
honour, 180, 235, 238, 246, 248, 253–254, 259, 266
hoof, 88, 151, 192
hoopoe, 94, 140, 163–164, 279
horn, 22, 76, 89, 111, 151, 176, 192, 235
horse, 14–16, 28, 35, 38, 68, 88, 99, 104, 107, 114, 117–118, 120–123, 132, 151, 155, 160–161, 192, 195, 263, 333
humours, 83–84, 92, 238, 252
hunger, 14, 117–118, 161, 223, 251, 253, 258, 285
hunting, 18, 35, 38, 41, 48, 96–97, 100, 102, 107, 115, 121, 130, 159–160, 162, 176, 178, 180, 184, 191, 227, 251, 253, 263–264, 326, 333
husbandry, 33, 148, 231
hybrid. *See* cross
hyena, 152, 155

idolatry, 208, 281
illness, 18, 21, 115, 162, 193, 237, 250–251, 257, 285–286, 289
imagination, 6–7, 22, 105, 138, 238
imam, 51–52, 110, 132, 163, 213, 194, 221, 312, 314, 341–342
immortality, 51, 53–54, 196, 274
imperfection, 68, 89, 124, 185, 300
infidel, 201, 209, 312
injustice, 1, 65, 102, 108, 121, 126, 128, 146, 149, 231, 241, 261, 268, 301, 314
inspiration, 44, 135, 138–139, 162, 175, 191, 218, 232–233, 236–238, 242, 244, 251, 255, 258, 273–278
instinct, 22, 44, 191, 233–234, 251, 277
intestine, 77, 79, 84, 86, 193, 288. *See also* bowel
iron, 16, 79, 100, 116, 118, 122, 137, 139, 152, 183, 223–224, 238, 329
irony, 13–14, 21, 174, 205, 314; dramatic, 5, 11, 216
irrigation, 32, 134, 204, 249, 329

jackal, 10, 20, 47, 152, 155, 158, 165, 222, 260
jihad, 30, 50, 304, 306
jinn, xix, 1–7, 10, 12–14, 20, 28, 30–31, 44–45, 48, 52–53, 73, 100–102, 106, 108, 110–111, 120, 125–133, 136–142, 151–152, 163–164, 175, 184, 186, 199–202, 205,

207–209, 213, 216–219, 232, 236–241, 247, 260, 262, 268, 271–272, 295–296, 299, 309–311, 313, 334
judge, 30, 67, 101, 107–108, 127–128, 139, 145–150, 155, 199, 231, 237–238, 269, 294, 334
judgement, divine, 20, 29–30, 103, 144, 169, 179, 182, 190, 212, 220–221, 227, 232, 239, 288, 311–312, 339–341

kalām, 211, 245
kidney, 77, 83–84, 86, 89, 193, 250
kin, 26–27, 119, 123, 203, 295
kindness, 15, 46, 106, 115–116, 148, 209, 223, 261, 270–272, 278, 291. *See also* compassion; generosity
king. *See* monarch
knowledge, xviii, xx, 23, 25, 34, 64, 69–70, 72, 91, 96, 99, 110–112, 129, 132–133, 136–141, 146, 162, 164, 169, 183, 188, 190, 197, 200, 210, 217, 225, 242–244, 247, 258, 267, 275, 277, 279–281, 289, 298, 307, 320, 338

lark, 18, 94, 163, 166, 227, 279, 323
law, 28, 125, 131–132, 137–138, 145–147, 160, 199, 205, 212, 231, 257, 266, 294
leaf, 66–67, 75, 88, 94, 176, 187, 234, 243, 245, 249, 275, 298; as clothing, 99, 109–110, 135
leisure 135, 204, 253
leopard, 35, 160, 222, 263
lice, 31, 187, 195, 299
lion, 10, 16, 20, 24, 35, 79, 88, 150–162, 192, 222–223, 233, 260, 263, 267
literalism, 107, 308
liver, 77, 81, 83–84, 89, 118, 193
lizard, 91, 187
locust, 80, 84–85, 164, 173, 197, 245, 299
logic, xix–xx, 10, 37, 181, 216
lore, 1, 24, 52, 137–140, 212, 218, 227, 255, 269, 296, 314
loyalty, 45, 153, 156, 237, 239
lung, 77, 81, 83, 85, 86, 289

macrocosm, xviii, 237, 274. *See also* microcosm
magic, 121, 126, 129, 134, 136–137, 141, 162, 218
magpie, 163
male and female, 68, 78, 84–85, 89, 94, 113, 134, 161, 172–173, 278, 284
martyr, 29, 116, 212–213, 220–221, 267. *See also* self-sacrifice
mathematics, xviii, xx, 1, 24, 93, 129, 214, 216, 328, 342
matter, xix, 66, 68, 72, 78, 84, 86, 90, 111, 187, 189, 197–198, 214–215, 237, 247, 287, 298, 306
medicine, 18, 32, 82–83, 93, 121, 194–195, 206, 216, 250, 252, 285–286, 290, 300, 329. *See also* physician
melancholy, 84, 94, 168, 237. *See also* humours
melody, 16, 188, 223. *See also* music
mercy 90, 117–119, 121, 126, 146, 188, 272; God's, 15, 24, 29, 102, 136, 140, 161, 205, 211, 232, 244, 253, 261, 274, 278, 280. *See also* compassion
metamorphosis, 17, 245–247
microcosm, xviii, xix, 274. *See also* macrocosm
midrash, 2, 5, 29, 124, 137–138, 174, 207, 256, 278, 296
milk, 14, 32, 47, 66, 116–117, 123, 148, 158, 224, 235, 248, 252, 278, 311
milling, 107, 117, 134, 249, 253
millipede, 76
mimicry, 154, 167, 181, 224
mineral, 63–67, 71–72, 132, 134, 183, 197, 206, 216, 219, 237–238, 242
miniver, 259
miracle, 72, 212, 241, 255–256, 299
mole, 75
monarch, 6, 10, 26, 44–46, 49, 51, 81, 102–103, 116, 127–128, 138, 147, 153, 161, 172–173, 178, 201, 204, 220, 223–224, 231, 237, 239, 240–241, 243, 270–272, 299, 303, 332. *See also* caliph
monotheism 36, 48, 51, 63, 71, 107, 120,

124–125, 137, 146, 166, 198, 200, 210, 215, 239, 260, 284, 301–302, 314, 339–340, 342
moon, 19, 93, 106, 116, 124–125, 170, 190, 197–198, 202, 225, 237, 273, 302, 310
morality. *See* ethics
mosquito, 18, 79, 173–174, 227
mouse, 76, 79, 159, 192, 194, 225, 297
mule, 14–15, 88, 99, 103–119, 161, 263, 294
music, 21, 84–85, 91–92, 97, 166, 171–172, 188, 296. *See also* melody
mystic, 72, 162, 215, 267, 289, 292–293, 314
myth, 99, 136, 162, 216, 274, 280, 335–336

nakedness, 33, 109, 134–135, 148, 151–152, 188, 190–191, 252–253, 259, 261–262, 291, 300
nation, 18–19, 50, 52, 108, 115, 119, 138, 173, 176, 204, 217–218, 225, 227, 265, 306–309
natural selection, 24–25, 31, 67, 75–76
naturalism, 25, 251
navigation, 96, 216, 335
nest, 22, 94–97, 162–163, 169, 234, 246, 250, 277
nightingale, 24, 48, 51, 163, 171–172, 248–251, 301, 311
nomad, 32, 99, 108, 148, 180, 307, 324
nostril, 16, 83, 85, 122, 174, 222, 235
nutriment 34, 66, 75–76, 83, 193, 196, 249, 262
nut, 67, 207

oasis, 204
obligation, 19, 34, 37, 39, 42–43, 50–51, 102, 125, 181, 212, 257, 305
occasionalism, 89–91, 245
occult, 136, 139, 221, 280–281
oesophagus, 79, 84, 88
offspring. *See* progeny
oil, 47, 121, 158, 194, 247
omen, 71, 81, 168, 177, 180, 189, 233, 241, 279, 282
omphalos, 203
ontology, 13, 73, 215, 301
oppression, 1, 20, 65, 108, 115, 119, 126, 129–130, 142, 146, 182, 236, 241, 253, 263, 301, 331, 334
orator, 150, 166, 193, 195, 242, 266, 269, 278–279, 301, 311
organ, 24, 26–27, 31, 35, 69, 77, 79, 81, 83–90, 94, 153, 175, 190–193, 196, 199, 235, 237–238, 297
ornament, 54, 134, 261
ostrich, 26–27, 30, 95, 163, 277
owl, 18, 21, 24, 175–176, 179–182, 186, 279
ox, 35, 89, 117, 120, 125–126, 183, 260
oyster, 24, 76, 297–298, 300

paganism, 71, 120, 137, 168, 180, 204, 211, 216–217, 237, 269, 281, 284, 292, 302, 330, 342
parable, 73, 207, 255, 291
paradise, 49, 72, 74, 133–134, 165, 178, 224, 274, 303–304, 306, 311, 337. *See also* heaven
parasite, 26, 34, 180, 193
parent, 26, 47, 89, 114, 123, 140, 164, 246, 261, 271–272, 276, 278–279, 302, 305, 331. *See also* child
parrot, 20, 27, 45, 175, 181, 224, 269, 271–272, 275, 282, 292, 295
partridge, 94, 163, 165, 278
pasture, 88, 100, 104, 114–115, 210, 243
peacock, 96, 163–172
penitence, 18, 30, 50, 165, 258, 286, 293, 305
perfection, 9, 20, 72, 77, 124–125, 138, 144, 198, 212, 300, 314
perfume, 260, 323, 335
pheasant, 80, 163, 166
philosopher, 10–12, 28, 40, 45, 53, 65, 71–72, 82, 97, 107, 127, 130–131, 137–138, 144–145, 155–156, 172, 190, 199–200, 202, 216–218, 221, 232–233, 247, 269, 271–273, 276, 282, 287, 289, 296, 298, 301, 310, 320, 332

phoenix, 162
physician, 123, 195, 250, 256, 269, 282, 285–286, 289–290, 320, 342; of the soul, 256–257. *See also* medicine
pietism, 2, 18, 21, 30, 51, 54, 176, 179, 181, 212, 214, 256, 266, 278, 282, 285, 292–294, 304, 312
pig, 4, 28, 34, 82, 88, 119–121, 132, 192, 208–209, 224, 263
pigeon, 96, 163, 165
pity, 14, 118–121, 148–149, 188, 263, 291. *See also* compassion; mercy
planet, 13, 19, 30, 45, 71, 78, 92–93, 124, 127, 144, 197, 215, 237–238, 281, 310, 333. *See also* heavenly (celestial) body
plant, 19, 29, 31, 39, 41, 63, 65–75, 86, 88, 96, 99, 101, 105, 132, 134–136, 166–167, 171, 184, 193, 197, 203–209, 216–217, 219, 225, 231, 235, 238, 242–243, 249, 251, 259, 262, 269, 273, 275, 290–291, 297
pleasure, 15, 41–42, 88, 143, 146, 166–167, 172, 175, 190, 201, 210, 235, 241, 246, 249–250, 254, 257
ploughing, 18, 99, 107, 134, 136, 227, 249, 253. *See also* agriculture
plumage, 22, 24, 70, 77, 86–87, 95–96, 98, 107, 109, 162, 164, 173, 175, 188, 261, 300
poet, poetry, 11, 24–25, 31, 40, 51, 116–117, 122, 125, 138–139, 157, 162, 168, 179, 241, 265, 267, 269, 273, 278–279, 289, 312
politics, 43, 45, 47, 49–50, 102, 126, 128, 150, 180, 228, 235–236, 303–304, 340
poverty, 119,190, 237, 244, 258, 291, 325
prayer, 18, 21, 95, 97, 101, 115, 139, 141, 161, 164–165, 167–169, 181–182, 186, 190, 207–208, 211–212, 242, 255–258, 267, 273, 282, 285–287, 292, 294, 299, 316
preacher, 52, 53, 163, 166, 266, 279, 293, 315
predator. *See* beast of prey
pride, 1–2, 7, 10, 12–13, 14–15, 21, 23, 25, 30, 33, 47, 54, 103, 106, 111, 113–114, 124, 127, 133, 139, 151, 173, 183, 204–205, 216, 220, 228, 245–261, 270, 282, 288–295, 309–312
proboscis, 26, 76, 79, 191, 235
progeny, 46–47, 67–68, 86, 89, 99, 103, 107–109, 113, 136, 143, 154, 165, 160, 207–208, 232, 234–235, 243, 246, 248, 253, 260, 271, 291, 331, 342. *See also* child
prophecy, prophet, 5, 10, 14, 29, 51–52, 103, 110, 119, 130–132, 136–138, 141, 147, 164–165, 184, 204, 206, 208–213, 218–221, 232, 238, 241, 251, 255–257, 267, 275, 280, 285, 288–289, 292, 294–295, 299, 310, 312, 314, 316, 332, 339
proportion, 26, 41, 96, 111–112, 122, 124, 198, 224, 310. *See also* symmetry
prose, 8–9, 157, 211
prosperity, 102, 186, 210, 215, 235, 323–329
prostration, 12, 165, 273, 293, 310
punishment, 113, 148, 208–209, 252, 260–262, 274, 284, 341. *See also* judgement; retribution
purity, physical, 66, 84, 235, 248, 311; spiritual, 1, 7, 18, 51–54, 63, 181, 201, 212, 226, 237, 256, 265, 269, 273, 282. 285, 312, 314–315
pyramid, 203, 281

quadruped, 70, 90, 109
quail, 94–95, 163, 208, 278

rabbit, 4, 6, 14, 19, 111–112, 121, 123, 192, 257
racecourse, 38
race. *See* ethnicity
ram, 14, 79, 111, 117, 139
raven, 21, 95, 163–164, 168, 258, 267, 279
reason, 11, 13, 21–22, 25–26, 35, 37, 43–45, 51, 54, 69, 82, 91, 100, 103, 107–109, 112, 117, 131, 135, 138, 148–149, 151, 156, 157, 175, 181, 191–192, 200, 214, 229, 233, 235, 238–240, 242, 251, 273–274, 288, 294
rebellion, 7, 12, 45, 100, 102–103, 107–108, 126, 141, 201, 205–206, 213, 220, 230,

239–240, 250, 252, 260, 321, 326–327, 335, 338–339, 341
religion, 47–51, 71, 115, 131–132, 137, 156, 184, 212, 215, 242, 260, 287, 289, 292–293, 301–307, 334. *See also* law
repentance, 27, 29, 119, 205, 258, 282, 284–285, 294, 299
reproduction, 30, 82, 86, 99, 107, 113, 196, 253
responsibility, 53–54, 114, 231, 236, 312, 341
resurrection, 29, 50–51, 80, 119, 142, 167, 203, 220, 247, 288, 291, 295, 305–306, 311, 312
retribution, 29, 54, 146, 165, 182, 249, 312. *See also* judgement
revelation, 47, 101, 162, 199, 208, 211–212, 216, 218, 237, 251, 258, 265, 279, 288. *See also* inspiration
revolution, 4, 13, 19, 29–30, 116, 124, 144, 153, 216, 220, 228, 265, 283, 327
rhinoceros, 27, 176, 179, 182
rib, 77, 87
riddle, 52, 279
ring-dove, 157, 163
river, 89, 94, 96, 97, 101, 104, 134, 169, 172, 184, 203–204, 206, 219, 249, 254, 307–308, 311, 324–329
roach, 34, 187
romance, 29, 32–33, 42, 85, 136, 173, 178, 253, 264
rumen, 77, 86–88, 193, 196

sacrifice, 38, 49–51, 120, 181, 209, 282, 285, 304–305
saint, 51–54, 212–213, 265, 267, 294, 312–314, 316
salamander, 187
salvation, 12, 30, 40, 64, 72, 74, 168, 221
sand-grouse, 46, 95, 170, 271, 279
sandpiper, 163, 171
satire, 3–6, 8, 9, 13, 16, 17, 21, 28, 157, 168, 221, 313
scales, 22, 77, 87, 183, 188, 261, 308
scarab, 173, 193
scholar, 110, 120, 126–127, 129, 131, 142, 145, 155, 217, 269, 282, 296, 300, 332
science, scientist, 1–2, 10, 25, 39, 52, 72, 89, 112–114, 155, 183, 195, 199, 203, 207, 214, 216–218, 233, 238, 242–244, 269, 288, 296–297, 314–315, 320–321, 342
scorpion, 76, 187, 194, 197, 225, 297
scripture, 5, 10, 117, 208–209, 233, 269, 281–282, 292, 314, 332, 337, 342
sculptor, 79
sea, 15, 17, 18, 27, 42, 68, 73, 75, 79, 99, 101, 104–105, 107, 131, 152, 163–164, 170, 182–183, 191, 200, 202, 207–208, 227, 229, 253, 259, 273, 308–309; sea-shore, 94, 126, 183, 226, 254
sea-serpent, 10, 16–18, 24, 30–31, 182–186, 196–197, 225–229, 309
season,15, 26, 68, 93–94, 111, 167, 230, 242, 246, 249, 282, 300, 326
sectarianism, 12, 48, 221, 265, 270, 301–306
self-sacrifice, 49–51, 304–305
sermon, 52, 166, 212, 255, 315, 323; Sermon on the Mount, 32, 167, 258
serpent. *See* snake
servant, 82, 115, 140, 163, 181, 201, 216, 220, 231, 272, 280, 295
sex, 15, 39, 86, 196, 257, 300
shame, 33, 73, 79, 135, 208, 250, 254–255, 261–262, 265, 268, 270–271, 293
sheep, 20, 24, 88–89, 99, 107, 114, 118, 121, 139, 157, 160–162, 173, 195, 222, 227, 233, 251, 260–263, 325
shell, 22, 73, 77, 86–87, 183, 192, 261, 308, 310
shepherd, 33, 45, 139, 152
ship, 7, 16, 73, 101–102, 104, 152, 182–183, 224
shout, 14, 41, 103, 117,122, 155
sight, 38, 70, 75–76, 96, 176, 199–200, 275
silk, 14, 22, 33, 259–261, 300; industry, 32, 219, 324
silkworm, 17, 245, 276, 297–298, 324
sin, 208–209, 255–257, 261, 268, 275, 338–341

sincerity, 1, 13, 34, 181–182, 275, 285, 293
skin, 6, 14, 38, 75, 77–78, 86, 96, 109–110, 112–113, 117, 121, 148, 152, 174, 200, 214, 261–263, 308, 329
skylark,18
slavery, 47, 69, 99–109, 113, 115, 129–120, 137, 145, 147–148, 151, 163, 204, 213, 228–229, 236, 238, 241–243, 247–250, 254–255, 259, 269, 271, 280, 290–291, 301, 307–311, 322, 327, 329
sleep, 73, 80, 159, 165, 178, 243–246, 250–251, 256, 260, 275–277
smell, 73–76, 96, 120–122, 164, 193, 244
snake, 35–36, 76–77, 91, 175, 187, 194–197, 208, 225, 290, 334
snow, 74–76, 187, 323
soil, 31, 41, 66, 73, 95, 101, 116, 134, 167, 203, 206, 224, 245, 326
song, 9, 17–18, 29, 85, 97, 134, 139, 163, 165–166, 170–172, 188, 190, 199, 226, 238, 253, 303
sorcerer, 121, 269, 280, 284. *See also* magic
soul, 12, 34, 40–41, 43, 48, 50, 63, 70, 82–83, 91, 104, 109, 129, 160, 170, 179, 182, 184, 188, 192, 215, 230, 233, 246, 274–275, 295, 297–298, 300–301, 304–306, 309; human, 7, 30, 43, 45, 53–54, 64, 72, 81, 131, 134–135, 155, 200, 249–257, 261–262, 273–274, 289–290, 293; of the spheres, 25, 71, 238–239; of the world, 67, 71–72, 162, 215, 274, 287
sovereignty, 6, 43–44, 70, 85, 103, 128, 140–141, 148, 153, 190, 202, 211, 218, 239, 256, 284
sparrow, 18, 95, 163, 227, 278
spectre, 200, 209, 296, 309
spider, 187, 191, 276
spirit, 12, 13, 21, 31, 65, 71, 100, 108, 131, 200–210, 209, 218, 228, 309. *See also* jinn
spirituality, 10, 12, 18, 20, 23, 30, 34, 49–54, 74, 89, 111, 138, 153, 182, 188, 191, 197, 211, 221, 266, 292, 298, 304–305
spleen 77, 83–84, 86, 89, 193, 237
spokesman 35, 50, 69, 102–112, 114–115, 127, 150–151, 156, 158, 188, 194, 203, 205, 212, 226, 230, 236, 241–242, 254–255, 258, 260–262, 265, 297, 301, 306, 319
starling, 97, 163
star, 12–13, 15, 19, 45, 71, 78, 104–106, 111, 116, 124–125, 143–144, 170, 197, 206, 237, 239, 273, 281–286, 302, 310, 313; see heavenly (celestial) body
stewardship, 53, 231, 264
stomach, 24, 66–67, 77, 79, 83–84, 86–89, 193, 196, 257, 289
stork, 96–97, 163
subjectivity, 28, 37, 39, 113, 215
submission, 30, 137, 284
summer, 94, 96, 99, 112, 134, 157, 169–170, 173, 206, 230, 243–245, 273, 320
sun, 17, 19, 41, 45, 74, 78, 93, 106, 124–125, 135, 164, 170, 176, 197, 218, 221, 227–228, 244, 251, 255–256, 273, 277, 291, 302, 320, 338. *See also* heavenly (celestial) body
survival, 6, 15, 33, 84, 88, 113, 124, 180, 196–197, 257
swallow, 17, 18, 22, 94–95, 97 , 163, 169, 276, 279
swarming creature, 45, 67, 76–77, 90, 150, 172, 187, 197, 232, 241, 246–247, 275, 277, 279, 299, 301, 309
swordfish, 183–184, 196, 226, 229, 309
sycophant, 32
symmetry, 13, 24, 31, 36, 51 91, 95, 98, 165, 185
syrup, 47, 158, 325

tail, 17, 48, 70, 77, 79, 82, 87, 96–98, 111, 122, 124, 154, 159, 164, 170, 187, 192, 194, 223–224, 227, 245, 308
talisman, 126, 134, 184, 216, 218, 269
tambourine, 154, 236
taste, 32, 73, 75–76, 96, 113, 135, 139, 158, 178, 193, 235, 248, 265, 275
tax, 204, 212, 231, 257–258, 291
taxonomy, 27, 187
teleology, 26, 35, 39, 43, 112
temple, 139–140, 205, 258, 321–322, 326, 332–333

termite, 139, 187, 276, 295–299
theodicy, 70, 190, 195, 268, 286, 340
theology, 21, 31, 64, 72, 75, 103, 129,132, 181, 214, 269, 278–279, 301–302, 312, 338, 340–341. *See also kalām*
theosophy, 137
theurgy, 137, 141
threshing, 99, 134, 167, 249
throne, 89, 102, 105, 140, 164, 174, 201, 204, 208, 309, 330, 331, 333–334
tick, 75, 187
tiger, 20, 79, 152–156, 160, 223, 263
toil, 27, 75, 99, 100, 104, 107, 134, 139, 151, 182, 193, 248–249, 252–254, 261–262, 277, 290–291, 298
toleration, 137, 182, 196, 228, 321, 332, 334, 340, 342
tongue, 52, 76, 89, 100, 142, 171, 184–185, 187, 201–202, 218–219, 221, 238, 275, 279, 292, 303, 307, 315, 319
touch, 74–76, 131, 149
trade, 18, 204, 212, 227, 231, 242, 249, 319. *See also* commerce
transcendence, 53, 125, 171, 200–202, 214
travel, 69, 73, 114, 126, 129, 168–170, 175–177, 179, 186, 267
treasurer, 231, 237, 292
tree, 73–75, 79, 94, 99, 101, 109, 134–135, 140, 162 166–167, 171–172, 187, 203–204, 206, 219, 224, 233–235, 238, 243, 245–246, 248, 253–254, 258–259, 261, 269, 273, 275–276, 304, 311–312
troops, 13, 46, 71, 140–141, 151–153, 192, 218, 222, 225–226, 230, 235–237, 243, 270–273, 309, 324
turtle-dove, 163
turtle, 84, 163, 183–185, 192, 309
tusk, 101–102, 108, 110–112, 118, 120, 191–192
tyranny, 10, 20–21, 31, 53, 102, 126, 128, 137, 142, 173–174, 205, 223, 263, 270, 275, 280–281, 283–284, 294, 299, 307, 331, 334

universe, 103, 155, 181, 188, 202, 212, 231, 239
urbanity, 32–33, 69, 148, 157, 291
utility, 6, 54. *See also* adaptation

vanity, 17, 21–23, 47, 146, 176, 229, 253
vassal, 13, 16, 46, 108, 153, 161, 178, 188, 222–223, 225–226, 230, 235, 237, 243, 270, 272, 322, 324, 326–327, 332–333, 335
vegetarianism, 19, 41, 99–100, 175, 260
venom, 36, 76, 194–196, 226
violence, 12, 54, 91, 131, 136, 139, 160–161, 174, 229, 236, 252, 270, 302
viper, 36, 187–188, 194–195, 290, 326. *See also* snake
virtue, 2, 13, 23, 44, 51–54, 64, 66, 102–103, 123, 125, 133, 136, 150, 156, 169, 180, 194–195, 205, 216, 218, 232, 242, 246, 253, 266, 269, 291, 307, 311–313, 315
vizier, 5, 27, 44, 73, 127, 140, 144–147, 163, 176, 184, 188, 202, 206–207, 218, 224, 268, 327, 334
vulture, 175, 193

wasp, 17, 20, 84, 98, 173–174, 246, 297
water creature, 17, 27, 227
water-wheel, 117, 249
weapon, 5, 16, 118, 122–123, 151–152, 173–174, 192, 223, 234–235, 256, 263–264, 305, 329
weasel, 27, 32, 152, 154, 160, 223
web, 191, 276
whale, 27, 183–185
wine, 175, 194, 214, 248, 295, 311, 335
wing, 76–77, 79, 84–85, 87, 95–98, 119, 162, 164–165, 169, 174–175, 188, 190–191, 224–225, 232, 234, 245, 295, 308
winter, 31, 76, 94, 99, 112, 134, 157, 165, 169–170, 173, 206, 230, 235, 243–246, 273, 287, 326
wisdom, 9, 11, 23, 34, 53, 70, 75, 85, 87, 90–91, 112, 114, 138, 150, 155, 157, 162, 191, 194–199, 216, 231, 234–236, 251, 275, 277, 279, 297–300, 309, 311, 313

wolf, 122, 154–155, 233
womb, 78, 79, 89, 134, 252, 277
wool, 14, 22, 77, 86–87, 109, 116, 118, 123, 148, 173, 188, 203, 209, 260–261, 264, 292, 300
worm, 14, 17–18, 26–27, 31, 74–76, 139, 166, 187, 190, 193, 198, 218, 227, 245–246, 260, 264, 276, 296–300, 324
worship, 17, 21–22, 52–53, 64, 80, 82, 97, 107, 133, 137,139, 140, 164, 168, 170, 176, 181–182, 186, 207–209, 212, 221, 255, 257–258, 269, 273, 279–280, 282, 287, 302, 309, 342

zodiac, 78, 92–93, 111, 144, 170, 206, 281
zoology, 6, 17, 87, 234, 257

Index Locorum

SCRIPTURE

Qur'an

1:6	72
2:30	64, 133, 183
2:30–36	133
2:31	135
2:34	132
2:36	274
2:61	208
2:62	342
2:101–102	294
2:102	138
2:111–115	303
2:112	137
2:115	258, 303
2:117	105, 189, 210
2:125	211
2:135	314
2:155–156	161
2:164	106
2:165	161
2:183–187	211
2:198	190
2:243	287
2:255	105
2:256	48, 303–304
2:258	173–174, 281
2:259	287
2:261	166
3:7	110, 112, 294
3:10	294
3:13	70, 234
3:17	190
3:33–34	255
3:47	210
3:59	210
3:95	314
3:97	211
3:110	102
3:140	116, 228
3:173	182
3:191	80
3:199	190
4:1	203
4:59	146
4:119	211
4:160	110
4:163	138
5:6	190
5:18	228
5:27–31, 32	160
5:31	258
5:33	209
5:54	220
5:57–60	208
5:69	167, 342
5:73	256
6:38	119
6:59	200
6:73	210
6:84	138
6:93	311–312
6:103	219
6:129	268
6:142	104
7:11–25	135–136
7:21	135
7:24	274

7:54 170
7:64 287
7:73–79 285
7:88–93 285
7:107, 108 208
7:130–141 142
7:133 186, 299
7:179 291
7:189 203
8:12 256
8:37 167
8:52 311–312
9:30 256
9:33 211
9:34 257–258
9:36–37 93
9:111 49, 304
9:126 126
9:129 105
10:14 201
10:61 200
10:90–94 142
10:98 284
10:99 304
11:6 119, 187, 199, 225, 307, 308, 309
11:45 67, 103
11:106–108 312
11:114 255–256
12 138
12:18 237
12:64 211, 244
12:105 81
13:2 106
14:33 273
14:46 174
14:48 125
14:50 312
15:30 274
15:45–48 311
16:4 89
16:5–7, 8 104
16:12 106
16:14–16 104
16:40 105, 210
16:66 235
16:68 258
16:68–70 233
16:80 203
17:1 72
17:5 220
17:44 243, 279
18:37 89
18:39 161
18:50 132
18:93–97 227
19:35 210
19:57 136
20:50 112, 245
20:116 132
21:22 239
21:23 232
21:51–70 137, 281
21:78–82 138–139
21:82 219
21:85 136
21:95–96 227
22:5 89
22:17 342
22:20–24 312
22:37 106
22:46 258
23:13 105
23:13–14 89
23:14 67
23:15–16 203
23:16 244
23:91 211
23:115 80
24:22 119
24:41 258, 279
25:31 132, 294
25:53 170
25:54 104, 203
26:69–104 137, 281
26:78–80 285–286
27:15–45 140
27:16 278
27:18 192
27:20, 22–25 164
27:33 220
27:38–40 141
27:40 299
27:51–52 179–180
28:38 281

28:88 20, 200
29:24 173–174
29:38 219
29:43 116, 228
29:45 255
29:60 258
30:9 20, 180
30:29 302
31:11–19 129
31:14 47, 271
31:20 273, 274
32:8 105
33:72 273
34:10–14 139
34:12–14 295
34:13 240
35:11 89
36:77 89
36:79 246–247
36:82 210
37:40–49 311
37:60–64 312
37:83–89 281
37:139–148 284
38:34–40 139
38:49–64 312
38:50–52 311
39:9 280
39:21 234
39:61 167
40:28–45 284
40:67 89
40:68210
40:80104
42:51 219
43:12 170
43:13 104
43:13–14 119
44:25–27 179
44:37 143
44:38 80
44:43–44 312
45:14 119
46:29 240
47:26 307
47:29 311–312
48:16 220
49:12 257
50:14 143
53:46 89
54:7 80
55:5–6 12, 124, 273
55:17, 19 170
55:58 134
56:24 209
56:52–53 312
57:20 257
61:4, 14 49, 305
68:11 257
69:6–7 178
69:17 105
69:18 309
70:4 144
72 101
72:1–2 141
72:1–19 240
72:8–9, 10 141
74:31 310
75:10 169
75:37 89
76:2 89
77:20 79
79:10–13 247
79:26 234
79:27–33 211
80:19 89
82:7–8 111
83:18–19 105
87:2–3 210
89:10–12 280
90:10–20 170
95:4 110
95:8 103
97 212
101:9 312
102:3 168
104:4–5 312
105:1–4 168
112 210

Hebrew Bible
Genesis
1:3 105
1:6–8 310
1:16 124
1:17–18 106

1:31 197
2:1–3 208
2:7 228
2:16–17 99
3:7 109–110
3:18 99
3:19 228, 229
3:21 109–110
4:10 160
6:11 132
9:13 99
18 313
38:6–26 228
Exodus
4:2–4, 7, 17 208
8:2–13 186
8:16 299
10:14 299
20:8–11 208
Leviticus
11:7 120
16:29 221
16:30–31 305
Numbers
21:6 219
22:28–30 5, 117
35:31–34 132
Deuteronomy
21:22–23 132
29 20
32:4 191
1 Kings
3:28 138
5:9–11 138
5:13 140, 278
10:1–13 140
2 Kings
18:18, 37 140
Isaiah
11:7 260
45:18 105–106
47 220
Jeremiah
9:23–24 114
25:9 220
27:6 220
43:10 220
Ezekiel
1:14 207
38:2–3, 14–18 227
39:1, 11 277
Hosea
14:2–3 305
Jonah
1:1 284
1:4–5 101
3:1–10 284
Psalms
19 200
23 152
36:10 215
49:13 266
50 140
73–83 140
93 200
93:2 208
102:7 176
103:14 228
104:29 228
114:4–6 139
Proverbs
6:6–11 244
Job
3:14 291
9:12 232
19:26 289
37:7 228
38–40 199
38:25–27 35
39:5–12 35
39:13–18 277
39:24 122
Lamentations
4:8 277
Ecclesiastes
2:4–23 290–291
3:14–15, 19 22
3:20 228
4:2 197
5:8 291
12:7 228
Nehemiah
6 342
1 Chronicles
6:24 140
15:17 140

2 Chronicles
4:18 140

New Testament
Matthew
6:26 258
7:19 167
10:34–39 305
16:24 305
Luke
9:23–26 305
Revelations
20:8 227
21:4 167

HADITH

Al-Fiqh al-akbar
I, 10 312
II, 23 312

Janā'iz of Tirmidhī
Bāb 70 312

Mishkāt al-maṣābiḥ
VII, I, 3 256

Muwaṭṭa' of Mālik
Kitāb al-Aqḍiyya,
Bāb 1 149

Ṣaḥīḥ Bukhārī
Book 72, hadith 780 292

Ṣaḥīḥ Muslim
Book 31, hadith 6177–6178
220

Waṣīyat Abī Ḥanīfa
§ 8 105
§18–19 312

RABBINIC LITERATURE

Targum Jonathan
Genesis
15:7 173

Midrash
Genesis Rabbah
10:7 174
Numbers Rabbah
20:15 5

Mishnah
Sanhedrin
4.5 160
Avot
3.10 89
4.1 304

Jerusalem Talmud
Berakhot 120
2
Babylonian Talmud
Shabbat
77b 79
Ta'anit
21b 191
Giṭṭin
56b 174
Baba Bathra
91a 173
Sanhedrin
38b 266
108b 191
Menuḥot
64b 121

Mystical Texts
Sefer Yetzirah 207

EPISTLES OF THE BRETHREN OF PURITY

Epistle 1 64, 92–93, 214
Epistle 5 91–92, 296
Epistle 9 64
Epistle 16 105
Epistle 21 63
Epistle 25 68, 78
Epistle 26 274

Epistle 28 72
Epistles 32–33 91
Epistle 34 274
Epistle 35 146
Epistle 38 72
Epistle 40 90
Epistle 42 303
Epistle 43 72
Epistle 45 137–138
Epistle 48 184, 228
Epistle 49 68

CLASSIC TEXTS

Aesop
Fables
210 79
269 79

Anaxagoras
Fragment 17 142

Anaximander
On the 'Physics' 228

Aristotle
De Anima
I.4.408a5 93
II.3 75
II.4.415b30–416a6 69
III.5 189, 215
III.12.434a30–32 75
De Generatione Animalium
II.1.731b 86
II.4.740a24–35 68
III.10 173
De Partibus Animalium
I.1.642a18–30 93
I.5.645b27 81
II.3.650a21–30 66–67
II.9.655b 234
II.17.661a16–21 76
III.1.661b 234
III.1.662b 175
III.14.674a23–674b15 88–89
III.14.674b19–36 88
IV.8.683a30–35 185
IV.10.686a27–b22 109
IV.10.687a3–16 69
IV.10.687a11–13 297
IV.12.693a11–15 90–91
De Plantis (pseudo-Aristotle)
I.2.817b25–818a1 66
II.3.825a4 74–75
Eudemian Ethics
VII.4.1248a17–29 189
Historia Animalium
I.1.488a3–5 175
I.1.488b 74
IV.3.527b 185
IV.7.532a 234
V.19.552a21–552b 74
V.21 173
VI.1.558b–559a 94
VIII.1.588b4–11 63
VIII.3 175
VIII.12.597b27–29 175
IX.40.923b 45
IX.50.632b1–11 88
On Melissus, Xenophanes, and Gorgias (pseudo-Aristotle)
2.975a25–29 228
Metaphysics
II.1.993b10–11 200
II.1.993b11–14 217
III.4.1000b9–12 228
V.6.1016b17–24 64
XII.6.1063a15–17 144
XII.10.1075a12–25 238–239
Nicomachaean Ethics
III.3.1112a28 178
VI.7.1141a21 215
De Caelo
II.12.292b 74
On Youth, Old Age, Life and Death, and Respiration
6.740a20 82
Physics
I.163.20 142
VIII.10.267b17 144
Politics
I.5.1254b10–11 115
I.8.1256b15 66
I.9.1256b23 115
I.13.1260a36–1260b1 253

III.5.1277b34–1278a14 253
III.5.1278a20 253
VII.9.1329a26–29 253
VII.12.1331a19–35 253

'Aṭṭār
Manṭiq al-ṭayr 162, 278

Augustine
Confessions
9.10.25 279

Avicenna
al-Ishārāt wa'l-tanbīhāt 314
Kitāb al-Shifā' 233
Liber de Anima
4.3 233
5.1 233

al-Baghdādī
Lubab al-ta'wīl fī ma'ānī al-tanzīl 287

Baḥyā ibn Paqūda 289
Kitāb al-Hidāya ilā farā'iḍ al-qulūb
II.3 196–197
II.5 166
IV.3 286

Baiḍāwī
Commentary, Sura 12 138

al-Baladī
Habala
2.47–48 80

al-Baqlī
'Arā'is al-bayān fī ḥaqā'iq al-Qur'ān 111
Livre de Bilawhar et Budasf 207

Bidpai
Pañcatantra 157, 162, 174, 334

I.110 103
I.14–15 150
I.75 152
I.365–395 155

Cicero
De Divinatione
I.52.119 282
II.10.25 282
De Natura Deorum
II.57.140 69–70

Darwin
Descent of Man 84–85, 113
Foundations of the Origin of Species 234
Origin of Species 75, 76, 234

Diogenes Laertius
Lives of the Eminent Philosophers
7.85–86 273

Epicurus
Principal Doctrines
8 100
15 34, 100
25 100
Vatican Fragments
21, 52 100

Erasmus
In Praise of Folly 85

al-Fārābī
On 'De Interpretatione'
IX 283
Fuṣūl al-madanī 241
§87 230
Kitāb Iḥṣā' al-'ulūm 218
Kitāb Mabādi' ārā' ahl al-madīna al-fāḍila
81, 241
Fī taḥṣīl al-ṣa'āda 115

Firdawsī
Shahnameh 162, 204, 325, 333, 335, 336

Galen
De Alimentorum Facultatibus 250

De Compositione Medicamentorum per Genera
III.2 82
De Locis Affectis 233
De Naturalibus Facultatibus
II.9 83
De Placitis Hippocratis et Platonis 82
De Temperamentis 93
De Usu Partium 82
I.2 151–152, 192
I.5 273
II.14–15 113
IV.4 83
IV.6 82
IV.15 83
VI.7 82
VI.9 84
VII.9 82
VII.14 81
VIII.4 82
Hygiene
I 80
Peri Ethon 273
Precis of the 'Timaeus' 70
On Simples
11 194
Summary of the 'Republic' 154
Therapeutica ad Glauconem
I 250

al-Ghazālī
Faḍā'iḥ al-bāṭiniyya 288
Iḥyā' 'ulūm al-dīn
Book 40 312
Mishkāt al-anwār 200, 219
Al-Munqidh min al-ḍalāl 111, 288, 301–302

Halevi
Kuzari 11
3.11 191

Hippocrates
De Dieta 250
De Insomniis 81
De Temperamentibus
1.9 82
Hobbes
The Elements of Law
I.19.5 235–236

al-Ḥujwīrī
Kashf al-maḥjūb 292, 304
'On Blame' 266

Ibn 'Arabī
Fuṣūṣ al-ḥikam 69, 272
Al-Futūḥāt al-Makkiyya 272

Ibn al-Jawzī
Talbīs Iblīs 293

Ibn al-Muqaffa'
Kalīla wa-Dimna 156–157, 162, 334
'The Innocent Camel' 155

Ibn Gabirol
Fons Vitae 11

Ibn Khaldūn
Muqaddimah 178
2.4 99
5.4 178
Ibn Ṭufayl
Ḥayy ibn Yaqẓān 68, 80, 82, 111, 206

Ibn Ya'fūr
Mufaḍḍaliyyāt 179

Isidore of Seville
Etymologies 12
1.9 118
1.12 114
1.26 121
1.43 122
2.3–6 150, 223
2.6 223
2.7 154
2.12 176
2.14–16 79
2.17 175

2.19 120
2.23–24 257
3.9 244
4.4 187
4.6–7 223
4.39–40 226
4.45–46 77
5.2 276
6.49 300
7.14–17 163
7.20 277
7.38–42 176
7.44 168
7.61–62 251
7.76 168
8.1 243
8.17 193

al-Jāḥiẓ
'On Lads and Lasses' 158
'On Singing-Girls' 157

al-Jayyānī
Al-Baḥr al-muḥīṭ 133

John Actuarius
De Urinis 84
De Spiritu Animali
II.1 83–84

al-Kalābādhī
Kitāb al-Ta'arruf li-madhhab ahl'l-taṣawwuf 212, 314

Kant
Critique of Practical Reason 125
Groundwork of the Metaphysic of Morals 37

al-Kindī
'Essay on How to Banish Sorrow' 73–74, 252, 291
'Essay on the Prostration of the Outermost Sphere... ' 273
'On First Philosophy' 217
Metaphysics 217

al-Kisā'ī

Qiṣaṣ al-anbiyā' 133, 137, 140, 164, 173, 178, 224, 284, 285

al-Khwārizmī
Sindhind 143

Lactantius
Divine Institutes
VII.4 194

Lucan
Pharsalia
I.371–374 263
IX.859–861 79

Lucretius
De Rerum Natura
I.10–23 100

Macrobius
Saturnalia
VIII 81

Maimonides
Guide to the Perplexed 9
I.11 208
II.35–40 138
III.12 34
III.12–13 106
III.13 35
III.25 34
III.29 173
Treatise on Resurrection 76

al-Maqrīzī
Kitāb al-Nizā' wa'l-takhāṣum 213

al-Māwardī
Aḥkām al-sulṭāniyya wa'l-wilāyāt al-dīniyya 146

al-Miṣrī
'Umdat al-sālik 263

Monawwar
Asrār al-tawḥīd fī Manāqib Abū Sa'īd 267

Montaigne
Essays
I, 48, 'Of War Horses' 123
II, 11, 'Of Cruelty' 117
II, 12, *Apology for Raymond Sebond* 21–23, 70, 113, 174, 223, 227, 229, 244, 267, 299, 300, 313

Nābigha al-Dhubyānī 273
Dīwān 125

Nicomachus of Gerasa
Arithmêtikê Eisagôgê 64, 91
II.17 92

Nizām al-Mulk
Siyāsat-nāma 128

Origen
De Principiis 202

Ovid
Metamorphoses
1.76 70

Paul of Aegina
The Seven Books 80, 84, 121, 194–195, 250, 251, 252, 300

Philo of Alexandria
De Opificio Mundi
1.31 125

Philoponus
De Caelo 125
De Opificio Mundi 125

Plato
Euthyphro
14 242
Laws
VII.846–849 253
Republic
I.342–343 152
I.473–496 156
I.351d 301
II.362 242
II.370–371 153–154
II.373 250
III.405–408 250
VI.507–VII.521 201
VII.525 214
Sophist
244b 301
Statesman
298 123
Symposium
211 301
Timaeus 125, 201
28 65
91–92 70

Pliny the Elder
Natural History
VII.2 261
VIII.10.28 78
VIII.10.29 79
VIII.17–21 223
VIII.25 154
VIII.26.67–68 298
VIII.34 257
VIII.64–65 114
VIII.65.159–162 122
VIII.72.206 120
IX.12.37–38 185
IX.51.97–98 185
IX.54.107 300
XI.5.13–14 243
XI.7.17 243
XI.10.20–26 243
XI.15.45 243
XI.18.56–57 173

Plotinus
Enneads
I. 7.1 215
I.8.2 215
V.1.5 215
V.3.17 306

VI.9.2 215
Plutarch
Moralia
'On the Eating of Flesh'
I.4 41

Porphyry
De Abstinentia
III.20 34–35

Proclus
On the First Book of Euclid's 'Elements' 214
Elements of Theology 214
Props. 1–13 301
On 'Alcibiades I' 214

Saadiah
The Book of Theodicy 14, 35, 80, 132
Kitāb al-Mukhtar fi'l-āmānāt wa'l-'i'tiqādāt
Introduction 288
I.2 25
X.4 293
X.10 166, 291

Sextus Empiricus
Outlines of Pyrrhonism 79, 146, 221

Shahrastānī
Kitāb al-Milal wa'l-niḥal 206

Simplicius
On Aristotle's 'Physics'
I.163.20 142

Spinoza
Ethics
I, P1–8 211
I, Appendix 40
III, P7 40
Short Treatise...
5.1 40

Suhrawardī
Philosophical Allegories and Mystical Treatises 162

Ṭabarī
Commentary on the Qur'an 173

al-Ṭabarsī
Majmū' al-bayān fī tafsīr al-Qur'ān 110

al-Tawḥīdī
'The Zoological Chapter'
§108 170
§144 170
§158 163

al-Tha'labī
'Arā'is al-majālis fī qiṣaṣ al-anbiyā' 133, 183, 192, 204

al-Tirmidhī
Kitāb Khatm al-awliyā' 64, 212, 304

Vergil
Aeneid
VII.781–783 117

Yaḥyā ibn'Adī
Tahdhīb al-akhlāq 63, 266